COMMON CORE ACHIEVE

Mastering Essential Test Readiness Skills

READING & WRITING

Bothell, WA • Chicago, IL • Columbus, OH • New York, NY

MHEonline.com

Send all inquiries to:
McGraw-Hill Education
8787 Orion Place
Columbus, OH 43240

ISBN: 978-0-02-143256-1
MHID: 0-02-143256-2

Printed in the United States of America.

4 5 6 7 8 9 QLM 17 16 15 14

Table of Contents

Chapter 6 Evaluate Textual Evidence 178

Chapter 7 Analyze Structure Across Texts 216

To the Student

Congratulations! If you are using this book, it means that you are taking a key step toward achieving an important new goal for yourself. You are preparing to take your high school equivalency test, an important step in the pathway toward career, educational, and lifelong well-being and success.

Common Core Achieve: Mastering Essential Test Readiness Skills is designed to help you learn or strengthen the skills you will need when you take your high school equivalency test. The program includes four core student modules—*Reading & Writing, Mathematics, Science,* and *Social Studies.* Each of these modules provides subject-level pretests and posttests, in-depth instruction and practice of the core skills and practices required for high school equivalency tests, and a number of additional features to help you master all the skills you need for success on test day and beyond.

How to Use This Book

Before beginning the lessons in each module, take the **Pretest**. This will give you a preview of the types of questions you will be answering on the high school equivalency test. More importantly, it will help you identify which skill areas you need to concentrate on most. Use the evaluation chart at the end of the Pretest to pinpoint the types of questions you have answered incorrectly and to determine which skills you need to work on. The evaluation chart will also help you identify where to go within the module for instruction and practice. You may decide to concentrate on specific areas of study or to work through the entire module. It is highly recommended that you work through the whole module to build a strong foundation in the core areas in which you will be tested.

Common Core Achieve: Mastering Essential Test Readiness Skills includes a number of features designed to familiarize you with high school equivalency tests and to prepare you for test taking. At the start of each chapter, the **Chapter Opener** provides an overview of the chapter content and a goal-setting activity. The lessons that follow include these features to help guide and enhance your learning:

- **Lesson Objectives** state what you will be able to accomplish after completing the lesson.
- **Key Terms and Vocabulary**, critical for understanding lesson content, is listed at the start of every lesson. All boldfaced words in the text can be found in the Glossary.
- The **Key Concept** summarizes the content that is the focus of the lesson.
- **Core Skills** are emphasized with direct instruction and practice in the context of the lesson. Each of the Core Skills aligns to the Common Core State Standards.
- Special features within the lessons include **21st Century Skills, Technology Skills, Workplace Skills, Language Skills,** and **Test-taking Skills** to help you activate high-level thinking skills by using real-word application of these skills.
- **Think about Reading** questions check your understanding of the content throughout the lesson.
- **Write to Learn** activities provide you with a purpose for practicing your writing skills.
- The end-of-lesson **Vocabulary Review** checks your understanding of important lesson vocabulary, and the **Skill Review** checks your understanding of the content and skills presented in the lesson.

- **Skill Practice** and **Writing Practice** exercises appear at the end of every lesson to help you apply your learning of content and skill fundamentals.

In addition to the above lesson-level features, this module also includes these features to help you check your understanding as you prepare for the test.

- The end-of-chapter **Review** and **Writer's Workshop** test your understanding of the chapter content and provide an opportunity to strengthen your writing skills. (These features are included in the *Reading & Writing* and *Social Studies* modules.)

- **Check Your Understanding** charts allow you to check your knowledge of the skills you have practiced and reference where you can go to review skills that you should revisit.

- The **Answer Key** explains the answers for the questions in the book.

- After you have worked through the book, take the **Posttest** to see how well you have learned the skills presented in this book.

Good luck with your studies, and remember: you are here because you have chosen to achieve important and exciting new goals for yourself. Every time you begin working within the materials, keep in mind that the skills you develop in *Common Core Achieve: Mastering Essential Test Readiness Skills* are not just important for passing the high school equivalency test; they are keys to lifelong success.

Directions: Read the following passage. Then choose the best answer to questions 1 through 4.

The pharaoh and other members of the royal family were at the top of ancient Egyptian society, followed by the upper class of priests and nobles. Priests took care of the temples and celebrated religious ceremonies, while nobles oversaw the government. The rest of the people were divided into educated professionals, such as scribes and doctors, and a broad working class. At the bottom of Egyptian society were the tenant farmers, servants, and slaves.

1. Which of the following best expresses the author's purpose for writing the paragraph?

A. to persuade readers to visit Egypt
B. to list the jobs done by ancient Egyptians
C. to entertain people with stories about life in ancient Egypt
D. to inform readers about the class structure in ancient Egypt

2. What is the function of the word *while* in the second sentence?

A. to introduce a cause
B. to introduce a contrast
C. to introduce a solution
D. to introduce the next step in a process

3. Which of the following is the best summary of the text?

A. People in ancient Egypt had different roles in society. Priests had religious duties, and nobles ran the government. Others worked in various jobs.
B. At the top of Egyptian society were the pharaoh and members of the royal family, followed by the upper class of priests and nobles. At the bottom were the tenant farmers, servants, and slaves.
C. In ancient Egypt, there were different classes. For instance, there were scribes and doctors, who were highly educated, and tenant farmers and servants, who were dependent on others for their livelihood.
D. Egyptian society was organized in a strict hierarchy headed by the pharaoh and royal family. Next came priests and nobles, then a professional class, an independent working class, and, lastly, dependent workers.

4. What type of details does the author use to support the main idea?

A. descriptions
B. examples
C. reasons
D. statistics

Directions: Read the following passage. Then choose the best answer to questions 5 through 9.

Jong-Kyu took a deep breath and gripped the overhanging rock with all his strength. Then, pushing off with his legs and pulling with his arms, he managed to launch himself up and past the lip of the overhang. For a moment he lay listening to his heart slow. When he could no longer hear it beating, he stood and looked down into the valley of his birth, his childhood—the valley of his greatest loss.

It was hard to pinpoint where it had happened. Time had torn down familiar landmarks and raised up strange ones. He thought, though, that broad tree might be the one they'd sheltered under during the storm. Closing his eyes, he let himself recall her face.

Mi-na's short hair was pasted against her head by the rain, and she was panting with laughter after the race for the shelter of the tree. He would tell her now, he decided, looking into her sparkling eyes. He would ask her to come with him when he left the valley to find work. Before he could speak, though, Mi-Na had sprinted away, calling to him to follow. Then, suddenly, thunder exploded around them, and his sweet, sweet girl was a blinding blaze of blue and gold.

Jong-Kyu opened his eyes. He could hear his heart again. No, that was not the tree, he thought. It had been farther to the left, maybe where the cell-phone factory stood now.

5. What structural technique is used in the passage?

A. alternating viewpoints
B. flashback
C. foreshadowing
D. parallel plots

6. Which word or phrase best describes the text structure of the last two sentences in the passage?

A. chronology
B. spatial description
C. order of importance
D. cause followed by effect

7. What is the dominant tone of the passage?

A. angry
B. hopeful
C. melancholy
D. threatening

8. What is the relationship between paragraph 1 and paragraph 3?

A. Paragraph 3 describes the loss mentioned in paragraph 1.
B. Paragraph 1 explains the cause of the event in paragraph 3.
C. Paragraph 1 introduces the characters that appear in paragraph 3.
D. The event in paragraph 3 happens after the event in paragraph 1.

9. Which of the following details from the passage supports a theme of the lingering effects of loss?

A. "Jong-Kyu took a deep breath and gripped the overhanging rock with all his strength."
B. "Time had torn down familiar landmarks and raised up strange ones."
C. "Mi-na's short hair was pasted against her head by the rain . . ."
D. "Closing his eyes, he let himself recall her face."

Directions: Read the following passage. Then choose the best answer to questions 10 through 13.

E-mail Message

From: Cathy Palmer
Sent: 2/15/2014
To: All Network Users
Subject: Formatting errors with e-mail

To all network users:

It has been brought to our attention that a formatting error occurs when sending e-mails from your machines. This error could impact what portions of your e-mail actually get sent.

If you insert an attachment by dragging the file into the body of the e-mail, any text below the attachment gets truncated out of the message and attached as a separate text file or HTML file. What this means is that, when sending attachments, any text that comes *after* the inserted file does not show up when you open it.

To prevent this problem from occurring, always use the Attach File button on your e-mail window, rather than dragging the file into the body of the text.

Thank you,
Network Services

10. Which of the following best explains why the author wrote this e-mail message?

A. to send attachments to the recipients
B. to explain what the Attach File button is for
C. to describe two ways to attach files to an e-mail message
D. to prevent further formatting errors in employees' e-mail messages

11. What is the overall structure of the e-mail message?

A. cause and effect
B. comparison
C. order of importance
D. problem and solution

12. Which of the following is NOT an effect that the writer hopes to achieve?

A. for recipients to stop attaching so many files to the e-mail messages they send
B. for recipients to use the Attach File button whenever they attach files to e-mail messages
C. for recipients to stop attaching files by dragging them into the body of an e-mail message
D. for recipients to understand why text has been disappearing from e-mail messages they have sent

13. What is the tone of the passage?

A. angry
B. apologetic
C. businesslike
D. optimistic

Directions: Read the following passage. Then choose the best answer to questions 14 through 17.

It was we, the people; not we, the white male citizens; nor yet we, the male citizens; but we, the whole people, who formed the Union. And we formed it, not to give the blessings of liberty, but to secure them; not to the half of ourselves and the half of our posterity, but to the whole people—women as well as men. And it is a downright mockery to talk to women of their enjoyment of the blessings of liberty while they are denied the use of the only means of securing them provided by this democratic-republican government—the ballot.

For any state to make sex a qualification that must ever result in the disfranchisement of one entire half of the people, is to pass a bill of attainder, or, an ex post facto law, and is therefore a violation of the supreme law of the land. By it the blessings of liberty are forever withheld from women and their female posterity.

—From "On Women's Right to the Suffrage" by Susan B. Anthony

14. What is the main idea of paragraph 2?

A. People who cannot vote are not free.
B. It is illegal for women to vote in many states.
C. Denying women the right to vote goes against the US Constitution.
D. Keeping women from voting is the same as condemning them without trial.

15. This passage uses sophisticated vocabulary and sentence structure to discuss an abstract concept, making it an example of

A. a complex text.
B. historical fiction.
C. literary nonfiction.
D. a rhetorical device.

16. Which phrase from the passage helps convey an angry tone?

A. "the male citizens"
B. "downright mockery"
C. "the blessings of liberty"
D. "supreme law of the land"

17. According to the passage, the only way to ensure one's liberty is by

A. voting.
B. achieving posterity.
C. passing laws.
D. reading the US Constitution.

Directions: Read the following passage. Then choose the best answer to questions 18 through 21.

> Many people think that dangerous team sports such as football and soccer are the best way for children to stay fit and to gain important team-building skills. Of course, it is true that children need physical exercise and opportunities to interact with others. However, dance is a better way to address these needs. Children who are involved in dance build tremendous strength, endurance, and flexibility in a calm and collaborative environment. In addition, they build their cognitive skills when they are memorizing choreography and team-building skills when they are performing in recitals.

18. The words *of course* at the beginning of sentence 2 introduce

A. a statement of agreement with an opposing argument.
B. a statement of disagreement with an opposing argument.
C. the assumption on which the author's argument is based.
D. the evidence that the author uses to refute an opposing argument.

19. Which of the following statements about the passage is true?

A. The author's evidence is relevant to the claim, but not sufficient.
B. The author's evidence is relevant to the claim and sufficient.
C. The author's evidence is not relevant to the claim or sufficient.
D. The author's evidence is relevant to the claim, but the sources are not credible.

20. Which of the following signal words or phrases in the passage indicates contrast?

A. however
B. in addition
C. of course
D. when

21. Which of the following is a hidden assumption that the author makes about dance?

A. It is active.
B. It is not dangerous.
C. It does not require strength.
D. It requires children to work together.

Directions: Read the following passage. Then choose the best answer to questions 22 through 26.

The Spectre

The immediate cause . . . of the prevalence of supernatural stories . . . was doubtless owing to the vicinity of Sleepy Hollow. There was a contagion in the very air that blew from that haunted region; it breathed forth an atmosphere of dreams and fancies infecting all the land. Several of the Sleepy Hollow people were present at Van Tassel's, and, as usual, were doling out their wild and wonderful legends. Many dismal tales were told about funeral trains, and mourning cries and wailings heard and seen about the great tree where the unfortunate Major André was taken. . . . Some mention was made also of the woman in white, that haunted the dark glen . . . and was often heard to shriek on winter nights before a storm, having perished there in the snow.

The chief part of the stories, however, turned upon the favorite spectre of Sleepy Hollow, the Headless Horseman, who . . . it was said, tethered his horse nightly among the graves in the churchyard.

The sequestered situation of this church seems always to have made it a favorite haunt of troubled spirits. It stands on a knoll, surrounded by locust-trees and lofty elms. . . . To look upon its grass-grown yard, where the sunbeams seem to sleep so quietly, one would think that there at least the dead might rest in peace. . . . Not far from the church, was . . . a wooden bridge . . . thickly shaded by overhanging trees, which cast a gloom about it, even in the daytime. . . . Such was one of the favorite haunts of the Headless Horseman, and the place where he was most frequently encountered. The tale was told of old Brouwer . . . how he met the Horseman . . . and was obliged to get up behind him; how they galloped . . . until they reached the bridge; when the Horseman suddenly turned into a skeleton, threw old Brouwer into the brook, and sprang away over the tree-tops with a clap of thunder.

—From "The Legend of Sleepy Hollow" by Washington Irving

22. How does the graveyard setting affect the story about the Headless Horseman?

A. The sunny, quiet churchyard provides a contrast to the frightening spectre.
B. The setting is necessary because it is a story about a ghost whose body was buried there.
C. All the ghost stories mentioned in the passage are set in the graveyard, so this one is too.
D. The story of the horseman is made more frightening because he appears in a secluded graveyard.

23. How can you tell that this passage is a work of fiction?

A. It is written in paragraphs.
B. It includes segments in chronological order.
C. It tells about imaginary events and characters.
D. It uses many details to describe people, places, and events.

24. This passage is from the beginning of a story. What will the rest of the story most likely be about?

A. the Headless Horseman
B. the Sleepy Hollow church
C. an evening at Van Tassel's
D. the adventures of old Brouwer

25. Which graphic organizer would be best for recording the characteristics of the headless horseman?

A. concept web
B. time line
C. two-column chart
D. Venn diagram

26. How does the writer make clear the transition between the first and second paragraphs?

A. The first paragraph is about stories, and so is the second one.
B. The second paragraph is about the Headless Horseman, but the first paragraph is not.
C. The word *however* in the second paragraph tells the reader that the two paragraphs are about opposing topics.
D. The second paragraph introduces the subject of "the chief part of the stories" described in the first paragraph.

Directions: Read the following passage. Then choose the best answer to questions 27 through 30.

(1) For the trip, each man was expected to furnish his own accoutrements [equipment]. (2) In saddles, we had the ordinary Texas make . . . (3) Our bridles were in keeping with the saddles, the reins as long as plough lines, while the bit was frequently ornamental and costly. (4) The indispensable slicker, a greatcoat of oiled canvas, was ever at hand, securely tied to our cantle strings. (5) Spurs were a matter of taste. (6) If a rider carried a quirt [short riding whip], he usually dispensed with spurs, though, when used, those with large, dull rowels [part of a spur: a turning wheel with sharp points] were the make commonly chosen. (7) In the matter of leggings, not over half our outfit had any, as a trail herd always kept in the open, and except for night herding, they were too warm in summer. (8) Our craft never used a cattle whip, but if emergency required, the loose end of a rope served instead and was more humane.

—From *The Log of a Cowboy* by Andy Adams

27. What is the purpose of the paragraph?

A. to tell a story about cowboys
B. to explain the work cowboys do
C. to describe cowboys' equipment
D. to introduce the main characters in a novel

28. Which of the following statements most accurately compares the impact of the photo and the text?

A. The photo has a greater impact because it illustrates the dramatic setting for cowboys' work.
B. The photo has a greater impact because it immediately shows all the equipment that cowboys use.
C. The text has a greater impact because it uses dramatic language to express cowboys' experiences.
D. The text has a greater impact because it provides deeper insight into cowboys' use of their equipment.

29. What is the antecedent of the pronoun *they* in sentence 7?

A. spurs
B. leggings
C. outfit
D. herd

30. Which details in the text support the idea that cowboys did not want to hurt the animals?

A. They used ornamental bits and long reins.
B. They wore slickers but seldom had leggings.
C. Their spurs had dull rowels, and they didn't use cattle whips.
D. They kept the herd in the open and sometimes herded at night.

Directions: Read the following passages about secondhand smoke. Then choose the best answer to questions 31 through 37.

Children and Secondhand Smoke

Breathing secondhand smoke can be harmful to children's health. [It has been linked to] asthma, Sudden Infant Death Syndrome (SIDS), bronchitis and pneumonia, and ear infections.

Children's exposure to secondhand smoke is responsible for

1. increases in the number of asthma attacks and severity of symptoms in 200,000 to 1 million children with asthma;
2. between 150,000 and 300,000 lower respiratory tract infections (for children under 18 months of age); and
3. respiratory tract infections resulting in 7,500 to 15,000 hospitalizations each year.

The developing lungs of young children are severely affected by exposure to secondhand smoke for several reasons, including that children are still developing physically, have higher breathing rates than adults, and have little control over their indoor environments. Children receiving high doses of secondhand smoke, such as those with smoking [parents], run the greatest risk of damaging health effects.

Join the millions of people who are protecting their children from secondhand smoke. You can become a child's hero by keeping a smoke-free home and car.

—from the U.S Environmental Protection Agency

A Letter to the Editor

The move toward smoke-free apartment buildings is discriminatory. Although it might be true that secondhand smoke is dangerous, there is no justification for telling people what they can or cannot do in their homes. As long as people are not smoking in a public place, they are harming no one but themselves. They say taxes on cigarettes go toward funding the treatment of smoking-related diseases, so smokers are also contributing to their own healthcare costs. Until cigarettes are banned entirely, smoking is legal, and the rights of smokers to enjoy a cigarette in their homes must be protected!

31. What is the purpose of the numbered list in "Children and Secondhand Smoke"?

A. to describe the progression of a smoking-related illness
B. to explain the three most important ways in which smoking can affect your health
C. to list statistics of children's respiratory illnesses from the most to the least prevalent
D. to identify the three groups of children who are most vulnerable to smoking-related illnesses

32. The argument in "Children and Secondhand Smoke" is based on what hidden assumption?

A. All parents smoke.
B. Children imitate their parents.
C. Parents want their children to be healthy.
D. Smoking around children can damage their health.

33. Which of the following best analyzes the validity of the argument in "Children and Secondhand Smoke"?

A. The evidence is contradictory, so the argument is invalid.
B. The author offers relevant and verifiable facts to present a valid argument.
C. The author offers a biased opinion that cannot be confirmed, resulting in an invalid argument.
D. The argument is based on a logical assumption but unsound reasoning.

34. Which of the following is an underlying assumption stated in the letter?

A. People have the right to do anything legal in private.
B. Secondhand smoke is illegal.
C. People pay taxes when they purchase cigarettes.
D. Smokers' health care costs are higher than others' costs.

35. Which of the following accurately contrasts the two arguments?

A. The EPA uses emotional language, but the letter writer does not.
B. The EPA's claim is stated explicitly, but the letter's claim is not.
C. The EPA demonstrates a negative bias; the letter writer shows a positive bias.
D. The EPA's argument is based on fact; the letter is based on opinion.

36. Read this sentence from "Children and Secondhand Smoke": "The developing lungs of young children are severely affected by exposure to secondhand smoke . . ." How might you rewrite the sentence in the active voice and keep the same meaning?

A. Smoking has severe effects on the developing lungs of young children.
B. Young children's lungs are still developing and are severely affected by secondhand smoke.
C. Exposure to secondhand smoke severely affects the developing lungs of young children.
D. Young children's lungs were severely affected by exposure to secondhand smoke.

Directions: Read the following passages about Cleopatra, a queen of Egypt. (It was once believed that Cleopatra committed suicide by holding an asp—a type of poisonous snake—to her chest until it bit her.) Then choose the best answer to questions 37 through 40.

Cleopatra: Peace, peace!
Dost thou not see my baby at my breast,
That sucks the nurse asleep?

—From *Antony and Cleopatra* by William Shakespeare

The story of Cleopatra's suicide is not without its detractors. Although classical historians believed that she died from the bite of an asp, later scholars thought it was more likely that her death came from the bite of a cobra. More recently, historians have challenged the notion that she committed suicide at all, suggesting instead that she was murdered by her enemy, Octavian.

37. What can you tell about the Shakespeare passage from the boldfaced word "Cleopatra" followed by a colon?

A. It is drama.
B. It is fiction.
C. It is a poem.
D. It is an essay.

38. What is the structure of the second passage?

A. cause and effect
B. compare and contrast
C. description
D. sequence

39. What example of figurative language does Shakespeare use?

A. He uses a simile, likening death to sleep.
B. He uses a metaphor, comparing an asp to a baby.
C. He uses dramatic language to exaggerate the event.
D. He uses repetition to emphasize Cleopatra's request for "peace."

40. Based on the two passages, which of the following statements is probably true?

A. Shakespeare's play presents a factual account of Cleopatra's suicide.
B. Shakespeare's play served as a reference source for the second passage.
C. Shakespeare's play contradicts the belief that Cleopatra died from a snake bite.
D. Shakespeare's play reflects the belief of earlier scholars that Cleopatra died from a snake bite.

Chapter 1

Identify Main Ideas and Details

Much of the information that people get during the workday is in the form of writing. Whether you read a memo, an e-mail, or a magazine article, you need to understand what it is about. You also need to understand the books and stories you read to get the most out of them.

As you read text at work, at home, or in class, you need to understand the main ideas and details of what you are reading. Being able to determine the main idea and theme of a passage means that you clearly understand what the text is about.

In this chapter you will study these topics:

Lesson 1.1

Determine the Main Idea

How do you determine what your employer is trying to communicate in a memo? How do you know what a piece of fiction is about? Learn how to determine the main idea, or the most important idea in a text.

Lesson 1.2

Identify Supporting Details

Supporting details provide information about the main idea of a text. How do you know which details in an e-mail or a biography support the main idea?

Learn how to identify details and distinguish those that support a main idea from those that do not.

Lesson 1.3

Identify Direct and Implied Main Ideas

How do you find the main idea when it is stated directly? How can you identify the main idea when it is only implied? Learn how to locate direct and implied main ideas.

Lesson 1.4

Summarize Details

How do you tell only the most important ideas from an article or a memo in your own words? Learn how to locate supporting details and then summarize them.

Lesson 1.5

Identify a Theme

Can you describe the message of a piece of fiction? Can you find examples in a story that illustrate its theme? Learn how to identify the theme of a passage and give evidence from text that supports the theme.

Goal Setting

What do you hope to learn in this chapter? Think carefully about when you have wanted or needed to find the most important ideas in a text. How can these lessons improve the way you understand text that you read? Apply your ideas to as many different kinds of text as you can.

Why do you think it is important to be able to identify main ideas and themes? How can this help you in everyday life?

LESSON 1.1 Determine the Main Idea

LESSON OBJECTIVES

- Determine the main ideas and supporting details of a text
- Identify main ideas in different types of texts

CORE SKILLS

- Determine Main Ideas
- Identify Main Ideas in Various Texts

Key Terms

main idea
most important idea in a paragraph or passage

supporting details
facts, opinions, examples, or other details that help explain the main idea

topic sentence
sentence stating the main idea of a paragraph or passage

Vocabulary

identify
find, pinpoint

informational text
passage meant to explain, describe, instruct, or persuade

literary text
passage based on imagination or reality that tells a story

Key Concept

The main idea is the most important idea in a paragraph or passage. A main idea can be found in many different kinds of texts.

Have you ever been asked to tell what a book or a movie was about? To do this, you had to figure out what the main idea, or the most important idea, in the work was. To find the main idea of any text, ask yourself the following question: What is the most important thing the writer is saying?

Main Ideas

Almost everything you read has a **main idea**, or the most important idea of the passage. It doesn't matter if you are reading a novel, a newspaper article, a textbook, a webpage, or a company's policy manual: the writer is trying to communicate one or more main ideas. A sentence that states the main idea of a paragraph or passage is known as a **topic sentence**.

Identify the Main Idea in Paragraphs

Understanding the structure of a paragraph will help you **identify**, or find, the main idea. A paragraph usually consists of a topic sentence and several other sentences that explain or give details about the topic. Often the topic sentence is the first sentence in a paragraph. However, the topic sentence may appear in the middle or at the end of a paragraph. Sometimes the topic sentence is not directly stated but suggested. All the other sentences within the paragraph focus on, or relate to, the topic sentence.

Suppose you were reading a paragraph on the topic of missing children. Within the paragraph, the author would focus on a single issue concerning the topic, such as the fact that the largest reported group of missing children is runaways. The following sentences are examples of other topic sentences, each of which could be expanded into a paragraph.

- A large number of children are kidnapped by relatives or friends rather than strangers.
- Stricter laws should be passed to punish people who abduct children.
- Fingerprinting and videotaping are two ways to help identify missing children.

- Grace Hechinger's book, *How to a Raise Street-Smart Child*, offers advice to families about facing the problems of child abduction.

Notice how each sentence makes a clear, definite statement about the topic of missing children. Authors often directly state the main idea when they are presenting information.

Determine the Main Idea

When you are reading a newspaper, you immediately notice the headlines:

Police Crack Down on Drug Ring

Blizzard Paralyzes City

Funding for Day-Care Centers Slashed

Baseball Players Threaten to Strike

Lottery Winner Takes All: A Cool Million

Headlines attract your attention. This is because they serve a very important purpose: they alert you to the content of the news story that follows. A headline tells you, in brief, what a story is mainly about. You expect newspaper articles to explain the headlines in more detail. The following example demonstrates this relationship between a headline and a news story.

Directions: Read the story, and write down the story's topic.

Woman Lifts Car Off Son

CALIFORNIA—Cynthia Burgess, a five-foot-three, 110-pound woman, lifted a Toyota weighing nearly a ton off her son, who was trapped under the car when the emergency brake was accidentally released. She described her show of strength as "no big deal."

If you wrote down that the story is about a woman who lifts a car off her son, you understood that the headline is the topic of the story.

Identify Details

Now look at how a topic sentence can be developed into a paragraph.

Grace Hechinger's book, *How to Raise a Street-Smart Child*, offers advice to families about facing the problems of child abduction. The author urges parents to discuss the subject of missing children openly. By honestly telling children about kidnappers, parents can teach their children how to avoid dangerous situations and to feel more secure. The author also suggests that parents establish rules to ensure their children's safety. Parents who want to protect their children from kidnappers will find this book invaluable.

As you can see, all the sentences in the paragraph relate to the main idea expressed in the boldfaced topic sentence. They explain the author's purpose and highlight what makes the book worth reading. In other words, they give details, such as facts, opinions, examples, and explanations, which help you understand the main idea. These are known as **supporting details**. Recognizing the main idea helps you organize your reading. Once you understand the major point of a paragraph, you can better understand how the remaining sentences are linked to the main idea.

WRITE TO LEARN

Write a one-paragraph newspaper article to go with one of the headlines listed near the top of this page. In your paragraph, include supporting details to help the reader understand the main idea expressed in the headline. Make sure that everything you write is related to the main idea.

CORE SKILL

Determine Main Ideas

To find the main idea and the topic sentence of a paragraph, follow this procedure:

1. Read the entire paragraph.
2. Ask yourself, "What is the author writing about?" This is the topic.
3. Ask yourself, "What is the author saying about the topic?" This is the main idea.
4. Look for a sentence that generally states the main idea. This is the topic sentence.

Find an article in a print or online magazine that interests you. With a partner, find the main idea of the entire article using the procedure above. Then look for the main idea in some of the paragraphs in the article.

LANGUAGE SKILL

Punctuation: Commas

Knowing how commas are used will help you understand the texts you read and help you write texts others can understand easily.

Use a comma

- to separate items in a series.
- after an introductory element.
- to separate text that provides additional details.
- to separate independent ideas.

However, unless you can state the reason for using a comma, don't put one in.

Read the sentences below, and place commas where necessary.

1. Although the meeting is in Philadelphia a teleconference is planned as well.
2. Jacob knew the consequences but he decided to speak up anyway.
3. Ms. Ortega an immigrant from Chile came to our class yesterday.
4. Our university's three largest schools are Architecture Business and Media.

As you read through the rest of the lesson, notice where commas are placed and ask yourself the reason for their placement.

Identify Unstated Main Ideas

Sometimes a main idea is not stated directly. When reading a passage that does not have a clear topic sentence, ask yourself: *What is the most important thing the writer is saying?* The answer is the main idea.

Read the following passage, and write a sentence stating its main idea.

> The pharaoh and other members of the royal family were at the top of Egyptian society, followed by the upper class of priests and nobles. Priests took care of the temples and celebrated religious ceremonies, while nobles oversaw the government. The rest of the people were divided into educated professionals, such as scribes and doctors, and a broad working class. At the bottom of Egyptian society were the tenant farmers, servants, and slaves.

The main idea of this passage is that Ancient Egyptian society had a clear class structure. This idea is not stated directly, but each sentence supports it.

Think about Reading

Directions: Read the sentences in the first column. For each sentence, draw a line to a. b. or c. to explain what kind of supporting detail the sentence provides.

1. The author urges parents to discuss the subject of missing children openly.
2. By honestly telling children about kidnappers, parents can teach their children how to avoid dangerous situations and to feel more secure.
3. The author also suggests that parents establish rules to ensure their children's safety.
4. Parents who want to protect their children from kidnappers will find this book invaluable.

a. It gives the author's opinion of Hechinger's book.

b. It gives the reason why Hechinger offers a particular piece of advice.

c. It gives an example of the advice Hechinger offers in the book.

Main Ideas in Various Texts

You encounter several different kinds of texts every day. Signs and notices are everywhere—at school, at work, and on the street. You may read books and newspapers, e-books and websites, e-mails and text messages. No matter what kind of text it is—a novel, a blog, or a manual—it is helpful to identify and understand its main ideas.

Different Types of Texts

In general, texts are literary or informational.

Literary texts tell a story. One type of literary text is fiction. Fiction focuses on characters and events that the author has imagined. Examples of fiction are novels and short stories. Literary texts can also be nonfiction. Nonfiction texts are about real people, places, and events. Examples of nonfiction literary texts are biographies, autobiographies, and memoirs. Just as in other texts, paragraphs and passages in literary texts focus on a main idea. They may also identify that main idea in one topic sentence.

Informational texts explain, describe, instruct, or try to persuade. There is a wide range of informational texts, from news reports to rental agreements. They are based on factual information, which often consists of details that support a main idea.

As you read the paragraph below, use a concept web like the one shown below to identify the main idea in the center circle and the details in the outer circles. You can find a blank concept map in the Graphic Organizer section at the back of the book.

> With varying degrees of success, many women around the world today struggle for equal rights. Historically, the following three factors have initiated the greatest number of improvements for women: violent revolution, world war, and the rigors of pioneering in an undeveloped land. In all three cases, the essential element that improved the status of women was a shortage of men, which required women to perform many of the tasks that had been reserved for men. As a result, women have achieved greater equality with men during periods of social adversity [challenges].

Concept Web

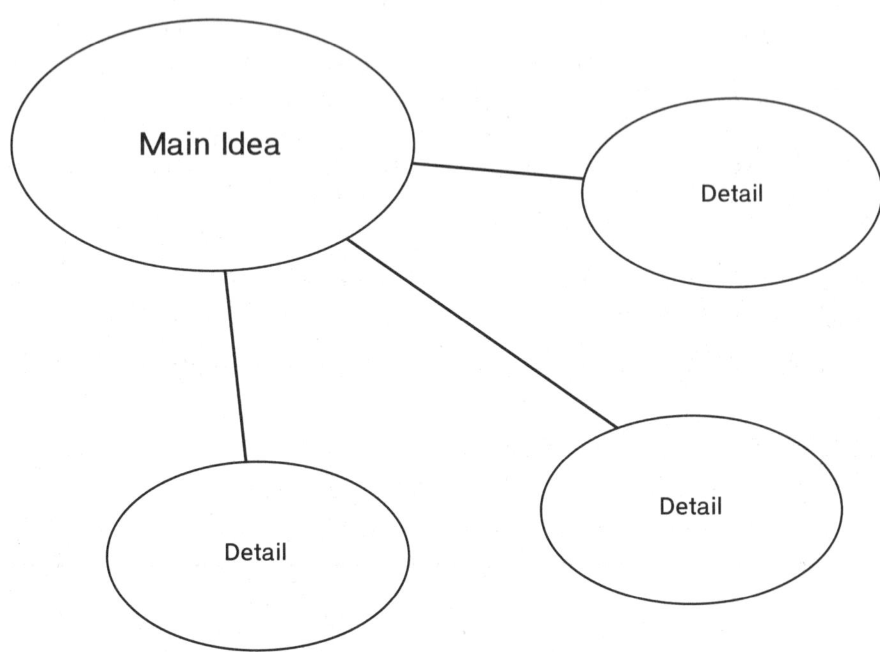

CORE SKILL

Identify Main Ideas in Various Texts

The topic sentence is not always the first sentence in a paragraph. Often in informational texts, key facts are presented first, leading to an ending that makes a point using the facts.

Read the paragraph about women's equality on this page. Ask yourself: *Which sentence do the facts in the paragraph support?* The answer is the topic sentence.

Decide which sentence is the topic sentence, and exchange and discuss your answers with a partner.

Directions: Read the following passage from the novel *The Log of a Cowboy* by Andy Adams. Underline the main idea.

(1) For the trip, each man was expected to furnish his own accoutrements [equipment]. (2) In saddles, we had the ordinary Texas make . . . (3) Our bridles were in keeping with the saddles, the reins as long as plough lines, while the bit was frequently ornamental and costly. (4) The indispensable slicker, a greatcoat of oiled canvas, was ever at hand, securely tied to our cantle strings. (5) Spurs were a matter of taste. (6) If a rider carried a quirt [short riding whip], he usually dispensed with spurs, though, when used, those with large, dull rowels [part of a spur: a turning wheel with sharp points] were the make commonly chosen. (7) In the matter of leggings, not over half our outfit had any, as a trail herd always kept in the open, and except for night herding, they were too warm in summer. (8) Our craft never used a cattle whip, but if emergency required, the loose end of a rope served instead and was more humane.

Think about Reading

Directions: Answer the following questions about the excerpt from *The Log of a Cowboy*.

1. Which sentence states the main idea?
2. How does the rest of the passage support the main idea?
3. List three details that support the main idea.

Joey Celis/Getty Images

Directions: Read the following bulletin board memo. Use the headings to help determine the main ideas.

MEMO

To: All employees

From: Maintenance

Date: April 5, 2014

Subject: Office Recycling

Kantaka Engineering Office Recycling Program

All employees should recycle following our company's established procedures. Separate the paper recyclables from nonpaper recyclables. Large green containers are for paper recyclables. Tall blue containers are for nonpaper recyclables. The containers are located in the copy/supply room. Every Friday, maintenance will collect all recyclables and bring them to the recycling center. The following items are recyclable:

Mixed Paper. White paper, envelopes, newsprint, colored paper, file folders, lined paper, computer paper, magazines, and shredded paper can be placed in the green containers.

Cardboard. Cardboard should be flattened, labeled, and placed next to a regular trash can for pickup by maintenance.

Bottles and Cans. Please clean all bottles and cans and place them in the blue containers.

E-Waste. Old/outdated electronics such as computers, monitors, and printers contain heavy metals that, if disposed of improperly, can be toxic to the environment. Call the Information Technology Department for disposal.

Think about Reading

Directions: Next to each statement, circle T if the statement is true or F if it is false.

1. T F Literary texts do not contain topic sentences.
2. T F Literary texts include both fiction and nonfiction texts.
3. T F Workplace texts may use headings to emphasize main ideas.

Summary

A passage or a paragraph often centers around one main idea. The main idea provides the overall focus of the passage. Often, a topic sentence states in general terms what the passage is about. Every other sentence in the passage includes supporting details that relate to the topic sentence and the main idea.

WORKPLACE SKILL

Communicating the Main Idea of a Memo

In the workplace, memos and e-mails are used to communicate important information to employees. They may be about procedures, meetings, changes in the organization, or other information that needs to be communicated. Read the memo on this page. Note that the section at the top of a memo tells the date, the subject, and the name of the sender. The subject line and headings within the memo can help you determine the main ideas. Ask yourself:

- What subject is given in the subject line?
- What is the title of the memo?
- What topics are mentioned in the headings?
- What details are included under the headings?

In your notebook, write an e-mail message identifying the main ideas in the memo to a coworker.

Vocabulary Review

Directions: Complete the sentences using the following key terms and vocabulary words.

identify	**informational text**	**literary text**
main idea	**supporting details**	**topic sentence**

1. The workers at the museum couldn't wait to ________________ the fossil.
2. Maya Angelou's memoir is a good example of a(n) ________________.
3. Nyah's teacher asked her to make sure each paragraph in her essay had a(n) ________________ expressed in a(n) ________________.
4. The speaker's story was so memorable because of the hilarious ________________ that brought the topic to life.
5. A workplace document is generally a(n) ________________.

Skill Review

Directions: Read the passage below. Then choose the best answer to each question.

> (1) The people had stopped moving out of church. (2) Whispers passed along, and a boding uneasiness took possession of every countenance. (3) Children were anxiously questioned, and young teachers. (4) They all said they had not noticed whether Tom and Becky were on board the ferryboat on the homeward trip; it was dark; no one thought of inquiring if anyone was missing. (5) One young man finally blurted out his fear that they were still in the cave! (6) Mrs. Thatcher swooned away. (7) Aunt Polly fell to crying and wringing her hands.
>
> —Mark Twain, *The Adventures of Tom Sawyer*

1. What is the main idea of the passage?
   A. People are worried about the church.
   B. People are worried because the children are being questioned.
   C. People are worried because Tom and Becky are missing.
   D. People are worried about the way Mrs. Thatcher and Aunt Polly are behaving.

2. Which words in sentences 2 and 3 indicate that people are worried?
   A. "whispers" and "young"
   B. "passed along" and "questioned"
   C. "took possession" and "teachers"
   D. "boding uneasiness" and "anxiously"

3. The events "people passing whispers," "Mrs. Thatcher swooning," and "Aunt Polly crying" indicate that
   A. people are concerned.
   B. no one asked about Tom and Becky.
   C. it had become dark outside.
   D. Tom and Becky are on the ferryboat.

4. Which of the following statements best describes how the reader would know that the main idea of the passage is unstated?
   A. There is a topic sentence at the beginning of the passage.
   B. There a topic sentence in the middle of the passage.
   C. There is a topic sentence at the end of the passage.
   D. There is no topic sentence in the passage.

Skill Practice

Directions: Read the passage below. Then choose the best answer to each question.

5 July, 1775.

I should have been more particular, but I thought you knew everything that passed here. The present state of the inhabitants of Boston is that of the most abject slaves, under the most cruel and despotic of tyrants. Among many instances I could mention, let me relate one. Upon the 17th of June, printed handbills were posted up at the corners of the streets, and upon houses, forbidding any inhabitants to go upon their houses, or upon any eminence [high place], on pain of death; the inhabitants dared not to look out of their houses, nor to be heard or seen to ask a question.

Our prisoners were brought over to the Long Wharf, and there lay all night, without any care of their wounds, or any resting-place but the pavements, until the next day, when they exchanged it for the jail, since which we hear they are civilly treated. Their living cannot be good, as they can have no fresh provisions; their beef, we hear, is all gone, and their wounded men die very fast, so that they have a report that the bullets were poisoned. Fish they cannot have, they have rendered it so difficult to procure; and the admiral is such a villain as to oblige every fishing schooner to pay a dollar every time it goes out.

The money that has been paid for passes is incredible. Some have given ten, twenty, thirty, and forty dollars, to get out with a small proportion of their things.

It is reported and believed that they have taken up a number of persons and committed them to jail, we know not for what in particular. Master Lovell is confined in the dungeon; a son of Mr. Edes is in jail, and one Wiburt, a ship-carpenter, is now upon trial for his life. God alone knows to what length these wretches will go, and will, I hope, restrain their malice.

—Abigail Adams, letter to her husband, John Adams

1. Which sentence best states the topic of the passage?

A. Adams thought her husband knew the conditions in Boston.

B. The inhabitants of Boston are slaves.

C. People in Boston are suffering.

D. People are leaving Boston.

2. Which sentence states the main idea of the 2nd paragraph?

A. Prisoners have to pay for their food.

B. Prisoners live in poor conditions.

C. Prisoners have been poisoned.

D. Prisoners are kept outside.

3. Which of the following events does the author use to support the idea that Bostonians are being treated unfairly?

A. Handbills were posted.

B. Prisoners were brought to the Long Wharf.

C. Fish was difficult to procure.

D. People were jailed for no reason.

4. Which definition best matches the use of the word **committed** in the final paragraph of the passage?

A. placed

B. dedicated

C. promised

D. recorded

Writing Practice

Directions: Find a news article in a print or an online newspaper on a specific current event. Write a topic sentence that gives the main idea of the article. Then, in two or three sentences, explain the key supporting details. Make sure all the key details in your summary support the main idea.

LESSON 1.2 Identify Supporting Details

LESSON OBJECTIVES

- Determine which details in a text support the main idea
- Use supporting details to make generalizations about a text

CORE SKILLS

- Identify Supporting Details
- Cite Details

Key Terms

generalization
broad statement

Vocabulary

description
statement of what someone or something is like

observe
watch carefully

visualize
form a mental picture

Key Concept

Supporting details are concrete ideas that develop the main idea in a passage. There are many types of supporting details.

In conversation, you often use supporting details to explain or to clarify a general comment. If you were telling someone that you enjoyed watching a certain TV show, you might give an example of your favorite episode. You could also describe major characters, offer reasons why the show is so entertaining, or report facts about the actors. Similarly, authors use examples, reasons, facts, and descriptions to support main ideas in their writing.

Supporting Details

Authors develop main ideas with different types of details. These supporting details may include descriptions, facts, reasons, and examples. A **description** is a statement that says what something or someone is like. It often gives sensory details such as color, shape, or scent.

In a descriptive passage, supporting details give information about the main idea. The author's purpose in developing a main idea through descriptive details is to help you **visualize** a person, place, object, or event. To visualize is to form a mental picture.

Facts are another type of supporting detail. Facts are statements that can be proved. Authors develop their main ideas with facts when their purpose is to explain or to persuade by conveying detailed and accurate information.

Examples and reasons are two more types of supporting details. You can more clearly understand the meaning of a general statement when you are given an example or a reason. Examples are specific illustration of an idea, and reasons are the explanation of an idea. Below are some examples of types of supporting details.

1. Experts estimate that the force of the Tunguska explosion was 1,000 times stronger than the atomic bomb dropped on Hiroshima.
2. By mid-morning, storm clouds darkened the sky, rain began to fall, and the winds started to pick up.

(Continued on page 21)

Glow Images

(Continued from page 20)

3. Marine debris is [a] persistent pollution problem in our ocean. Marine debris injures and kills marine life, interferes with navigation safety, and poses a threat to human health. (National Oceanic and Atmospheric Administration)

Think about Reading

Directions: Read the sentences in the box on the previous page and the sentences above to identify which sentences are descriptions, which ones are facts, and which ones are reasons or examples. Write the type of supporting detail next to the number of the sentence below. Remember that a supporting detail can fit into more than one category. For example, a detail could be a fact and a reason or example.

1. ____________ 2. ____________ 3. ____________

Differentiating between Types of Supporting Details

To support the main idea, a writer does not usually use only description, only facts, only examples, or only reasons. He or she uses a mixture of them.

Directions: Read the passage about marine debris below. Underline the main idea, and write the kinds of details the author uses to support it.

> Marine debris is [a] persistent pollution problem in our ocean. Marine debris injures and kills marine life, interferes with navigation safety, and poses a threat to human health. Our oceans and waterways are polluted with a wide variety of marine debris, ranging from soda cans and plastic bags to derelict fishing gear and abandoned vessels. Today, there is no place on Earth immune to this problem.
>
> —The National Oceanic and Atmospheric Administration

In this passage, the main idea is stated in the first sentence: "Marine debris is [a] persistent pollution problem in our ocean." In the second sentence, the writer lists reasons why marine debris is a problem. The third sentence provides examples of marine debris.

Directions: Read the passage, and underline each supporting detail. What types of details does the writer use?

The Great Galveston Hurricane of 1900

By mid-morning, storm clouds darkened the sky, rain began to fall, and the winds started to pick up. The frightening hurricane hit full-force by late afternoon and became increasingly worse as complete darkness fell. The terrified residents of Galveston huddled together in their houses and slowly climbed to upper floors and then attics as the water level crept up in the city. Eventually, the winds of the hurricane rose to 135 miles per hour—a category 4 storm by today's meteorological standards. The high winds drove a fifteen-foot storm surge over the city, swamping everything it crossed.

If you recognized that the writer used description and facts to discuss the hurricane, you have grasped how writers use details to support main ideas.

CORE SKILL

Identify Supporting Details

Supporting details can describe, provide factual information, or give examples or reasons to support the main idea.

To identify supporting details in a passage, follow these steps:

1. Read the entire passage.
2. Ask yourself: *What is the author writing about?* This is the main idea.
3. Then ask yourself: *What pieces of information describe, provide factual information, illustrate, or explain and expand the main idea?* These are the supporting details.

Working with a partner, take turns choosing paragraphs in a newspaper or magazine article. Have one partner find the main idea and the other select the details that support it. Then switch roles.

WRITE TO LEARN

Write a short paragraph on the topic "My Favorite Place." Use description, factual information, reasons, or examples as details to support your main idea of why a certain place is your favorite. At the end of the paragraph write what type of detail you chose to use and why.

LANGUAGE SKILL

Use Complete Sentences

A complete sentence must have a subject and a predicate. The subject names the person or thing that the sentence is about. The predicate, which always includes a verb, tells what the subject is or what the subject is doing.

In the sentence, "A caterpillar inched across the yard," *caterpillar* is the subject, and *inched across the yard* is the predicate.

If the subject or predicate is missing, the group of words is not a complete sentence; it is a fragment.

A fragment may be missing the subject or the predicate.

- *Buried the bone*
- *The great and powerful ox*

It is also possible for a fragment to contain a subject and a predicate but be unable to stand alone. This occurs when it follows a subordinating conjunction, such as *after, when, if,* or *because.*

- *after the lightning flashed*

Which of the following are complete sentences?

A. Where the horses run free.

B. Lighting the fire.

C. Rain falls.

D. Won't he come home?

Finish any fragments to make them complete sentences.

Think about Reading

Directions: On the lines below, write three supporting details from the passage about the Galveston hurricane. Be sure to include both types of details: description and fact. After each one, write what type of detail it is.

1. ______________________________
2. ______________________________
3. ______________________________

Using Details to Make Generalizations

As you **observe**, or carefully watch, the world around you, you can make **generalizations**, or broad statements, based on details in your environment. Making generalizations is a way of drawing conclusions based on your knowledge of what you experience. Details, whether in reading or in your environment, provide the information you need to more fully understand your experience. In this section, you will learn how to cite details to make generalizations about a text.

Directions: Study the photograph of the beach. What details do you observe? What do these details tell you about the shoreline and the ocean?

LCDR Eric Johnson, NOAA Corps, NOAA/Dept. of Commerce

You can observe from the photo that the beach is polluted. If you saw other photographs showing people dumping trash in the ocean, you could generalize that people cause beaches to become polluted. The details that you put together and cite to make this generalization would be the debris on the beach and the people dumping their trash.

In a similar way, when you read a text, you use supporting details to make generalizations about the author's ideas. Supporting details provide the information you need to understand the main idea of the text more fully. For example, you can use supporting details to help you find the meaning of a term or concept in your reading that you do not fully understand.

Directions: Read the passage below, which describes a very particular type of pollution and how it occurs. Which supporting details in the passage help you generalize that nutrients can harm ocean life?

Sometimes it is not the type of material, but its concentration, that determines if it is a pollutant. For example, nutrients such as nitrogen and phosphorus are essential elements for plant growth. However, if they are overabundant in a body of water, they can stimulate an overgrowth of algae called an algal bloom. Some algal blooms are considered to be harmful because they can have a negative effect on living organisms. An excess of nutrients entering a body of water, either through natural or human activities, can also result in hypoxic or dead zones. When large amounts of algae sink and decompose in the water, the decomposition process consumes oxygen and depletes the supply available to healthy marine life. Most of the marine life that lives in these areas either dies, or, if they are mobile such as fish, leave the area. Habitats that would normally be teeming with life become, essentially, biological deserts.

—The National Oceanic and Atmospheric Administration

Think about Reading

Directions: Reread the passage above about a type of ocean pollution that involves excess nutrients. List four details that help you understand what *dead zones* are and how they are formed. Then write a sentence explaining the concept of *dead zones* in your own words.

1. ______________________________
2. ______________________________
3. ______________________________
4. ______________________________

Explanation of *dead zones*: ______________________________

____

Summary

Supporting details help readers understand the main idea of a text. To identify the supporting details, ask yourself: *What pieces of information describe, provide factual information about, give examples of, explain, or expand the main idea?* These are the supporting details.

The supporting details in a text can also give you the information you need to make a generalization about the text and to help you reveal unstated information and clarify its meaning.

CORE SKILL

Cite Details

As you have learned, supporting details can help you determine the main idea, as well as hint at information that is not directly stated, allowing you to generalize about the meaning of the passage.

Reread the paragraph about the Galveston hurricane. What is the main idea?

The main idea of the passage could be stated: "The Galveston hurricane was devastating." Cite details by making a list of all the supporting details that helped you determine this main idea. Then compare your list of details with a partner's.

Next, try citing details that might help you generalize about the nature of hurricanes.

The description of the hurricane consisted of details about high winds and rain and the fact that 135 miles per hour winds constitute a category 4 storm. These details allow you to generalize that hurricanes are an extreme type of storm.

Vocabulary Review

Directions: Fill in the blank with the word that best completes each of the sentences below.

description **generalization** **observe** **visualize**

1. The author provided enough detail about the setting so the reader could ________________ it.
2. When we put together details in our environment, we can make a ________________ about what we are observing.
3. If you closely ________________ your surroundings, then you will be able to better understand what you are experiencing.
4. Write a ________________ about a place so your reader will be able to experience what it is like there.

Skill Review

Directions: Read the passage below. Then complete the activities.

Only extremely fast-moving shock waves can break off branches without knocking down a whole tree. After an atomic bomb was dropped on Hiroshima, Japan, in 1945, people observed a similar phenomenon. Experts estimate that the force of the Tunguska explosion was 1,000 times stronger than the atomic bomb dropped on Hiroshima. If the blast had occurred over a populated area, it would have been catastrophic.

1. What is the main idea of the passage?
   A. The Tunguska explosion did not cause much damage.
   B. The Tungaska explosion had a greater effect than an atomic bomb.
   C. The Tunguska explosion knocked down many trees.
   D. An atomic bomb was dropped at Tunguska.

2. List two supporting details that helped you determine the main idea.
   A. ________________
   B. ________________

Skill Practice

Directions: Read the passage below. Then choose the best answer to each question.

> As I see it, it is not going to be easy to attain unanimity with respect to our different concepts of government and human rights. The struggle is bound to be difficult and one in which we must be firm but patient. If we adhere faithfully to our principles, I think it is possible for us to maintain freedom and to do so peacefully and without recourse to force.
>
> The future must see the broadening of human rights throughout the world. People who have glimpsed freedom will never be content until they have secured it for themselves. In a truest sense, human rights are a fundamental object of law and government in a just society.
>
> Human rights exist to the degree that they are respected by people in relations with each other and by governments in relations with their citizens.
>
> —From "The Struggle for Human Rights" speech by Eleanor Roosevelt

1. Which detail does not support the main idea that expanding human rights is an important mission?

A. It is not going to be easy to attain unanimity with respect to our different concepts of government and human rights.

B. People who have glimpsed freedom will never be content until they have secured it for themselves.

C. The future must see the broadening of human rights throughout the world.

D. Human rights are a fundamental object of law and government in a just society.

2. What kind of supporting detail is provided in this sentence: "People who have glimpsed freedom will never be content until they have secured it for themselves"?

A. description

B. example

C. fact

D. reason

Writing Practice

Directions: Write a paragraph describing an event you witnessed or participated in that was particularly interesting or significant. Use at least three types of supporting details in your paragraph to help the reader experience and understand the interest or significance of the event.

LESSON 1.3 Identify Direct and Implied Main Ideas

LESSON OBJECTIVES

- Recognize the difference between direct and implied main ideas
- Identify implied main ideas and their supporting details

CORE SKILLS

- Determine Implied Main Ideas
- Use Details to Deduce Central and Supporting Ideas

Key Terms

deduce
figure out

implied
expressed indirectly

Vocabulary

collaboration
the act of working together with others

emphasize
stress or highlight

Key Concept

A main idea may be stated directly in a topic sentence or sentences, or it may be implied. An implied main idea must be inferred from supporting details.

Have you ever told your friends a story about something that happened to you? You may have announced the point of your story right away. For example, you may have said, "Yesterday was the luckiest day of my life," and then gone on to describe all the things that made it lucky. Or you may have told your story one detail at a time and let your friends figure out the point of the story as you went along. In the first case, you stated your main idea directly; in the second, you implied the main idea.

Direct and Implied Main Ideas

When you read a text passage, usually one idea emerges as central. This main idea may be stated directly in one or more sentences. For example, in a newspaper article, the main idea is often stated in the first sentence or the headline. Note how the first sentence of the following paragraph tells the reader the main idea. The remaining sentences provide details about that idea, such as the magnitude of the earthquake and some history about a tsunami related to another earthquake in the region.

> A strong earthquake has struck in the Indian Ocean, raising fears of a tsunami in South Asian coastal communities. The magnitude 7.8 quake caused no immediate damage. However, countries in this region were devastated by a massive tsunami following a 9.0 quake off the island of Sumatra in December 2004, and today's quake has led many to flee low-lying areas.

Sometimes, however, an author does not directly state the main idea. Instead, the main idea is **implied**, or expressed indirectly. In such cases, you must **deduce**, or figure out, the main idea. Each detail presents a part of what the passage is about. To identify an implied main idea, think about all the details and determine how they are related.

Directions: Read the passage below from "The Gift of the Magi" by O. Henry. In this passage, the main idea is not directly stated. Underline the details that offer clues to the implied main idea.

For there lay The Combs—the set of combs, side and back, that Della had worshipped long in a Broadway window. Beautiful combs, pure tortoise shell, with jeweled rims—just the shade to wear in the beautiful vanished hair. They were expensive combs, she knew, and her heart had simply craved and yearned over them without the least hope of possession. And now, they were hers, but the tresses that should have adorned the coveted adornments were gone.

—From "The Gift of the Magi" by O. Henry

In the passage, you learn that Della loved the combs, which she now owns. You also learn that her tresses, or long hair, have been cut. These details help you determine the implied main idea: "Della finally owns the combs she always wanted, but now she cannot use them."

Implied Main Ideas and Supporting Details

When you read a passage with an implied main idea, often some of the sentences contain key phrases that serve as stronger clues to determining the main idea than others. It is important to recognize these sentences because they tie all the ideas together.

Directions: In the passage below, some sentences offer clues to the main idea, whereas others do not. Read the passage about the early days of the settlers in the Great Plains before poor farming practices and drought led this area to become the Dust Bowl. See whether you can identify the implied main idea, paying close attention to the ideas each sentence suggests.

What the settlers to the Great Plains could not see were the deep networks of roots that tightly anchored the fertile soil. The roots were so thick and matted it took steel plows, invented by John Deere in 1837, to cut through them. But to the farmers the back-breaking effort was worth it as grain prices had soared in the late 1920s and early 30s. Parts of the country were experiencing an economic depression, but not the Great Plains farmers. Their grain was golden.

—From *Black Blizzards* by Linda Perl

Remember that often, some of the sentences in a passage provide more clues to tie all of the ideas together than do other sentences. Locate those sentences and use them to help you deduce the main idea. The implied main idea of the passage could be stated, "The Great Plains farmers worked hard and prospered."

CORE SKILL

Determine Implied Main Ideas

To identify an implied main idea of a passage, follow these steps:

1. Read the entire passage.
2. Look for details that tell what the passage is about.
3. Determine how the details are related.
4. Identify any key phrases that tie the ideas together.
5. Determine what idea connects all the details.

Select a paragraph from a novel, short story, or article. Read it, and determine whether the main idea is directly stated or implied. If the main idea is stated, find the sentence that best states the main idea. If the main idea is implied, follow the steps above to identify it, and state it in your own words. Repeat the process with two or three different paragraphs.

WRITE TO LEARN

Write a paragraph with an implied main idea. Compose a one-paragraph description of something in the room in which you are sitting without directly naming the object. In your paragraph, make sure that you use many details that would help a reader figure out what you are writing about.

Exchange paragraphs with a partner, and determine the main idea of each other's paragraphs.

21st CENTURY SKILL

Communication and Collaboration

Every time you talk with a friend or send a text, you are using communication skills. Working jointly with others to accomplish shared goals is called **collaboration**.

Today, with all the ways we have to communicate and collaborate, it is more important than ever to be thoughtful when interacting with others. Sometimes it is hard to tell what people mean while speaking and in writing. Read and apply the tips below for communicating and collaborating in future endeavors.

Tips for Communicating

- Express ideas clearly.
- Listen carefully.
- Acknowledge other people's values and opinions.

Tips for Collaborating

- Respect the people you are working with.
- Be open-minded and willing to compromise.
- Share responsibility.

Write a short e-mail to a supervisor or colleague describing a problem at work, using the above tips. Use details to describe the problem clearly. Be careful that your words do not imply ideas you do not wish to communicate. Consider how your words may affect the recipient of the message.

Think about Reading

Directions: Read the following sentences, and place a checkmark beside the sentence or sentences that tie together the ideas that the farmers worked hard *and* prospered.

1. ________ "What the settlers to the Great Plains could not see were the deep networks of roots that tightly anchored the fertile soil."
2. ________ "The roots were so thick and matted it took steel plows, invented by John Deere in 1837, to cut through them."
3. ________ "But to the farmers the back-breaking effort was worth it as grain prices had soared in the late 1920s and early 30s."
4 ________ "Parts of the country were experiencing an economic depression, but not the Great Plains farmers."

Using Details to Deduce Central and Supporting Ideas

You have observed how supporting details are clues to discovering an implied main idea. These details also serve another purpose. Certain phrases and sentences hint at information that is not directly stated. From these specific details, you can draw conclusions that enable you to interpret a passage.

Every day, you use clues from your surrounding environment and your interactions with others to interpret situations. Imagine that you are seeking work and that you receive a message asking you to call the Human Resources Department of a company where you interviewed for a job. When you call, the director says, "Congratulations!" What would you deduce from the situation? You would probably expect the director to offer you a job.

Directions: Read the two scenarios below. For each, decide what you would deduce about the situation, and then list several details that helped you come to that conclusion. Write your answers in your notebook.

1. Observation: As a woman walks toward the door of a small clothing store, a high-pitched alarm goes off. The store manager races after the woman and grabs her arm. A sweater, stuffed inside the woman's coat, drops to the floor.
2. Observation: After a concert, people in the audience loudly clap their hands and cheer. Some stand and yell, "Bravo! Bravo!"

In reading, as in real life, the inferences that you make depend largely upon your powers of observation—your ability to spot important details or clues.

Directions: Read the excerpt below from the novel *Winesburg, Ohio* by Sherwood Anderson. What kinds of descriptive details does the author **emphasize**, or stress, in this passage? The details underlined below provide clues to the implied main idea.

> (1) Ray Pearson arose and stood staring. (2) He was almost a foot shorter than Hal, and when the younger man came and put his two hands on the older man's shoulders they made a picture. (3) There they stood in the big empty field with the quiet corn shocks standing in rows behind them and the red and yellow hills in the distance, and from being just two indifferent workmen they had become all alive to each other. (4) Hal sensed it and because that was his way he laughed.
>
> —From *Winesburg, Ohio* by Sherwood Anderson

The author describes two men and their relationship with one another, in terms of age, height, and occupation. The author also emphasizes the setting in which they are working. All these details help you deduce that the passage is about the relationship between the two men.

Think about Reading

Directions: Use the supporting details to deduce the answers to the following questions about the excerpt from *Winesburg, Ohio*.

1. How do Ray and Hal know each other?
2. Sherwood Anderson describes the moment at which Ray and Hal become __________.
3. Which sentence provides the best evidence that their relationship has changed?

Summary

An author does not always directly state the main idea of a text. Sometimes the main idea is implied. If you cannot find the main idea directly stated, you must look at the important details to determine how they are connected. Look for key sentences or phrases that tie all the important ideas together. Supporting details in a passage offer clues to an implied main idea and also to deducing other information that is not directly stated.

CORE SKILL

Use Details to Deduce Central and Supporting Ideas

In passages with implied main ideas, think about how the supporting details relate to one another to deduce what the passage is about. Ask yourself:

- Do the details have a common topic?
- Does the author emphasize particular details through techniques such as repetition?
- What does this emphasis tell you about the topic?

Read the paragraph from *Winesburg, Ohio* on this page. Using the questions above, determine and write the implied main idea. Then compare answers with a partner. If you have written different main ideas, review the details in the passage, work through the questions again together, and decide on the main idea.

Vocabulary Review

Directions: Match each term on the left with its definition on the right by drawing a line between the two.

1. implied	figure out
2. deduce	the act of working together
3. emphasize	expressed indirectly
4. collaboration	stress or highlight

Skill Review

Directions: Read the passage below. Then choose the best answer to each question.

Now, there were two possessions of the James Dillingham Youngs in which they both took a mighty pride. One was Jim's gold watch that had been his father's and his grandfather's. The other was Della's hair. Had the queen of Sheba lived in the flat across the airshaft, Della would have let her hair hang out the window some day to dry just to depreciate Her Majesty's jewels and gifts. Had King Solomon been the janitor, with all his treasures piled up in the basement, Jim would have pulled out his watch every time he passed, just to see him pluck at his beard from envy.

—From "The Gift of the Magi" by O. Henry

1. Which phrase from the passage most directly and completely states the main idea?

A. "Della would have let her hair hang out the window some day to dry just to depreciate Her Majesty's jewels and gifts."

B. "Now, there were two possessions of the James Dillingham Youngs in which they both took a mighty pride."

C. "One was Jim's gold watch that had been his father's and his grandfather's."

D. "The other was Della's hair."

2. Which detail best supports the idea that Della's hair was a prized possession?

A. They took pride in two possessions.

B. The queen of Sheba lived across the airshaft.

C. Della's hair would depreciate a queen's jewels.

D. The queen of Sheba had jewels and gifts.

3. Which detail best supports the idea that Jim's watch was a prized possession?

A. They took pride in two possessions.

B. King Solomon was the building janitor.

C. The king kept his treasures piled in the basement.

D. Seeing Jim's watch would have made Solomon envious.

Skill Practice

Directions: Read the passage below. Then choose the best answer to each question.

Some talked of gray, bewhiskered hordes who were advancing with relentless curses and chewing tobacco with unspeakable valor; tremendous bodies of fierce soldiery who were sweeping along like the Huns. Others spoke of tattered and eternally hungry men who fired despondent powders. "They'll charge through hell's fire an' brimstone t' git a holt on a haversack, an' sech stomachs ain't a'lastin' long," he was told. From the stories, the youth imagined the red, live bones sticking out through slits in the faded uniforms.

—From *The Red Badge of Courage* by Stephen Crane

1. Which statement about this passage is true?

A. The passage has no main idea.

B. The passage has a main idea that is directly stated.

C. The main idea has to be deduced from supporting details.

D. One of the sentences ties all the supporting ideas together.

2. Which idea does the author emphasize in the first sentence?

A. Veterans were brave.

B. Veterans were sorry to see the war end.

C. Veterans were reluctant to speak of their pasts.

D. Veterans described enemy soldiers the same way.

3. Based on the supporting details, what impression of war does the passage give?

A. War is glorious.

B. War is frightening.

C. War makes men vicious.

D. People become immune to the effects of war.

Writing Practice

Directions: Find two passages in a short story or a novel. In one of the passages, the main idea should be directly stated. In the other passage, the main idea should be implied. Read the two passages carefully.

A. For the passage in which the main idea is directly stated, write the topic sentence that states the main idea. Then write one or two sentences explaining how the supporting details in the passage relate to this main idea.

B. For the passage with the implied main idea, deduce the main idea using the supporting details and write the implied main idea in your own words. Then write one or two sentences explaining how the supporting details in the passage relate to this main idea.

LESSON 1.4 Summarize Details

LESSON OBJECTIVES

- Develop a summary of a short passage
- Summarize longer, more complex passages

CORE SKILLS

- Summarize Key Information
- Summarize a Text

Key Terms

paraphrase
to restate information in one's own words

summarize
to describe the main points in a concise manner

Vocabulary

comprehensive
complete; including most or all

concise
brief and to the point

skim
to read quickly, looking for main ideas and specific information

Key Concept

Explaining the most important ideas in a passage in a concise way is called summarizing. A summary includes the main idea and the key supporting details.

Have you ever read a great book and told a friend about it? You probably didn't describe the entire book from beginning to end. Instead, you picked the most important points or events in the book, probably starting with the main idea. Then you described some of the key details that support that main idea and made the book interesting. What you told your friend is a summary, or a concise version, of the book.

Summarizing Key Information

A summary provides a snapshot of a passage to tell what it is about. For this reason, tests often ask for summaries as demonstrations of understanding. Being able to summarize requires accurate understanding of the main ideas, key supporting details, and author's opinion—whether implicit or explicit—in a text. Summarizing requires you to capture the main points of a text without inserting your feelings or opinions about the topic.

Identifying Main Idea and Supporting Details

When you **summarize**, you describe the main points in a **concise** way, or in a manner that is brief and to the point. The key to summarizing a passage is figuring out what information is most important to remember.

When the main idea of a passage is stated, you have a clue about what information is most important in the passage. A topic sentence can often tell you what the main idea is. When you have determined the main idea, look for the key supporting details. These are the details that directly support and provide additional information about the main idea, as opposed to minor details, which may be interesting but are not directly relevant to the author's central point. Key details build upon one another, whether in sequence or through other relationships, to form and support the main idea and flow of ideas in a text.

Read the passage below from a book by William Hornaday.

> Between the Rocky Mountains and the States lying along the Mississippi River on the west, from Minnesota to Louisiana, the whole country was one vast buffalo range. [It was] inhabited by millions of buffaloes. One could fill a volume with the records of plainsmen and pioneers who penetrated or crossed that vast region between 1800 and 1870. [Many] were surprised, astounded, and frequently dismayed by the tens of thousands of buffaloes they observed, avoided, or escaped from. The buffaloes lived and moved as no other quadrupeds ever have. [They traveled] in great multitudes, like grand armies in review, covering scores of square miles at once. They were so numerous they frequently stopped boats in the rivers [and] threatened to overwhelm travelers on the plains. In later years, [they] derailed locomotives and cars, until railway engineers learned by experience the wisdom of stopping their trains whenever there were buffaloes crossing the track.
>
> —from "The Extermination of the American Bison" by William T. Hornaday

In the passage, the first sentence or two most completely states the main idea, which is that huge numbers of buffalo covered the American West. Now try summarizing the most important supporting details in a few concise sentences—these are the details that support the main idea and explain what the passage is about.

It is sometimes helpful to look for categories into which you can group details. In the paragraph above, there are two major categories of details. In the first category are details that describe how many buffalo there were. The second category contains details that describe what happened when travelers and settlers encountered these large herds.

Summarize in your own words the following details from the first category:

- The buffaloes lived and moved as no other quadrupeds ever have.
- [They traveled] in great multitudes, like grand armies in review, covering scores of square miles at once.

One possible summary is "Bison were unique among quadrupeds in that they lived and moved in huge herds."

Think about Reading

Directions: Reread the passage about buffalo. Complete the activities below.

1. In a notebook, list three details from the passage that describe what happened when travelers and settlers encountered these large herds.
2. Choose the sentence below that best paraphrases the details you have listed in your notebook.

   A. Buffalo moved like armies crossing the plains.

   B. Buffalo herds frequently disrupted travelers and commerce in the West.

   C. Buffalo were useful for their meat and hides.

   D. No other animal affected settlers as much as the buffalo.

CORE SKILL

Summarize Key Information

To summarize key information, you must identify the most important points and the information that supports them. This begins with understanding the main idea. To ensure you understand the main idea, **paraphrase**, or restate it in your own words. Use your paraphrase to find the most important supporting details. If the main idea is not directly stated, figure out the implied main idea by looking at the details in the passage to determine what the details are mainly about.

To summarize key information in a passage, follow this procedure:

1. **Skim**, or quickly read, the text to find the main idea.
2. Paraphrase the main idea.
3. Identify key details (they may be from more than one category).
4. Paraphrase these details in concise sentences.

Find a paragraph in a newspaper or magazine article. Follow the procedure above to summarize the main idea and key details into concise sentences.

CORE SKILL

Summarize a Text

To develop a summary of a text, follow the four steps for identifying and paraphrasing the main idea and key details of a passage. Then add two more:

1. Write a concise description in your own words that includes the paraphrased main idea and details.
2. Make grammatical changes to improve sentence flow.

Remember not to add your own opinion or feelings to your summary. If the author of the text expresses an opinion, however, it is important to include the author's opinion in your summary.

Find a political commentary. Follow the procedure above to summarize the text in no more than one paragraph. Remember to give the author's opinion, not your own.

WRITE TO LEARN

Follow the six steps to write a short summary of the passage by the prison teacher. Remember to paraphrase the main idea *in your own words.* Then identify, paraphrase, and rewrite the most important supporting details in a few concise sentences. Make the author's sympathies clear.

Summarizing a Text

Up to now, you have been identifying and paraphrasing key information in text, which are important steps toward creating a summary. Now you will combine what you have learned to write a complete summary of a passage.

Directions: Read the passage below. Determine the main idea, and write a sentence stating it in your own words.

> Tuesday mornings I strip myself of all worldly trappings—jewelry, keys, cell phone, money, identification. From the moment I step through the first of four electronic gates, I am cut off from anything outside. The "trap," as this doorway is called in prison parlance, is a portal in and out of the larger world. What lies beyond is a closed community about which little is known by those who live in the surrounding towns. There is not much of beauty behind these fences of chain link and coiled wire. Few things grow, except the dry grass of the yard and a few sparse border plantings tended by inmates as we walk past. Occasionally, a starling alights on the lawn, or a flock of geese flies over with their plaintive honking. I am here for a mere two hours each week, but the students I teach live in this stripped-down world 24 hours a day, 7 days a week, most without respite.

If your statement indicates that prison inmates live in a bleak and unattractive environment cut off from the outside world, then you have correctly restated the main idea.

Now reread the passage, and underline the key details. The first one you will notice is that the author has to give up all his or her possessions before entering the prison. The author gives examples of these possessions, but the examples support the key detail, not the main idea. You can leave them out of your summary.

Now, examine the author's word choice and the supporting details he or she includes when describing the prison's surroundings. How does the author feel about the life the inmates lead inside the prison?

One clue you may notice is the word *strip* in the first line. This word implies that, having given up "all worldly trappings," the author feels naked and vulnerable. You may also notice that the examples given of occasional moments of beauty are birds, which can fly away at any time—in stark contrast to the inmates, who cannot leave. These choices show that the author feels sympathy for the prisoners he or she teaches each week, not because they are convicted of a crime, but because they must spend all their time in such bleak, unrelenting surroundings.

Make sure that your summary briefly explains the author's attitude and how it is conveyed.

Using Text Features to Identify Main Ideas and Key Details

A useful tool in summarizing informational passages such as articles, memos, and instructions is text features. Boldfaced or italicized text, titles, section headings, and paragraph breaks provide clues about what information is most important. Text features such as headings and subheadings can reveal the main idea of a section or paragraph; italicized words and bullets indicate key details. Use text features to help you identify main ideas and key details. Then combine them into a **comprehensive**, or complete, summary.

Directions: Read the memo below, and identify the useful text features.

> # MEMO
>
> **To:** All employees
>
> **From:** Maintenance
>
> **Date:** April 5, 2014
>
> **Subject:** Office Recycling
>
> **Kantaka Engineering Office Recycling Program**
>
> All employees should recycle following our company's established procedures. Separate the paper recyclables from nonpaper recyclables. Large green containers are for paper recyclables. Tall blue containers are for nonpaper recyclables. The containers are located in the copy/supply room. Every Friday, maintenance will collect all recyclables and bring them to the recycling center. The following items are recyclable:
>
> **Mixed Paper.** White paper, envelopes, newsprint, colored paper, file folders, lined paper, computer paper, magazines, and shredded paper can be placed in the green containers.
>
> **Cardboard.** Cardboard should be flattened, labeled, and placed next to a regular trash can, for pickup by maintenance.
>
> **Bottles and Cans.** Please clean all bottles and cans and place them in the blue containers.
>
> **E-Waste.** Old/outdated electronics such as computers, monitors, and printers contain heavy metals, that, if disposed of improperly, can be toxic to the environment. Call the Information Technology Department for disposal.

Think about Reading

Directions: Read the following list of text features. Place a checkmark beside the features that are relevant to creating a summary of the memo above.

_______ **1.** Sender and recipient lines

_______ **2.** Subject line

_______ **3.** Title

_______ **4.** Boldfaced headings

_______ **5.** List of examples of mixed paper

_______ **6.** Capitalized words

TEST-TAKING SKILLS

Understand the Question

When taking a test, take the time to understand each question before answering it. Follow these steps.

- Read the directions carefully.
- Be sure you know what the question is asking.
- Have a strategy for answering questions.

There are two effective strategies for answering questions about a passage or a graphic. One method involves reading the passage or looking over the graphic once before reading the questions. Another method involves skimming the questions before reading the passage or looking at the graphic to give you an idea of what information to look for.

Regardless of which method you use, be sure to refer to the passage or graphic to confirm your answer choice. Summarize the information in the passage or graphic to make sure you understand it.

Working with a partner, choose a passage from this lesson, or from your other reading. Write a test question with three answer choices for your partner on a piece of paper. Exchange papers, and use what you have learned about test-taking skills to answer your partner's question. Then check the answers.

Summary

A summary concisely captures the most important information in a passage, including the main idea and key supporting details. Paraphrasing the main idea can help you determine which details are key. These details, which can sometimes be grouped into categories, tell what the passage is mainly about. Summarizing as you read can help you understand longer texts and complex passages.

Informational passages sometimes provide features such as titles, headings, numbered paragraphs, and boldfaced or italicized words that help you identify important ideas and details as you summarize text.

Vocabulary Review

Directions: Fill in the blanks with the key terms and vocabulary words from the word bank that best complete the sentences in the description of writing a summary.

paraphrase **summarize** **comprehensive** **concise** **skim**

When you 1) ________________ a text, you write the most important information in a 2) ________________ manner. First, 3) ________________ the text to determine the main idea and 4) ________________ the main idea using your own words. Use the main idea to locate key supporting details and combine these details into a 5) ________________ summary.

Skill Review

Directions: Read the passage. Then mark each of the statements below True (T) or False (F).

Trudy sliced through the water with a powerful crawl stroke all morning. A phonograph on one tugboat played lively songs and everyone cheered her along. However, by noon heavy rain was pelting the sea, and a strong wind was pushing Trudy off course. Several people on the tugboats became seasick due to the rough waters.

Twelve hours into her swim, the weather had become dire. Mr. Burgess had urged Trudy to quit several times. One friend yelled from a tugboat, "Trudy, you must come out!" Despite the discomfort of the boat passengers, Trudy refused to quit. She playfully rolled onto her back and quipped, "What for?"

Finally the shore of Kingsdown, England, was in sight. Trudy pushed herself to complete the last draining yards and then wobbled onto the beach. She had crossed the Channel in fourteen and a half hours. Not only had she had done it, but she made it in record time!

—From *Swimming the English Channel* by Mallory Garrison

________ **1.** One of the sentences in the passage states the complete main idea.

________ **2.** To summarize the passage, you would need to find the main idea and key details in each paragraph.

________ **3.** A good paraphrase of the passage's main idea might be: "Despite many challenges, Trudy swam the Channel in record time."

________ **4.** Trudy's use of the crawl stroke is a key detail that should be included in the summary.

Skill Practice

Directions: Read the passage below. Then choose the best answer to each question.

Federal agencies and institutions responsible for the enforcement of equal opportunity laws need the authority of a Constitutional amendment. The 1964 Civil Rights Act and the 1963 Equal Pay Act are not enough; they are limited in their coverage—for instance, one excludes teachers, and the other leaves out administrative and professional women. The Equal Employment Opportunity Commission has not proven to be an adequate device, with its power limited to investigation, conciliation, and recommendation to the Justice Department. In its cases involving sexual discrimination, it has failed in more than one-half. The Justice Department has been even less effective. It has intervened in only one case involving discrimination on the basis of sex, and this was on a procedural point. In a second case, in which both sexual and racial discrimination were alleged, the racial bias charge was given far greater weight.

—From Equal Rights Amendment speech by Shirley Chisholm

1. Which of the following sentences is the best paraphrase of the passage's main idea?

A. A Constitutional Amendment is needed to protect women's rights.

B. A Constitutional Amendment is needed to prevent racial discrimination.

C. The Justice Department has not been effective in preventing discrimination.

D. Sexual and racial discrimination are problems in the world today.

2. Which detail should be part of a comprehensive summary?

A. The Equal Pay Act was passed in 1963.

B. The Justice Department rarely hears cases of sexual discrimination.

C. Charges of racial bias are more important than charges of sexual bias.

D. The Equal Employment Opportunity Commission investigates complaints.

Writing Practice

Directions: Open a book, magazine, or newspaper and randomly choose an article or passage several paragraphs long. Write a comprehensive summary of the passage, using the procedure you have learned.

LESSON 1.5 Identify a Theme

LESSON OBJECTIVES

- Identify the theme of a fictional passage
- Synthesize multiple main ideas to determine the theme

CORE SKILLS

- Synthesize Details That Relate to the Theme
- Understand the Relationship among Ideas

Key Terms

theme
underlying message in a work of fiction

Vocabulary

conflict
a struggle between opposing forces in a story or play, usually resolved by the end of the work

perspective
particular standpoint or point of view

synthesize
combine parts or elements to form a new whole

Key Concept

The theme is the underlying meaning of a story. An author reveals the theme in a work of fiction through characters, setting, language, and other literary elements.

Have you ever gone to an art exhibit where all of the work expressed a certain idea or meaning, such as photographs of the innocence of childhood or paintings showing the diversity of the American landscape? This underlying idea that ties the works together is the exhibit's theme. Works of literature, such as short stories and novels, also have themes that tie the passages together with a coherent meaning.

Using Fictional Elements to Determine Theme

A **theme** is the central message in a literary text. Themes in short stories and novels express beliefs and opinions about life. A theme can reflect the author's attitudes toward political or social issues and his or her perceptions about human nature and relationships.

Although the theme is rarely directly stated by the author, sometimes a character's comments may reveal the theme. In most cases, however, the theme will not be stated by the characters or by the narrator. Instead, you will have to determine the story's meaning by interpreting the significance of the fictional elements—setting, plot, characterization, point of view, language, and **conflict**. The conflict may be a struggle between opposing forces or characters, or even an internal struggle within an individual character.

The action of a story is often observed through the eyes of a particular character. This is what is meant by *point of view*. Sometimes the story is told in first person; that is, by a character in the story. Other times, it is told in third person, or by an outside observer, but from one point of view. In some cases, however, the point of view may shift from character to character.

After analyzing all the fictional elements, you need to **synthesize** (combine elements to create a new idea) these details to determine the theme.

Christopher Kerrigan/McGraw-Hill Education

When you read a novel, story, or poem or see a play, key and minor details provide information about aspects such as the setting, the plot, the conflict, and the characters and their motivations. Even the language itself provides clues. The author chooses words and uses techniques such as repetition and metaphor to call readers' attention to important themes. It is in the process of fitting all these different aspects together that you will recognize those themes.

Begin by listing the details about the literary elements and language. Look for repeated ideas or patterns, and ask yourself what they have in common. Bear in mind that what they have in common may be a pattern of contrasts. This is the case in the passage below. Remember, too, that some of the important details and relationships may be implied rather than stated.

Directions: Read the passage. As you read, make a list of the details about the settings that the narrator describes.

> The sun filtering through my blinds is nothing like the glare on the rubble of Cervantes Boulevard after the earthquake. But for a moment I'm fooled. Even the realization that I'm seventeen and no longer a child does nothing to calm me. Whenever I have this dream, it brings the real earthquake back with astonishing clarity.
>
> I guess it goes to show how surfaces can be deceiving. San Francisco is 3,000 miles and another lifetime away. Here on our safe suburban street, I have the biggest, brightest room in a big, bright comfortable house. I claimed it as soon as my sister, Mimi, moved away, which was basically as soon as she could. And I keep it in perfect order. There are no visible signs in my life here in Boston of what we have been through—the splintering of my family, the chaos, our losses, and my mother's now healed injuries. No outward signs, no, nothing at all, except the fact that ever since my four-year-old self blacked out in that earthquake, I have been unable to speak.

The passage is set in a bedroom in a suburban house, but it also refers to another setting—San Francisco, where an earthquake took place in the past. How do these two settings conflict with one another? Which do we experience? Which one is not described? How might this indicate a theme? The suburban setting is visible, whereas the earthquake setting is in the narrator's mind. Thus, you can see that the fictional element of setting sets up an opposition that might point to the theme.

Directions: Reread the passage above. Look at the words the author uses. Underline the words with the same or similar meanings.

Words such as "surfaces," "visible," and "outward" emphasize the author's ideas about what is visible as opposed to what is hidden. They also serve as clues to the theme. Just as the author describes a visible and a hidden setting, the language suggests a theme that appearances are deceiving. In the passage, the narrator's world appears bright, happy, and healthy, but hidden behind this façade are persistent memories of loss, turmoil, and pain.

CORE SKILL

Synthesize Details That Relate to the Theme

The theme of a story might be directly stated by the author or characters, or it might be implied. The reader needs to find and synthesize details to determine the theme, if it is not stated. Pay close attention to how the following suggest a theme:

- Setting
- Plot events
- Characters' traits or actions
- Characters' observations about life and human behavior
- Narrator's observations about life and human behavior
- Language and choice of words

With a partner, discuss how character traits or actions indicate the theme in the passage on this page. Together, write a sentence summarizing your ideas. Share your sentence with another pair.

WRITE TO LEARN

Choose a short story that you have read recently, or find one in a library. O. Henry is a good author to try. Read the story, and determine whether the theme is stated or implied. If it is stated, locate the statement of the theme. If it is implied, use the fictional elements of setting, plot, characterization, point of view, conflict, and language to determine the theme, and state it in your own words. Write a short paragraph about the short story you read, explaining how the author uses fictional elements to indicate and emphasize theme.

CORE SKILL

Understand the Relationship among Ideas

To determine the theme of longer works, such as novels or plays, you need to be constantly on the lookout for clues based on the author's use of fictional elements.

Themes may announce themselves slowly over the course of a work. Because themes are generally complex and sophisticated, you might need to read many paragraphs, pages, or chapters to determine a text's theme.

To find the theme of a longer work:

- Determine the main idea of each paragraph.
- Synthesize the multiple main ideas.
- State a larger theme that includes the entire work.

Before using the process above to determine the theme of a longer work, apply the process to a short text. Read a short story in a magazine or a collection you have at home. Apply the process above to determine the main idea for each paragraph, and then synthesize the multiple main ideas to see how they relate to and suggest an overall theme. For each paragraph, write the main idea. Then write the ideas that tie them together. State the theme in one concise sentence.

Think about Reading

Directions: Read the passage on the previous page again. Then answer the questions below.

Which sentence in the passage best describes the tension between the earthquake in the narrator's past and the appearance of the narrator's present life? How does this relate to the theme?

Synthesizing Multiple Main Ideas to Determine the Theme

Paragraphs are the building blocks of writing. An author's task is to skillfully link the ideas of the paragraphs so they logically reveal the theme. Each paragraph may have its own central idea, and to understand the theme of a complete work, you need to be able to pull these main ideas together and see how they relate to one another.

Directions: Read the passage below and at the top of the next page. Notice that many of the details in the first paragraph are seen from the **perspective**, or point of view, of the dog Spitz, who is under attack. How might you state the main idea of this paragraph?

Now focus on the language and action in the second paragraph. In this paragraph, the perspective shifts back to Buck, the dominant dog. Which details show you that the scene is being viewed primarily through Buck's eyes?

But Buck possessed a quality that made for greatness—imagination. He fought by instinct, but he could fight by head as well. He rushed, as though attempting the old shoulder trick, but at the last instant swept low to the snow and in. His teeth closed on Spitz's left fore leg. There was a crunch of breaking bone, and the white dog faced him on three legs. Thrice he tried to knock him over, then repeated the trick and broke the right foreleg. Despite the pain and helplessness, Spitz struggled madly to keep up. He saw the silent circle, with gleaming eyes, lolling tongues, and silvery breaths drifting upward, closing in upon him as he had seen similar circles close in upon beaten antagonists in the past. Only this time he was the one who was beaten.

(Continued on page 41)

(Continued from page 40)

There was no hope for him. Buck was inexorable. Mercy was a thing reserved for gentler climes. He maneuvered for the final rush. The circle had tightened till he could feel the breaths of the huskies on his flanks. He could see them, beyond Spitz and to either side, half crouching for the spring, their eyes fixed upon him. A pause seemed to fall. Every animal was motionless as though turned to stone. Only Spitz quivered and bristled as he staggered back and forth, snarling with horrible menace, as though to frighten off impending death. Then Buck sprang in and out; but while he was in, shoulder had at last squarely met shoulder. The dark circle became a dot on the moon-flooded snow as Spitz disappeared from view. Buck stood and looked on, the successful champion, the dominant primordial beast who had made his kill and found it good.

—From *The Call of the Wild* by Jack London

Think about Reading

Directions: Read the passage from Jack London's *Call of the Wild* again. In a notebook, answer the questions below.

1. What is the main idea of the first paragraph?
2. What is the main idea of the second paragraph?
3. Synthesize the two main ideas to suggest an overall theme for the passage.

Summary

The theme is the underlying meaning of a fictional work. You can determine the theme of a passage by identifying and synthesizing the most important details, including setting, plot, conflict, point of view, character and author observations, and language.

The theme in a longer work of fiction can be determined by first identifying the main ideas presented in each paragraph or passage, finding the ideas and fictional elements that tie the passages together, and then synthesizing them into an overall theme. By synthesizing multiple main ideas, you will be able to identify larger themes, and deepen your understanding of the meaning of the work.

21st CENTURY SKILL

Social and Cross- Cultural Skills

Meeting the challenges of the information age and the global workforce requires mastering social and cross-cultural skills. It is important to learn to interact effectively with people of different cultures and circumstances and to use your own social and cultural background to contribute to shared projects.

Understanding the literary elements of language, setting, and point of view can help you gain insight into cultural and social backgrounds that are different from your own. For example, people from different cultural backgrounds sometimes speak different languages, and meaning can be embedded in language. Answer the questions below:

1. How might understanding the concept of setting help you understand people who are unlike you?
   - **A.** Where someone has lived can affect the decisions they make.
   - **B.** Everyone has worked in many different settings.
   - **C.** Certain types of environments promote positive thinking.
2. Which statement below demonstrates how point of view can relate to cross-cultural understanding?
   - **A.** People can never agree because they have different perspectives.
   - **B.** People from different backgrounds might view the same event differently.
   - **C.** Even people from different backgrounds agree on most issues.

Vocabulary Review

Directions: Circle the best word to complete each sentence below.

1. The (theme, conflict) in a story refers to a struggle between opposing forces or characters.
2. When you (perspective, synthesize) two things, you put them together to make a new whole.
3. The (theme, conflict) of a story is an underlying message that is often complex and sophisticated.
4. Each character in a story has his or her own (perspective, synthesize).

Skill Review

Directions: Read the passage below. Then complete each activity.

Call me Ishmael. Some years ago—never mind how long precisely—having little or no money in my purse, and nothing particular to interest me on shore, I thought I would sail about a little and see the watery part of the world. It is a way I have of driving off the spleen and regulating the circulation. Whenever I find myself growing grim about the mouth; whenever it is a damp, drizzly November in my soul; whenever I find myself involuntarily pausing before coffin warehouses, and bringing up the rear of every funeral I meet; and especially whenever my hypos get such an upper hand of me, that it requires a strong moral principle to prevent me from deliberately stepping into the street, and methodically knocking people's hats off—then, I account it high time to get to sea as soon as I can. This is my substitute for pistol and ball. With a philosophical flourish Cato throws himself upon his sword; I quietly take to the ship. There is nothing surprising in this. If they but knew it, almost all men in their degree, some time or other, cherish very nearly the same feelings towards the ocean with me.

—From *Moby Dick* by Herman Melville

1. Fill in the blanks with the word or phrase that best completes each sentence below.

   A. The __________ of the passage might be stated as, "The ocean has the power to transform people."

   B. The narrator goes to the sea whenever he is feeling __________.

   C. The narrator believes most people __________ with him about the ocean.

2. Cite two details from the passage that relate to its theme.

   A. ______________________________

   B. ______________________________

Skill Practice

Directions: Read the passage below. Then choose the best answer to each question.

"Why don't you say you'd have a splendid, wise, good husband and some angelic little children? You know your castle wouldn't be perfect without," said blunt Jo, who had no tender fancies yet, and rather scorned romance, except in books.

"You'd have nothing but horses, inkstands, and novels in yours," answered Meg petulantly.

"Wouldn't I though? I'd have a stable full of Arabian steeds, rooms piled high with books, and I'd write out of a magic inkstand, so that my works should be as famous as Laurie's music. I want to do something splendid before I go into my castle, something heroic or wonderful that won't be forgotten after I'm dead. I don't know what, but I'm on the watch for it, and mean to astonish you all some day. I think I shall write books, and get rich and famous, that would suit me, so that is my favorite dream."

—From *Little Women* by Louisa May Alcott

1. Which sentence below is the best statement of the theme of the passage?

A. Everyone's dreams are of equal value.

B. Most people need a little magic to be successful.

C. People should strive for their own version of greatness.

D. It's okay to disagree with another person.

2. Which detail describes something that is not a part of Jo's dream.

A. a splendid wise, good husband

B. a stable full of Arabian steeds

C. being rich and famous

D. writing books

Writing Practice

Directions: Write a short story of at least two paragraphs. If you have trouble thinking of a story, you may base your story on one you've read before, as long as you use your own words. You may also tell an incident from your life as though it were a fictional story. In your story, include the following elements:

1. A beginning, middle, and end
2. A different main idea for each paragraph
3. A theme that is either stated in the story or implied
4. Details that clearly support your theme

Share your story with a partner, and determine the theme in each other's work.

Directions: Read the following passage. Then choose the best answer to questions 1 and 2.

The crops that we grow for food need specific conditions to thrive, including the right temperature and enough water. A changing climate could have both positive and negative effects on crops. For example, the northern parts of the United States have generally cool temperatures, so warmer weather could help certain crops grow. In southern areas where temperatures are already hot, even more heat could hurt crop growth. Global climate change will also affect agriculture and food supply in many other ways.

—From *A Student's Guide to Global Climate Change,*
U.S. Environmental Protection Agency website

1. Using supporting details, what generalization could you make about the information in the passage?

A. Crops do better overall in a colder climate.

B. Cold weather is harmful to crops.

C. Climate change will provide the right temperature conditions for crop growth.

D. Climate change will affect crops in different ways.

2. Which of the following choices names the two types of supporting details the author uses to develop the idea, "A changing climate could have both positive and negative effects on crops?"

A. facts and questions

B. descriptions and reasons

C. examples and facts

D. questions and reasons

Directions: Read the following passage. Then complete activities 3 through 5.

5 July, 1775.

I should have been more particular, but I thought you knew everything that passed here. The present state of the inhabitants of Boston is that of the most abject slaves, under the most cruel and despotic of tyrants. Among many instances I could mention, let me relate one. Upon the 17th of June, printed handbills were posted up at the corners of the streets, and upon houses, forbidding any inhabitants to go upon their houses, or upon any eminence [high place], on pain of death; the inhabitants dared not to look out of their houses, nor to be heard or seen to ask a question.

Our prisoners were brought over to the Long Wharf, and there lay all night, without any care of their wounds, or any resting-place but the pavements, until the next day, when they exchanged it for the jail, since which we hear they are civilly treated. Their living cannot be good, as they can have no fresh provisions; their beef, we hear, is all gone, and their wounded men die very fast, so that they have a report that the bullets were poisoned. Fish they cannot have, they have rendered it so difficult to procure; and the admiral is such a villain as to oblige every fishing schooner to pay a dollar every time it goes out.

The money that has been paid for passes is incredible. Some have given ten, twenty, thirty, and forty dollars, to get out with a small proportion of their things.

It is reported and believed that they have taken up a number of persons and committed them to jail, we know not for what in particular. Master Lovell is confined in the dungeon; a son of Mr. Edes is in jail, and one Wiburt, a ship-carpenter, is now upon trial for his life. God alone knows to what length these wretches will go, and will, I hope, restrain their malice.

—From "A Letter to her Husband, John Adams" by Abigail Adam

3. Which statement from the passage best states the main idea?

A. "I should have been more particular, but I thought you knew everything that passed here."

B. "The present state of the inhabitants of Boston is that of the most abject slaves . . ."

C. "Our prisoners were brought over to the Long Wharf, and there lay all night, without any care of their wounds, or any resting-place but the pavements . . ."

D. "It is reported and believed that they have taken up a number of persons and committed them to jail . . ."

4. Fill in the blanks below with the best choice from the word bank.

text	Boston	main idea

A. No matter what type of __________ you read, it is helpful to identify the main idea.

B. Abigail Adams is telling John Adams about the plight of residents of __________ .

C. The __________ is that the treatment of all citizens is cruel.

5. Which of the following best summarizes the key information in the second paragraph of the passage?

A. Prisoners are not cared for properly. They have no treatment for wounds, no place to sleep, and are not given enough good food.

B. Fishermen are suffering. It is difficult to catch fish, and fishing boats are taxed.

C. Most of the wounded men are dying. The bullets may have been poisoned, and their wounds are not being treated.

D. Many people have been sent to jail without being charged. Innocent people are being confined in jails and dungeons and put on trial.

Directions: Read the following passage. Then complete activities 6 through 8.

"Miss Woodhouse, as you will not give me your opinion, I must do as well as I can by myself; and I have now quite determined, and really almost made up my mind—to refuse Mr. Martin. Do you think I am right?"

"Perfectly, perfectly right, my dearest Harriet; you are doing just what you ought. While you were at all in suspense I kept my feelings to myself, but now that you are so completely decided I have no hesitation in approving. . . . It would have grieved me to lose your acquaintance, which must have been the consequence of your marrying Mr. Martin. . . . I could not have visited Mrs. Robert Martin, of Abbey-Mill Farm . . ."

Harriet had not surmised her own danger, but the idea of it struck her forcibly.

"You could not have visited me!" she cried, looking aghast. "No, to be sure you could not; but I never thought of that before. That would have been too dreadful!—What an escape!—Dear Miss Woodhouse, I would not give up the pleasure and honour of being intimate with you for any thing in the world."

"Indeed, Harriet, it would have been a severe pang to lose you; but it must have been. You would have thrown yourself out of all good society. I must have given you up."

"Dear me!—How should I ever have borne it! It would have killed me never to come to Hartfield any more!"

"Dear affectionate creature! . . . *You* confined to the society of the illiterate and vulgar all your life! I wonder how the young man could have the assurance to ask it. He must have a pretty good opinion of himself."

(Continued on page 46)

(Continued from page 45)

"I do not think he is conceited either, in general," said Harriet, her conscience opposing such censure; "at least, he is very good natured, and I shall always feel much obliged to him, and have a great regard for—but that is quite a different thing from—and you know, though he may like me, it does not follow that I should—and certainly I must confess that since my visiting here I have seen people—and if one comes to compare them . . . However, I do really think Mr. Martin a very amiable young man, and have a great opinion of him . . . but as to leaving you, it is what I would not do upon any consideration."

"Thank you, thank you, my own sweet little friend . . . A woman is not to marry a man merely because she is asked, or because he is attached to her, and can write a tolerable letter."

—From *Emma* by Jane Austen

6. Fill in the blanks below with the best choice from the word bank.

Harriet	**opinion**
Miss Woodhouse	**marriage**

A. Harriet greatly values her friend's ________ .

B. ________ has a favorable opinion of Mr. Martin.

C. ________ implies that Mr. Martin is not good enough for her friend.

D. The passage implies that Harriet has been persuaded against her will into a decision about her ________ .

7. Use supporting details to choose the sentence below that best states the implied main idea of the passage.

A. Marriage is unimportant to Harriet.

B. Miss Woodhouse helped Harriet make the right decision.

C. Harriet would have refused Mr. Martin even without Miss Woodhouse's input.

D. Miss Woodhouse did not have Harriet's happiness foremost in her mind.

8. Fill in the blanks in the paragraph below to complete the summary of the Jane Austen passage.

society	**friendship**	**marry**	**character**	**happiness**

In counseling Harriet about whether or not to marry Mr. Martin, Miss Woodhouse implies that she does not have Harriet's [A.] ________ in mind. Miss Woodhouse tells Harriet that she would have to end her [B.] ________ with her and that Harriet would be excluded from good [C.] ________ if she married him. Then she questions Mr. Martin's [D.] ________, even though Harriet shows that she regards him highly. In the end, Miss Woodhouse persuades Harriet to refuse to [E.] ________ Mr. Martin, but the main reason is because Harriet has been made to choose between Miss Woodhouse and Mr. Martin.

Directions: Read the following passage. Then choose the best answer to questions 9 and 10.

As she lay thinking and mourning, the suggestion began to creep into her mind that there was an undefinable something about this boy that was lacking in Tom Canty, mad or sane. . . . What if the boy were really not her son, after all? Oh, absurd! She almost smiled at the idea, spite of her griefs and troubles. No matter, she found that it was an idea that would not 'down,' but persisted in haunting her. . . . At last she perceived that there was not going to be any peace for her until she should devise a test that should prove, clearly and without question, whether this lad was her son or not, and so banish these wearing and worrying doubts. . . . And while she listened, the measured breathing was broken by a soft, startled cry, such as one utters in a troubled dream. This chance occurrence

(Continued on page 47)

(Continued from page 46)

furnished her instantly with a plan worth all her laboured tests combined. . . . Since that day, when he was little, that the powder burst in his face, he hath never been startled of a sudden out of his dreams or out of his thinkings, but he hath cast his hand before his eyes, even as he did that day; and not as others would do it, with the palm inward, but always with the palm turned outward—I have seen it a hundred times, and it hath never varied nor ever failed. "Yes, I shall soon know, now!"

—From *The Prince and the Pauper* by Mark Twain

9. Which of the following is NOT a main idea in the passage?

A. The main character wishes that Tom Canty were her son.

B. The main character decides she must fashion a test for Tom Canty.

C. The main character questions whether Tom Canty is her son.

D. The main character figures out how to tell whether or not Tom Canty is her son.

10. Synthesize the multiple main ideas to determine which of the following best states the theme.

A. There is something strange about living with someone who is not related to you.

B. You can solve any problem if you put your mind to it and work hard enough.

C. Some detail will always reveal the difference between people, no matter how outwardly similar they may be.

D. A mother should always love her child despite his or her shortcomings.

Check Your Understanding

On the following chart, circle the number of any item you answered incorrectly. In the third column, you will see the pages that you can review to study the content covered in the question. Pay particular attention to reviewing those lessons in which you missed half or more of the questions.

Lesson	Core Skill	Item Number(s)	Review Page(s)
Lesson 1.1: Determine the Main Idea	Determine Main Ideas	3, 4, 9	13–14
	Identify Main Ideas in Various Texts	3, 4	15–17
Lesson 1.2: Identify Supporting Details	Identify Supporting Details	1	21–22
	Cite Details	2	23
Lesson 1.3: Identify Direct and Implied Main Ideas	Determine Implied Main Ideas	7	27–28
	Use Details to Deduce Central and Supporting Ideas	6, 7	29
Lesson 1.4: Summarize Details	Summarize Key Information	5, 8	33–34
	Summarize a Text	8	35
Lesson 1.5: Identify a Theme	Cite Details That Relate to Theme	10	39
	Synthesize Multiple Main Ideas	10	40–41

WRITE ABOUT The Gift of the Magi

Read *The Gift of the Magi* by O. Henry on page 307. Write an essay in which you

1. identify its theme
2. summarize its main ideas and key details
3. explain what the main ideas and key details say about the theme

BEFORE YOU WRITE Relate Main Ideas and Details to the Theme

Use a concept web to take notes on the main ideas. You can find an example of a concept web in the Graphic Organizer section at the back of the book. Label the center circle "Theme" and the outer circles "Main Idea." Extend the web by adding the key supporting details for each main idea. As you read, write the main ideas and their supporting details in the web. Look for an idea to which O. Henry returns several times. This is the theme. Put the theme in the central circle.

When you have finished, review your concept web. Ask yourself: *What do the main ideas and key supporting details say about the theme?* Use your answers to develop a topic sentence for your essay.

TIP Use Present Tense in Your Essay

The simple present tense is used to show action or a state of being that is happening now or happens regularly. The simple present tense is also used when a statement is always true.

The sun rises every day.

I need a cup of coffee.

The simple present tense is often used to discuss what happens in a passage or what the author says. The underlined verbs in the sentences below indicate simple present tense.

Della sells her hair so that she can buy her husband's gift.

Twain explains the reasons for the steamboat's demise.

As you summarize the main ideas and details of the passage, use verbs in the simple present tense.

WHILE YOU WRITE Summarize Main Ideas and Key Details

You have identified the theme and created a topic sentence for your essay. Next, you need to summarize the main ideas and key details that support those ideas. Look at your concept web again. Around the central circle, you have four clusters. Each cluster contains a main idea surrounded by its supporting details. Write a sentence or two explaining each cluster.

Next, ask yourself *Which cluster is presented first in the text? Which is presented second?* Use the sentences you have written to create your summary. Place them in the same order as they are in the story.

Finally, explain what the main ideas and key details say about the theme. Think about how the main ideas illustrate the theme. For example, if the main idea of a section of a passage is "the hero persuades the townspeople not to seek revenge on the wrongly accused man," you might say that this idea shows the theme "good conquers evil" by having a good person prevent other people from doing a bad thing. Try to write your explanation in no more than one or two sentences.

TIP Watch Out for . . . the Comma Splice

A comma splice occurs when you join two independent ideas, or clauses, with a comma. Here's an example:

A tornado is a dangerous storm, a hailstorm can be dangerous, too.

The two complete clauses are "A tornado is a dangerous storm" and "a hailstorm can be dangerous, too." Both clauses have a complete subject and a complete verb and can stand alone. However, the comma is placed in a way that makes the sentence grammatically incorrect.

There are a number of ways to correct a comma splice:

- Divide the comma splice into two separate sentences by replacing the first comma with a period and changing the first letter of the second clause to upper case.
- Join the two clauses into a single sentence with a semicolon.
- Add a comma and a coordinating conjunction (words that connect ideas), such as *and*, *but*, or *so*.
- Add a subordinating conjunction (words that introduce clauses that cannot stand alone in a sentence) and use a comma if necessary. Common subordinating conjunctions include *although*, *because*, *before*, *if*, *when*, and *unless*.

AFTER YOU WRITE Check Your Work

Reread the writing assignment. Then read your essay carefully three times.

The first time you read, ask yourself whether you have completed the writing assignment correctly. Have you (1) identified the theme of the story, (2) summarized its main ideas and key details, and (3) explained what the main ideas and key details say about the theme?

Then read the essay again. Did you use present tense when summarizing and paraphrasing the story?

Reread the essay one last time. Did you use correct grammar, spelling, and punctuation? Do you see any errors? Did you type the words you meant to use?

Before submitting your essay, have another student read it and provide you with feedback.

Chapter 2

Analyze Relationships within Texts

Whether you are reading a spine-tingling mystery novel or the directions for putting together your new furniture, you need to understand how the ideas in a text work together. In some texts, ideas or events are arranged in sequence. When reading other texts, you might have to figure out how one person, event, or idea affects another. As you read for class, for work, or just for fun, you need to identify relationships within texts to deepen your understanding of what you read.

Hero/Corbis/Glow Images

In this chapter you will study these topics:

Lesson 2.1

Sequence Events

Can you determine the order of events in a story or article? Do you understand how steps and important information are arranged in instructions or directions? Identifying the order, or sequence, can help you better understand a text.

Lesson 2.2

Infer Relationships between Events, People, and Ideas

Writers don't always directly state everything a reader needs to know to understand the text. Sometimes you need to use your own knowledge as well as information in the text to make inferences, or understand what is not directly stated. Can you figure out the connections among events, people, and ideas when you read?

Lesson 2.3

Analyze Relationships between Ideas

Are you able to relate key events to the plot of a story? Can you determine how other story elements, such as characters and themes, are connected? Can you explain how a setting or context shapes the text? Learn how to draw conclusions and make generalizations to analyze relationships between ideas.

Lesson 2.4

Determine Implicit Relationships between Ideas

When you read an article about two related incidents, can you see how the events are related? Does the writer use proximity, punctuation, or text patterns to show the relationships? Look carefully at details and use what you already know about a topic to understand unstated relationships among ideas in a text.

Lesson 2.5

Analyze the Role of Details in Complex Texts

Can you distinguish between simple and complex texts? Are you able to identify details that support and explain broad or complicated ideas? Learn how to analyze the role of details in complex texts.

Goal Setting

Recall a time when you have wanted to understand why or how something happened in a book, television show, or movie. Analyzing relationships among ideas can help you fully understand the events in a story.

How would a deeper understanding of a text help increase your appreciation of it?

Why is it important to understand the relationships within texts? How can this help you become a better reader?

LESSON 2.1 Sequence Events

LESSON OBJECTIVES

- Determine the sequence of events in narrative passages
- Identify sequence in procedural texts

CORE SKILLS

- Sequence Information
- Use Text Features

Key Terms

sequence
order

transition
a change from one event or idea to another

Vocabulary

chronological
in time order

flashback
interruption of a time sequence to tell what happened earlier

process
a series of actions leading to an end

time line
a diagram that shows events in the order they occurred

Key Concept

The sequence of events is the order in which the events in a text occur.

The order in which ideas appear in a text affects the reader's understanding. Imagine reading a diary or a news report that is out of order or trying to follow a recipe that does not tell you when to complete each step. How would that affect your understanding of the texts or the outcome of the recipe? Sequence in a text is important to the reader's comprehension.

Sequence of Time

When you read, it is important to determine how a passage is organized. Often events are described in the order in which they occurred. The ordering of events in texts helps you understand how one action or event relates to another. Without some type of order, text would be confusing.

Chronological Order

When you are reading an exciting book or watching a movie, you look forward to discovering what comes next in the **sequence**, or order, of events. Usually stories are told in **chronological** order. In chronological order, events are organized according to when they occurred. This sequential order helps the reader or observer follow the unfolding action. Readers often can determine the order of events in a passage by identifying a signal word or phrase that calls attention to a **transition**, or a change from one event or idea to another. Transition signal words and phrases help the reader move from one part of a story to the next.

Examples of transition words and phrases used to show time order include *first, second, next, finally, at a later time, before,* and *then.*

One device authors use that breaks from strict chronological order is **flashback**. In a flashback, an author interrupts the story to tell about an event in the past. An author may use a flashback to reveal a character's motivations or to explore the causes of an event. However it is used, a flashback gives the reader deeper insight into the characters, events, or ideas in the text.

OJO Images/Getty Images

Directions: Read the passage. Then answer the questions.

Jong-Kyu took a deep breath and gripped the overhanging rock with all his strength. Then, pushing off with his legs and pulling with his arms, he managed to launch himself up and past the lip of the overhang. For a moment he lay listening to his heart slow. When he could no longer hear it beating, he stood and looked down into the valley of his birth, his childhood—the valley of his greatest loss.

It was hard to pinpoint where it had happened. Time had torn down familiar landmarks and raised up strange ones. He thought, though, that broad tree might be the one they'd sheltered under during the storm. Closing his eyes, he let himself recall her face.

Mi-na's short hair was pasted against her head by the rain, and she was panting with laughter after the race for the shelter of the tree. He would tell her now, he decided, looking into her sparkling eyes. He would ask her to come with him when he left the valley to find work. Before he could speak, though, Mi-Na had sprinted away, calling to him to follow. Then, suddenly, thunder exploded around them, and his sweet, sweet girl was a blinding blaze of blue and gold.

Jong-Kyu opened his eyes. He could hear his heart again. No, that was not the tree, he thought. It had been farther to the left, maybe where the cell-phone factory stood now.

Think about Reading

1. Which words signal to the reader that the first paragraph is arranged in time order?
2. What does Jong-Kyu do right after he pulls himself onto the overhanging rock?
3. What does the author explain in the flashback?
4. How does the author signal that Jong-Kyu's flashback has ended?
5. What happens right before the thunder explodes?

Sequence in a Process

Narrative writing is not the only type of text that uses sequence. In fact, sequence might be even more important in text that describes a **process**, or a series of actions leading to an end. Instruction manuals and recipes, for example, would be extremely confusing if they did not clearly describe a series of steps in sequence.

CORE SKILL

Sequence Information

A narrative text can take the form of fiction or nonfiction, as long as it tells a story of some kind. Most narrative texts present events in chronological order. However, sometimes a text will step back in time to fill in details (flashback), and sometimes a text will look ahead and hint at something that will happen later (foreshadow). To keep track of events that are not told in chronological order, readers can jot down notes about the sequence.

Find a narrative text in a print or online magazine or newspaper that spans several years. Take notes about the order of events. Then create a **time line** like the one below to record the main events in sequence. A time line is a graphic organizer that shows when important events happened.

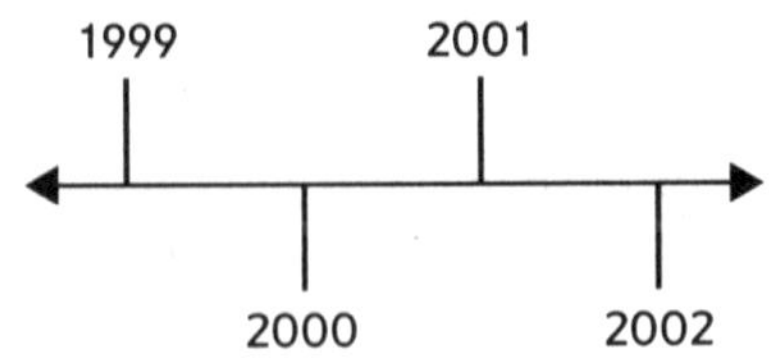

WRITE TO LEARN

Write instructions for a familiar household task, such as making a bed or doing laundry. Exchange and discuss your instructions with a partner to check that your instructions are clear.

WORKPLACE SKILL

Describe a Procedure

Many workplace documents require that the reader understand a sequence of events to accomplish a task. For example, an office document may describe the procedure for completing new-employee forms, the steps to follow in the event of an emergency, or the guidelines for filing a complaint.

Read the Student Complaints section of the State University Procedures Manual. Write a paragraph summarizing the steps the university must follow if a student files a complaint.

Directions: Read the following passage. Then create a flowchart that shows the steps for making the sandwich. You can find an example of a flowchart in the Graphic Organizer section at the back of the book.

> First, gather lunch meat, mustard, sliced cheese, tomato, onion, lettuce, and two slices of bread. Slice the onion and tomato thinly. Then spread mustard on one slice of bread. Layer the other ingredients as you prefer. Finally, place the second slice of bread on top. Finish by cutting the sandwich in half.

In the description of how to make a sandwich, notice the transition words *first, then, finally,* and *finish.* They emphasize the order of the steps. Even without those words, though, the description would make sense. Why? Because the steps are organized in a logical sequence.

Procedural Documents

A process, which can also be called a procedure, might be written in paragraph form as shown in the example above, or it may be presented as a list. At home or in the workplace, you will encounter many documents that give instructions for completing procedures. They often include text features such as numbers and boldface type to help readers navigate the steps. Many procedural documents also include diagrams to help readers visualize the process.

Directions: Read the passage. If the Resident Assistant cannot resolve the complaint, what should be done next?

State University Procedures Manual

Section 5.35 Student Complaints

When the University receives a written complaint from a student, procedures must be followed for forwarding the complaint.

1. The **Resident Assistant** must inform the student filing a complaint that he or she will receive a response to the complaint within fifteen calendar days. If the complaint is not resolved at this level, the complaint should be sent to each of the following levels until satisfaction among all parties is reached.
2. If the issue is not resolved with the Resident Assistant, the complaint should be forwarded to the **Assistant Director of Residential Life**.
3. If the issue is still unresolved, the complaint will next go to the **Director of Residential Life**.
4. After that, an unresolved complaint will be forwarded to the **Vice President of Student Affairs**. The university official must send his or her decision to the student within fifteen days from the date the complaint was received.

Directions: Read the following passage. Underline the transition words that show time order.

> If you want to satisfy yourself of this characteristic of the horse, and learn something of importance concerning the peculiarities of his nature, etc., turn him into the barn-yard, or a large stable will do, and then gather up something that you know will frighten him; a red blanket, buffalo robe, or something of that kind. Hold it up so that he can see it; he will stick up his head and snort. Then throw it down somewhere in the center of the lot or barn, and walk off to one side. Watch his motions, and study his nature. If he is frightened at the object, he will not rest until he has touched it with his nose. You will see him begin to walk around the robe and snort, all the time getting a little closer, as if drawn up by some magic spell, until he finally gets within reach of it. He will then very cautiously stretch out his neck as far as he can reach, merely touching it with his nose, as though he thought it was ready to fly at him. But after he has repeated these touches a few times, for the first [time] (though he has been looking at it all the time) he seems to have an idea what it is. But now he has found, by the sense of feeling, that it is nothing that will do him any harm, and he is ready to play with it. And if you watch him closely, you will see him take hold of it with his teeth, and raise it up and pull at it. And in a few minutes you can see that he has not that same wild look about his eye, but stands like a horse biting at some familiar stump.
>
> —From *The Arabian Art of Taming and Training Wild and Vicious Horses* by P. R. Kincaid

Think about Reading

Directions: Answer the following questions about the excerpt from *The Arabian Art of Taming and Training Wild and Vicious Horses.*

1. What should you do after you hold up the blanket?
2. What will the horse do after he is in reach of the blanket?
3. What will the horse do after he discovers that the blanket will not harm him?

Summary

Understanding the order of events or ideas in a narrative or informative text is important to your comprehension of the material. Ideas and information in texts are often organized in chronological, or time, order. Transition words and text features can help you understand how a text is organized.

CORE SKILL

Use Text Features

A full page of informational text without visual interruption can be difficult to understand. That's why informational texts often have features that serve as visual guides to support readers' comprehension of the text. Some commonly used text features are boldfaced or italicized type, headings, subheadings, numbering, and bullets.

With a partner, write a list of the text features used in the Student Complaints procedural document on the previous page. Then discuss how each feature helps readers understand the text.

Vocabulary Review

Directions: Match each word with its definition.

1. _________ **sequence**
2. _________ **transition**
3. _________ **chronological**
4. _________ **time line**
5. _________ **flashback**
6. _________ **process**

a. a diagram that shows events in the order they occurred

b. a series of actions leading to an end

c. interruption of a time sequence to tell what happened earlier

d. order

e. in time order

f. a change from one event or idea to another

Skill Review

Directions: Read the passage below. Then choose the best answer to each question.

(1) In December 1944, the Japanese army sent Lieutenant Hiroo Onoda to a remote Philippine island called Lubang. For 29 years, Lt. Onoda hid in the jungle and waited for the Japanese army to retake the island.

(2) In 1942, Onoda attended the Japanese Imperial Army intelligence school. Then he was assigned to lead a mission to destroy an airfield and a pier on Lubang Island. Soon after he arrived, the Allied army gained control of Lubang. Lt. Onoda and three of his men retreated into the jungle. They refused to surrender even when the war ended in August 1945. Lt. Onoda's commander, Major Taniguchi, had ordered Lt. Onoda to continue the mission even if the Japanese army surrendered.

(3) Philippine locals, the army, and relatives tried to tell the men that the war was over. However, the men believed that each message was a trick. Over the years, Lt. Onoda's companions deserted the group or were killed in skirmishes with locals and the Philippine police. By 1972 Lt. Onoda was alone.

(4) In 1974 a young Japanese man tracked him down and arranged for Major Taniguchi to meet Lt. Onoda on Lubang. On March 9, 1974, Major Taniguchi ordered Lt. Onoda to surrender.

1. What happened ***before*** Onoda was sent to Lubang?

A. Onoda hid in the jungle.

B. Onoda refused to surrender.

C. Onoda attended the Japanese Imperial Army intelligence school.

D. Onoda's companions were killed in skirmishes with locals and the police.

2. When did Lt. Onoda surrender?

A. 1942

B. 1944

C. 1972

D. 1974

3. Which paragraph interrupts the chronological order of the passage?

A. Paragraph 1

B. Paragraph 2

C. Paragraph 3

D. Paragraph 4

Skill Practice

Directions: Read the passage below. Then choose the best answer to each question.

We walked down the path to the well-house, attracted by the fragrance of the honeysuckle with which it was covered. Some one was drawing water and my teacher placed my hand under the spout. As the cool stream gushed over one hand she spelled into the other the word *water*, first slowly, then rapidly. I stood still, my whole attention fixed upon the motions of her fingers. Suddenly I felt a misty consciousness as of something forgotten—a thrill of returning thought; and somehow the mystery of language was revealed to me. I knew then that "w-a-t-e-r" meant the wonderful cool something that was flowing over my hand. That living word awakened my soul, gave it light, hope, joy, set it free! There were barriers still, it is true, but barriers that could in time be swept away.

—From *Story of My Life* by Helen Keller

1. When does Helen's teacher spell the word *water*?

A. at the same time the water flows over Helen's hand

B. after the water flowed over Helen's hand

C. before the water flows over Helen's hand

D. at the same time as Helen draws water

2. What happens when Helen understands what "w-a-t-e-r" means?

A. She learns how to draw water.

B. The mystery of language is revealed to her.

C. She feels like she has forgotten something.

D. She no longer has any barriers.

3. Why does Keller choose to tell about that day in sequence?

A. to show how one event leads to another

B. to compare this day with the day before

C. to show that Helen's teacher cares about her

D. to explain the effects of Helen's illness

4. How do the day's events change Helen?

A. She learns to spell.

B. She begins to like her teacher.

C. Her soul is set free.

D. She can speak again.

Writing Practice

Directions: Write a paragraph about an event that changed your life in a positive way. Tell about the details in chronological order. Include a flashback if it can provide the reader with a deeper understanding of the story. Be sure to use transition words to make the order of events clear.

LESSON 2.2 Infer Relationships between Events, People, and Ideas

LESSON OBJECTIVES

- Infer relationships within a text
- Provide examples and evidence from the text to support inferences

CORE SKILLS

- Make Inferences
- Cite Evidence

Key Terms

cite
make reference to

infer
come to a conclusion based on evidence and prior knowledge

Vocabulary

explicit
clearly stated

imply
suggest

valid
justified, appropriate, meaningful

Key Concept

Making an inference is determining the most likely explanation for the given information.

Most writers do not directly explain all the important details in a story. For instance, if you are reading a mystery novel, you will likely make inferences to figure out who the criminal is. When making inferences—that is, using text evidence and prior knowledge to figure things out—you discover how the people, events, and ideas in a text relate to one another. For example, the author may show a relationship between two people by telling how they are alike or different. Two events may be related because one event causes the other to happen. Two ideas may relate when one idea adds new information about the other idea.

Inferring a Writer's Meaning

Readers use details in a passage to figure out the author's meaning. **Explicit** details are clearly stated and help a reader come to a sound conclusion about characters or events. But sometimes an author will **imply**, or suggest, ideas rather than explain them directly. In this case, the reader must make inferences to identify relationships among text elements and to understand the author's message.

When you **infer**, you draw a conclusion based on information in the text plus what you already know from life. In other words, you make a logical guess. A successful reader uses explicit details and implied information as clues to the author's message. Look at the examples.

Explicit Details

Hearing a deep rumble of thunder, Kacy looked up and saw thick, dark clouds rolling in her direction; she hurried inside before the storm hit.

Here, the author provides a vivid description of rumbling thunder and thick dark clouds before directly stating that a storm is approaching. The relationship between the weather conditions and Kacy's actions is clearly stated.

(Continued on page 59)

(Continued from page 58)

Implied Information

The Carsons work at their store from sunrise to sunset, but they always have beautifully maintained flowerbeds and a manicured lawn.

In this case, the relationship between ideas in the text is not obvious. Readers must make an inference about how the Carsons maintain a beautiful yard while working all day at their store. Although it is not stated, readers might logically infer that the Carsons hire a gardener because they are not home during daylight hours to tend the yard themselves.

Once you make an inference, check its accuracy. Ask yourself: *Is there enough evidence to support my conclusion? Have I overlooked any facts or clues?* If your conclusion is based on sufficient evidence, your inference is **valid**, or justified.

Directions: Read the paragraph. Write a detail that supports the inference that many people are willing to take their chances in the music business.

> Every year thousands of people record songs; however, statistics show that a small percentage of recordings released yearly make money. Only a few new artists make it to the Top 40. The success rate of new musicians is less than 1 percent.

If you wrote *every year thousands of people record songs*, you correctly identified a detail that supports the inference.

Directions: As you read the passage below, ask yourself: *How does the author imply that Jethro feels embarrassed when talking to people?*

> Jethro always felt content at home among his books. Through them, he could escape the drudgery of life as a farmer and learn about faraway lands he longed to visit. But his contentedness vanished when he had to go to the grocery store or feed shop. In contrast to the easy conversations he found in his books, a real exchange usually ended with him spluttering and turning red. He often crawled home, ashamed and discouraged, without buying everything he needed.

CORE SKILL

Make Inferences

When you read, look for information and relationships that the author implies but does not directly state. Think about what you know from your experience, and then make a logical guess about what is happening in the text.

Read the paragraph about Jethro, and make an inference about his personality. Then write a short paragraph that requires readers to make a logical guess. Trade paragraphs with a partner and make inferences about each other's writing.

TEST-TAKING SKILL

Gather Information

Gathering information is a basic test-taking skill that helps you focus to complete a test in the time allotted.

There are several strategies for finding an answer in a reading passage. First, you can scan the passage for key words that relate to the question. If the question asks for a detail about a character, look quickly through the passage to find the character's name or a pronoun (*he*, *she*, *it*) that designates the character. Details likely surround those words.

Another way to gather information is to analyze what the question is asking for. If you have a question about the main idea of a passage, you will need to skim the entire passage and ask yourself what it is about. Seek out any available topic sentences or groups of details.

Gathering information becomes simpler when you have a strategy that matches the question type.

WRITE TO LEARN

Write a short paragraph about a character from a favorite book. Include explicit details as well as information that will allow readers to infer something about the character. Exchange papers with a partner, and then discuss the details in each passage and the inference each of you made.

Think about Reading

Directions: Reread the passage about Jethro. Then choose the best answer to each question.

1. Which detail best supports the inference that Jethro feels embarrassed when talking to people?
   A. "Jethro always felt content among his books."
   B. "He could escape the drudgery of life as a farmer."
   C. "His contentedness vanished when he had to go to the grocery "store or feed shop."
   D. "A real exchange usually ended with him spluttering and turning red."
2. What is another valid inference you could make about Jethro?
   A. Jethro does not like to work.
   B. Jethro does not like being a farmer.
   C. Jethro does not like spending money.
   D. Jethro does not remember what to buy at the store.

Citing Evidence

Like crime-scene detectives, readers use a number of strategies to connect all the related evidence, or clues, and build understanding. Readers can use different kinds of evidence to support their inferences. Three types of evidence are facts and statistics, opinions, and examples.

Facts and Statistics Facts and statistics can be checked for accuracy:

- *Texting takes a driver's eyes off the road for an average of 4.6 seconds.*
- *The sport of windsurfing will be part of the 2016 Olympic Games.*

Opinions Opinions are personal views that cannot be verified:

- *Laws that limit sound inhibit freedom of expression.*
- *Loud music should be banned within the city limits.*

Examples Examples illustrate a writer's point:

- *Banks make money from interest, such as the interest you pay on a loan.*
- *There are many interesting places to visit in New York City, including the Empire State Building and Central Park.*

Think about Reading

Directions: Identify each piece of evidence as a fact, opinion, or example.

1. Sugary snacks should not be sold in school cafeterias. ________
2. Healthier snack options include fruit, whole-grain crackers, and low-fat cheese or yogurt. ________
3. By law, chain restaurants in New York City must list calorie counts next to each menu item. ________

Directions: Read the following passage. Underline the opinion the author expresses about Alfred Nobel.

What does a stick of dynamite have to do with a world-famous peace prize? The story begins in the 19th century with Alfred Nobel, a Swedish chemist and engineer. The Nobel family owned an explosives plant in which both Alfred and his younger brother worked. The plant manufactured liquid nitroglycerin. After his brother was killed in an experiment that went awry, Alfred became determined to develop a safer explosive.

In 1867 Alfred was granted a patent for a new explosive he named "dynamite." Soon, dynamite, along with the recently invented pneumatic drill, was being used worldwide to aid in the construction of roads and bridges. The invention of dynamite turned Alfred Nobel into a rich man but not a happy one, for he regretted the often warlike applications of his explosive. He had meant for dynamite to be used in safe and peaceful endeavors, but suddenly men were using it as a tool of aggression. When Alfred died, he left his fortune to give prizes to people who do their best for humanity in the fields of physics, chemistry, medicine, literature, and peace. Nobel was one of the world's greatest humanitarians.

You should have underlined the following sentence: *Nobel was one of the world's greatest humanitarians.*

Think about Reading

Directions: Answer the question below about Alfred Nobel.

What evidence in the passage implies that Nobel wanted to make up for the fact that his invention was used for war and aggression?

Summary

Writers often describe relationships between people, events, or ideas in a passage without providing explicit details. Readers gain understanding by combining evidence from the text with what they already know to make a valid inference. Recognizing various kinds of evidence is a skill that will help you build your understanding of literary and informational texts.

CORE SKILL

Cite Evidence

When an author states an opinion, that opinion should be supported by evidence. As you read a passage, ask yourself whether the author's opinion is valid. It is important to be able to **cite**, or make reference to, exactly which evidence in the text led you to accept the author's opinion as logical.

Take a look at the passage about Nobel. What evidence does the author use to support his or her opinion about how Nobel felt?

Read an editorial in a print or online newspaper or magazine. Write the opinion that the writer expresses in the article. Then cite the evidence the author uses to support the opinion. Tell whether or not you think the writer's opinion is valid, based on the evidence.

Vocabulary Review

Directions: Write a key term or a vocabulary word to complete each definition.

cite **explicit** **imply** **infer** **valid**

1. Something that is clearly stated is ________________.
2. If evidence is logically sound, it is ________________.
3. When you make a reference to something, you ________________ it.
4. To ________________ means to come to a conclusion based on evidence and prior knowledge.
5. When you express something indirectly, you ________________ it.

Skill Review

Directions: Read the passage below. Then choose the best answer to each question.

In August 2013, part of the New York City subway system was shut down. What was the reason? Some kittens had wandered onto the tracks! People waiting at a subway station reported seeing the kittens frolicking along the tracks. Engineers turned off the subway's third rail, which provides electric power to the trains as they zip along to their destinations. Their fear was that the furry little creatures would be run over or electrocuted. Some subway riders, who were typically perturbed and disgruntled when their trains didn't run on time, waited patiently for 90 minutes until the kittens had been rescued. Then the trains began to run again, and subway riders finally made it to their destination.

1. Which detail best supports the inference that people sympathized with the kittens?
   A. Part of the New York City subway system was shut down.
   B. Kittens were frolicking on the tracks.
   C. Riders waited patiently until the kittens were rescued.
   D. The trains began to run again.

2. Which of the following is a valid inference?
   A. The engineers cared about the kittens' safety.
   B. Many cats live in New York City subway tunnels.
   C. All the subway riders were happy to wait until the trains ran again.
   D. The third rail provides power to many of the skyscrapers in New York City.

3. Which sentence shows a relationship between events in the passage?
   A. Subways have a third rail, and the kittens were electrocuted.
   B. Millions of people ride the New York City subways every day, and trains are often delayed.
   C. Engineers were called in to turn off the subway's electric power, so riders were perturbed and disgruntled.
   D. Kittens were on the subway tracks, so riders were delayed.

Skill Practice

Directions: Read the passage below. Then match each inference with the detail that supports it.

Doctors say it is a common problem: many people are not getting enough healthful sleep. There is a growing concern that stress and unhealthful habits are to blame, preventing many of us from getting the sleep we need in order to function well in our everyday lives. That is the bad news; the good news is that doctors believe that there is much people can do about the problem.

First of all, doctors say, you should always pay attention to your sleep pattern. Do you stay up late, and then have difficulty falling asleep? Do you fall asleep quickly, only to awaken several times a night? If you become aware of your sleeping pattern, you can make adjustments that will lead to a better night's sleep.

Did you know that what you eat can affect how you sleep? If you eat a large, spicy dinner, your sleep might be interrupted. In addition, doctors say it is better to eat smaller meals throughout the day rather than one huge meal shortly before bed. The body reacts better and allows us more restful sleep.

Can you ever get too much sleep? Teenagers don't seem to think so. But doctors say that too much sleep is sometimes a more serious problem. People who sleep a great deal during the day may have some kind of physical illness that they are unaware of. Or perhaps depression is the cause. Either way, it is a problem that warrants a visit to the doctor.

Inference

1. Your diet may be affecting how you sleep.
2. People who get a lot of sleep may actually be sick.
3. Sleeping is not as easy as it may seem for many people.
4. Difficulty sleeping is a problem that can be solved.

Supporting Detail

a. "People who sleep a great deal during the day may have some kind of physical illness that they are unaware of."

b. "Doctors say it is a common problem; many people are not getting enough healthful sleep."

c. "If you become aware of your sleeping pattern, you can make adjustments that will lead to a better night's sleep."

d. "It is better to eat smaller meals throughout the day rather than one huge meal shortly before bed."

Writing Practice

Directions: Find a short story in a magazine or literature collection. After reading the story, write an inference that you made based on evidence in the text. Then write two or three details from the story. Explain how each detail relates to and supports your inference. Make sure your inference is valid based on the evidence that you cite.

LESSON 2.3 Analyze Relationships between Ideas

LESSON OBJECTIVES

- Identify the literary elements that create the framework of a text
- Analyze relationships within texts (the connections between characters, plot, events, setting, or ideas)

CORE SKILLS

- Identify Literary Elements
- Analyze the Relationship between Plot and Setting

Key Terms

characterization
the way an author reveals characters' traits

narrative
a story

Vocabulary

analyze
closely examine

conflict
an internal or external struggle

dynamic
showing change or growth

Key Concept

Relationships exist between different text elements—between characters, between characters and setting, between plot and setting, or between ideas.

Have you ever heard of "getting lost in a book"? This phrase describes the imaginary journey you take when you read a good story. You may encounter danger, adventure, romance, or humor along the way. You may meet characters that you root for or against as they struggle with challenges. You may be transported to another world through the author's description of a particular time and place. Recognizing connections among the characters, setting, plot, and theme of a story makes reading a richer experience.

Literary Elements

Character, plot, setting, and theme are key elements in literature. They are the *who, what, where, when,* and *why* of a story. Recognizing these elements and how they relate to one another can help you understand literary text.

Narrative

A story is sometimes called a **narrative** because the events of the story are narrated, or told, by a storyteller. A good narrative blends literary elements in a way that produces a reaction—such as fear, shock, intrigue, or joy—from the reader.

The elements of a narrative include characters, plot (the series of events in a story), setting (the time and place in which the story occurs) and theme (the message or moral). Together, these elements form the basic framework of a story.

The characters, setting, and plot are usually easy to identify in a narrative. However, recognizing the theme may be more difficult. How do you figure it out? Think about what the characters are like, what they do and say, and how they resolve their problems. You can also ask yourself: *What lesson did the characters learn? What is the author trying to tell me about life? What does the author most want me to know about this topic?* Answering these questions will help you discover a narrative's theme.

Characterization

All characters exhibit personality traits—even characters who aren't human. Character traits are qualities such as ambition, aggression, kindness, timidity, and cleverness. Sometimes character traits are described directly by the narrator. Personality traits might also be revealed by what a character says and does, what other characters say about the character, and how a character deals with problems. Characters that change or grow as a result of their experiences are called **dynamic** characters. The way that an author reveals a character's traits is called **characterization**.

As you read the following passage, notice the difference between the characterization of the lady with the dog and the characterization of Gurov. Through Gurov's observations, the reader gets a physical description of the lady and learns about her daily habits. In contrast, the reader must infer Gurov's character traits from his actions and from his thoughts about the lady.

> It was said that a new person had appeared on the sea-front: a lady with a little dog. Dmitri Dmitritch Gurov, who had by then been a fortnight at Yalta, and so was fairly at home there, had begun to take an interest in new arrivals. Sitting in Verney's pavilion, he saw, walking on the sea-front, a fair-haired young lady of medium height, wearing a beret; a white Pomeranian dog was running behind her.
>
> And afterwards he met her in the public gardens and in the square several times a day. She was walking alone, always wearing the same beret, and always with the same white dog; no one knew who she was, and every one called her simply "the lady with the dog. "
>
> "If she is here alone without a husband or friends, it wouldn't be amiss to make her acquaintance, " Gurov reflected.
>
> —From "The Lady with the Dog" by Anton Chekhov, translated by Constance Garnett

The plot and setting of a narrative influence what readers learn about a character. How a character behaves in a particular setting or in response to particular events reveals certain personality traits. The reader knows from the passage that Gurov has already spent two weeks in the seaside resort and that he spends his time sitting in the pavilion and walking in the gardens. It is not mentioned that he spends any time with other people. Based on this information, he appears to be a quiet, shy man who has enough money to take a long vacation. Also, it can be inferred that he is not impulsive because he thinks carefully about whether or not he should approach the lady with the dog.

CORE SKILL

Identify Literary Elements

As you read a narrative, look for the literary elements that give the story its foundation. Ask yourself:

- *Who are the main characters?*
- *Where and when does the action take place?*
- *What are the key events of the plot?*
- *What is the author's message?*

Think about a familiar book or story you have read, such as *The Great Gatsby, The Wizard of Oz,* or *Huckleberry Finn.* Answer the questions above without naming the story's title. Share your analysis with a partner. Can he or she identify the story from the literary elements you identified?

WRITE TO LEARN

Write a story in three or four paragraphs with a main character, a setting, a plot, and a theme. Exchange stories with a partner, and identify the literary elements in each other's work.

CORE SKILL

Analyze the Relationship between Plot and Setting

A plot is a series of events that includes at least one conflict and complications that a character encounters throughout a story.

The events and conflicts a character experiences are directly connected to the setting of a story. For example, suppose a plot entails a thief breaking into an art museum. The motives and methods for robbing a small seaside mariner museum, the National Gallery of Art in Washington, DC, or an American Indian art collection in a southwestern desert town would be very different.

Think about a story you have read recently, and imagine a different setting for the action. Write a few sentences explaining how the plot would be different if the setting changed.

One of the main components of plot is **conflict**. A conflict is an external or internal struggle that one or more characters face. It may be a character's problem with another character *(Sam needed the car, but his brother had borrowed it.)*, with society *(Thomas Jefferson felt that the laws were unfair.)*, or with nature *(Sara tried to remain calm as the floodwaters washed out the bridge ahead of her.)*. A character may also have an inner struggle with his or her beliefs or feelings *(Jill didn't know whether to tell Anna; it might hurt her feelings.)*. By the end of a story, there is usually a resolution, which means that the character comes to terms with the conflict in some way.

Think about Reading

Directions: Reread the passage from "The Lady with the Dog" on the previous page. In a notebook answer the questions below.

1. What is the relationship between the lady and the other characters?
2. Gurov lives in a time when it is frowned upon to approach someone you do not know. What is Gurov's conflict concerning the lady with the dog? Is it internal or external?

Analyzing Relationships in Text

As you read a narrative, it's helpful to **analyze**, or examine, relationships among the literary elements to build a better understanding of the text. For example, you might analyze how the setting influences the characters and plot, how events reveal the characters' traits, and how all these elements help communicate the theme.

Directions: Read the passage. What conflict is the character experiencing? How does that relate to the setting? What theme, or message, do these story elements communicate?

> Growing up, I lived in a small farmhouse on a dairy farm. Each morning before school, I would go out and complete my chores, which included collecting eggs from our chickens and milking our cows. On dark, cold days, I would often dream of a life in the big city, a life without chores around every corner. Determined to leave, I saved every penny I had and at the age of 19, I boarded a bus for New York City.

You should have noted that the conflict is that the character is unhappy living on a dairy farm. This conflict relates directly to the setting because it is the daily chores required on a dairy farm and the weather that make the character want to leave. If you said the setting and the character's internal conflict communicate a message about the importance of perseverance or determination, then you understood the theme of the passage.

As you examine a story closely, meaningful connections among characters, settings, and plot often emerge.

Directions: Read the following passage. What is Carrie's conflict? Is it external or internal?

> Once across the river and into the wholesale district, she glanced about her for some likely door at which to apply. As she contemplated the wide windows and imposing signs, she became conscious of being gazed upon and understood for what she was—a wage-seeker. She had never done this thing before, and lacked courage. . . . Over the way stood a great six-story structure, labeled Storm and King, which she viewed with rising hope. It was a wholesale dry goods concern and employed women. She could see them moving about now and then upon the upper floors. This place she decided to enter, no matter what. She crossed over and walked directly toward the entrance. As she did so, two men came out and paused in the door. A telegraph messenger in blue dashed past her and up the few steps that led to the entrance and disappeared. Several pedestrians out of the hurrying throng which filled the sidewalks passed about her as she paused, hesitating. She looked helplessly around, and then, seeing herself observed, retreated. . . . Her feet carried her mechanically forward, every foot of her progress being a satisfactory portion of a flight which she gladly made.
>
> —From *Sister Carrie* by Theodore Dreiser

You should have noted that Carrie's internal conflict was the need to get a job versus the lack of courage to ask for one.

Think about Reading

Directions Answer the following questions about the excerpt from *Sister Carrie.*

1. How does the setting influence Carrie's actions?
2. What does Carrie's attitude toward getting a job reveal about her?
3. What is the theme of the passage?

Summary

The elements of a narrative—characters, setting, plot, and theme—form the foundation of a story. The ability to identify these elements and to analyze relationships among them helps readers gain a better understanding of literary texts.

21st CENTURY SKILL

Media Literacy

In our multimedia culture, we get information and entertainment from words on paper and through powerful images and sounds. You can read a book in print or on a computer or tablet. You can listen to it with an MP3 player or watch it in video form. However, a story may change from one medium to another.

You may have already noticed the difference if, for example, you read a Harry Potter book and then saw the film adaptation, in which some of the events were missing or different. Writers of movies, films, and plays often adapt a book to fit the intended audience and the time allotted.

With a partner, make a storyboard, or visual plan, to adapt "The Lady with the Dog" into a short film. What visual clues (for example, clothing, body language, and props) will you use for characterization and to establish the setting? Will you film in black and white or color? What shots will you use (close-ups or panoramas) and why? Discuss your storyboard in a small group.

Vocabulary Review

Directions: Match each key term or vocabulary word with its definition.

1. narrative	**a.** showing change or growth
2. characterization	**b.** closely examine
3. analyze	**c.** an internal or external struggle
4. dynamic	**d.** the way an author reveals the characters' traits
5. conflict	**e.** a story

Skill Review

Directions: Read the passage below. Then complete the activities.

Her marriage to Leonce Pontellier was purely an accident, in this respect resembling many other marriages which masquerade as the decrees of Fate. It was in the midst of her secret great passion that she met him. He fell in love, as men are in the habit of doing, and pressed his suit with an earnestness and an ardor which left nothing to be desired. He pleased her; his absolute devotion flattered her. She fancied there was a sympathy of thought and taste between them, in which fancy she was mistaken. Add to this the violent opposition of her father and her sister Margaret to her marriage with a Catholic, and we need seek no further for the motives which led her to accept Mr. Pontellier for her husband.

The acme of this bliss, which would have been a marriage with the tragedian, was not for her in this world. As the devoted wife of a man who worshipped her, she felt she would take her place with a certain dignity in the world of reality, closing the portals forever behind her upon the realm of romance and dreams.

But it was not long before the tragedian had gone to join the cavalry officer and the engaged young man and a few others; Edna found herself face to face with the realities. She grew fond of her husband, realizing with some unaccountable satisfaction that no trace of passion or excessive and fictitious warmth colored her affection, thereby threatening its dissolution.

—From *The Awakening* by Kate Chopin

1. Which phrase best shows that Edna is a dynamic character?

A. Edna's marriage was purely an accident.

B. She grew fond of her husband.

C. She left to join the cavalry officer.

D. Her marriage resembled many other marriages.

2. The __________ of this excerpt is that, despite her family's disapproval, Edna marries a man she does not love, but who loves her, only to discover later that her marriage is __________.

3. Which phrase best states the theme of the passage?

A. The reality of loneliness

B. The dangers of ignorance

C. The battle of good and evil

D. The unpredictability of human emotion

Skill Practice

Directions: Read the excerpt from *The Secret Garden*. Then choose the best answer to each question.

They drew the chair under the plum-tree, which was snow-white with blossoms and musical with bees. It was like a king's canopy, a fairy king's. There were flowering cherry-trees near and apple-trees whose buds were pink and white, and here and there one had burst open wide. Between the blossoming branches of the canopy, bits of blue sky looked down like wonderful eyes.

Mary and Dickon worked a little here and there, and Colin watched them. They brought him things to look at—buds which were opening, buds which were tight closed, bits of twig whose leaves were just showing green, the feather of a woodpecker which had dropped on the grass, the empty shell of some bird early hatched. Dickon pushed the chair slowly round and round the garden, stopping every other moment to let him look at wonders springing out of the earth or trailing down from trees. It was like being taken in state round the country of a magic king and queen and shown all the mysterious riches it contained. . . .

Colin had been instructed as to the law of whispers and low voices several days before. He liked the mysteriousness of it and did his best, but in the midst of excited enjoyment it is rather difficult never to laugh above a whisper. . . .

Mary . . . was a great believer in Magic. Secretly she quite believed that Dickon worked Magic, of course good Magic, on everything near him and that was why people liked him so much and wild creatures knew he was their friend. She wondered, indeed, if it were not possible that his gift had brought the robin just at the right moment when Colin asked that dangerous question. She felt that his Magic was working all the afternoon and making Colin look like an entirely different boy. It did not seem possible that he could be the crazy creature who had screamed and beaten and bitten his pillow. Even his ivory whiteness seemed to change. The faint glow of color which had shown on his face and neck and hands when he first got inside the garden really never quite died away. He looked as if he were made of flesh instead of ivory or wax.

—From *The Secret Garden* by Frances Hodgson Burnett

1. Which quote from the passage is an example of characterization?

A. "It was like a king's canopy, a fairy king's."

B. "bits of blue sky looked down like wonderful eyes."

C. "it is rather difficult never to laugh above a whisper"

D. "Mary . . . was a great believer in Magic."

2. Which event is NOT related to the setting?

A. They drew the chair under the plum-tree

B. Colin screamed and beat and bit his pillow.

C. Dickon pushed the chair slowly round and round the garden.

D. They brought him things to look at—buds which were opening . . .

3. What message does the author communicate about the "secret garden"?

A. Gardens can grow anywhere.

B. No one can grow a garden alone.

C. It takes magic to grow a beautiful garden.

D. The beauty of nature can transform people.

Writing Practice

Directions: Read a short story in a magazine or literature anthology. Write a brief summary in which you identify the characters, setting, conflict, and theme. Then write three or four sentences explaining how the setting affects the plot.

LESSON 2.4 Determine Implicit Relationships between Ideas

LESSON OBJECTIVES

- Identify implied relationships between ideas
- Cite evidence to support implied relationships

CORE SKILLS

- Determine Implied Relationships between Ideas
- Predict Outcomes

Key Terms

inference
a logical guess based on stated details in the text plus what you already know

predict
foretell

Vocabulary

outcome
result, effect

proximity
closeness, quality of being near or next to

Key Concept

Like ideas, relationships between ideas in a text may be implied. When this occurs, readers must find clues in the text to help them understand how the ideas connect.

When you assemble a jigsaw puzzle, you look for pieces that will fit together and for patterns of color and shape that belong next to each other; then you connect them. When you read, you sometimes have to figure out how different pieces of the text fit together to communicate the writer's message. You may need to look for patterns and other clues to completely understand how one idea connects to others in the text.

Interpreting Implied Relationships between Ideas

Authors often imply how two ideas relate to one another without directly stating their relationship. To completely understand the author's message, you need to make an **inference**, or a logical guess, about the relationship between ideas. You can do this by looking for clues in the text, such as punctuation, **proximity** (closeness), and patterns.

Directions: As you read, circle any punctuation marks that offer clues about the relationship between ideas. Take notes on how the ideas are placed in the paragraph. Which ideas are near one another? What patterns do you notice?

> Umpires in American baseball are often yelled at by managers; umpires in Japanese baseball are treated with much more respect. In America, a dubious call by an ump can cause managers to launch into tirades loaded with unprintable words. Japanese managers, on the other hand, politely inquire as to whether the umpire is quite certain about the call he has made. American managers sometimes become literally hopping mad, and often they are thrown out of the game for their antics. A Japanese manager remains calm even though he may be angry.

Did you notice the semicolon (;) in the first line of the passage? Semicolons are used to connect sentences whose ideas are closely related. When you see a semicolon in text, ask yourself: *What is the relationship between these two ideas?*

Look at the word patterns in the two sentences separated by the semicolon. You will see that the writer has used very similar phrasing: "Umpires in American baseball are . . ." and "Umpires in Japanese baseball are . . ." This pattern is another clue that the ideas are closely related. The repetition emphasizes that a comparison is being made between the two nationalities.

As you read the rest of the paragraph, you probably noticed a similar pattern—pairs of sentences in which the first is about American baseball and the second is about Japanese baseball. Note that each pair of sentences addresses the same topic. For example, the third pair describes how baseball managers express anger.

Thus, even though the writer never states that that he or she is comparing how American and Japanese baseball managers treat umpires, the relationship among the ideas is made clear through punctuation, proximity, and word and sentence patterns.

In addition to text clues, you may also need to use prior knowledge to understand implied relationships between ideas.

Directions: Read the following passage about the Pony Express. In the last sentence, the writer mentions the Pacific Telegraph line. What do you know about the telegraph that helps you interpret the relationship implied in the last line?

> The Pony Express has been romanticized in tales about the early western United States, but it actually played an extremely practical role. It was begun in 1860 as a way to carry mail between Missouri and California. The Pony Express used the fastest mode of communication available—a man on a horse. It was a kind of relay race across the country. There were relief stations about every 15 miles to give the rider food, water, and a fresh horse. After riding for about 75 miles, the messenger handed his mail pouch to the next man in the relay, who continued the route. After just 19 months, the Pony Express ended operations in October 1861, when the Pacific Telegraph line was completed.

You probably know that a telegraph is an electrical means of sending and receiving messages over long distances. This knowledge helps you interpret the relationship between the Pony Express and the Pacific Telegraph line, even though this relationship is not explicitly stated in the text.

CORE SKILL

Determine Implied Relationships between Ideas

Some relationships are not stated directly in a text; they are suggested. Readers must use clues in the text plus their own experience to infer the relationship that the author is implying. To identify an implied relationship, follow these steps:

1. Read the entire passage. Note clearly stated ideas and relationships. They may be clues to unstated relationships.
2. Where a relationship is not stated, ask yourself: *Why does the author include these ideas?*
3. Notice how the ideas are presented in the text. Ask yourself: *Why are these ideas near one another? Do the sentences have similar structures? What punctuation is used?*
4. Then ask yourself: *Is the author comparing the ideas? Does one cause the other? Is one an example of the other? Do they form a sequence?*
5. Consider what you already know about the topic, and apply that to ideas presented in the text.

Find a short passage in print or online. With a partner, find and underline the explicit details. Use what you both know about the topic from experience to infer the relationship that the author is implying between people or events.

CORE SKILL

Predicting Outcomes

Authors often imply that one action causes another action to happen. Read these sentences: *It rained for three days. Farmers watched anxiously as the river rose.* Even though the author does not state that the rain caused the river to rise, the relationship between these events is easy to recognize. It's also possible to make a reasonable prediction based on the text. Because "farmers watched anxiously as the river rose," readers can predict that if the river overflows, it will cause damage to crops, fences, or other features of a farm.

Here's how to predict an outcome:

1. Read the entire passage.
2. Note explicit and implicit relationships between ideas.
3. Ask yourself: *What could happen as a result of this event or action? Can I make a reasonable prediction?*
4. Review the ideas, relationships, and patterns in the text. Make sure the outcome you predicted could logically follow from what you have read.

Look at the paragraph about the settlement of the Americas. The author states that the Spanish conquistadors who colonized Central and South America were on a mission to spread Catholicism. Based on that information, what prediction can you make about the most popular religion in Central and South America today? What prediction can you make about the most common language spoken on these continents? Discuss your ideas with a partner.

Think about Reading

Directions: Reread the passage about the Pony Express. Then circle the appropriate words in the sentence below to explain the implied relationship between the Pony Express and the Pacific Telegraph line.

> The writer implies that the telegraph (imitated, replaced, stopped) the Pony Express (and, because, but) telegraph wires sent long-distance messages (faster than, so that, while) they could be delivered on horseback.

Citing Evidence of Implied Relationships

When you recognize implied relationships between ideas, it is often possible to infer ideas that are deliberately left unstated in the text. In the paragraph below, for example, the pattern of ideas creates an expectation, so readers are able to infer what the author does not state.

> The Europeans who settled North America came mostly from Northern Europe, especially England, but those who colonized Central and South America came from Southern Europe, predominantly Spain. Most of the English were settlers; most of the Spanish were soldiers. The English settlers hoped to find prosperity and religious freedom in North America; the Spanish conquistadors were under orders to bring back wealth for their rulers and to spread Catholicism throughout the New World. Most important of all, the English brought their families with them.

At the beginning of the paragraph, the author establishes a pattern contrasting the settlement of North America and Central and South America. Because of this, the author does not need to say that the Spanish soldiers came without their families. This inference can be made because of the relationship between other details in the passage.

Readers can take the inferences they make a step further and **predict**, or foretell, an **outcome**, or result. When making predictions, just as when making inferences, you combine evidence from the text with what you already know. Use this information to predict what you will read or what will happen next in a text.

Directions: Read the following passage, and predict an outcome. In your notebook, cite the evidence you used to make your prediction.

> A tsunami is caused by an undersea earthquake. Waves speed toward land at hundreds of miles per hour, building 100-foot-tall crests as they go. Eventually, the huge waves crash on shore and swallow everything in their path, causing tremendous destruction. Scientists monitor undersea activity and can usually estimate the time a tsunami will hit a particular area. People living in tsunami danger zones know what to do when the alarm sounds.

Did you predict that when the alarm sounds, people evacuate the area, moving to higher ground? This is a reasonable prediction based on evidence in the text (tsunamis have "100-foot-tall crests" and "swallow everything in their path") and what you already know about the danger associated with tsunamis.

Directions: Read the following passage. Note relationships among ideas, and make a prediction. Write the information in your notebook.

Sea Otters at Risk

Sea otters that live in coastal waters have the thickest fur of any mammal. There are between 850,000 and 1 million hairs per square inch on a sea otter's skin; humans have only about 100,000 hairs on their entire head! To stay warm in freezing water, otters blow air into their fur. The trapped air keeps the animals warm and buoyant.

Hundreds of years ago, sea otters thrived along the Pacific coast, from southern California to Alaska. However, fur traders killed them by the millions, and by 1900 the species faced near extinction. Legislators enacted laws to protect sea otters, allowing a rebound in population, and now nearly 80,000 again frolic along the Pacific coastline.

Today, oil spills put sea otters at great risk. If toxic oil gets on their thick fur, they ingest it while grooming and die. Even if they do not swallow the oil, oil-covered fur loses its insulating ability, and the otters die from hypothermia. The oil also poisons much of their food source, leaving survivors at risk of starvation.

Industrial chemicals are another major threat. The bodies of more than a hundred dead otters found off California's coast contained a chemical used to prevent barnacles from sticking to boats. Some people wonder: could sea otters be an early warning sign that pollution is poisoning the ocean's entire ecosystem?

Did you note that after millions of sea otters were killed, legislators enacted laws to protect them in the early 1900s? Based on this relationship, you may have predicted that lawmakers might enact new laws to protect coastal waters from pollution in an effort to protect sea otters.

Think about Reading

Directions: Reread the passage about sea otters. In a notebook, write which details show an implied relationship between human activities and threats to sea otters.

Summary

Writers often imply, or hint at, relationships between ideas. Readers can use clues such as proximity, punctuation, and text patterns to make inferences about how ideas are related. Often by figuring out the relationships between details in a text, readers can predict an outcome.

WRITE TO LEARN

Write a comparison of two people, places, or things without stating that you are comparing them. Use proximity, punctuation, and sentence patterns to indicate comparison.

21st CENTURY SKILL

Global Awareness

Throughout the world, thousands of animal species are threatened or endangered. Endangered species are at the brink of extinction now; threatened species are likely to be at the brink in the near future. The major threats to these animals are loss of habitat and overhunting. To get a global perspective of the situation, go to an Internet site such as the World Wildlife Fund.

Choose an endangered or threatened species that interests you. Use a search engine to find information about the animal. In a notebook, record the animal species, the area of the world in which it is threatened or endangered, and any details about efforts to save the animal. Report your findings to the class, inferring relationships among the ideas and making a prediction about the animal's future.

Vocabulary Review

Directions: Read the clue beside each scrambled key term or vocabulary word. Then unscramble the word, and write it correctly on the line.

1. DRETICP	This means to foretell what will happen in the future.	______________
2. RYTOXIIPM	This means closeness or nearness.	______________
3. CUTOMOE	This is an effect or result of something that happens.	______________
4. FIRECENNE	This is a process of using details in the text plus your own knowledge.	______________

Skill Review

Directions: Read the passage. Then choose the best answer to each question.

Is Organic Better?

While shopping for groceries, you may have had to choose between standard and organic foods. People usually buy standard foods because of a wider selection and cheaper prices. However, more and more people believe organic foods are better for your body and worth a higher price.

A standard McIntosh apple may look identical to an organic McIntosh apple. How are the two different? Standard food farmers may use artificial chemicals on their crops. For example, farmers may use pesticides to kill insects and control weeds. Some farmers even use chemicals to increase the amount of food they grow. In contrast, organic farmers use no artificial chemicals. They use alternative methods to protect crops and make their fields productive. For example, organic farmers spray milk on zucchini and grapes to kill mold. They coat apple tree branches with vegetable oil so insects cannot lay eggs there. And organic farmers use glue traps to keep insects away from the plants.

On standard farms, animals may be raised in cramped conditions that promote disease. The feed given to livestock may have chemicals added to prevent or treat diseases or to make the animals bigger and more productive. Conditions on organic farms are much different. Regulations prevent farmers from keeping livestock shut in, so livestock roam free in pastures or open yards. Livestock are given only chemical-free feed.

Today most experts agree that organic and standard foods can be part of a healthy diet. However, food grown without chemicals is bound to be safer. But for now, the choice to "go organic" is personal.

1. Which detail BEST supports an implied relationship between how organic farms are run and organic food being more healthful?

A. Foods are low in fat.

B. Organic foods cost more.

C. No artificial chemicals are used.

D. Organic apples look just like standard apples.

2. Which could you logically predict based on evidence in the passage?

A. Cows on organic farms grow taller.

B. Cows on organic farms get more exercise.

C. Cows on organic farms are kept in large barns.

D. Cows on organic farms live longer than cows on standard farms.

Skill Practice

Directions: Read the passage below. Then choose the best answer to each question.

The age at which a teenager can get a driver's license ranges from 14 years, 3 months in the state of South Dakota to 17 years in New Jersey. If most experts had their way, teens would have to wait until they were 17—or even 18—to get a license. The Insurance Institute for Highway Safety says that car accidents are the leading cause of death among teenagers and that raising the driving age would save lives.

The experts could be right. New Jersey is the only state that gives driver's licenses as late as 17, and the number of crash-related deaths in that state is 18 per 100,000 teens. In Connecticut, where teenagers can get a learner's permit at 16 and get their license four months later, the death rate is 26 per 100,000. The statistics don't lie. They tell us that raising the driving age saves lives.

But is it age or a lack of driving experience that causes the problem? I believe it is a lack of experience, because driving is not a skill that can be mastered overnight. Instead of raising the age at which teens can get a license, why not increase the amount of time a teenager must practice driving before getting a driver's license? In that way, teens would get more practice, and by the time they are ready to drive on their own, they will have put in many supervised hours behind the wheel.

Doing something just because it is good for you may not be popular, but it is part of growing up. Teens may have to accept that they will not be given a license until they have had plenty of practice. This will help keep them and other drivers safe.

1. Which statement implies a relationship between teen driving and safety?

A. Safe driving is a skill that anyone can learn over time.

B. Teen drivers in New Jersey are older and have fewer accidents.

C. Teens in Connecticut can get a license at age 16 and four months.

D. Changes to the age at which a teen can get a license will not be well received.

2. Which does the writer imply would cut down on deaths among teenagers?

A. raising the age at which teens are allowed to get a license

B. lowering the age at which teens are allowed to get a license

C. raising the amount of time teens must practice before getting a license

D. lowering the amount of time teens need to practice before getting a license

Writing Practice

Directions: Write a short passage about something that interests you. Be sure to show relationships between ideas, including an implied relationship that allows readers to predict an outcome. Remember that this can be done by establishing a text pattern or by implying that one action causes another action to happen.

LESSON 2.5 Analyze the Role of Details in Complex Texts

LESSON OBJECTIVES

- Identify the characteristics of complex texts
- Explain the role of details in complex texts

CORE SKILLS

- Comprehend Complex Texts
- Use Details to Analyze Complex Texts

Key Terms

complex
complicated; difficult to understand and explain

scan
to read quickly

Vocabulary

complement
to complete or add to something

conclusions
reasonable judgments

Key Concept

The details in complex informational and literary texts provide clues to the main ideas, significance of events, and relationships implied by the author.

Have you ever read an article and then said to yourself, "What was that about? I don't get it." It happens to many people as they read more complicated texts, but being able to read complex texts is vital for success in college, the workplace, and life in general. Readers who take a careful and purposeful approach to reading know how to analyze details in a text to gain a deeper understanding of the author's message.

Complex Text

A **complex** text is complicated, or difficult to understand and explain. It might include technical or advanced vocabulary, long and elaborate sentences, or sophisticated ideas. It might be about an unfamiliar subject or explore abstract ideas such as love, success, patriotism, or morality.

Other characteristics of complex texts include an implicit purpose, more than one level of meaning, multiple themes or a sophisticated theme, and uncommon text structures. In general, a complex text requires readers to apply their knowledge about language, literature, and life experiences to fully comprehend the author's meaning.

Read the examples that follow. The first presents information in a straightforward manner; the sentence structure and vocabulary are simple. The second example is a complex presentation of the same idea; the sentence structure and vocabulary are more advanced.

> **Straightforward text:** In the early days of the Algonquin people, humans and animals thrived. They lived in a land where the climate was mild all year long.
>
> **Complex text:** Initially, the Algonquin populace—human beings and wildlife alike—bourgeoned in an environment that was perennially temperate.

The two sentences below were written in 1775 by Alexander Hamilton, one of America's founding fathers. What features make the text complex?

> "The origin of all civil government . . . must be a voluntary compact between the rulers and the ruled. [It] must be liable to such limitations as are necessary [to secure] the absolute rights of the latter, for what [right] can any man or set of men have to govern others except their own consent?"

Think about Reading

Directions: Reread the quote from Alexander Hamilton. In a notebook, write two or three sentences explaining the features that make the text complex.

Understanding Complex Text

To understand complex texts, be an active reader. This involves identifying and thinking about important details that reveal meaning. Here's how.

Scan and predict. Scan the text, or look it over quickly, to get an idea of what it is about. Read the title if there is one, and look at any photos or illustrations. Watch for words that appear in a special font or sections that are numbered. Note details that tell *who, what, when, where, why,* and *how.* Use this information to predict what you will learn from the text.

Make connections. Use prior knowledge, or what you already know, to help you connect to the text. Ask yourself: *Does this remind me of something that happened to me or to someone I know? Did I read about this or see something about it on TV? Is something happening in the world today that is similar?*

Visualize. Create a mental image of the details. Using your senses (sight, hearing, sound, taste, touch) helps you understand and remember details.

Check structure. How is the text organized? Does it compare and contrast people or things? Does it present a problem and suggest solutions? Does it describe events in chronological order, or do you need to figure out the order of events?

Ask questions. Ask relevant questions as you read. For example, you might ask, "Why is that important?" or "What does this word mean?" Write your questions on sticky notes, and place them next to the text. Continue reading or reread to find answers to your questions. Add the answers to your sticky notes.

Summarize. Paraphrase, or restate in your own words, the most important ideas. This makes it easier for you to remember and understand what you read.

Actively read the passage on the next page about two ancient structures. The writer includes information about the structures being World Heritage sites to **complement**—complete, or add details about—the main topic.

CORE SKILL

Comprehend Complex Texts

To understand a complex text, be an active reader and look for clues. Follow this procedure:

1. Begin by scanning the entire text. Ask yourself: *What key words do I see? What are the major sections of the text? How is the text organized? What will I learn?*
2. As you read, look for details that connect to something you already know.
3. Make a list of questions that occur to you as you read. Then review the text, looking for answers to your questions.

In a print or online source, find a complex passage that interests you. With a partner, discuss what makes the passage complex. Then follow the procedure above to figure out the text's meaning. Compare your findings with those of your partner.

WRITE TO LEARN

Write a paragraph defining the abstract concept *success.* Use examples and other details to explain what success means to you. Then exchange papers with a partner, and read each other's paragraphs. Discuss the challenges associated with writing and reading complex ideas.

LANGUAGE SKILLS

Pronoun-antecedent Agreement

When reading complex text, it is important to identify and clarify relationships among the people, places, and things that are presented. Active readers make sure they understand the relationship between pronouns and their antecedents. A pronoun takes the place of a noun (the antecedent) that has already been named. Common pronouns include *he, she we, you, they, it, his, her,* and *ours*. A pronoun must agree with its antecedent in number and person.

Incorrect: Every man in the meeting kept raising their voice.

Correct: Every man in the meeting kept raising his voice.

Incorrect: If a person hits a parked car, you should leave a note.

Correct: If a person hits a parked car, he or she should leave a note.

Look at the passage about the Taj Mahal and the Great Pyramid. The pronoun *they* is used twice in the first paragraph and once in the second. Work with a partner to identify the antecedent to *they* each time the pronoun is used. Then discuss how you were able to identify the antecedent in each case.

Directions: Read the following passage. Circle the important details that indicate the importance of the ancient structures.

> The Taj Mahal and the Great Pyramid have something in common besides being ancient examples of monumental architecture. Both have been scheduled for destruction. When Arab Muslims took over Egypt centuries ago, they had plans to dismantle the Great Pyramid for its limestone. But before the plan could be put into effect, they found limestone that was easier to obtain at a nearby quarry, so the Great Pyramid was left alone.
>
> Likewise, a British businessperson in India in 1830 expressed interest in taking down the Taj Mahal for its valuable marble. Wrecking crews were hired, and the demolition date was set. However, protesters pointed out that the temple was a cultural achievement without parallel, and they stopped the destruction in the nick of time.
>
> In the 1980s, the Taj Mahal was named a World Heritage site, and in 1996, India's Supreme Court banned the use of coal near the site to protect the beautiful white-marble monument from pollution. The Great Pyramid has been a World Heritage site since 1979.

Did you circle the details about the building materials used (limestone for the Pyramid, marble for the Taj Mahal), and each structure's status as a World Heritage site? These details convey the importance of the two structures.

Think about Reading

Directions: Reread the passage above about two ancient wonders. Then write the answer to this question in your notebook: What does the phrase "a cultural achievement without parallel" mean?

Analyzing Complex Literary Texts

You have learned that identifying and analyzing important details can help you understand complex informational texts. The same procedure—reaching **conclusions**, or reasonable judgments, based on important details—can help you understand complex literary texts, such as poems or short stories.

The poem on the next page, written by Walt Whitman, is about Ulysses S. Grant, but it also treats abstract themes—heroism and democracy—and relies on readers' familiarity with events of the time. As with many complex texts, it is helpful for readers to recall their prior knowledge of the subject or author.

In this case, readers might recall that Grant served as a lieutenant general in the US Civil War. As commander of the Union armies, he was the one who accepted the Confederate surrender at Appomattox Courthouse. Grant's popularity led to his being elected president in 1868. When he left office, Grant traveled around the world and was treated like—and received by—royalty.

It is also helpful for readers to know that Whitman, who had served as a volunteer nurse during the Civil War, wrote many patriotic poems. In addition, Whitman was a champion of the "average" man and admired Grant's ability to be a typical American and an extraordinary figure at the same time.

The poem is complex not only because of the abstract themes and historical topic, but also because of the way it is written. Note, for example, that Whitman combines many details in one long sentence. Also, some of the words and spellings he uses may be unfamiliar. The complex structure and unusual vocabulary make the poem difficult for some readers to understand.

Directions: Read the poem. In it, Whitman lists several important qualities of Grant, but there is one quality that impresses him most. Underline the word that introduces Whitman's explanation of that quality. Then write a sentence summarizing that quality as you understand it.

What Best I See in Thee

To U. S. G. return'd from his World's Tour

1 What best I see in thee
2 Is not that where thou mov'st down history's great highways,
3 Ever undimm'd by time shoots warlike victory's dazzle,
4 Or that thou sat'st where Washington sat, ruling the land in peace,
5 Or thou the man whom feudal Europe fêted, venerable Asia swarm'd upon
6 Who walk'd with kings with even pace the round world's promenade;
7 But that in foreign lands, in all thy walks with kings,
8 Those prairie sovereigns of the West, Kansas, Missouri, Illinois,
9 Ohio's, Indiana's millions, comrades, farmers, soldiers, all to the front,
10 Invisibly with thee walking with kings with even pace the round world's promenade,
11 Were all so justified.

—From *The Patriotic Poems of Walt Whitman*

Whitman mentions Grant's many historical roles—as a great military hero (line 3), the country's leader (line 4), and an international celebrity (lines 5–6). "But," he says (line 7), these are not Grant's best qualities. Instead, what is best about Grant is that he represents all Americans (lines 8–10) and that, by celebrating Grant, the world had celebrated and "justified" common farmers, soldiers and others from all parts of the United States (line 11). In the poem, Whitman portrays Grant as an embodiment of democracy.

Summary

A complex text may contain technical or unfamiliar vocabulary, elaborate sentences, and advanced ideas. To understand complex texts, be an active reader. This includes scanning before you read to get a sense of the text's structure and subject matter, asking questions and identifying important details as you read, and summarizing the main points after you read.

CORE SKILL

Use Details to Analyze Complex Texts

When you analyze a complex text, identify details that communicate the writer's message. Follow these steps:

1. Scan the text to get an idea of what it is about.
2. Read the entire passage.
3. Ask yourself: *What is the writer's main idea? Which details support that idea? What are the most important points for me to remember?*
4. Make notes as you read. List key ideas, important vocabulary, and significant names, places, and dates.
5. Use your notes to write a summary of the text. Be sure to include the main idea and key points.

In an online or print source, read Walt Whitman's famous poem for Abraham Lincoln, "Oh Captain, My Captain." Follow the procedure above to write a summary of the poet's message.

Vocabulary Review

Directions: Match each word with its definition.

1. scan	**a.** to complete or add to something
2. complex	**b.** to read quickly
3. complement	**c.** reasonable judgments
4. conclusions	**d.** complicated; difficult to understand or explain

Skill Review

Directions: Read the passage below. Then choose the best answer to each question.

The Spectre

The immediate cause . . . of the prevalence of supernatural stories . . . was doubtless owing to the vicinity of Sleepy Hollow. There was a contagion in the very air that blew from that haunted region; it breathed forth an atmosphere of dreams and fancies infecting all the land. Several of the Sleepy Hollow people were present at Van Tassel's, and, as usual, were doling out their wild and wonderful legends. Many dismal tales were told about funeral trains, and mourning cries and wailings heard and seen about the great tree where the unfortunate Major André was taken. . . . Some mention was made also of the woman in white, that haunted the dark glen . . . and was often heard to shriek on winter nights before a storm, having perished there in the snow.

The chief part of the stories, however, turned upon the favorite spectre of Sleepy Hollow, the Headless Horseman, who . . . it was said, tethered his horse nightly among the graves in the churchyard.

The sequestered situation of this church seems always to have made it a favorite haunt of troubled spirits. It stands on a knoll, surrounded by locust-trees and lofty elms. . . . To look upon its grass-grown yard, where the sunbeams seem to sleep so quietly, one would think that there at least the dead might rest in peace. . . . not far from the church, was . . . a wooden bridge . . . thickly shaded by overhanging trees, which cast a gloom about it, even in the daytime. . . . Such was one of the favorite haunts of the Headless Horseman, and the place where he was most frequently encountered. The tale was told of old Brouwer . . . how he met the Horseman . . . and was obliged to get up behind him; how they galloped . . . until they reached the bridge; when the Horseman suddenly turned into a skeleton, threw old Brouwer into the brook, and sprang away over the tree-tops with a clap of thunder.

—From "The Legend of Sleepy Hollow" by Washington Irving

1. What explanation does the author give for why the woman in white shrieked before winter storms?

A. She was married on a winter evening in Sleepy Hollow.

B. She died in the glen on a snowy night.

C. She saw the Headless Horseman riding through the glen.

D. She died on the wooden bridge under the overhanging trees.

2. According to the author, which word best describes the atmosphere of Sleepy Hollow?

A. unfriendly

B. cheerful

C. dreamlike

D. enthusiastic

3. What is the meaning of the word *spectre* as used in the passage?

A. hero

B. ghost

C. dancer

D. soldier

Skill Practice

Directions: Read the passage below. Then choose the best answer to each question.

Invasion of the Plant and Animal Snatchers

Across the landscape they silently creep, powerful forces that are almost impossible to overcome. They aggressively conquer ponds and streams, destroy pastoral meadows, invade neighborhood canals . . . and maybe your backyard. They are invasive species, aggressive predators that dine on native plants and feast on helpless fish and wildlife, creating a growing ecological nightmare.

The first nonnative plants and animals were brought over by colonists. Today exotic animals can be purchased from pet stores or through a growing Internet market. Invasive species can also arrive through the ballast ejected from oceangoing ships, or as an innocent seed wedged in the shoe of an international traveler. According to the US Fish and Wildlife Service, approximately 50,000 nonnative species have been documented.

One of the more popular nonnative species is the Burmese python. Often python owners discover their exotic pet has outgrown its enclosure—and sometimes the owner's interests. The imperfect solution? Release the python into the wild where it quickly hunts and devours native rabbits, raccoons, and rats—upsetting the ecosystem's balance.

Lionfish, native to the South Pacific, were first sighted along the southeastern U.S. coast in the 1980s. As nonnatives, they have few natural predators. One favorite meal of the lionfish is the native parrotfish, which thrives on algae. Without parrotfish, algae become a health hazard, particularly to fragile coral reefs.

In 1890 the American Acclimatization Society released European starlings into New York's Central Park in an effort to populate the landscape with birds referenced by Shakespeare (*Henry IV*, Part I). Today starlings cause more than $800 million per year in damage to agriculture and $6 million in damage to aircraft. The starlings move together in droves, taking over the nests of other birds, eating their eggs and any weaker wildlife that might get in their way.

1. Scan the passage to answer this question: In which area do Lionfish originate?

A. south Florida

B. western Europe

C. the North Atlantic

D. the South Pacific

2. Which detail BEST supports the author's message that invasive species are destructive?

A. Today exotic animals can be purchased on the Internet.

B. Invasive species can arrive in ballast ejected from oceangoing ships.

C. Released Burmese pythons eat native rabbits, upsetting the ecosystem's balance.

D. European starlings were introduced to New York's Central park in 1890.

Writing Practice

Directions: Write a short informational or literary passage about something you are interested in. Make your passage complex by including things such as technical terms, compound or complex sentences, abstract ideas, or an unusual text structure. Make your writing sophisticated, yet clear enough for active readers to comprehend its meaning.

Directions: Read the following passage. Then choose the best answer to questions 1 through 3.

"After a long talk with the harbor-master, Captain Leclere left Naples greatly disturbed in mind. In twenty-four hours he was attacked by a fever, and died three days afterwards. We performed the usual burial service, and he is at his rest, sewn up in his hammock with a thirty-six pound shot at his head and his heels, off El Giglio Island. We bring to his widow his sword and cross of honor. It was worth while, truly," added the young man with a melancholy smile, "to make war against the English for ten years, and to die in his bed at last, like everybody else."

"Why, you see, Edmond," replied the owner, who appeared more comforted at every moment, "we are all mortal, and the old must make way for the young."

—From *The Count of Monte Cristo* by Alexandre Dumas

1. How does the setting of the story contribute to the plot?

A. The setting is a harbor in Naples where Leclere delivers goods.

B. The setting is the sea off El Giglio Island, where Leclere is buried.

C. The setting is the Leclere's family home, where the narrator brings the captain's things.

D. The setting is a country home off the coast of England, where Leclere's crew is vacationing.

2. Which of the following is a valid inference readers could make about the young man in the story?

A. He is British.

B. He was born in Naples.

C. He is Captain Leclere's son.

D. He replaced Leclere as captain of the ship.

3. Which phrase best states the theme of the passage?

A. the circle of life

B. believe in yourself

C. the illusion of power

D. honesty is the best policy

Directions: Read the following passage. Then choose the best answer to questions 4 through 6.

The sun had not yet peeked over the crest of the mountain above Harjanti's small Indonesian village when she awoke with excitement. Today was the opportunity she had been waiting and working for—market day.

Three months prior, Harjanti had discovered exotic gray doves for sale at the market. She was determined to have one. But how would she procure the money?

Rice paddies, vegetable gardens, a goat, and a few chickens provided an ample living for Harjanti's family, but there was little expendable income. Harjanti then recalled a story that her husband had told her about how he gathered bark from wild cinnamon trees as a youth. He had sold the cinnamon in the marketplace and earned money to buy a sturdy young milking goat for his family.

Harjanti, with a gleam in her eye, went to her husband and asked him whether people still bought cinnamon in the marketplace. He responded affirmatively. Harjanti explained her idea—she could gather cinnamon bark and sell it at the market for enough money to buy a beautiful gray dove!

The next morning Harjanti and her husband traversed the narrow, winding road that led up the mountain to a cluster of cinnamon trees. He demonstrated how to gather the inner bark and explained that when the pieces dried, they would curl up tightly and turn brown, and then they would be ready to sell.

(Continued on page 83)

(Continued from page 82)

For the next few weeks Harjanti visited the cinnamon grove every day. At last she had gathered enough bark, dried it, and cut it into short sticks. Finally the day had come to sell her large bundle of cinnamon at the market and buy her precious bird.

As Harjanti waited impatiently that morning for the other women from the village to get ready for market, she heard her sister calling her. As it turned out, Harjanti's niece had a fever, and her sister had an important appointment in town. She asked Harjanti to stay at home with the sick girl. She told Harjanti she would just have to sell cinnamon at the market another day, but they both knew that the next market day would not come for a long time.

—from "Harjanti's Dilemma" by Ann Oliver

4. How does the author organize the story?

A. by comparing and contrasting events

B. by telling events in chronological order

C. by presenting problems and solutions

D. by ranking events in the order of their importance

5. Which event is NOT part of the story's plot?

A. Harjanti's niece becomes ill.

B. Harjanti sees doves for sale at the market.

C. Harjanti's husband shows her how to gather cinnamon bark.

D. Harjanti sells her cinnamon bark.

6. What is Harjanti's conflict at the end of the story?

A. an internal conflict with her belief about poverty

B. an external conflict with her husband about buying a dove

C. an internal conflict about whether to help her sister or go to the market

D. an external conflict with nature as she tries to strip the bark from cinnamon trees

Directions: Read the following passage. Then choose the best answer to questions 7 and 8.

MEMO

To: All Employees

From: Human Resources

Subject: Blossom Flower Company anti-harassment policy

Human Resources would like to remind all employees of company policy regarding harassment.

Harassment is defined as behavior considered offensive, hostile, or disruptive to an employee. Examples of harassment include

- threats
- physical assault
- derogatory jokes or slurs
- objectionable posted materials

An employee who believes he or she is the victim of harassment should report the incident immediately to a Human Resources (HR) contact. If harassment is confirmed, the accused is to be informed immediately of that decision. He or she will be subject to timely and appropriate disciplinary action.

7. Which text feature does the author use in the passage?
   A. italic type
   B. subheads
   C. bulleted list
   D. boldfaced words

8. What conclusion can you logically infer from reading this memo?
   A. Someone at the company has reported possible harassment.
   B. The company does not have good enough business standards.
   C. Someone at the company likes to tell jokes during lunch time.
   D. There are more female than male employees in the company.

Directions: Read the following passage. Then choose the best answer to questions 9 and 10.

I turned as noiselessly as possible, and becoming every now and then rigid with the fear of being discovered, as a branch cracked or a leaf rustled, I pushed back into the bushes. It was long before I grew bolder, and dared to move freely. My only idea for the moment was to get away from these foul beings. . . . Then suddenly . . . I saw with an unpleasant start two clumsy legs among the trees, walking with noiseless footsteps parallel with my course, and perhaps thirty yards away from me. The head and upper part of the body were hidden by a tangle of creeper. . . . Then looking hard, I distinguished . . . the head and body of the brute I had seen. . . . There was an emerald flash in his eyes as he glanced at me from the shadow of the trees, a half-luminous colour that vanished as he turned his head again. . . .

"Who are you?" said I.

He tried to meet my gaze. "No!" he said suddenly, and turning went bounding away from me through the undergrowth. . . .

The sun had set some minutes since, the swift dusk of the tropics was already fading out of the eastern sky. . . . Unless I would spend the night among the unknown dangers of the mysterious forest, I must hasten back to the enclosure. . . . I gave one more look into the blue shadows that had swallowed up this odd creature, and then retraced my way down the slope towards the stream, going as I judged in the direction from which I had come.

. . . The colourless clearness that comes after the sunset flush was darkling; the blue sky above grew momentarily deeper, and the little stars one by one pierced the attenuated light; the interspaces of the trees, the gaps in the further vegetation, that had been hazy blue in the daylight, grew black and mysterious. I pushed on. The colour vanished from the world. The tree-tops rose against the luminous blue sky in inky silhouette, and all below that outline melted into one formless blackness. . . . I began to be tormented by a faint rustling upon my right hand. I thought at first it was fancy, for whenever I stopped there was silence, save for the evening breeze in the tree-tops. Then when I turned to hurry on again there was an echo to my footsteps.

I turned away from the thickets, keeping to the more open ground, and endeavouring by sudden turns now and then to surprise something in the act of creeping upon me. I saw nothing, and nevertheless my sense of another presence grew steadily. . . . I felt assured now that my tawny-faced antagonist was stalking me once more; and coupled with that was another unpleasant realisation, that I had lost my way.

—From *The Island of Doctor Moreau* by H. G. Wells

9. Which event from the text is an example of foreshadowing?

A. "I turned as noiselessly as possible"

B. "I gave one more look into the blue shadows"

C. "the blue sky above grew momentarily deeper"

D. "going as I judged in the direction from which I had come"

10. Which could you logically predict after reading this passage?

A. The creature will get lost, too.

B. The creature will climb a tree.

C. The creature is human.

D. The creature cannot see the narrator.

Check Your Understanding

On the following chart, circle the number of any item you answered incorrectly. In the third column, you will see the pages that you can review to study the content covered in the question. Pay particular attention to reviewing those lessons in which you missed half or more of the questions.

Lesson	Core Skill	Item Number(s)	Review Page(s)
Lesson 2.1: Sequence Events	Sequence Information	4	52–53
	Use Text Features	7	54–55
Lesson 2.2: Infer Relationships between Events, People, and Ideas	Make Inferences	2, 8	58–59
	Cite Evidence	10	60–61
Lesson 2.3: Analyze Relationships between Ideas	Identify Literary Elements	3, 5, 6, 9	64–65
	Analyze the Relationship between Plot and Setting	1	66–67
Lesson 2.4: Determine Implicit Relationships between Ideas	Determine Implied Relationships between Ideas	2, 8	70–71
	Predict Outcomes	10	72–73
Lesson 2.5: Analyze the Role of Details in Complex Texts	Comprehend Complex Texts	2, 8	76–77
	Use Details to Analyze Complex Texts	1, 10	78–79

WRITE ABOUT A Company Policy

Read the passage on page 309 about falls in the workplace. Then think about a workplace environment or other public place that you know well. Write a memo to employees that

1. outlines the potential for falls in the place you chose
2. identifies two or three ways that employees can make the place safer
3. describes the company's policy, or plan of action, for preventing and responding to injuries from falls.

BEFORE YOU WRITE Create a Flow Chart

First, research general information about falls in the workplace. You may want to research the following:

- Injuries that can be sustained in falls
- How falls can be prevented
- What to do in case of a fall

Search the Internet to locate information about falls. Use search terms such as *falls in the workplace* or *preventing falls* for more ideas.

Then select a specific company or workplace and find its safety policy that includes information about falls. Create a flow chart to record the steps in the safety policy on how to respond to falls. You can find an example of a flow chart in the Graphic Organizer section at the back of the book.

When you have finished, review your flow chart. Ask yourself: *Are these steps in the correct order? Did I include all the main steps in the policy?* Use your flow chart to help you draft your memo.

TIP Use Present and Future Tense Accurately in Writing

The simple present tense is used to show action or a state of being that is happening now or happens regularly. The simple present tense is also used when a statement is always true.

- Maria loves reading.
- I need to go to work.

The future tense is used to discuss events or actions that will happen in the future. The underlined verbs in these sentences indicate the future tense:

- The company will implement the policy next month.
- Employees will have three weeks of vacation time.

As you write your company memo, use the present tense to describe actions that are currently happening. Use the future tense to discuss actions or events that will happen in the future.

WHILE YOU WRITE Indicate Sequence of Events

You have researched and identified the main steps in preventing and responding to falls in the workplace. Start by writing a sentence or two introducing the policy about falls in your memo and explaining why the company is implementing it. Be sure to include a statement that explains the potential for falls in the place you chose.

Now you need to expand on the steps of the safety policy that you will describe in your memo. First, explain the preventive measure to be taken. Next, describe the steps to be taken in case of a fall. To do this, revisit your flow chart. Write two or three sentences elaborating on each step in the plan. *Which step happens first? What happens next?* Use the sentences you have written to create the body of your memo. Be sure to use sequence words such as *first, next, then, last, finally,* and *after* to show the relationship among the ideas in your memo. For example, *First, call an ambulance if needed.*

Finally, write a few sentences restating the company's reason for the policy and the safety benefits the company hopes to achieve.

TIP **Remember to . . . Use Commas after Introductory Words, Phrases, and Clauses**

Use commas after introductory words, phrases, and dependent clauses to separate the introductory element from the main part of the sentence. A dependent clause is a group of words that has a subject and a predicate but does not express a complete idea.

Here are some examples of introductory words, phrases, and clauses:

- <u>Carefully,</u> the driver backed the truck into the entrance. (introductory adverb)
- <u>Unfortunately for Liz,</u> she slipped and hurt herself. (introductory adverbial phrase)
- <u>When the batteries are in position,</u> slide the rear panel back into place. (dependent clause)

AFTER YOU WRITE Check Your Work

Reread the writing assignment. Then read your memo carefully three times.

The first time you read, ask yourself if you have completed the writing assignment correctly. Have you (1) outlined the potential for falls in the place you chose, (2) identified two or three ways that employees can make the workplace safer, and (3) described the company's policy on preventing and responding to injuries from falls?

Then read your memo again. Did you use sequence words to indicate the relationship among ideas? Did you use the present tense to describe actions or events that are happening now and future tense to describe those that will happen in the future?

Reread the memo one last time. Did you use correct grammar, spelling, and punctuation? Did you remember to use a comma after introductory words, phrases, and dependent clauses? Do you see any errors? Did you type the words you meant to use?

Before submitting your memo, have another student read it and provide you with feedback.

Chapter 3

©Fancy Photography/Veer

Interpret Words in Context

When writing, authors decide not only what to say, but also how to say it. The words they choose are important because even the simplest word choice can have a big impact on the meaning of the text and the reader's response. An author may use words and phrases that express precise, literal meanings; connotative meanings that are suggested; or figurative language that means more than the literal meaning of the words. Recognizing how an author's words convey his or her message can help you better understand and enjoy what you read.

In this chapter you will study these topics:

Lesson 3.1

Determine Connotative and Figurative Meanings

When reading, can you always understand exactly what an author means? An author may use creative language that goes beyond the literal meaning of particular words. Learn to recognize how authors use connotative meaning and figurative language to help you understand what you read.

Lesson 3.2

Analyze Tone

How does an author feel about the subject that he or she is writing about? The tone of the text expresses the writer's attitude. Learn how to analyze tone by looking closely at authors' word choices, sentence structure, and language style.

Lesson 3.3

Analyze Word Choice

Have you ever read something that made you feel sad, amused, or frightened? If you have, the author's choice of words helped make you feel this way. Certain words can have a particular effect on the reader. Learn how an author's word choices help make readers remember the text and feel and think a certain way.

Goal Setting

Think back to a time when an author's choice of words confused you. How did you figure out what the author was trying to communicate? How might these lessons help you understand an author's use of language?

Why do you think it is important to understand how specific words, phrases, and language impact a text? How can this help you when reading texts in everyday life? How can this help improve your writing?

LESSON 3.1 Determine Connotative and Figurative Meanings

LESSON OBJECTIVES

- Identify connotative and figurative meanings in various texts
- Understand connotative and figurative language through context

CORE SKILLS

- Analyze and Evaluate Word Choice
- Interpret Words and Phrases

Key Terms

connotative
suggested by a word or phrase

figurative
meaning more than its literal sense

Vocabulary

context
the words, phrases, and sentences that surround a word

homophones
words that sound the same but are spelled differently and have different meanings

mood
the emotions that a reader feels when reading a text

tone
the expression of a writer's attitude through stylistic choices

Key Concept

The connotative meaning of a word or phrase is the meaning suggested by the word. Figurative language includes words or phrases that imply more than their literal meaning.

Have you ever read a book and wondered how an author chooses the words he or she uses? For example, why would an author choose gleeful instead of happy. Careful word choice helps authors communicate meaning and mood more effectively. To recognize how an author is using creative language in a text, ask yourself: How do these words make me think or feel?

Identifying Connotative and Figurative Meaning

Authors choose their words carefully. The **connotative**, or suggested, meaning of a word or phrase affects the meaning of a text. **Figurative** language, which suggests more than the literal meaning of a word or phrase, goes even further to enrich text meaning. Thoughtful word choices allow writers to communicate ideas precisely in various types of texts.

Connotative Meaning and Word Choice

Knowing the literal meaning of a word or phrase is important for understanding a text, but words can have different levels of meaning. Connotative meaning is the feeling or image a word brings to mind. For example, *stink* and *scent* refer to an odor, but each word makes a reader think or visualize something different. *Scent* may bring to mind a beautiful flower, while *stink* may evoke garbage. As you read, think about the different levels of meaning of words and phrases in the text.

Tone, or the expression of a writer's attitude, is communicated through word choices and other stylistic choices. A writer may make different choices when arguing a political issue, discussing company policies, or describing an adventure.

Carefully chosen words set the **mood**, or the atmosphere of the text, which makes the reader feel certain emotions when reading. It can make the reader feel sad, angry, scared, or amused. A change in word choice can convey a different mood and change the meaning of a text.

As you read, notice how the writer's word choices connote, or suggest, a meaning that contributes to the tone and mood of a passage.

Directions: Read this passage. As you read, list specific words the writer uses to connote, or suggest, a meaning that sets the tone and mood of the passage.

A Little Repair

After Anjel screwed the last panel back in place, she held her breath and waited, but nothing happened. She stared, clutching her screwdriver, but the lights were distinctly dim and the speakers were deafeningly silent. Blinking back tears from her eyes, Anjel considered each of the steps she had just completed. She'd connected every wire and rebooted each system exactly as the schematic indicated. Just as she was coming to the conclusion that her original design was fundamentally flawed, she heard a small whirring sound. The check lights on the android's fingertips began lighting from yellow to green, and the eyes opened suddenly. Anjel dropped her screwdriver, ignoring the clatter of metal on tile, and waited for her android to speak.

Did you note that at first the mood is one of anxiousness and then it changes to surprise? The author states that Anjel is "clutching her screwdriver." The word *clutching* describes a strong grip. It suggests that Anjel feels anxious or nervous. A word such as *holding* would not convey these feelings, so it would not be a good choice. Then Anjel "dropped her screwdriver" and ignored "the clatter of metal on tile." The word *clatter* connotes an unpleasant noise. By stating that Anjel was "blinking back tears," the author also helps readers picture how frustrated she feels.

Figurative Language

Figurative language implies more than just the words' literal meaning and the words do not always mean what they say. Examples of figurative language, often called "figures of speech," include similes, metaphors, and personification.

- A **simile** is a comparison using the word *like* or *as*: The new sports car was like a spaceship.
- A **metaphor** is a direct comparison: The new sports car was a sleek spaceship.
- **Personification** likens an animal or object to a human being. It may be stated directly, as in *The building was a friendly soldier, guarding the neighborhood* (the sentence states that the building was a soldier), or implied, as in *We moored under towering smokestacks whose breath blackened the city* (the word breath implies that the smokestacks are alive).

Understanding Connotative and Figurative Meanings in Various Texts

How can you interpret what the author intends to suggest by his or her choice of particular words? How can you interpret the meaning of an unfamiliar figure of speech in a text? Search for **context** clues in surrounding words, phrases, and sentences. The context in which the writer uses particular words will help you determine what he or she means.

CORE SKILL

Analyze and Evaluate Word Choice

To analyze and evaluate word choices, follow this procedure:

1. Read the entire passage.
2. Ask yourself: *What is the author's tone? What mood do you, the reader, feel?*
3. List action and descriptive words the author uses.
4. Ask yourself: *Which words help create the mood in the passage? Would other words work in their place?*
5. *Determine whether the word choices were effective and conveyed the tone the author intended.*

Find a story in print or online that interests you. With a partner, follow the procedure above. Discuss the mood of the passage and suggest words the author might have used that would create a different mood.

WRITE TO LEARN

Write a one-paragraph description of your favorite place to visit. For example, it could be a city, a park, or a friend's home. Choose your words carefully to set a mood for the reader. To add interest, include connotative words or figurative language, such as similes, metaphors, or personification.

CORE SKILL

Interpret Words and Phrases

How can you interpret the meaning of language used to create a mood if some words or phrases are unfamiliar? Read the entire text. Ask yourself how you feel when you read it. Look for context clues to help you figure out any unknown words. Remember, *context* is the other words and sentences that surround a word.

Read this short passage, and then answer the questions below.

> Senator Feldman marched onto the stage, his body stiff with outrage. In a loud voice that was almost a shout, he claimed to be incensed at allegations that his campaign staff had mishandled funds. The senator declared angrily, "This is a plot by my opponent to discredit me because I am ahead in the polls."

1. What mood does the word *marched* suggest?
2. What meaning does the word *incensed* connote?

When you first read a text, try to get a sense of the author's intention. Ask yourself: How does the author want me to feel? What is the author's tone?

Then look for words that fit the author's intention. Verb selection is an important element of connotative language. The right action word can make the difference between a dull text and a compelling text that engages the reader and communicates exactly what the author wants to express.

Directions: Read the passage, and then underline the phrases that show personification.

Mount Washington

The day started out like a hiker's dream: a cool late autumn breeze and a cloudless sky ensured that the trek would be a pleasant one despite the rugged terrain. This was the type of day you experience on Mount Washington only once or twice during this season. The sun was already beginning its descent, but the summit was only a quarter mile away. It would be worth the race against time to finally reach the top. To reach the summit of Mount Washington, the highest peak in New Hampshire, had always been a dream of mine. At this point, to turn around before reaching the summit post would be a severe disappointment. As I started along the trail again, a furious cluster of black clouds suddenly appeared, swallowing the peak of the next mountain and shutting out what remained of the sunlight. The rapidly advancing shadows of the clouds darkened the tree line below me. I knew what this meant: I needed to find shelter immediately. A sense of dread made me realize that I wasn't fully prepared to spend the night on the mountain. I hoped my gear and my willpower would hold out, and I steeled myself for the long, cold night ahead.

If you underlined "race against time" or "a furious cluster of black clouds suddenly appeared, swallowing the peak of the next mountain," you understood that the author gave time the human ability to race and gave the clouds the human ability to feel fury and swallow.

Think about Reading

Directions: Complete the activities below.

1. What other words might the author have chosen? Match each word from the passage with a word or phrase that connotes the same meaning.

From the Text	Alternatives
"dread"	in haste
"cloudless"	dismay
"rapidly"	clear blue

2. What is the mood of the passage?

A good writer selects language that connects with the reader. For example, a writer may use figures of speech to compare something to objects or situations that are familiar to most readers. In this way, the author collaborates with the reader and the message of the text is understood.

Directions: Read the following passage. Underline examples of figurative language, and identify what type of figurative language they are.

When the first light went out at 6:45, the Texas sun had just poked its nose over the horizon and the hundreds of Navy training planes nestling on the ramp looked like gray ghosts in the dim morning light. Mounting the steps to the squadron control tower a few minutes earlier, I had noticed, far off to the north in the dew-infested haze, a scowling bank of black clouds. I remember feeling relieved that I wasn't flying that day. I had, instead, drawn the assignment as tower duty officer. Later I would have been happy to trade places with almost anyone in the squadron.

In the glass-encased tower atop the hanger, all the disconnected threads of the complex operations of a warm naval-air-training squadron were gathered and loosely held. Here, we were in direct radio contact with hundreds of practicing pilots. This day one would survive an experience that dozens of others would never forget.

Think about Reading

Directions: Answer each question about the author's word choices.

1. The phrase "a scowling bank of black clouds" is an example of which type of figure of speech?
2. How does this figure of speech help readers understand the passage?
   A. It helps readers visualize the setting.
   B. It describes what old Navy planes look like.
   C. It helps readers understand the phrase *dew-infested.*
3. What kind of figurative language does the author use to describe the Navy training planes on the ramp? Explain your answer.

Summary

Authors choose words carefully to express their attitude about a subject and connect with the reader. Writers often use connotative meaning to suggest the meaning of a word or phrase. They also use figurative language to imply more than a literal meaning. Pay attention to the words and phrases an author chooses to use. Consider how the passage would be different if the author had chosen different words.

LANGUAGE SKILL

Spelling Homophones

Homophones are words that sound the same but are spelled differently and have different meanings. When you read, it is fairly easy to recognize the difference. However, when you write, it can be difficult to decide which word to use. For example, the words *there, their,* and *they're* are commonly confused. *There* refers to a place or is used to point out an idea. *Their* is the possessive pronoun of them. *They're* is a contraction of they are.

- *There* are two ways to get *there.*
- *Their* mother has to drive them.
- *They're* not happy about it.

Its and *it's* also commonly cause confusion. *It's* is the contraction of *it is*. *Its* is the possessive form of *it*. When choosing one of these words while writing, check whether the sentence makes sense with *it is*. If it does not, use *its*.

- The dog lost *its* collar. (*It is* does not make sense.)
- I like that car, but *it's* too expensive. (*It is* makes sense.)

Select the correct homophone to complete each sentence.

1. Bill and Sam are working on (*there, they're, their*) report.
2. I hope the (*whether, weather*) is good for Friday's game.
3. The (*brakes, breaks*) failed on my car, so I took it (*two, too, to*) the mechanic.

As you read, notice any word that has a homophone.

Vocabulary Review

Directions: Complete the sentences using the following key terms and vocabulary words.

connotative	**context**	**figurative**
homophones	**mood**	**tone**

1. The word *stinky* has a ________________ meaning of something very nasty and unpleasant smelling.
2. The other words and sentences around a word create a frame, or ________________, for it.
3. The author's ________________ in the story was serious and helped create a very frightening ________________.
4. The words *sail* and *sale* are ________________.
5. If I say you are as quiet as a mouse, I am using ________________ language known as a simile.

Skill Review

Directions: Read the passage below. Then choose the best answer to each question.

(1) For years, our Glenbrook Gladiators had the best football team in the state. (2) This year was no exception, thanks to Coach Mantini. (3) We won the first three games of the season, and if we sustained the momentum, we would be state champs again. (4) Then Coach got really sick, and soon he was as thin as a rail. (5) Doctors insisted he stay home and rest for the rest of the season.

(6) The school hired a new coach. (7) We liked Coach Cruz, but our team spirit was low and it showed; we lost the next three games! (8) Then one day Coach Cruz said, "I know Coach Mantini believed in you guys, and I do too. (9) If we win, you will make him proud and let him know he's done a great job with you." (10) Coach Cruz was a beacon of light, helping us see that by winning we would confirm that Coach Mantini was a great coach. (11) Well, the pep talk worked. (12) Last night we won!

1. What is the attitude expressed in the tone of the passage?
   A. amused
   B. hopeful
   C. irritated
   D. carefree

2. Which sentence in the passage contains a simile?
   A. Sentence 2
   B. Sentence 4
   C. Sentence 7
   D. Sentence 9

3. Which word could the author have used in sentence 5 instead of *insisted*?
   A. thought
   B. disagreed
   C. demanded
   D. recognized

4. Which of these phrases from the passage contains a metaphor?
   A. "but our team spirit was low"
   B. "soon he was as thin as a rail"
   C. "Coach Cruz was a beacon of light"
   D. "And if we sustained the momentum"

Skill Practice

Directions: Read the passage below. Then choose the best answer to each question.

The Shore

Jana parked her jalopy in the already-crowded lot and eagerly jumped out. She tugged her chair, umbrella, and beach bag from the trunk, distributed them about her person, and took off like Marco Polo on his first expedition to China. But, unlike Marco Polo, Jana wasn't going from Italy to China. She was going from Philadelphia to Wildwood, New Jersey, for the first time. At long last, she was going to The Shore, the wondrous, almost mythical, larger-than-life Shore. Jana had been waiting an eternity for this indulgence and was so excited that her stomach felt like a swarm of butterflies. Even so, with the chair wedged under her right arm, the umbrella clutched in her left hand, and the bulky beach bag bouncing against her hip in time with her steps, the four-block slog felt like a journey to the farthest reaches of Earth.

Jana didn't hit her stride until the second corner, when she first smelled the water. Her body became a huge sponge, greedily soaking in the salty, humid air. She crested a rise and could see the beach in front of her, studded with sunbathers. The breeze greeted her skin with its tiny granules of salt and sand. She became aware of a growing symphony—the wondrous crashing of the waves mixed with the cacophony of sound from sunbathers' voices, transistor radios, and vendors hawking their wares. Hurriedly, she removed her sandals and plunged up to her ankles into the warm, pillow-soft sand. For a moment, Jana just stood there, reveling in her first impressions of The Shore. Then, suddenly, she let her gear fall to the sand and bounded like an excited puppy toward the sea.

1. What is the connotative meaning of *jalopy*?

A. van

B. old wreck

C. sports car

D. limousine

2. What metaphor did the author use about Jana's body?

A. She hit her stride.

B. She removed her sandals.

C. She became a huge sponge.

D. She became aware of a growing symphony.

3. What is the attitude expressed in the tone of the passage?

A. fearful

B. sarcastic

C. indifferent

D. exhilarated

Writing Practice

Directions: Find a short newspaper report on a topic of local interest. Rewrite it using connotative and figurative language to evoke a positive or a negative response in the reader.

LESSON 3.2 Analyze Tone

LESSON OBJECTIVES

- Identify the tone of a text
- Explain how authors of various genres establish tone

CORE SKILLS

- Analyze Word Choice
- Interpret Words and Phrases to Draw Conclusions

Key Terms

purpose
an author's reason for writing a text

Vocabulary

interpret
explain the meaning of something, or understand something

persuade
convince someone to agree

transmit
pass on

Key Concept

Tone is the expression of a writer's attitude through stylistic choices.

When you speak, your tone of voice helps convey your message. Think about the tone you use when speaking in different circumstances. To make someone laugh, you may use a playful tone. To ask a friend for an important favor, your tone may be urgent. Authors also use tone in their writing. The tone an author conveys in a text is much like the tone of voice that a speaker conveys. A poet may convey a reflective tone. The author of a mystery story may use a serious or threatening tone.

Identifying Author's Tone

Three important factors have a major influence on an author's tone—topic, purpose, and genre.

Topic When an author chooses a topic, he or she has an attitude about that topic. That attitude is the author's feeling or emotion about the topic. It may be positive, negative, or neutral. The author may find the topic to be ridiculous, tragic, amusing, or gravely serious. Part of good writing is conveying this attitude in the text with tone. The author's style choices when writing about a topic express how he or she feels about the topic.

Purpose An author's purpose helps determine the tone in a text. The author must decide how to approach the subject to achieve his or her goal. For example, the goal of a workplace e-mail may be to explain a new office policy, so the tone is serious and directive. The goal of a short essay may be to amuse the reader, so the tone is light and humorous. In either case, the tone communicates the author's intention.

Genre Almost all text fits into recognized genres, or categories, of writing. Recognizing the genre of a passage gives you an immediate clue to its tone. For example, readers know that the tone of an office memo is usually neutral and businesslike, while the tone of a thriller is often anxious and urgent.

Style techniques such as sentence structure and word choice help **transmit**, or pass on, an author's tone. When the writer of an e-mail chooses short, directive sentences and harsh words, the tone may be angry. However, when the writer uses longer sentences and descriptive words, the tone of the e-mail may be instructive. For example, "See me in my office now" has an angry tone. In contrast, "It's a good idea to communicate regularly with your supervisor" seeks to teach office workers how to interact effectively, and its tone is neutral and instructive.

A writer's word choice depends on the purpose of the text. Some words are used to **persuade**, or convince, readers to agree with the writer's ideas; other words simply provide information in an unbiased way.

Recognizing the writer's tone helps the reader understand the text and the writer's purpose.

Directions: Read the passage below, paying attention to the author's tone. Underline words that help convey tone.

> The wind howled past the window, setting the torn screen in the bedroom window flapping. The window frame shook, and Camilla thought it was likely to come off before the storm was over. Outside in the wilderness that surrounded the cabin, some creature cried out a primitive wail, protesting the storm. With shaking hands, Camilla tightened the lock on the window and hoped that whatever foul beast was out there wouldn't come any closer.

The passage begins with the phrase "The wind howled." Note that the window screen is not just broken, it's "torn." The words *howled* and *torn* transmit a threatening tone. These words and others in the paragraph may make the reader feel nervous or frightened.

Directions: Read the passage. As you read, underline words and phrases that indicate the author's attitude toward Emmett.

> Emmett handed in his paper and exited the classroom, making no effort to be quiet or to keep from disturbing the other students still taking the test.
>
> "Don't feel like you have to work as fast as Emmett," the teacher said after Emmett was outside. "Quicker doesn't always mean better."
>
> The other students looked relieved and bent their heads back down over their essays. Some students looked confused about how anyone could finish an essay test as swiftly as Emmett always seemed to.
>
> Emmett strolled around campus, enjoying the crisp autumn air and smiling to himself contentedly. He was certain he would get an A on his essay, even though he had finished it in less than half the time allotted. No one else he knew wrote as quickly as he did, and Emmett thought it was good to show the teacher that he could think faster than the other students. Emmett felt that quicker meant better almost all the time.

CORE SKILL

Analyze Word Choice

Word choice helps create the tone of a text. Carefully chosen words communicate the attitude of the author.

To analyze word choices in a passage, follow this procedure:

1. Read the entire passage.
2. List the action and descriptive words used in the passage.
3. Ask yourself what particular tone these words suggest.

Find a passage in print or online in which the author's purpose is to entertain readers. With a partner, follow the procedure above. Discuss how the genre, purpose, word choice, and text structure help the author set the tone of the passage.

WRITE TO LEARN

Write a one-paragraph description of an incident involving an unnamed real person or a fictional character. Do not state your attitude explicitly. Choose your words and sentence structures carefully to help readers identify your attitude toward the incident and the person.

After writing, exchange papers with a partner. Identify the tone used in each other's paragraph.

CORE SKILL

Interpret Words and Phrases to Draw Conclusions

Authors use tone to convey an attitude and persuade readers to draw a particular conclusion. To draw an accurate conclusion, the reader needs to be able to interpret the authors' words and phrases.

To interpret words and phrases in a passage, first read the entire text. Think about how the author wants you to feel. Look for particular words and phrases that help convey the tone of the passage.

Reread the passage about Chez Robert and the person who answered the phone. What tone does the author convey toward that person and toward the restaurant in general?

If you said indignant, angry, bitter, disappointed, or mocking, you understood that the author was not happy with the restaurant's service, beginning with that phone call.

Find a restaurant or movie review in print or online. As you read it, note the author's tone. What conclusion does the author want you to draw? Did you? Which words helped you draw that conclusion?

Think about Reading

What is the author's tone in the passage about Emmett? What does the tone convey about his or her attitude toward Emmett? Explain how you know. Write your answer in a notebook.

Analyzing Tone in Various Texts

When you first read a text, identify the genre and try to get a general sense of the author's purpose. Ask yourself: *What is the genre of this text? What tone might I expect in this genre? How does the author feel about this topic?*

Then look for language that suggests the tone the author is trying to convey. Note words and phrases that convey how the author feels. Taking notice of the author's style choices will give you a clue as to what the author's purpose may be. To **interpret**, or understand, the tone, look for the following features:

- Sentence structure: Are the sentences short or long?
- Formal vs. informal language: Is the language professional or casual?
- Imagery: What descriptions provide mental pictures for a reader?
- Figurative language: What comparisons are being made?

Finally, consider how the words and language support the author's purpose. For example, does the simple sentence structure of a repair manual make the text easy to understand? Does the imagery in a short story contribute to the scary tone the author wants to project? Does the formality of a workplace document communicate the writer's seriousness? Interpreting tone helps you understand the author's reason for writing the text.

Directions: Read the following passage. Identify the genre of the text and the author's purpose for writing the text. As you read, note how the author's choice of words transmits a clear tone to the reader.

When we made our call for dinner reservations at Chez Robert, we probably should have known from the cold, snippy attitude of the person answering the phone that this dining experience would be terrible. Still, we're always willing to give a new restaurant a try.

Well, make no mistake about it: going to Chez Robert will be a waste of your hard-earned money. Unless you're happy to be berated for the way you like your steak and are willing to wait an hour and a half for the privilege of being served three peas on a lettuce leaf to tide you over, you're better off going to the local burger joint. The hunk of gray leather that finally arrived a half-hour later, drowned in raspberry-colored glue masquerading as a sauce, we can honestly say, was not worth the wait.

We've never been treated so badly at a restaurant in our entire reviewing career. Please, do us the favor of avoiding the loss of two precious hours of your life while staring at the fake-marble paneling at Chez Robert and wondering whether the chef traveled to Paris to kill a cow. We'll never get those hours back, but we'd like to think we did it for you.

Directions: Read the two short passages below. Notice the individual words and phrases used in each passage. Use the author's stylistic choices to identify the tone of each passage. Then compare your answers with those of a partner.

1. As I walked down the street, I could hear footsteps approaching from behind me. They drew closer and closer. I looked around, but no one was there. Then I saw the shadow.
2. Last week's fire left several families homeless. Friends and neighbors kindly took them in, and many concerned citizens generously donated food, clothing, and furniture to replace what was lost. Today an amazing number of people showed up to help rebuild the homes with supplies donated by local businesses. See the whole story tonight at 11 on Channel 88 News.

Think about Reading

Directions: Reread the two passages above, and then complete the following activities.

1. Look at the first passage. Order these words from the most accurate description of the tone in the passage to the least accurate.

   ________ relaxed ________ interested

   ________ scared ________ indifferent
2. What was the author's purpose for writing the first passage?
3. How do the word choices and sentence structure in the first passage convey the author's purpose for writing the text?
4. Which word best describes the author's tone in the second passage?

   A. angry **C.** admiring

   B. embarrassed **D.** worried
5. What is the author's purpose for writing the second passage?
6. How do the author's word choices in the second passage convey the author's purpose?

Summary

Tone is the expression of the attitude a writer has toward a topic using stylistic choices. Different genres typically have different tones. To analyze tone in a text, identify the genre of the text. Also think about how the author conveys his or her emotions about the topic. Examine the author's word choices, sentence structure, and language style. The author's purpose for writing the text is more easily understood when readers identify the tone.

21st CENTURY SKILL

Interact Effectively with Others

While searching for a job, it is necessary to interact appropriately with business contacts and potential employers. Basic social skills should be expressed in business correspondences like the cover letter on page 100.

Using the appropriate tone in a business letter is a necessary social skill that will serve you well even after you get the job. It helps establish good working relationships with supervisors and coworkers.

At work, you may also need to determine a supervisor's purpose for writing a memo, letter, or assessment of your work. To understand the author's intention, ask yourself: *What does he or she want to accomplish with this document? How does it affect me? Am I supposed to do something in response?* The author's word choices and language are important clues to the effect he or she wants to achieve.

Find an online sample of a letter of recommendation or cover letter. Read the document with a partner. Discuss the tone of the document and important words and phrases that help the author set the tone. Then share your document and your findings with the class.

Vocabulary Review

Directions: Draw a line from each word to its definition.

1. **persuade**	**a.** explain the meaning of something
2. **purpose**	**b.** pass on
3. **transmit**	**c.** convince someone to agree
4. **interpret**	**d.** reason

Skill Review

Directions: Read the passage below. Then choose the best answer to each question.

Dear Ms. Moreno:

(1) In response to your recent advertisement in the *Chicago Sun-Times*, I am writing to express my interest in the nurse assistant position currently available at Sunny Days Senior Home.

(2) I have extensive experience in the health care field. (3) I have held positions as a nurse assistant at hospitals, outpatient centers, and doctors' offices. (4) I believe this field experience, as well as my Nurse Assistant Certification, would make me a valuable candidate for the position at Sunny Days Senior Home. (5) In addition to practical experience and education, I have a strong work ethic, a cooperative attitude, team spirit, and a desire to help others, which I believe would make me an exemplary staff member.

(6) I would appreciate the opportunity to discuss my qualifications with you at a mutually convenient time. (7) Thank you in advance for your time and consideration, and I look forward to speaking with you.

Respectfully yours,

Rima Freeman

Encl: résumé

1. What is the tone of the passage?

A. casual

B. amused

C. pessimistic

D. professional

2. Which sentence states the author's main purpose for writing the letter?

A. sentence 1

B. sentence 2

C. sentence 4

D. sentence 7

3. How does sentence 6 help convey the author's tone?

A. It adds to the angry tone of the letter.

B. It adds to the casual tone of the letter.

C. It adds to the professional tone of the letter.

D. It adds a friendly note to the tone of the letter.

Skill Practice

Directions: Read the passage below. Then choose the best answer to each question.

E-mail Message

From: Lily Chin
Sent: 11/22/2014
To: All Employees
Subject: Mandatory Intranet Password Change

The following message is sent on behalf of our information technology group.

Between January 1 and February 1 of next year, you will be prompted via e-mail to change your password. When you receive this prompt, you must log on to our intranet password reset system. Use your current user ID and password, and follow the instructions to change your password. You will not be able to access the system until you change your password.

Your security questions and answers as well as your Personal Identification Number (PIN) will be in the IT security system. If you forget your password or are locked out, you may reset it by using your security questions and PIN. If you call the Help Desk to have your password reset, please identify yourself as an employee and inform them that you will need your password reset. The Help Desk will reset your password and give you a temporary password, which you can then use to access the system and create your new password.

Thank you for your attention to this matter.

Lily Chin

Information Technology Coordinator

1. What is the tone of the passage?
   A. hostile
   B. serious
   C. flippant
   D. desperate

2. Which of the following words or phrases in the e-mail best helps the author achieve her purpose?
   A. via e-mail
   B. prompted
   C. may reset
   D. you must log on

Writing Practice

Directions: Think about a place, a book, or a movie that you are familiar with. Summarize it in a short paragraph. Choose your purpose for writing and use careful word choices to convey that purpose in your tone. Exchange paragraphs with a partner. Can you identify each other's purpose and tone?

LESSON 3.3 Analyze Word Choice

LESSON OBJECTIVES

- Explain how word choice affects the understanding of a text
- Give examples of the impact that an author's word choice has on a text

CORE SKILLS

- Analyze Word Choice
- Evaluate Word Choice

Key Terms

impact
have an effect on

style
a writer's use of language

Vocabulary

affects
influences

depicts
describes in words

emotions
feelings

similes
comparisons that use *like* or *as*

Key Concept

To communicate accurately, authors make careful decisions about the words they use.

Have you ever read a book that made you laugh or feel sad? The author carefully chose words to keep you interested and curious about what would happen next. Whether they make up a play, a poem, or even an e-mail, the words and phrases that an author chooses are designed to set a mood and to get a particular reaction from the reader.

Choosing the Right Word

An author's word choice has an effect on you as a reader. When you explore and analyze a writer's choice of words, you gain a better understanding of what the writer wants you to understand, think, or feel. You also gain a better understanding of the meaning of the text.

Word choice is an element of **style**, the writer's use of language. Good writers select words that create a mood to make readers feel a certain way such as sad, angry, frightened, or amused. Writers also choose words to persuade readers to agree with their point of view or to keep their text unbiased.

Words that describe a fictional character or a real person can reflect a story's mood and have an effect on the reader. For example: "The boy's black eyes were like a snake's, and they burned like cold fire." To describe the boy's eyes, the writer uses **similes**, comparisons that use the word *like* or *as*: "like a snake's (eyes)" and "like cold fire." They describe, or **depict**, the boy as a scary person and create a feeling of fear. If the description had been "The boy had dark eyes," the reader would have had little or no emotional response. Using descriptive words is part of many writers' styles.

In workplace documents, word choice can mean the difference between employees accomplishing a task correctly and incorrectly. For example: During the fire drill, it is mandatory that employees use only Exits 12-14.

The author's word choice expresses a tone that reinforces the seriousness of the message. The writer uses the word *mandatory* to inform readers that using the proper exits during the fire drill is required of everyone. The formal tone of the sentence is conveyed in that word choice.

How Word Choice Affects Understanding

Word choices **impact**, or have an effect on, the meaning of a text. As a result they also impact the reader's understanding and interpretation of the text.

People who write business e-mails must choose their words carefully to make sure their meaning is clear. One change in word choice can cause readers to misunderstand what is expected of them.

Read the e-mail below by a writer who is concerned that employees are not sending all the information they intend to send in their e-mails. The writer chooses clear words and direct language to ensure that the reader understands the problem and can accurately follow the instructions at the end of the e-mail.

First, the writer addresses "all network users." Then the writer states the problem, describing what happens if an attachment is inserted incorrectly.

Next, the writer restates the problem in simpler language. The phrase "What this means" signals an explanation, and the writer provides the reader with information about how to avoid the problem.

E-mail Message

From: Cathy Palmer
Sent: 2/15/2014
To: All Network Users
Subject: Formatting errors with e-mail

To all network users:

It has been brought to our attention that a formatting error occurs when sending e-mails from your machines. This error could impact what portions of your e-mail actually get sent.

If you insert an attachment by dragging the file into the body of the e-mail, any text below the attachment gets truncated out of the message and attached as a separate text file or HTML file. What this means is that, when sending attachments, any text that comes *after* the inserted file does not show up when you open it.

To prevent this problem from occurring, always use the Attach File button on your e-mail window, rather than dragging the file into the body of the text.

Thank you,

Network Services

Think about Reading

Directions: In a notebook, answer the following question about the passage.

What tone does the choice of a word like *truncated* transmit in this e-mail message?

CORE SKILL

Analyze Word Choice

Word choice can determine whether or not a text captures the reader's attention. Word choice also **affects**, or influences, how readers understand and interpret the author's purpose.

To analyze an author's word choice, follow this procedure:

1. Read the entire text.
2. Ask yourself: *What is the author's intention? What mood does the author set?*
3. Scan the text for words that express the author's purpose (i.e.: prevent, benefit, warn, congratulate,) or signal the mood of the text (i.e.; gloomy, mysterious, thrilling, romantic).
4. Think about how the text would differ if the author had made other word choices.

Find a short informational passage in print or online. Discuss with a partner the author's purpose for writing and how his or her word choices did or did not meet that purpose. How would using similar yet different words affect the text?

WRITE TO LEARN

Write a paragraph about something that interests you, such as a type of cuisine, a professional sport, or a medical advance. Choose your words carefully to set a mood. Then exchange paragraphs with a partner and rewrite each other's work, making different word choices to express the same ideas. Is the effect the same? Explain.

TEST-TAKING SKILL

Evaluate the Answer

When you take a test, evaluate the answer choices before selecting your answer. Reread the question and each answer choice, one at a time. After each choice, ask yourself: *Does this choice correctly answer the question?* If you find that more than one choice answers the question, ask yourself: *Which choice BEST answers the question?* That answer choice is the correct one.

Reread the passage about Grenada. Then read the following question and evaluate the answer choices to find the right one.

Which choice of words BEST conveys how dangerous Ivan was?

a. After passing Grenada, Ivan continued to strengthen.

b. A prison was damaged and some inmates escaped.

c. Many structures were built of concrete.

d. In Jamaica, about half a million people would have to evacuate.

If your answer was *d*, you evaluated all the choices and found the one that uses a precise word (*evacuate*) to signal extreme danger.

Analyzing and Evaluating Word Choice in Various Texts

When you analyze word choice in a text, you explain the impact that particular words have on the audience. Each type of text has a specific audience. For example, the audience for an instructional booklet would not be the same as the audience for a murder mystery.

Writers also choose words based on their purpose for writing the text. For example, the author of a story that has a humorous tone aims to amuse readers with funny expressions; the author of a tragic news story uses a style that will relate the gravity of the event. Through word choice, the author connects with readers' feelings, or **emotions**.

Directions: Read the passage about Grenada. What emotions does it generate?

Ivan Strikes Hard in Grenada

On September 7, 2004, Hurricane Ivan struck the island of Grenada in the West Indies. The worst hurricane Grenada had experienced in almost ten years, Ivan left at least 12 dead, devastated the island's agriculture, and destroyed countless structures, including 90 percent of islanders' homes. Although many of these structures had been built of concrete, the storm reduced them to rubble.

The country's prime minister, Keith Mitchell, who was among those who lost their homes, said that the storm had been "beyond imagination." He also confirmed that the country's centuries-old prison had been damaged so severely that inmates had escaped and many were still at large.

Ivan continued to strengthen after leaving Grenada, and more damage is expected as its 140-mile-per-hour winds churn through the Caribbean. The U.S. Hurricane Center in Miami, Florida, warned that it could make direct hits on Jamaica, Cuba, and the southern United States. Jamaica has already warned that about half a million people will have to be evacuated.

The author of this news story uses intense words to express the destruction caused by Hurricane Ivan in Grenada in 2004. In the beginning, the author states that Ivan was "The worst hurricane Grenada had experienced in almost ten years." If you are familiar with Grenada's history of hurricanes, these words have a strong impact, but they might have much less impact if you are not familiar with Grenada.

The author depicts the damage in a way that enables readers to understand the gravity of the situation and to sympathize with the victims. For example, the author includes the detail that the prime minister "was among those who lost their homes," and later states that prison "inmates had escaped and many were still at large." These words are intended to have an emotional impact on the reader by stirring feelings of sympathy or fear.

As you read, you should also evaluate the author's word choice. When you evaluate word choice, you judge for yourself how well the author's words meet his or her purpose or impact the audience. Ask yourself: *Does this particular word help convey the author's message? Did the author choose a word that does not imply what he or she thinks it does? Could the author have chosen a different word to better convey his or her message to readers? Which word might have been better? Why?*

Think about Reading

Directions: Read the passage about Grenada again, and then answer the following questions.

1. Circle the words in the box that describe the mood the author's word choice creates in the passage?

bleak	**expectant**	**hopeful**	**stable**

2. What impact does the author intend to have on readers by describing the prime minister as "among those who lost their homes"?
   A. Readers will decide to help rebuild homes.
   B. Readers will feel compassion for the prime minister.
   C. Readers will worry about their own homes.

3. Explain how the author conveys how strong Hurricane Ivan is, and identify which of the author's word choices help convey that idea.

____

____

____

Summary

Writers choose words and phrases that will have a specific impact on readers. Good word choice creates the author's desired effect and gives the audience a clear understanding of the author's purpose. When analyzing an author's word choice, ask yourself: *What is the author's purpose for writing? Who is the audience? Which words does the author use to create a particular effect?* After you identify an author's purpose and word choice, evaluate how the words affect your understanding of the text and achieve the author's intention.

CORE SKILL

Evaluate Word Choice

The author's word choice in a text makes the difference between a memorable text that people want to reread and one that holds no interest for the reader.

To evaluate an author's word choice, follow this procedure:

1. Read the first few sentences of a text.
2. Ask yourself: *Why did the author choose these words and phrases? Do these particular words and phrases capture my interest? Do they make me want to find out more?*
3. Think about whether the author has succeeded in engaging you. Note the specific words and phrases that helped the author accomplish this.

Choose a passage from your favorite story or book of fiction. Follow the procedure above. Place sticky notes next to words and phrases that especially make the text memorable. Share your notes and reactions to the author's word choices with a partner.

Vocabulary Review

Directions: Draw a line from each word to its definition.

1. affects	**a.** comparisons that use *like* or *as*
2. depicts	**b.** feelings
3. impact	**c.** the writer's use of language
4. similes	**d.** describes in words
5. style	**e.** influences
6. emotions	**f.** have an effect on

Skill Review

Directions: Read the passage. Then use a word from the box to complete each sentence.

Raymond Chen has been working for the SS&G Accounting firm for 15 years as an accounting manager. He is an honest associate who is respected by all the clerks he supervises. Raymond is punctual and dependable, priding himself on providing monthly reports to his boss, the district account director, on schedule. This month's report is due by 10:00 A.M. Friday. It is already 9:30 A.M. on Friday, and Raymond is not receiving any cooperation from Rosalind Osei, who is supposed to supply him with the information he needs to complete the report. Rosalind also reports to the district account director. Raymond considers his options on how to best resolve the current situation.

easygoing	enraged	nervous	prompt	unhelpful	unhurried

1. The author's word choices help convey a ________________ tone.
2. Instead of *punctual*, the author could have used ________________ to describe Raymond.
3. By stating that "Raymond is not receiving any cooperation from Rosalind Osei," the author implies that Rosalind is ________________ .

Skill Practice

Directions: Read the passage below. Then choose the best answer to each question that follows.

> Wilbur, having used his turn in the unsuccessful attempt on the 14th, the right to the first trial now belonged to me. After running the motor a few minutes to heat it up, I released the wire that held the machine to the track, and the machine started forward into the wind. Wilbur ran at the side of the machine, holding the wing to balance it on the track. Unlike the start on the 14th, made in a calm, the machine, facing a 27-mile wind, started very slowly. . . .
>
> The course of the flight up and down was exceedingly erratic, partly due to the irregularity of the air, and partly to lack of experience in handling this machine. . . . This flight lasted only 12 seconds, but it was nevertheless the first in the history of the world in which a machine carrying a man had raised itself by its own power into the air in full flight, had sailed forward without reduction of speed, and had finally landed at a point as high as that from which it started.
>
> —from "How We Made the First Flight" by Orville Wright

1. What is the mood of the passage?

A. silly

B. brooding

C. unfeeling

D. triumphant

2. Which words did the author choose to convey that the ride was bumpy?

A. holding the wing to balance it

B. the unsuccessful attempt on the 14th

C. the flight up and down was exceedingly erratic

D. released the wire that held the machine to the track

3. Which feature does the author's style NOT include?

A. a simile

B. descriptive words

C. long sentences

D. action words

Writing Practice

Directions: Write a short passage about a real or imaginary event. Choose your words carefully to set a mood and to make the action come alive. Try to use descriptive words that will appeal to your reader's emotions.

Directions: Read the following passage. Then choose the best answer to questions 1 through 4.

The first impressions, on entering this city, are decidedly favourable. It possesses a character essentially different from that of New York. It has not so much business, nor so much animation; but there is, in Philadelphia, a freedom from mere display; an evidence of solidity, of which its more commercial rival is nearly destitute.

All the streets are spacious. . . . The private houses are characterized by elegant neatness; the steps and window-sills of many of them are of grey marble, and they have large mats placed before the doors. The streets are carefully swept, as well as the foot-paths, which are paved with brick. . . . The principal street is one hundred feet wide; and the others vary from eighty to fifty. In the foot-paths a great inconvenience is experienced by the injudicious mode in which cellars are constructed, the openings of which project into the street; and also by the slovenly practice of the store or shopkeepers placing great quantities of loose goods on the outside of their doors.

Philadelphia stands on the bank of the river Delaware; and, in 1795, when Mr. Weld was there, its appearance, as approached from the water, was not very prepossessing. Nothing was visible but confused heaps of wooden store-houses, crowded upon each other, and wharfs, which projected a considerable way into the river. The wharfs were built of wood; they jutted out, in every direction, and were well adapted for the accommodation of shipping; the largest merchant vessels being able to lie close alongside of them. Behind the wharfs, and parallel to the river, runs a street called Water-street. This is the first street which the stranger in America usually enters, after landing; and (says Mr. Weld) it will not give him a very favourable opinion either of the neatness or commodiousness of the public ways of Philadelphia. Such stenches, at times, prevail in it, owing in part to the quantity of filth and dirt that is suffered to remain on the pavement, and in part to what is deposited in waste-houses, of which there are several in the street, that it is really dreadful to pass through it. It was here, in the year 1793, that the malignant yellow fever broke out, which made such terrible ravages among the inhabitants; and, in the summer season, in general, this street is extremely unhealthy.

—From *Travels in North America* by William Bingley

1. What was the author's purpose for writing this passage?

A. to suggest that people visit Philadelphia

B. to inform people about some parts of Philadelphia

C. to entertain readers with a funny story about Philadelphia

D. to persuade local leaders to clean up the city of Philadelphia

2. Which word best describes the author's tone in the passage?

A. bitter

B. ashamed

C. admiring

D. judgmental

3. Which of the following words has the same denotation, or literal meaning, but a less negative connotation than *stench*?

A. color

B. aroma

C. texture

D. consistency

4. What was the author's reason for using the words "spacious" and "elegant neatness" in the second paragraph?

A. to denote that Philadelphia is not like New York

B. to depict scenes of the Delaware River

C. to help readers experience Water Street in Philadelphia

D. to help readers visualize the nice parts of Philadelphia

Directions: Read the following passage. Then choose the best answer to questions 5 through 7.

My fellow citizens, today we celebrate the mystery of American renewal. . . . When our Founders boldly declared America's independence to the world and our purposes to the Almighty, they knew that America, to endure, would have to change; not change for change's sake but change to preserve America's ideals: life, liberty, the pursuit of happiness. Though we marched to the music of our time, our mission is timeless. Each generation of Americans must define what it means to be an American.

. . . Today, a generation raised in the shadows of the cold war assumes new responsibilities in a world warmed by the sunshine of freedom but threatened still by ancient hatreds and new plagues. Raised in unrivaled prosperity, we inherit an economy that is still the world s strongest but is weakened by business failures, stagnant wages, increasing inequality, and deep divisions among our own people.

When George Washington first took the oath I have just sworn to uphold, news traveled slowly across the land by horseback and across the ocean by boat. Now, the sights and sounds of this ceremony are broadcast instantaneously to billions around the world. Communications and commerce are global. Investment is mobile. Technology is almost magical. And ambition for a better life is now universal.

We earn our livelihood in America today in peaceful competition with people all across the Earth. Profound and powerful forces are shaking and remaking our world. And the urgent question of our time is whether we can make change our friend and not our enemy. This new world has already enriched the lives of millions of Americans who are able to compete and win in it. But when most people are working harder for less; when others cannot work at all; when the cost of health care devastates families and threatens to bankrupt our enterprises, great and small; when the fear of crime robs law-abiding citizens of their freedom; and when millions of poor children cannot even imagine the lives we are calling them to lead, we have not made change our friend.

We know we have to face hard truths and take strong steps. . . . Though our challenges are fearsome, so are our strengths. Americans have ever been a restless, questing, hopeful people. And we must bring to our task today the vision and will of those who came before us. . . . Thomas Jefferson believed that to preserve the very foundations of our Nation, we would need dramatic change from time to time. Well, my fellow Americans, this is our time. Let us embrace it.

. . . Today we do more than celebrate America. We rededicate ourselves to the very idea of America, an idea born in revolution and renewed through two centuries of challenge; an idea tempered by the knowledge that, but for fate, we, the fortunate, and the unfortunate might have been each other; an idea ennobled by the faith that our Nation can summon from its myriad diversity the deepest measure of unity; an idea infused with the conviction that America's long, heroic journey must go forever upward.

And so, my fellow Americans, as we stand at the edge of the 21st century, let us begin anew with energy and hope, with faith and discipline. And let us work until our work is done. . . .

—From Bill Clinton's Inaugural Speech, January 20, 1993

5. Why might the author have chosen to use the word *myriad* in the sixth paragraph?

A. To highlight the lack of diversity

B. To make a plea for diversity

C. To define the term *diversity*

D. To emphasize the great degree of diversity

6. Which word best describes the mood that the author's tone creates through word choice?

A. playful

B. hopeful

C. foreboding

D. disappointed

7. The phrase "the sunshine of freedom" is an example of which figure of speech the author uses to engage readers?

A. a simile

B. a metaphor

C. connotation

D. personification

Directions: Read the following passage. Then choose the best answer to questions 8 through 10.

The Law of the Jungle . . . is as perfect as time and custom can make it. . . . Mowgli spent a great part of his life in the Seeonee Wolf-Pack, learning the Law from Baloo, the Brown Bear; and it was Baloo who told him, when the boy grew impatient at the constant orders, that the Law was like the Giant Creeper, because it dropped across every one's back and no one could escape. "When thou hast lived as long as I have, Little Brother, thou wilt see how all the Jungle obeys at least one Law. And that will be no pleasant sight," said Baloo.

This talk went in at one ear and out at the other, for a boy who spends his life eating and sleeping does not worry about anything till it actually stares him in the face. But, one year, Baloo's words came true, and Mowgli saw all the Jungle working under the Law.

It began when the winter Rains failed almost entirely, and Ikki, the Porcupine, meeting Mowgli in a bamboo-thicket, told him that the wild yams were drying up. . . . So Mowgli laughed and said, "What is that to me?"

"Not much NOW," said Ikki, rattling his quills in a stiff, uncomfortable way, "but later we shall see. Is there any more diving into the deep rock-pool below the Bee-Rocks, Little Brother?"

"No. The foolish water is going all away, and I do not wish to break my head," said Mowgli, who, in those days, was quite sure that he knew as much as any five of the Jungle People put together.

"That is thy loss. A small crack might let in some wisdom." Ikki ducked quickly to prevent Mowgli from pulling his nose-bristles, and Mowgli told Baloo what Ikki had said. Baloo looked very grave, and mumbled half to himself: "If I were alone I would change my hunting-grounds now, before the others began to think. And yet—hunting among strangers ends in fighting; and they might hurt the Man-cub. . . ."

—From "How Fear Came" by Rudyard Kipling

8. Which statement is an example of the author's use of personification in the passage?

A. Wild yams dry up.

B. Mowgli speaks like a human.

C. Baloo and Ikki speak like humans.

D. Water moves away from the deep rock-pool.

9. Which word best describes the author's tone in the passage?

A. mocking

B. whimsical

C. depressing

D. embarrassed

10. What does the author imply by stating that "they might hurt the Man-cub"?

A. Baloo might hurt Mowgli.

B. Ikki's quill might hurt Mowgli.

C. Mowgli could be in danger.

D. Mowgli might pull Ikki's nose bristles.

Check Your Understanding

On the following chart, circle the number of any item you answered incorrectly. In the third column, you will see the pages that you can review to study the content covered in the question. Pay particular attention to reviewing those lessons in which you missed half or more of the questions.

Lesson	Core Skill	Item Number(s)	Review Page(s)
Lesson 3.1 Determine Connotative and Figurative Meanings	Analyze and Evaluate Word Choice	3, 4, 5, 6	90–91
	Interpret Words and Phrases	3, 7, 8, 10	91–93
Lesson 3.2 Analyze Tone	Analyze Word Choice	4, 5, 6	96–97
	Interpret Words and Phrases to Draw Conclusions	1, 2, 6, 9, 10	98–99
Lesson 3.3 Analyze Word Choice	Analyze Word Choice	4, 5	102–103
	Evaluate Word Choice	5, 6	104–105

WRITE ABOUT An Historic Speech

Read *What It Means to Be Colored in the Capital of the United States*, a speech by Mary E. Church Terrell, on page 310. Write an essay in which you

1. identify the tone of the speech
2. cite examples of connotative and figurative language in the speech
3. explain how the speaker's word choices affect her message and her listeners or readers.

BEFORE YOU WRITE Identify Words that Convey Tone

Use a concept web to take notes as you read the speech. You can find an example of a concept web in the Graphic Organizer section at the back of the book. The web will help you organize ideas for your essay. Label the center circle "Tone." In the outer circles, write at least six examples of connotative or figurative language or other word choices that express the author's tone, or attitude toward the subject. Remember that the connotative meaning of a word is its suggested or implied meaning and that figurative language includes words and phrases that imply more than their literal meaning. Add circles to the concept web as necessary. As you read, think about how those words and phrases shape the author's message. In the center circle, write one or two words to describe the tone, such as *playful, casual, serious, amused, indifferent,* or *pessimistic.*

When you have finished, review your concept web. Ask yourself: *How is the author's choice of words important to the message of the text?* Use your answer to form a topic sentence for your essay.

TIP Use the Subjunctive Mood in Writing

The subjunctive mood is a verb form used to express urgency and things that are not certain such as wishes, possibilities, doubts, or suggestions. These words describe situations that are conditional, and often the word *if* is used to show that one thing must happen before the other can. For example:

- If I were taller, I could reach that branch.

  or

- I wish I were taller so I could reach that branch.

The writer sets a condition (being taller) for making something happen (reaching the branch). To show that this situation is not a fact, or reality, the writer uses the subjunctive "I wish I were" instead of "I wish I was." For verbs other than forms of "to be," the subjunctive mood is usually made by dropping the -s ending for third-person singular subjects (he/she/it).

- She suggested that he buy a variety of items.

Here are some more examples of the subjunctive mood:

- It is vital that she be involved in the stage production. (urgency)
- If Martha were here, the cake would not have burned. (possible, but not a fact)
- I recommend that he remain at home until the fever is gone. (suggestion)
- The author wishes she were judged by her ability, not her color. (wish)

As you write your essay, you can use the subjunctive mood (1) to describe actions the author believes would happen *if* the conditions were right or (2) to suggest how the use of different wording might have affected the tone and message of the speech.

WHILE YOU WRITE Understand Word Choice

You have identified the tone of the speech and created a topic sentence for your essay. Now expand on your idea. Start by writing a sentence or two explaining the tone and what mood, or feeling, the author's tone creates. Remember that *tone* is the expression of the author's attitude toward the subject through stylistic choices; *mood* is the feeling a reader or listener gets from the author's words.

Next, develop key details to support your idea. Look at your concept web again. Around the central circle, you have six or more outer circles. Each of the outer circles contains an example of the author's word choices, such as connotative words or figurative language. Write a sentence or two about each word choice.

Then write a few sentences to explain how the author's word choices affect her message and her audience. For example, by using the connotative word *menial* instead of a synonym such as *unskilled* or *humble*, she stresses that people of color were considered lowly or subservient. Why did she choose the word *menial* rather than one of the other words? Did it make her speech more persuasive? If so, how?

Finally, write a concluding statement. In it, restate the author's tone and how the author's word choices built that tone.

TIP Remember to . . . Use Quotation Marks

When you write about a speech, you often quote the author's exact words. To write a direct quotation, the speaker's words should be enclosed in quotation marks (" "). The end mark, if it is part of the quote, should be placed within the quotation marks.

- "How do you feel today?" the doctor asked.

An indirect quotation also communicates someone's message, but it does not repeat the speaker's exact words. Quotation marks are not needed. Sometimes an indirect quotation is a question that a speaker has asked. Because the quotation is presented as a statement and not as a question, its end mark should be a period instead of a question mark.

- The doctor asked how Rachel was feeling.

If a phrase identifying the speaker comes before a quote, place a comma after the phrase and before the opening quotation mark.

- The doctor said, "It sounds like you have a cold."

If the phrase comes after a quote that is a statement, use a comma inside the quotation marks.

- "Your cold should improve in a few days," said Dr. Lehman.

AFTER YOU WRITE Check Your Work

Reread the writing assignment. Then read your essay carefully three times.

The first time you read, ask yourself whether you have completed the writing assignment correctly. Have you (1) identified the tone of the speech, (2) cited examples of connotative and figurative language in the speech, and (3) explained how the author's word choices influence her message and her audience?

Then read your essay again. Did you remember to use quotation marks to identify direct quotations of the speaker's words? Did you use other punctuation correctly with the quotation marks? Did you use the subjunctive mood to describe ideas, actions, or events that are conditional?

Reread the essay one last time. Did you use correct grammar, spelling, and punctuation? Do you see any errors? Did you type the words you meant to use?

Before submitting your essay, have another student read it and provide you with feedback.

Chapter 4

Juice Images/Glow Images

Examine Text Structure

Whether writing an article, an essay, a poem, a memo, an e-mail, or a novel, writers develop ideas using a structure that helps the reader find meaning. From one sentence to the next and from one paragraph to the next, understanding the development of ideas is crucial to figuring out the most important points in a text.

In this chapter you will study these topics:

Lesson 4.1

Analyze the Development of Ideas

Writers organize information in texts in certain ways to meet their goals and purposes. They choose which information to mention first, which information to leave till the end, which ideas to link together, and which words to use to link them. Learn how writers develop ideas in various texts.

Lesson 4.2

Analyze How Structure Impacts Key Ideas

Writers use many different organizational patterns. They may focus on the steps in a process, the causes of an event, the relative importance of several ideas, or the solution to a problem. They choose the structure that will best communicate their most important ideas. Learn how to identify ways in which structure impacts key ideas in texts.

Lesson 4.3

Analyze the Effects of Transitional and Signal Words

Transitional and signal words help the reader move through the ideas in a text. They show relationships between ideas in different sentences, paragraphs, and sections of a piece of writing. Locating and understanding transitional and signal words will help you understand the author's ideas and purpose for writing a text.

Goal Setting

How does the organization of the steps in a set of directions help you get from one place to another? Think about other texts where the structure has helped you understand the important ideas. How can this chapter improve the way you read all types of texts?

Why do you think it is important to recognize and use different types of structure in texts? How can this be helpful in everyday life?

LESSON 4.1 Analyze the Development of Ideas

LESSON OBJECTIVES

- Identify different types of text structure
- Explain how the structure of text supports the development of ideas

CORE SKILLS

- Recognize Organization
- Analyze Text Structure

Key Terms

organization
the way text is arranged

text structure
the pattern a writer uses to organize ideas in a text

Vocabulary

compare
identify the ways in which two or more things are alike

contrast
identify the ways in which two or more things differ

Key Concept

Every piece of writing has a structure. Writers develop their ideas in texts through organization.

Have you ever read a news article? Have you ever listened to a speech by a politician? You may have noticed that news articles tend to put the most important information first. A political speech, in contrast, may put it at the end. Depending on their goals, writers organize information in different ways to communicate their ideas to the reader.

Identifying Text Structure

Text structure is the pattern a writer uses to organize ideas in a text. The **organization**, or the way a text is arranged, helps the writer develop ideas. In a text, the sentences and paragraphs should fit together logically. This structure helps the reader understand the ideas in the text.

A common type of text structure is sequence. Stories and other narratives relate events in the order in which they happened. Recipes, directions, and procedures are presented in a series of ordered steps. Often, such texts include words such as *first, second, next,* and *last.*

Another way writers organize their writing is by comparing two or more things or ideas. A writer who wants to describe two ideas might **compare** them—or list the ways in which they are alike. The writer might also **contrast** them—or list the ways in which in which they are different. Comparisons and contrasts often use words such as *although, both,* and *in contrast.*

A third way to organize a text is through cause and effect. A factor that makes something happen is a cause. A result of one or more causes is an effect. Sometimes writers use the cause-and-effect text structure to discuss the relationship between events. Words and phrases such as *so, therefore, since,* and *as a result* identify cause-and-effect structure.

Description is yet another type of text structure. Writers describe people, events, and scenes in detail to present a vivid picture. Sometimes a writer describes an overall impression of a scene with details to bring it to life. At other times, he or she may start with the detail that immediately catches the eye and then move to less noticeable features.

Ingram Publishing

Another structure used to describe a person or place begins with one feature and then describes what is seen as the eye moves right or left, up or down—much as a video camera might move. A descriptive text frequently uses words and phrases that express spatial relationships, such as *above, to the right,* and *next to.*

Sometimes a writer explains a problem or problems and goes on to discuss one or more solutions. This structure is known as problem and solution. Words and phrases such as *in order to* and *so that* typify problem and solution texts.

Here are some examples of the five types of text structures.

- **Sequence:** First, wash the lettuce carefully. Then cut it into small strips with a sharp knife. Finally, place it on top of the finished tacos.
- **Compare and Contrast:** Although pasta and rice can be similar in color, they are very different foods.
- **Cause and Effect:** As a result of food shortages around the world, many people are going hungry.
- **Description:** As we rounded the corner, the first thing we saw was the massive stone fountain in the middle of the square. Colored lights played on it, turning the water leaf green one moment and blood red the next. To the right of the fountain stood a knot of people, oddly motionless. Then we noticed the soggy bundle of clothing at their feet.
- **Problem and Solution:** In this region the prevailing southwesterly winds can lead to severe erosion. In order to shield your crops, plant a row of sturdy trees along the southern and western borders of each planted field.

Directions: Read the passage, and write the numbers of the sentences that describe a contrast.

(1) The United Nations and the United States are both governed by elected leaders. (2) Whereas the United Nations (UN) is headed by a secretary-general, the United States is headed by a president. (3) The secretary-general is elected by the members of the UN General Assembly, which includes a representative from each member country. (4) The UN General Assembly currently consists of 193 members. (5) The secretary-general serves for five years, and at the end of this time, he or she can be re-elected to another term. (6) In contrast to the five-year term of the secretary-general, the president of the United States serves for a term of four years. (7) The president of the United States is not elected by members of the UN General Assembly; he or she is elected by the voters. (8) Although there have been eight secretaries-general since the UN was established in 1945, there have been 44 presidents since the United States became a country in 1776.

If you wrote the numbers 2, 6, and 8, you correctly identified the sentences that show contrast.

WRITE TO LEARN

Write a paragraph telling someone the steps for a hobby, like baking a pie or fly fishing, that you do well using sequence text structure. Make sure that your paragraph has at least five steps. Be sure to use sequence words such as *first, second, next,* and *last* to show the order of the steps.

CORE SKILL

Recognize Organization

Writers organize texts to support the development of ideas. To figure out how a writer organized a text, ask yourself the following questions:

1. Why did the writer begin with this sentence?
2. Why did the writer include this paragraph?
3. Why did the writer end with this sentence?

Read the passage about the United Nations again. Ask yourself the first question from the list above. Discuss with a partner why the writer began with a sentence comparing the United States and the United Nations.

CORE SKILL

Analyze Text Structure

To figure out the structure of a text, ask yourself the following questions:

1. *What is the purpose of this piece? To give directions? To compare and contrast two ideas or things? To relate causes and effects? To describe something? To solve a problem?*
2. *Does the piece contain any words that are specific to its text structure? For example, does it contain words such as* first, second, cause, effect, as a result, so that, compare, *or* contrast?

Find a document in print or online. Using the procedure above, decide what the purpose of the piece is. Then find and list any words that are specific to its structure.

Think about Reading

Directions: In a notebook, write the type of text structure that would include each sentence below.

1. As a result of high winds, power lines came down.
2. The mountains rose abruptly from the desert floor, and their peaks seemed to brush the clouds.
3. Although the original American flag had 13 stars, today's flag has 50 stars.
4. First, open the can and drain the beans. Then wash the beans and set the can aside.

Variations in Organization

Often, a text's organization includes more than one structure. For instance, a persuasive essay may describe a problem, then examine its causes and effects, and go on to compare possible solutions before finally recommending a course of action.

A text may also include variations on a particular structure. A good example is chronological order, also known as time order. Often chronological order expresses a clear sequence, relating what happened first, second, third, and so on. However, writers sometimes interrupt a sequence to move forward or backward in time. They may also speed up or slow down the speed at which time passes.

When writers interrupt the sequence to introduce events that took place before the story began, this is called a flashback. Flashbacks let writers add details from the past that help readers understand the information in the present.

Another way that writers express time is through pacing. A slow pace moves gradually through events, using plenty of details and description. A faster pace moves through events quickly in order to arrive at an important moment.

Flashback: The car slowed to a stop in front of the hospital. My thoughts raced back to the last time I was in the hospital. I had broken my arm falling off a horse, and the pain ran through me like fire.

Slow Pace: Light washed over the room, revealing the room item by item. A pair of paint-spattered overalls hung in the closet. The bed was unmade, the corner of a blanket trailed across the footboard, and pillows littered the floor.

Fast Pace: The car sped through the city, sliding under yellow lights mile after mile. In three hours, we were at the airport. With bags swinging by my side, I rushed onto the plane and breathed a sigh of relief.

Think about Reading

Directions: Look at the examples of slow and fast pacing above. The two paragraphs have the same number of sentences and are about the same length. In a notebook, write a sentence or two explaining what elements influence the pacing in each.

Directions: Read the memo about new rules in an apartment community. Identify the different text structures the writer uses.

> # MEMO
>
> **To:** All Scenic Acres Apartment Homes Residents
> **From:** Sharon Headley, Property Manager
> **Date:** 1/3/2014
> **Subject:** Noise Complaints
>
> It has come to my attention that there have been several noise complaints in recent weeks. Most recently, a retirement party last week involved loud music and unruly behavior that disrupted the entire community. Fairview Police responded to at least four noise complaints as a result of that party, and our complex has been fined. This type of reckless and irresponsible behavior cannot continue.
>
> We have developed a four-pronged plan to keep Scenic Acres the premier apartment community in Fairview. First, in order to ensure the safety of all of our residents, the property managers are instituting an 8 P.M. curfew for anyone under 18. Second, there will be no loud music in public areas after 10 P.M. Third, the entire complex will observe quiet hours after 11 P.M. Finally, all parties and other social events must be reviewed by the property management staff one week before the event.
>
> Anyone who violates these new rules is subject to fines and possible eviction from the community. We hope that these new policies will improve the quality of life for all residents. If there are any questions, please don't hesitate to contact the rental office.

Think about Reading

Directions: In a notebook, answer the following questions about the memo.

1. Which sentence shows the final step in the four-pronged plan?
2. Which cause led to the four-pronged plan?
3. Why did the author include the third paragraph?

Summary

The structure of a text helps the reader understand the ideas the text presents. Ask yourself these questions to help you identify a text's structure: *What is the purpose of this piece? Are there words in the text that provide clues to its structure?* Authors organize their writing to support the development of their ideas. The organization of a text can include different structures or variations on structures.

WORKPLACE SKILL

Interpreting Professional Documents

Workplace documents, such as memos, letters, agendas, and e-mail messages, have a specific structure. If you are reading a memo, there is usually a line that says *Subject*. This line tells you the topic of the memo.

Another workplace document, an agenda, has a certain order because it lists the sequence of events. The structure of an agenda will let you know what will happen in a meeting or at a conference. An agenda may use a numbered list to tell the reader what will be discussed and in what order.

Look online for an example of a meeting agenda. Then in your notebook, write an agenda for a meeting about an important issue in your community. Be sure to include at least four items in your agenda.

Vocabulary Review

Directions: Complete the sentences using the following key terms or vocabulary.

compare **contrast** **organization** **text structure**

1. In ________________ with Chicago's population of 2.7 million, New York City boasts 12 million residents.
2. When figuring out the ________________ of ideas in a text, it is important to look at the beginning, middle, and end.
3. To ________________ two objects, it is important to figure out how they are similar.
4. Cause and effect is one ________________ that writers use to express particular ideas.

Skill Review

Directions: Read the passage below. Then choose the best answer to each question.

> It was we, the people; not we, the white male citizens; nor yet we, the male citizens; but we, the whole people, who formed the Union. And we formed it, not to give the blessings of liberty, but to secure them; not to the half of ourselves and the half of our posterity, but to the whole people—women as well as men. And it is a downright mockery to talk to women of their enjoyment of the blessings of liberty while they are denied the use of the only means of securing them provided by this democratic-republican government—the ballot.
>
> For any state to make sex a qualification that must ever result in the disfranchisement of one entire half of the people, is to pass a bill of attainder, or, an ex post facto law, and is therefore a violation of the supreme law of the land. By it the blessings of liberty are forever withheld from women and their female posterity.
>
> —From "On Women's Right to the Suffrage" by Susan B. Anthony

1. Why did Anthony include the first paragraph in this passage?
   A. To show the cause of women's voting inequalities in the United States
   B. To show the effect of women not being able to vote in the United States
   C. To compare women's rights in the United States with women's rights in other countries
   D. To establish the tradition of freedom in the United States and contrast it with the treatment of women

2. Why did Anthony include the second paragraph in the passage?
   A. To show the cause of voting conflicts in the United States
   B. To describe how different states have different women's voting rights
   C. To contrast the different types of laws that deny women the right to vote
   D. To compare women being denied the right to vote to violating the law of the land

Skill Practice

Directions: Read the passage below. Then choose the best answer to each question.

Rosalia watched with wonder as the snow fell gently on the frozen ground, flake by flake, collecting in a mound below her first-floor dorm room. It was the first snowfall that she had seen in her life, ever since she had left the wet heat of Guatemala City behind six months ago for college in New York City. Rosalia had read once that snowflakes were like fingerprints—no two were the same. She squinted through the frosted window glass that separated her from the frigid outdoors to see whether the rule was true.

Rosalia looked at the winter clothing that she'd bought when she arrived: a puffy parka, wool gloves, a scarf, and a hat. She hadn't needed them during the humid Manhattan summer that was so much like the familiar climate in Guatemala City. But no matter how much she wanted summer to hang on, winter came, and snow wasn't far behind. Rosalia zipped the coat up to her chin, pulled her gloves over her long fingers, and slipped the hat over her curly hair. Finally, she wrapped the scarf around her neck and face the way her roommate from New Hampshire had shown her. In the mirror, small slivers of her caramel-colored skin were visible beneath her hat and scarf. She opened the door of the dorm and watched the sea of people that passed on the street. She felt invincible in her new winter clothes and bounded down the steps to join the crowd.

1. Why did the writer include the first paragraph of the passage?

A. To compare Guatemala City and Manhattan

B. To show the effect of Rosalia missing Guatemala

C. To describe how Rosalia experiences her first snowfall

D. To contrast how Rosalia has been doing in college to how other students are doing

2. Which sentence from the passage describes Rosalia's last step in preparing to go outside?

A. But no matter how much she wanted summer to hang on, winter came, and snow wasn't far behind.

B. Rosalia zipped the coat up to her chin, pulled her gloves over her long fingers, and slipped the hat over her curly hair.

C. Finally, she wrapped the scarf around her neck and face the way her roommate from New Hampshire had shown her.

D. In the mirror, small slivers of her caramel-colored skin were visible beneath her hat and scarf.

3. Which of the following sentences from the passage is a comparison?

A. Rosalia had read once that snowflakes were like fingerprints—no two were the same.

B. She squinted through the frosted window glass that separated her from the frigid outdoors to see whether the rule was true.

C. Rosalia zipped the coat up to her chin, pulled her gloves over her long fingers, and slipped the hat over her curly hair.

D. She felt invincible in her new winter clothes and bounded down the steps to join the crowd.

Writing Practice

Directions: Find an article in a print or online source about an environmental problem. Then in two to three sentences, write the causes of the problem. Next, write the effects of the problem. Be sure that the causes you chose lead to these effects.

LESSON 4.2 Analyze How Structure Impacts Key Ideas

LESSON OBJECTIVES

- Distinguish which text structures best communicate different types of ideas
- Identify how text structure impacts key ideas in a text

CORE SKILLS

- Analyze the Relationship between Paragraphs
- Understand Organization

Key Terms

distinguish
notice a difference

Vocabulary

character
a person in a novel, story, or play

plot
the series of events that make up a story

setting
the time and place in which the action of a story occurs

stanzas
groups of lines in a poem

Key Concept

Authors structure what they write in order to communicate and reinforce key ideas.

Have you ever written a poem? Have you also written an essay? If you have, you probably noticed that poems and essays are quite different. One main difference is that they have different text structures. Texts are structured in ways that help writers communicate important ideas.

Distinguishing between Text Structures

Authors of different types of texts—nonfiction, fiction, drama, and poetry—choose the structure that will best communicate the information in their text. One way to **distinguish**, or notice a difference, between various text structures is to understand which structures are common to which types of texts.

The list below reviews the types of text structures.

- **Sequence** Sequencing things is placing them in order. Often, sequence is thought of as time order, the order in which things occur. This structure is suited to writing stories of any kind. For example, sequence structure is often used in books about history, which tell the story of past events. It is also frequently used in short stories and novels, which usually tell stories about fictional events. Time order is also used to describe processes, so you will find it in instruction manuals, recipes, and directions.

  Another type of sequence is order of importance. Order of importance is often used in texts that seek to persuade the reader, such as an argument or a speech. In a persuasive text, the writer might start with the least important point and end with the most important one. This text structure helps persuade the reader by building to a strong conclusion.
- **Compare and contrast** Many different types of texts use this structure. A novel might contrast two people, a presentation might compare two business plans, or an informative text might compare and contrast two paintings. The comparison can be made point by point or subject by subject.

©Image Source/PunchStock

- **Cause and Effect** Cause-and-effect structure is common in history texts. It is also frequently found in investigative articles, biographies, autobiographies, and other texts that analyze events. This structure can focus on multiple causes of one event, on multiple effects that one event causes, or on a chain of related events, in which each event causes another, such as falling dominoes. In the workplace, reports frequently use cause-and-effect structure to analyze marketing, financial, and other company issues.
- **Description** Description may be impressionistic or detailed. It includes sensory details of what is seen, touched, or heard. It gives details on spatial relationships and appearances. It is common in fiction, but also in news reports, marketing pieces, travel writing, and many other texts.
- **Problem and Solution** This text structure may focus on how one solution can solve one or more problems or on how one problem might be addressed by one or more solutions. It is perhaps most familiar from user manuals, which often contain a troubleshooting guide. Other texts where problem and solution structure is common are recommendation reports and advertising.

Almost no text longer than one or two paragraphs will use only one structure. The structure within a paragraph may differ from that of the text as a whole. Still, each paragraph fits into the overall structure because it relates to the thesis, or main idea of the text, and builds on the ideas in the preceding paragraph or paragraphs. For example, a report with an overall problem-and-solution structure may include a description of the problem as well as an analysis of its causes and effects.

Directions: Read the following speech. Identify the overall text structure. Then write down how the fourth paragraph fits into the text as a whole and develops ideas from the third paragraph.

To those old allies whose cultural and spiritual origins we share, we pledge the loyalty of faithful friends. United, there is little we cannot do in a host of cooperative ventures. Divided, there is little we can do—for we dare not meet a powerful challenge at odds and split asunder.

To those new states whom we welcome to the ranks of the free, we pledge our word that one form of colonial control shall not have passed away merely to be replaced by a far more iron tyranny. We shall not always expect to find them supporting our view. But we shall always hope to find them strongly supporting their own freedom—and to remember that, in the past, those who foolishly sought power by riding the back of the tiger ended up inside.

To those peoples in the huts and villages of half the globe struggling to break the bonds of mass misery, we pledge our best efforts to help them help themselves . . . because it is right. If a free society cannot help the many who are poor, it cannot save the few who are rich.

(Continued on page 124)

CORE SKILL

Analyze the Relationship between Paragraphs

Paragraphs build from one to another to develop the writer's ideas. Follow these steps to figure out how the relationships between paragraphs are used to express ideas.

1. Read the entire text. Think about the important ideas in the text. Ask yourself: *Are the details in a sequence? Is the writer comparing ideas or things? Does one event cause the next?*
2. Read the first paragraph. Ask yourself: *What are the ideas that the first paragraph presents? Does it open with a strong statement? Does it suggest that a certain structure might follow?*
3. Read the second paragraph. Ask yourself: *Does the second paragraph develop ideas from the first? How?*
4. Read the third paragraph. Then think about how it relates to the second.
5. Follow this same process with the remaining paragraphs.

With a partner, locate a famous speech online, such as President Richard Nixon's Checkers speech and Rev. Dr. Martin Luther King, Jr.'s "I Have a Dream" speech. Look at the first paragraph, and identify the ideas the speaker presents. Then read the rest of the speech to see whether the ideas build on the ideas in the first paragraph. Write a brief explanation of what the relationship is between the paragraphs in the speech.

WRITE TO LEARN

Write a two-paragraph speech about an issue that is important to your community. You might want to write about adding stop signs at busy intersections, having a farmer's market, or making composting mandatory. Be sure that the ideas from the first paragraph are directly connected to ideas in the second paragraph.

21st CENTURY SKILL

Media Literacy

Media literacy is the ability to understand how and why media messages are constructed. Understanding text structure is a helpful tool in media literacy.

When looking at media, such as advertisements, think about what the text is trying to influence you to do, think, or feel. Examine the connection between images and text. What do you notice first—the text or the image? How does the image add to the text? Then read the message and figure out what emotions the text is trying to make you feel. How is the message impacted by the images? Does this emotional appeal of the message impact whether or not you want to buy what the ad is selling? Why or why not?

Find a print advertisement that includes text and an image. With a partner, follow the process above and analyze the ad. Join with another pair and share your analyses.

(Continued from page 123)

> To our sister republics south of our border, we offer a special pledge . . . to assist free men and free governments in casting off the chains of poverty. But this peaceful revolution of hope cannot become the prey of hostile powers. Let all our neighbors know that we shall join with them to oppose aggression or subversion anywhere in the Americas. And let every other power know that this Hemisphere intends to remain the master of its own house.
>
> —From Inaugural Address by John F. Kennedy

Each paragraph addresses a group of nations, beginning with old allies and ending with the new Latin American republics. In the fourth paragraph Kennedy pledges to help these new republics break free from poverty; this idea builds on his promise in the third paragraph to help the poor help themselves. If you wrote this, then you understood how the fourth paragraph built upon the third paragraph and how both fit into the overall thesis of how the United States is committed to helping nations that embrace freedom.

Think about Reading

Directions: Place a checkmark beside the dominant text structure used in Kennedy's speech.

1. _______ time order

2. _______ order of importance

3. _______ compare and contrast

4. _______ cause and effect

5. _______ description

6. _______ problem and solution

Text Structure and Key Ideas

Text structure can be used by a writer to emphasize certain ideas. In literary and informational texts, writers use text structure to place information in strategic places so readers will understand the ideas in the text.

Text Structure in Nonfiction

Nonfiction uses all the text structures listed on pages 122 and 123, such as sequence and cause and effect.

In any text, the writer positions the main idea where it will have the most impact or provide information when needed. For example, a persuasive text often ends with the most important idea. The writer hopes the reader will remember that thought or act on the emotion it evoked. In a problem and solution text, the writer wants you to understand the problem before proposing the solution, so the problem is described and analyzed first. Because you understand the problem already, when you read the solution, you can understand it and its potential effectiveness better because you already understand the problem.

Like longer texts, well-written individual paragraphs are also carefully structured to emphasize important ideas and essential concepts.

Text Structure in Fiction and Poetry

Most novels and stories are written in paragraphs, which are groups of sentences. Poems are made up of **stanzas**, or groups of lines. In novels and stories, each paragraph is built on information from the paragraph before it. Stories contain important elements, including **character** (the people in the story), **setting** (where and when the story takes place), and **plot** (the events of the story). These elements are introduced early so that readers can pay attention to how the characters develop or how the plot progresses. Identifying these story elements helps the reader understand the message in the story.

Directions: Read the following sentences from the beginning of a story. Underline the key idea in the paragraph.

> Francesca walked into the glass elevator and pressed the oval for the top floor. Her heartbeat was a drum in her chest. She was five minutes late for her meeting with Mr. Sanders, and she wasn't looking forward to what he was going to say.

The key idea is at the end. The paragraph introduces the main character and the setting, and the last sentence sets up the conflict. The last sentence also raises readers' expectations about what might happen in the next paragraph.

In a poem, the order of the stanzas is also significant. Like prose, or text written in sentences and paragraphs, a poem may state its main idea in the first stanza or in the last one; the main idea may also be implied. Other stanzas help develop the poet's main idea. Also, like a writer creating paragraphs, a poet positions the ideas in each stanza strategically to aid readers' understanding and to emphasize key ideas.

Directions: Read the passage. Underline words that involve sound. How do these relate to the key ideas in the paragraph?

> We could hear the market before we stepped through the doorway. Oh, the noise! The butchers to the left were trying to drown out the calls of the farmers to the right. We hurried on, leaving the shouts of "Fresh pork" and "Winter apples" behind us and moving into the territory of "Christmas turkeys" and "Local stilton." Sellers hawked their wares, and buyers clamored for attention. There seemed to be no escape from the noise. Then at last, we reached the solace of the bookstalls and stepped inside. Oh, the quiet!

Think about Reading

Directions: After reading about the covered market, answer the following questions. Write your answers in a notebook.

1. What is the key idea the writer wants to communicate about the market and about the bookstalls?
2. Which text structures are used in this passage? How does the writer use structure to emphasize the key ideas?

CORE SKILL

Understand Organization

Text structure impacts the key ideas in a text. In fiction, each paragraph connects to the paragraphs before and after it. In addition, each paragraph must connect to the thesis that governs the entire text.

The structure of a poem is not much different. The poet often introduces a concept in the first stanza, and the other stanzas build on this idea.

Select a poem that you have read before and examine how it is organized. Where does the poet place the topic? Is the main idea stated? If it is, where? How does the poet emphasize important supporting ideas? How do the stanzas build on the earlier stanzas? Write the answers to these questions in your notebook.

Discuss your poem and analysis with a partner.

Summary

Writers choose different structures—sequence, cause and effect, compare and contrast, description, and problem and solution—for different types of texts. Prose texts are organized in paragraphs, and poems are organized in stanzas. Writers use structure to influence how readers perceive key ideas.

Vocabulary Review

Directions: For each key term or vocabulary word, draw a line to its definition.

1. setting	**a.** notice a difference
2. character	**b.** group of lines in a poem
3. distinguish	**c.** the series of events that make up a story
4. stanza	**d.** the time and place in which story's action occurs
5. plot	**e.** a person in a novel, story, or play

Skill Review

Directions: Read the passage below. Then choose the best answer to each question.

On the first day of tenth grade at Sun Valley High, Sheila met Georgia—a brown-haired girl with deep brown eyes who would soon become her best friend. They had both lived in suburban Indianapolis for three years without meeting each other, and they had both moved to California. Since their parents were in the military, they were used to moving around a lot. Even though they had so much in common, they met each other only when they set foot inside Mr. Rivera's trigonometry class. The bad news about Mr. Rivera—how he assigned hours of homework every night and gave tests that made people cry—had been circulated around school before they reached the classroom door.

A few months into their new friendship, Georgia told Sheila she had terrible news. Sheila incorrectly assumed that Georgia had failed Mr. Rivera's most recent quiz on triangles, but Georgia's swollen eyes told a different story. Georgia said that she and her family would be moving again. Sheila sat, frozen, at the cafeteria table that had become theirs. She didn't know what she would do without Georgia.

1. How does the information in the second paragraph develop information from the first paragraph?

A. The second paragraph provides more information about the setting from the first paragraph.

B. The second paragraph continues introducing characters from the first paragraph.

C. The second paragraph introduces character talked about in the first paragraph.

D. The second paragraph presents the plot that the first paragraph suggests.

2. Which story elements does the writer introduce in the first paragraph?

A. character and plot

B. character, setting, and plot

C. setting and plot

D. setting and character

3. Which text structure best describes the way the passage is organized?

A. sequence

B. compare and contrast

C. problem and solution

D. cause and effect

Skill Practice

Directions: Read the passage below. Then choose the best answer to each question.

Popular award-winning author Sherman Alexie was born on the Spokane Indian Reservation in Wellpinit, Washington in 1966. His mother was a Spokane Indian, and his father was a Coeur d'Alene Indian. While Alexie was young and attending reservation schools, he had a life-changing moment. He opened one of the textbooks assigned to him and saw his mother's name written in it. At that moment, Alexie was determined not to let his future be determined by the limited resources of reservation schools. By the time he was of high-school age, he attended school off the reservation in nearby Rearden, Washington. Upon graduation, he received a scholarship to Gonzaga University. Two years later, he transferred to Washington State University in Pullman and enrolled in pre-med courses.

While at Washington State, Alexie discovered his love for poetry and writing instead of medicine. To reflect these interests, he changed his major to American Studies. Soon afterward, he received the Washington State Arts Commission Poetry Fellowship and the National Endowment for the Arts Poetry Fellowship. Alexie's writing focuses on Native American life on and off the reservation, and many of his pieces draw on his own upbringing on the Spokane Indian Reservation. Alexie wrote several short-story collections, including *The Lone Ranger and Tonto Fistfight in Heaven* in 1993 and *Reservation Blues* in 1995. He has written many award-winning novels, poetry collections, and short-story collections. His young-adult novel *The Absolutely True Diary of a Part-Time Indian* won the prestigious National Book Award in 2007.

1. What is the relationship between the first and second paragraph?

A. The second paragraph discusses Alexie's writing, and the first paragraph discusses Alexie's early life.

B. The second paragraph discusses Alexie's awards, and the first paragraph discusses Alexie's education.

C. The second paragraph discusses Alexie's publications, and the first paragraph discusses Alexie's parents.

D. The second paragraph discusses Alexie's poetry, and the first paragraph discusses Alexie's novels.

2. Which text structure best describes the way this passage is organized?

A. cause and effect

B. problem and solution

C. time order

D. order of importance

Writing Practice

Directions: Find a news article in a print or online newspaper about an issue in your community, your state, the country, or the world. First write the problem. Then write a paragraph describing three possible solutions to that problem using the problem and solution text structure. Be sure that each sentence connects to the next sentence.

LESSON 4.3 Analyze the Effects of Transitional and Signal Words

LESSON OBJECTIVES

- Locate transitions between words, phrases, and sentences
- Analyze how signal words impact understanding

CORE SKILLS

- Determine the Relationship among Ideas
- Analyze Transitions between Paragraphs

Key Terms

signal words
words and phrases that clarify relationships between ideas within and between sentences and paragraphs

transitions
movement from one idea to the next within and between paragraphs

Vocabulary

conclusion
final section of a text; an ending

specific
concrete; distinct

Key Concept

Writers use certain words and phrases to link ideas within sentences and between sentences.

Think about the last time you gave someone directions. You probably said things like "Next, turn right on Smithson. When you reach the second traffic light, turn left. Then, look for a large gate on the right." Words such as next, when, and then are called signal words. Even if you're not aware of it, you use signal words all the time. Signal words clarify the relationships between ideas. When you are telling stories, giving directions, or explaining a process, signal words and phrases help you show how your ideas relate to one another and help your listener understand those relationships correctly.

Locating Transitions

Well-written paragraphs lead the reader from one idea to the next. One way a writer marks a **transition**, or movement from one idea to the next, is by using **signal words** and phrases. Signal words and phrases highlight and clarify **specific**, or distinct, relationships within and between sentences and paragraphs. These relationships include: addition, time order, relative location, relative importance, cause and effect, comparison, contrast, example, and **conclusion**. A conclusion is the final part of a text or a summation.

A signal word is a clue that a shift is taking place in the text from one idea to the next. Here are some common signal words and phrases by category.

Signal Words

Addition: *additionally, also, besides, in addition, moreover, too*

In addition to moving to Wisconsin, Carmen started a new job.

Time order: *after, as soon as, at first, before, finally, first, last, immediately, meanwhile, often, next, when*

- After winning the lottery, Tariq bought a new car.

(Continued on page 129)

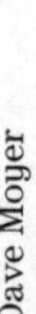

(Continued from page 128)

Relative Location: *around, at the top, below, beside, beyond, in front of, inside, nearby, opposite, outside, over, there, within*

- Inside the house, a large dinner table is the first thing you will see.

Relative Importance: *first, more importantly, most important, primarily*

- There are many reasons for researching a prospective employer, and the most important one is to know whether you really want to work there.

Cause and Effect: *as a result, because, consequently, for that reason, if . . . then, since, so, therefore*

- As a result of cutting down trees for many years, forests are dwindling.

Comparison: *also, both, just as, like, likewise, neither, similarly*

- Both teams played well in the tournament.

Contrast: *but, even so, however, in spite of, nevertheless, on the other hand, unlike*

- Unlike apples and oranges, bananas do not grow on trees.

Example: *for example, for instance, including, such as*

- Many sports teams are named after animals; for example, two high school football teams are the Dolphins and the Jaguars.

Conclusion: *consequently, finally, in brief, in conclusion, lastly, thus*

- In conclusion, voters should understand all candidates' platforms before casting their ballots.

Directions: Read the passage, and circle the signal words in it.

Anyone can walk all the way from Georgia to Maine on a long-distance trail called the Appalachian Trail. Really determined hikers can cover the distance in a single summer if they begin in early spring and hike straight through until October. The well-marked Appalachian Trail has been enjoyed by serious hikers for decades. Similarly, the newer, but even more spectacular Pacific Crest Trail attracts hikers on the West Coast. It also runs for thousands of miles and offers a remarkable outdoor experience for hardy walkers. Consequently, both trails are perfect for seasoned hikers to enjoy the majesty of the great outdoors.

If you circled *similarly, but, also,* and *consequently, both* you have correctly identified the signal words.

CORE SKILL

Determine the Relationship among Ideas

To figure out the relationship among ideas in a text, follow this procedure:

1. Locate transitions by identifying signal words. Signal words don't always come at the beginning of a sentence; sometimes they are in the middle.
2. Decide which type of relationship the signal words indicate. Does it show a comparison? Does it reveal a change in time?

Find a document, either in print or online, that describes a complex national problem. Using the procedure above, locate the transitions. Then decide which types of relationship the signal words indicate.

WRITE TO LEARN

Write a paragraph describing what you like to do on a free day. Use transitions and signal words that show time relationships. Make sure that your paragraph contains at least six activities. Be sure to use time order signal words such as *after, as soon as, at first, before, finally, first, last, immediately, meanwhile, often, next,* and *when.*

CORE SKILL

Analyze Transitions between Paragraphs

Transitions reveal important relationships between sentences and paragraphs. When transitions come between paragraphs, the writer wants you to think about how ideas in one paragraph are connected to the other.

A transition can present a cause and then shift to an effect. It can present contrasting information in two or more paragraphs and indicate this relationship by using signal words or phrases that explain the contrast. It might move from a less important point to a more important one, or move from one step in a process to the next.

Find an informational text in print or online. Ask yourself: *What relationship exists between the paragraphs?* Make a note of your answer. If there are signal words that mark the transitions, underline them. If there are no signal words, write how the transitions are expressed.

Think about Reading

Directions: Read the sentences, and underline the signal words.

1. Reading the paragraph below will answer some of your questions.
2. Three days after the flood, the family was allowed back in the house.
3. Low humidity, high temperatures, and strong winds can cause forest fires.
4. Caffeine can be found in many beverages, including coffee, tea, and cola.

Analyzing Transitions

Regardless of where transitions come in a passage, they mark a place where you should stop and pay attention to how the text is changing. Although writers often highlight transitions using signal words or phrases to alert the reader that a new idea is being introduced, this is not always the case.

For instance, a writer might talk about the physical size of New York City in one sentence and the physical size of Los Angeles in the next. To link the two sentences, a signal phrase such as "in contrast" might be used. However, even if the signal phrase is not used, the transition should still be apparent because the sentences about the subjects being compared are next to each other and the points of comparison are addressed in a similar order.

Look at the example below. As you read it, ask yourself: *What relationships exist between the ideas? How are the transitions expressed?*

> New York is an island city with nowhere to go; it has to grow upward rather than outward. Surrounded by land, Los Angeles hugs the ground and just continues spreading.

The first sentence discusses New York. It begins with a geographical fact about New York City—that it is built on an island. After the semicolon, the sentence states a result of this: that New York has built tall buildings to expand on the island.

The second sentence discusses Los Angeles. Again, it begins with a geographical fact—that the city is surrounded by land. As with the sentence about New York, the sentence about Los Angeles explains the result of the city's geography: It has grown outward rather than upward.

The contrast is not made explicit through the use of a signal word, but the order of the ideas and the placement of the two ideas beside one another make the transitions clear.

As you read, look for transitions and how the author clarifies them. Examine any signal words or phrases to see how they help you understand transitions.

Directions: As you read "Maya Lin's Vision," underline the signal words that indicate transitions in the text, and determine what category each belongs to.

Maya Lin's Vision

When the average person thinks of a memorial or a monument, stone statues of generals on horses or renderings of famous buildings in American history immediately come to mind. But Maya Ying Lin changed all previous perceptions of what a memorial should be. A 21-year-old architecture student at Yale University at the time, Lin entered a nationwide competition to design the Vietnam Veterans War Memorial in 1980. Her concept of "a park within a park" beat 1,421 other entries.

Unlike other memorials, Lin's memorial consists of two long walls that meet at the center. In addition, the memorial is made of polished black granite. Its surface acts as a mirror, allowing visitors to see their reflections among the etched names of more than 58,000 soldiers who lost their lives. Furthermore, the memorial is invisible from the nearby street because it is built into the ground. Only when approaching it can you see the unique design concept in its intended form. The wall starts small, beginning with the first casualty in 1959. It expands into the ground as the number of deaths reaches its apex. Then it gradually gets smaller again, ending with the war's final death in 1975.

Think about Reading

Directions: Reread the passage "Maya Lin's Vision." In a notebook, write a paragraph that answers these questions.

1. What type of relationship do the signal words in the first sentence of the first paragraph establish?
2. What transition does the signal word "unlike" emphasize?

Summary

Certain words and phrases signal transitions between ideas in a text. They are designed to help the reader understand how those ideas connect. Transitions can occur within sentences or paragraphs or between them. Signal words and phrases express relationships about time order, relative location, comparison, contrast, cause and effect, example, order of importance, and conclusion. Analyzing these terms helps you understand a text by identifying the relationships between ideas.

WORKPLACE SKILL

Use Signal Words to Organize Information

A flowchart is often used to illustrate the transitions in workplace processes. Look at the flowchart below. The steps are connected by arrows to describe the relationship between the steps. If you wanted to describe the relationship between the first two steps in words, you might say, "After the project is assigned, the timeline is created." The signal word *after* takes the place of the arrow in the chart.

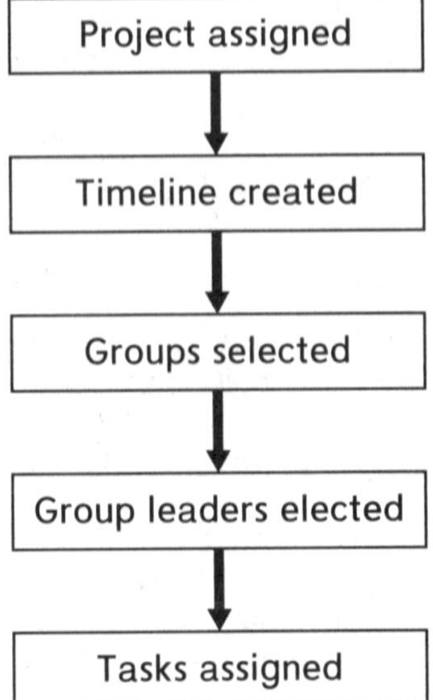

Signal words are used in workplace documents to organize information. Paying attention to them can help you decide what to do first. Signal words can also help you understand which ideas are the most important.

Work with a partner to create a paragraph describing the process shown in the flowchart above. Use signal words to introduce the steps.

Vocabulary Review

Directions: Draw a line from each key term or vocabulary word to its definition.

1. signal words	**a.** movement between one idea and the next within and between paragraphs
2. specific	**b.** final section of a text; an ending
3. transitions	**c.** concrete; distinct
4. conclusion	**d.** words and phrases that clarify relationships within and between sentences

Skill Review

Directions: Read the passage below. Then complete the activities.

Student Council President: Candidate #1, Sarah

Candidate Platform

First, I hope to increase student participation at all school events such as pep rallies, sporting events, and formal dances. The way I hope to do this is by keeping a website and encouraging club leaders to update it every week. The only way to participate is to know when things are happening, and I hope to keep you informed about everything.

Second, we all know that cafeteria food leaves a lot to be desired. Since my part-time job is at Burger Heaven, I've already talked to them about delivering food to the cafeteria every Tuesday. All the money we collect from the burger sale will be used for semi-formal and formal dances.

Finally, the system for selection of honors and advanced classes is outdated. Unlike general ed classes, which everyone has to take, honors classes should be scheduled differently. My proposal is that students who have averages of A- or higher should receive preferential treatment. They should be allowed to register for these selective classes first and leave the rest of the spots open for the general lottery. Consequently, the environment in those classes will be more conducive to learning.

In conclusion, I know that I will be a forward-thinking leader who will take us into next year with vision and enthusiasm. Next Wednesday, please remember to vote for Sarah Reed-Finnegan. Sarah is your choice!

1. Why does the writer use the signal phrase "in conclusion" at the beginning of the last paragraph?

A. to state why Sarah is running for student council president

B. to give another example of Sarah's school leadership

C. to show that Sarah is coming to a close and restating her qualities

D. to compare Sarah's qualities with her opponents' qualities

2. The signal word __________ in the second paragraph transitions to a cause explaining why Sarah can replace the cafeteria food, and the rest of the paragraph is about how Burger Heaven can support the school.

Skill Practice

Directions: Read the passage below. Then complete the activities.

Trial by Jury

A trial by jury is one of the most interesting facets of the United States justice system. Most citizens over 18 are eligible to serve on a jury, although there are certain factors that render a potential juror ineligible for service. Prior felony conviction and the inability to communicate in English are two of these.

The first step in serving as a juror is receiving a jury duty summons by mail. If selected to serve, you must report to the courthouse, where you may be called to join a juror pool. A juror pool is a group of potential jurors from which the trial jurors will be drawn. Juror selection, which is a process of determining individual jurors' suitability, may take a day or longer, depending on the nature of the case to be tried. Missing jury duty can result in fines and possibly jail time. For that reason, it is important for every citizen to comply with the jury summons. However, jury duty is not only legally required, it is also a civic duty that guarantees civil rights.

When selected to be on a jury, jurors hear statements by both sides: the prosecution and the defense. The prosecution's job is to present the case against the defendant and convince the jurors of guilt beyond a reasonable doubt. Jurors can only convict when the prosecution has proved beyond a shadow of a doubt that the accused is responsible for the crime. Therefore, the prosecution's evidence must clearly and definitively prove that the defendant is guilty.

In contrast, the defense team does not have to prove the defendant's innocence. Instead, it is the defense's job to cast doubt on the prosecution's case. To do this, the defense may try to poke holes in the prosecution's arguments. *Could someone else have committed this crime? Is the witness sure that the defendant was the person fleeing the scene?* The defense presents questions such as these and offers its own witnesses to support its theory of the crime.

When the prosecution and defense have presented their closing arguments, the jury deliberates until they reach a verdict. In all criminal cases, the jury must unanimously agree on that decision. When the jury has reached a verdict, all parties are called back into the courtroom, where the foreperson reads the verdict. Finally, the judge thanks the jury for its service, and the jurors are dismissed.

In conclusion, jury selection and service are essential if the justice system is to function properly. Juries ensure due process of the law and that every defendant receives a fair trial, judged by a group of his or her peers.

1. The transition between the second and third paragraphs is a __________ relationship, and the transition between the third and fourth paragraphs is a __________ relationship.

2. Which sentence from the passage contains a signal word that shows a conclusion?

A. "A trial by jury is one of the most interesting facets of the United States justice system."

B. "Missing jury duty can result in fines and possibly jail time."

C. "The defense presents questions such as these and offers its own witnesses to support its theory of the crime."

D. "Finally, the judge thanks the jury for its service, and the jurors are dismissed."

Writing Practice

Find an article in a print or online source about a war that the United States was involved in. In a paragraph, write five major events that led to the war. Use signal words and phrases to highlight transitions between ideas.

Directions: Read the following passage. Then choose the best answer to questions 1 through 3.

Daniel Inouye was born in Honolulu, Hawaii in 1924. Like many other immigrants of their time, his paternal grandparents moved from Japan to Hawaii to work on sugar plantations. Inouye's parents recognized the importance of education for their children starting at an early age. During that time, however, pathways for Asian American children to succeed in education were limited. In his late teens, Inouye discovered an interest in medicine and decided that he wanted to be a surgeon. When he was 17, Inouye was volunteering for the Red Cross during the attack on Pearl Harbor. Although he and his friends wanted to defend the country they called home, the United States didn't allow American-born children of Japanese immigrants the opportunity to serve in the military. Inouye sensed the depth of this injustice. He and others petitioned the White House to change their policy. Finally, the United States allowed Japanese-American men to serve in segregated units. When Inouye received the news that he would be allowed to serve, he dropped out of his pre-med program at the University of Hawaii and joined the 442nd Regimental Combat Team; Inouye's unit was comprised of all Japanese-American soldiers.

Inouye served in World War II starting in 1943. In 1945, he was wounded in combat, and surgeons had to amputate his right arm. This injury ended Inouye's dream of becoming a surgeon, but it opened the door to a new opportunity. When Inouye returned to Hawaii, he continued studying at the University of Hawaii, but he switched his major to government and economics. After graduating in 1950, he attended George Washington University Law School. He returned to Hawaii and began practicing law, eventually winning a spot as the first U.S. Representative from Hawaii after Hawaii became a state in 1959. In 1962, Inouye was elected to the United States Senate. He served a long and illustrious career in the Senate, serving in chairman roles on committees including the Senate Intelligence Committee, the Senate Committee on Indian Affairs, a committee investigating the Iran-Contra Affair, and the Senate Committee on Appropriations.

In 2000, Inouye and 21 other members of the 442nd Regimental Combat Team were awarded the National Medal of Honor—the nation's highest military award. Soon thereafter, he was elected to his ninth Senate term. When Senator Robert Byrd of West Virginia died in 2010, Inouye became the President Pro Tempore of the Senate—the third in line to succeed the president after the Vice President and the Speaker of the House.

When Inouye died in December 2012 at the age of 88, he became the Senate's second-longest serving member, holding the office for 49 years. After his death, Inouye was awarded the Presidential Medal of Freedom—the nation's highest civilian honor.

1. How does the information in the third paragraph connect to the information in the first two paragraphs?

A. The third paragraph provides information about Inouye's life in the Senate, and this relates to the first two paragraphs about Inouye's path to the Senate.

B. The third paragraph provides information about Inouye's later achievements, and the first two paragraphs show the early successes that led to these later achievements.

C. The third paragraph provides information about the aftermath of World War II, and the first two paragraphs describe Inouye's role in World War II.

D. The third paragraph describes the awards that the 442nd Regimental Combat Team received, and the first two paragraphs describe Inouye's role on this team.

2. Why does the author include this sentence in the first paragraph: "Inouye sensed the depth of this injustice"?

A. to show what caused Inouye to petition the White House to change its policy

B. to show the effect of Inouye serving in the Red Cross

C. to show the problem that Inouye faced while serving with the 442nd Regimental Combat Team

D. to contrast Inouye's views on the White House with his views on the Red Cross

3. What relationship does the word *like* signal in the first paragraph?

   A. a contrast between Inouye's grandparents' life on a sugar plantation and Inouye's work in the Senate

   B. a comparison between Inouye's grandparents' life in Japan and Inouye's life in Hawaii

   C. a comparison between Inouye's grandparents and other immigrants from Japan

   D. a contrast between the sugar plantations in Hawaii and sugar plantations in Japan

Directions: Read the following passage. Then choose the best answer to questions 4 and 5.

Franklin was a rather large man, and is supposed to have been about five feet ten inches in height. In his youth he was stout, and in old age corpulent and heavy, with rounded shoulders. The portraits of him reveal a very vigorous-looking man, with a thick upper arm and a figure which, even in old age, was full and rounded. In fact, this rounded contour is his most striking characteristic, as the angular outline is the characteristic of Lincoln. Franklin's figure was a series of harmonious curves, which make pictures of him always pleasing. These curves extended over his head and even to the lines of his face, softening the expression, slightly veiling the iron resolution, and entirely consistent with the wide sympathies, varied powers, infinite shrewdness, and vast experience which we know he possessed.

In his earliest portrait as a youth of twenty he looks as if his bones were large; but in later portraits this largeness of bone which he might have had from his Massachusetts origin is not so evident. He was, however, very muscular, and prided himself on it. When he was a young printer, as he tells us in his Autobiography, he could carry with ease a large form of letters in each hand up and down stairs. In his old age, when past eighty, he is described as insisting on lifting unaided heavy books and dictionaries to show the strength he still retained.

—From *The True Benjamin Franklin* by George Sydney Fisher

4. Which text structures are used in this passage?

   A. problem and solution and cause and effect

   B. compare and contrast and description

   C. problem and solution and compare and contrast

   D. sequence and cause and effect

5. Why did the writer include the second paragraph of the passage?

   A. to describe how Franklin looked as a young man

   B. to compare and contrast Franklin's appearance and abilities as a young and older man

   C. to show how Franklin solved the problem of carrying heavy letters upstairs

   D. to show the effect of Franklin's physical activities as a young man

Directions: Read the following passage. Then choose the best answer to questions 6 and 7.

My Neighbour's Garden

Why in my neighbour's garden
Are the flowers more sweet than mine?
I had never such bloom of roses,
Such yellow and pink woodbine.

Why in my neighbour's garden
Are the fruits all red and gold,
While here the grapes are bitter
That hang for my fingers' hold?

Why in my neighbour's garden
Do the birds all fly to sing?
Over the fence between us
One would think 'twas always spring.

I thought my own wide garden
Once more sweet and fair than all,
Till I saw the gold and crimson
Just over my neighbour's wall.

But now I want his thrushes,
And now I want his vine,
If I cannot have his cherries
That grow more red than mine.

The serpent 'neath his apples
Will tempt me to my fall,
And then—I'll steal my neighbour's fruit
Across the garden wall.

—From "My Neighbour's Garden"
by Dora Sigerson

6. Which text structure best describes the first and second stanzas?

A. cause and effect

B. compare and contrast

C. order of events

D. problem and solution

7. Repeating the question "Why in my neighbour's garden. . .?" helps the poet emphasize the idea that the

A. speaker needs to tend his or her garden.

B. neighbour works in his or her garden a lot.

C. neighbour and the speaker aren't friends.

D. speaker in the poem is feeling envious.

Directions: Read the following passage. Then complete activities 8 through 10.

Report of Brigadier General T. J. "Stonewall" Jackson CS Army, commanding First Brigade, Army of the Shenandoah Headquarters First Brigade, Camp near Manassas, Va., July 23, 1861

(1) Major: I have the honor to submit the following report of the operations of my brigade on the 21st.

(2) About 4 in the morning I received notice from General Longstreet that he needed a re-enforcement of two regiments, which were accordingly ordered.

(3) Immediately I received an order from General Beauregard to move to the support of General Bonham. Next to move the support to General Cocke. Finally, to take such position as would enable me to re-enforce either, as circumstances might require.

(4) Meanwhile, in the position last indicated, I received a request from General Cocke to guard the stone bridge, and immediately moved forward to effect the object in view.

(5) Subsequently ascertaining that General Bee, who was on the left of our line, was hard pressed, I marched to his assistance, notifying him at the same time that I was advancing to his support. But, before arriving within cannon range of the enemy, I met General Bee's forces falling back. I continued to advance with the understanding that he would form in my rear. His battery, under its dauntless commander, Captain Imboden, reversed and advanced with my brigade.

(Continued on page 137)

(Continued from page 136)

(6) . . . General Bee, with his rallied troops, soon marched to my support and as re-enforcements continued to arrive General Beauregard posted them so as to strengthen the flanks of my brigade. . . . The brigade, in connection with other troops, took seven field pieces in addition to the battery captured by Colonel Cummings. . . .

Your most obedient servant,

T. J. JACKSON,
Brigadier-General, Provisional Army, Confederate States

8. The signal word *immediately* at the beginning of the third paragraph shows the following relationship between the second and third paragraphs:

A. a change in time between events

B. a contrast between the events

C. an effect of the causes presented in the second paragraph

D. a conclusion in the third paragraph as a result of the second paragraph

9. Which signal words or phrases does the writer use in the sixth paragraph?

A. *soon* and *in addition*

B. *continued* and *posted*

C. *in connection* and *took*

D. *with* and *other*

10. The text structure of this piece is __________. Three signal words that are specific to its text structure are __________, __________, and __________.

Check Your Understanding

On the following chart, circle the number of any item you answered incorrectly. In the third column, you will see the pages that you can review to study the content covered in the question. Pay particular attention to reviewing those lessons in which you missed half or more of the questions.

Lesson	Core Skill	Item Number(s)	Review Page(s)
Lesson 4.1: Analyze the Development of Ideas	Recognize Organization	4, 5	116–117
	Analyze Text Structure	10	118–119
Lesson 4.2: Analyze How Structure Impacts Key Ideas	Analyze the Relationship between Paragraphs	1, 10	122–124
	Understand Organization	5, 6, 7	124–125
Lesson 4.3: Analyze the Effect of Transitional and Signal Words	Determine the Relationship among Ideas	2, 3, 4, 9, 10	128–129
	Analyze Transitions between Paragraphs	8, 9	130–131

WRITE ABOUT A Current Events Issue

Research a current events topic such as global warming, genetically modified crops, or campaign funding. After investigating your topic, take a position on it. Write an essay that

1. describes a current events issue
2. states your opinion about it
3. supports your opinion with research.

BEFORE YOU WRITE Create an Outline

Use an outline based on the format below to help you organize the ideas in your essay. In your outline, you will need to take a position on one side of your current events issue. Your opinion will be the thesis of your essay. Write your opinion next to the word "Thesis" in your outline. In the "Essay Points" section, write the points that you plan to use to support your opinion. Determine two or three points you want to make in your essay and write each sequentially next to the capital letters (first point next to A., second point next to B., and so on). Below each point, write facts, details, statistics, quotes, or paraphrases from your research that supports the point.

I. Thesis [statement of your position]

II. Essay Points

  A. [first point]

    1. facts, details, statistics, quotes, or paraphrases (add numbers for additional evidence)

  B. [second point]

    1. facts, details, statistics, quotes, or paraphrases

  C. [third point]

    1. facts details, statistics, quotes, or paraphrases

When you have finished, ask yourself: *Do all the points support an aspect of my position? Does all the evidence support the points? Does the order in the outline match the order that makes sense for my essay?* If all these answers are yes, then you have a good outline.

TIP Match Verb Tense and Sentence Structure in Paraphrases

To paraphrase means to use your own words to restate someone else's ideas. Paraphrasing is an important part of writing original work because your essay should not contain direct text from another source unless it is identified as a quotation. When you incorporate paraphrases into your essay, changing the wording may also require you to make changes in verb tense and sentence structure. Look at this sentence:

Brown states, "One day, genetically modified foods will make up most of the food supply."

Now look at these possible paraphrases:

- *In the future, says Brown, our diet will consist mainly of genetically modified foods.* (Despite the changes in wording, changes in sentence structure are minimal and the tense remains the same.)
- *In 1986 Brown predicted that the majority of our food would someday come from genetically modified sources.* (The date at the beginning requires the past tense throughout the sentence.)
- *According to Brown, we can all expect to be eating mostly genetically modified foods in the future.* (Changes in sentence structure include an infinitive phrase, which includes the word "to" plus a verb.)

WHILE YOU WRITE Explain Your Position Clearly and Logically

Now you are ready to begin writing. Begin by thinking about your evidence and reviewing your outline.

Use your thesis statement to make your perspective clear to the reader. For example, *Food companies that use genetically modified ingredients must label them to protect the consumer.* Notice that this sentence makes clear the topic (genetically modified foods), the writer's opinion (food companies should have to label these foods), and the perspective (health).

Next, examine your outline. Look at the order the topics and the evidence are listed in. Is it logical? How will it affect the reader's understanding? Does the most important idea come last or first? Change the order if necessary to make the most effective presentation.

Then write your essay, using the outline as a guide. As you write, make sure the structure you use reflects the relationships among the ideas in your essay. Use transition words to make the structure clear to the readers. Ask yourself: *What's the relationship between my pieces of evidence? Is it a time order relationship? In a time order structure, I can use transition words such as* first, next, after, *and* finally. *Is it a cause-and-effect relationship? If so, I can use transition words such as* since, so, *and* as a result. Ask yourself the same questions about the relationships between the paragraphs. Use transition words to make the relationships between your sentences and paragraphs clear to the reader.

Conclude your essay with a restatement of the issue. Summarize your main points, and restate your position.

TIP Remember to . . . Cite Your Sources

When you include ideas, facts, statistics, or words from your research, tell the reader where that information comes from. When you cite a source, you assure your readers that your evidence is valid. Provide them with information on how they can find that source to read more.

In-text citations are citations that you place in the body of your essay. When citing a print book or article with one author, you must use parentheses, the author's last name, the date of publication, and the page number. Here's an example of an in-text citation from a print book:

- "Raising large amounts of private funds for a political campaign is problematic because it makes some individuals think that they own the candidate" (Ohlen 2003, 18).

Notice that the citation comes after the quotation but before the period.

AFTER YOU WRITE Check Your Work

Reread the writing assignment. Then read your essay carefully three times.

The first time you read, ask yourself whether you have completed the writing assignment correctly. Have you (1) researched a current events topic, (2) stated your opinion, and (3) supported your opinion with evidence from your research? Is your evidence thorough and complete? Does the organization of your points make sense?

Then read your essay again. Did you use appropriate text structure, including transitional words and phrases within and between paragraphs? Did you cite your sources?

Read the essay one last time. Did you use correct grammar, spelling, and punctuation? Do you see any errors? Did you type the words you meant to use?

Before submitting your essay, have another student read it and provide you with feedback.

Chapter 5

Assess How Point of View Shapes Informational Text

Have you ever read an article that you thought was factual, only to realize partway through that the story was made up for the audience's entertainment? Readers' comprehension of a text isn't complete without understanding the author's purpose for writing it. Whatever an author writes—a news story, a memo, a novel, or an advertisement—he or she has a purpose for writing and a point of view about the topic. The author's point of view affects the text's content, structure, and style.

Ingram Publishing

In this chapter you will study these topics:

Lesson 5.1

Determine Author's Purpose and Point of View

Whether it is to entertain, inform, or persuade, all writers have a reason for writing and a particular way of looking at their topics. The reason for writing is the author's purpose, and his or her attitude toward the topic is the point of view. Learn how to determine the author's purpose and point of view in a text.

Lesson 5.2

Analyze How Author's Purpose Determines Structure

Texts are structured in a variety of ways. For example, many historical texts are organized chronologically, and many advertisements present a problem followed by a solution. Learn about the relationship between the author's purpose and the structure of a text.

Lesson 5.3

Infer Author's Purpose

Although some authors state their purpose for writing, others do not. If the purpose is not stated, how can you figure it out? Learn how to use evidence from a text, along with your prior knowledge of the topic, to infer the author's purpose.

Lesson 5.4

Analyze How Authors Differentiate Their Positions

Writers often acknowledge an opposing viewpoint when expressing their own perspective or opinion. Why would a writer present contradictory evidence? Learn how authors support their point of view by contrasting it with others.

Lesson 5.5

Analyze Author's Intention and Effect

How do writers use language to communicate effectively and produce a desired effect? Learn about the choices authors make to achieve their purpose and engage readers.

Goal Setting

When you read, it is useful to know why an author has written the text and how he or she feels about the topic. Think about types of texts you commonly read or listen to. How can this chapter increase your understanding of texts such as news articles, advertisements, and political speeches?

Why is it important to be able to identify a writer or speaker's purpose and point of view? How can this ability benefit you when reading communications at work from a supervisor, a coworker, or a customer?

LESSON 5.1 Determine Author's Purpose and Point of View

LESSON OBJECTIVES

- Identify the author's purpose
- Identify the author's point of view

CORE SKILLS

- Determine Author's Purpose
- Establish Point of View

Key Terms

author's purpose
the author's reason for writing a text

point of view
a writer's attitude toward a topic

Vocabulary

implicitly
not directly

neutral
not favoring one side or position

Key Concept

Authors have a reason for writing, and they often have an opinion about the topic of their writing.

Think about an article you have read recently. What was its purpose? Was it intended to inform you about a topic, to persuade you to think or do something, or to entertain you? What was the author's attitude toward the topic? Was it positive, negative, or neither? Every text is written for one or more reasons, and in many cases the author expresses an attitude about the topic. In persuasive writing, such as a letter to the editor, the author's attitude is generally apparent to the reader; however, in other forms of writing, the writer's attitude may be less obvious.

Identifying an Author's Purpose

The **author's purpose** is his or her reason for writing something. The reason might be to entertain, to persuade, or to inform readers. When an author writes to entertain, he or she often includes detailed descriptions and figurative language to make the text more enjoyable for readers. An author who writes to persuade provides reasons why the reader should agree with his or her opinion. If the author's purpose is to inform, his or her writing should be straightforward and clear.

Identifying an author's purpose helps you understand and evaluate different kinds of text. As you read, ask yourself: *Why did the author write this?* Keep that question in mind as you read the following passage.

> Your heart rate tells you how many times per minute your heart is beating and can vary depending on your activities. To determine your heart rate, find your pulse by lightly pressing on the inside of your wrist or the side of your neck. Your pulse is the gentle beat you can feel just below your skin. Count the beats for six seconds and multiply that number by 10 to calculate your heart rate.

To identify the author's purpose, look for clues in the text. The text contains facts about what a heart rate is and information about how to find it. Facts are clues that the author's purpose is to inform. Another clue is that the writing is clear and straightforward. The text contains no evidence that the author is trying to entertain or persuade the reader. Therefore, you can determine that the author's purpose is to inform.

BananaStock/Jupiterimages

Keep in mind that an author sometimes has more than one purpose for writing. For example, an informative article may also be entertaining.

Directions Read the following passage, and write a few sentences explaining what the author's purposes are and how you identified them.

> Only the scrape of our boots against rock and loose pebbles broke the silence as we moved deeper into the cave, carved into limestone more than 300 million years ago. Breathing had become an effort. The air, long stagnant from being kept in this tomblike cave, burned our throats and left a rancid taste. Foul-smelling and heavy, it stuck in our lungs after each intake of breath. The miner's lamps on our helmets cut a thin slice out of the thick, black gloom around us. It was hard to believe that the caves had first been mapped back in 1872.

If you wrote that the author's purposes are to inform and to entertain, you understand that the author includes facts in order to inform as well as vivid details and figurative language in order to entertain.

Directions: Read the passage below and write the author's purposes. Back up your claim with evidence from the text.

> The Portuguese explorer Ferdinand Magellan should be known as the greatest navigator of all time. The fleet under his command discovered the Strait of Magellan, a passageway at the tip of South America that connects the Atlantic and Pacific Oceans. Although he died before the voyage was completed, Magellan's navigational planning helped his crew finish their trip around the world. Magellan's discovery of the Strait of Magellan helped other explorers learn more about the Pacific Ocean. The most important result of his long voyage was proving that the world is round.

If you wrote that the author's purposes are to inform and to persuade, you understand that the passage contains facts and persuasive language.

Think about Reading

Directions: Read the following sentences from the passage above. Next to each sentence, circle either *I* for *inform* or *P* for *persuade* to indicate which purpose it serves.

1. I P The Portuguese explorer Ferdinand Magellan should be known as the greatest navigator of all time.
2. I P The fleet under his command discovered the Strait of Magellan.
3. I P The most important result of his long voyage was proving that the world is round.

CORE SKILL

Determine Author's Purpose

To determine an author's purpose for writing, follow this procedure:

1. As you read, ask yourself: *Why did the author write this?*
2. Look for facts, which are clues that the author's purpose is to inform.
3. Look for calls to action, such as *must* and *should*, that are supported by evidence. These are clues that the author's purpose is to persuade.
4. Look for figurative language and other literary techniques that appeal to readers' imaginations. This is a clue that the author's purpose is to entertain.

Reread the passage about cave exploration. Underline the text that indicates that one purpose of the passage is to entertain.

WRITE TO LEARN

What would the paragraph about cave exploration be like if it were written only to inform? Rewrite the passage without the language meant to entertain the reader.

CORE SKILL

Establish Point of View

The author's point of view can be expressed explicitly or implicitly. Recognizing whether the author's attitude is positive or negative can help you infer an implicit point of view.

To determine an author's point of view, follow this procedure:

1. Read the entire text.
2. Ask yourself: *Did the author express a personal opinion?* If so, that is his or her point of view.
3. If the author did not state an opinion, ask yourself: *Did the author choose words that express a negative or a positive attitude?* Use this information to help you establish the author's opinion.

Find a letter to the editor in a print or an online newspaper. With a partner, determine the letter writer's point of view. Then discuss whether the point of view is explicit or implicit.

Recognizing an Author's Point of View

When you read any piece of writing, it's important to recognize the author's **point of view**. Point of view is a writer's attitude toward a topic.

In nonfiction writing, an author might or might not express a point of view. Some nonfiction writing is **neutral**, which means that the author does not express or imply an opinion. However, in some nonfiction writing and in persuasive writing, writers do express or imply an attitude toward the subject matter.

When an author expresses an attitude, his or her point of view can be positive or negative. The author's attitude may be communicated explicitly or **implicitly**—that is, directly or indirectly. When a writer chooses words that say exactly how he or she feels about something, the point of view is explicitly stated. When a writer uses subtle word choices and does not directly state his or her opinion, the point of view is implicitly expressed.

For example, consider the following sentences:

- All students will benefit from having the option to walk to school.
- Arabella A. Mansfield, the first woman lawyer in the United States, began practicing law in Mount Pleasant, Iowa, in 1853.
- Banning cell phone use during school hours is an unrealistic expectation.

In the first sentence, the author's positive attitude toward students walking to school is indicated by the word *benefit*. The second sentence is neutral because the writer does not state or suggest a point of view. The phrase *unrealistic expectation* in the last sentence explicitly expresses the author's negative point of view toward banning cell phones at school.

Directions: Read the passage below. Write a summary of the evidence that tells you the author has a negative point of view about comic storytellers. Is the author's point of view implicit or explicit? Explain your reasoning.

> Comic storytellers announce that a story is one of the funniest they have ever heard. Then they blurt it out with impatient delight and are the first to laugh at the end. Sometimes, if they get a laugh, they are so happy that they will repeat the point of the story and glance around from face to face, hoping to collect a second laugh. It is a pathetic thing to see.

The author's point of view is explicitly expressed. It is clear from the final sentence, "It is a pathetic thing to see," that the author has a negative attitude toward comic storytellers. Another clue is the negative phrase such as "blurt it out with impatient delight." This evidence makes it obvious that the author dislikes comic storytellers.

Directions: Read the memo to Eduardo Hernandez. Underline any information in the text that helps you determine the author's point of view.

MEMO

To: Eduardo Hernandez, Director of Marketing

From: Odion Carter, Market Research Coordinator

Date: May 22

Subject: Choconana Cereal Launch

Market research has demonstrated that our current product launch for Choconana cereal needs to be revised. Our target audience for this cereal is children between the ages of 8 and 12. This age group no longer watches morning or afternoon cartoons. However, most use the Internet every day. They spend about six hours per week surfing the web and visiting social media sites.

I strongly recommend that we shift our focus and funds from television advertising to Internet advertising. This will help us represent Choconana cereal as a relevant product for our core age group. It will also ensure that our target audience is exposed to the product and help establish the overall Grain Goodness cereal group as a youth-friendly brand.

Attachments: Focus Group Results, January–April
Survey Analysis, January–April

Think about Reading

Directions: Answer each question about the author's point of view.

1. What is the author's point of view about advertising Choconana cereal on television versus on the Internet?
2. Is this point of view explicit or implicit? How do you know?

Summary

Every author has a purpose, or reason, for writing. It may be to entertain, to inform, to persuade, or a combination of these purposes. Answering the question "Why did the author write this?" helps readers determine the purpose. In addition, authors often express a point of view, or attitude, toward their topic. To determine whether the author's attitude is positive, negative, or neutral, readers should pay close attention to the author's word choices.

WORKPLACE SKILL

Determine the Purpose of Workplace Documents

Workplace documents, like any other type of writing, have a purpose. The purpose of a workplace document must be clear so that all readers understand the content and know what is expected of them.

Employers use memos—*memo* is short for *memorandum*—to inform employees about company plans and policies. Memos can also be used to describe company procedures or to persuade employees to act in a certain way.

Read the memo to Eduardo Hernandez. In a notebook, write three or four sentences that state the purpose of the memo and the evidence you used to determine the purpose.

Vocabulary Review

Directions: Complete each sentence using one of the following key terms and vocabulary words.

author's purpose **implicitly** **neutral** **point of view**

1. The reviewer used words like *fantastic* and *memorable* to express his positive ______________ toward the movie.
2. The journalist's article was ______________, presenting all the facts but expressing no opinion.
3. In an encyclopedia entry, the ______________ is to inform readers.
4. Ms. Clark's memo did not clearly state her opinion of the new rules, but she expressed her disapproval ______________.

Skill Review

Directions: Read the passage below. Then choose the best answer to each question.

In 1793 the war between France and Great Britain increased the hazards of the American sailor's life. Both sides preyed on American shipping for the supplies and ships they so badly needed. Great Britain also began stopping American ships on the high seas and kidnapping sailors. The British sorely needed sailors for their navy. Claiming that those removed from American ships were lawful subjects of the Crown, the English were not fussy about credentials. Although American sailors took to carrying identification papers, these papers failed to impress their captors.

1. What is (are) the author's purpose(s) for writing this passage?

   A. strictly to inform the reader
   B. to inform and to express an opinion
   C. strictly to entertain the reader
   D. to entertain and inform

2. Which excerpt from the passage provides the strongest clue to the author's point of view?

   A. "Both sides preyed on American shipping . . ."
   B. "The British sorely needed sailors for their navy."
   C. ". . . American sailors took to carrying identification papers . . ."
   D. ". . . the war between France and Great Britain increased the hazards of the American sailor's life."

Skill Practice

Directions: Read the passage below. Then choose the best answer to each question.

The Centers for Disease Control and Prevention (CDC) guidelines for adults tell us that we need a minimum of 75 minutes of vigorous aerobic activity per week. Running is one of the easiest ways to add this kind of activity to your life. But what if you've tried running and hated it? Or maybe you were successful the first couple of times you ran, and then gave up when it got hard. What, exactly, does "vigorous" mean? Do you really need to be huffing and puffing for 75 whole minutes a week?

The good news is you do not need to put yourself in the stroke zone in order to meet your weekly requirement for exercise, and running doesn't have to be painful. If you follow these simple steps, you will meet the physical activity requirement, you will avoid newbie injuries, and you may actually start to enjoy running.

Step 1: Make a plan. Set aside three days a week for running. Allow 30 minutes so you have time to warm up and cool down in addition to the 25 minutes of running.

Step 2: Warm up for a few minutes with a brisk walk. Your body needs to wake up, and your muscles need the added blood flow before you start to run.

Step 3: Now, start running just a bit faster than you walked in the warm-up. Think of it as a football jog: athletes jogging off the field don't run at top speed. As you run, listen to your body and your breathing. Try saying something out loud. If you can't keep a normal conversational tone, switch to a walk to catch your breath. When your breathing is more controlled, start running again. Alternate running and walking, moderating your activity level according to your body's ability to let you breathe and talk at the same time.

Step 4: After 25 minutes of alternating running and brisk walking, take a few minutes to cool down with a slower walk. Complete your cool-down with a few gentle stretches.

This is as vigorous as you need to get in order to gain the health benefits of running. As you progress each week, you should gradually run more and walk less, but your pace can stay casual and fun. Compare yourself to no one but yourself, and you'll get a little better each time.

1. Which of the following is one of the author's purposes for writing?

A. to make the reader laugh

B. to express the opinion that running is the best form of exercise

C. to inform the reader about how to start running without getting injured

D. to persuade the reader that running is difficult and dangerous for most people

2. Which statement best describes the author's point of view?

A. The author implies that everyone must follow the CDC guidelines.

B. The author implies that only running is an effective way to get exercise.

C. The author states explicitly that running is an easy way of getting exercise.

D. The author states explicitly that exercise is not as necessary as the CDC says it is.

Writing Practice

Directions: Find an article in a print or an online newspaper or magazine. In your notebook, write a short essay in which you summarize the article, identify the author's purpose and point of view, and identify whether the point of view is expressed implicitly or explicitly. Support your claims with evidence from the text.

LESSON 5.2 Analyze How Author's Purpose Determines Structure

LESSON OBJECTIVES

- Analyze how the structure of informational texts supports the author's purpose
- Analyze how the structure of literary texts supports the author's purpose

CORE SKILLS

- Analyze Text Structure
- Determine Author's Purpose

Key Terms

parallel plots
a narrative device in which two characters experience similar or contrasting stories at the same time in the narrative

problem-and-solution structure
an organizational pattern that presents something that needs to be dealt with and how to deal with it

Vocabulary

determine
identify through investigation or reasoning

effective
producing the desired result

Key Concept

Authors choose specific text structures to clarify what they want to say. The text structures engage the reader and help the authors achieve a purpose.

When you read about a historical event, you might expect the narrative to proceed in time order from the first action to the last. But this is not always the case. Sometimes writers take detours to explain ideas and events more clearly or to have a desired effect on readers. Authors choose a text structure that helps them accomplish their purpose.

Text Structure in Informational Passages

Every piece of writing is created for a purpose. One way an author communicates his or her purpose is by organizing the text in a particular way. This organization is known as text structure. A text can have an overall structure, and different structures can be used within passages or individual paragraphs.

An author chooses a particular text structure depending on his or her purpose for writing. For example, a journalist who wants to inform readers about an event may organize the article chronologically (in time order). Authors typically use a text structure that enhances their purpose and delivers their message clearly. These are the main types of text structures for informational texts:

Sequence The author describes events in the order in which they occurred or need to occur, or in order of importance.

Compare and Contrast The author compares two or more subjects or topics, describing how they are alike and different.

Cause and Effect The author explains the relationship between the cause of an event or phenomenon and the conditions or events that occur as a result.

Description The author describes a topic in detail by listing traits or qualities.

(Continued on page 149)

(Continued from page 148)

Problem and Solution The author presents a problem and offers or describes a solution. Multiple problems may be addressed in one text. Similarly, a text may suggest more than one solution.

Directions: Read the following text. Then identify the author's purpose and the text structure in the first paragraph.

> The case that came to be known as *Brown* v. *Board of Education* was actually the name given to five separate cases that were heard by the U.S. Supreme Court concerning the issue of segregation in public schools. . . . While the facts of each case are different, the main issue was the constitutionality of state-sponsored segregation in public schools. Once again, Thurgood Marshall and the NAACP Legal Defense and Education Fund handled these cases.
>
> When the cases came before the Supreme Court in 1952, the court consolidated all five cases under the name of Brown v. Board of Education. Marshall personally argued the case before the court. Although he raised a variety of legal issues on appeal, the most common one was that separate school systems for blacks and whites were inherently unequal. Thus, they violate the "equal protection clause" of the Fourteenth Amendment to the U.S. Constitution.
>
> Meeting to decide the case, the justices of the Supreme Court realized that they were deeply divided over the issues raised. . . . Unable to come to a solution by June 1953 (the end of the court's 1952-1953 term), the court decided to rehear the case in December 1953. . . . After the case was reheard in 1953, Chief Justice Warren was able to . . . bring all of the justices to agree to support a unanimous decision declaring segregation in public schools unconstitutional.
>
> —From "History of *Brown* v. *Board of Education*," US Department of Courts

The first paragraph serves as an introduction to the rest of the passage. It is clear that the author's purpose is to inform readers about the case of *Brown* v. *Board of Education*. The writer wants readers to know the basic background of the case before providing more information.

The text structure used in the first paragraph is description. The first sentence introduces the topic—the *Brown* v. *Board of Education* case. The remaining sentences provide details that describe it. The text structure helps the author achieve his or her purpose of providing background information about the case.

 Think about Reading

Directions: Read each author's purpose below. In your notebook, write which text structure would be most appropriate for the purpose. Explain your reasoning.

1. to persuade readers that dogs are better than cats
2. to explain why telephones were invented
3. to describe what happened in a movie

CORE SKILL

Analyze Text Structure

Determine (identify through investigation or reasoning) the structure of the third paragraph in the passage. Ask yourself: *Are events listed in chronological order? Are a problem and its solution described? Is the author comparing two things? Are a cause and its effect described? Is a topic presented and described in detail?*

The paragraph has two structures: problem-and-solution and sequence (chronological order). The paragraph describes a problem—the justices could not agree—and two solutions: The justices waited to rehear the case, and Warren brought the court together. The author describes events in chronological order to help readers understand the length of time required for justices to reach a decision.

Write three or four sentences describing the structure of the passage's second paragraph. Support your analysis with details from the text.

WRITE TO LEARN

Write a short essay describing the similarities and differences between cause-and-effect structure and sequence structure. Provide examples to illustrate each type of structure. Then identify which text structure (see the list on pages 148 and 149) you used in your essay, and explain why you chose it.

TECHNOLOGY SKILL

Use Computer Applications

This lesson includes boldface subheadings, numbered and bulleted lists, and italic text. These features help give the text structure and convey its purpose—to inform readers. You can create these features and more with most word-processing applications.

Choose an informational text you have written, and enhance the text's structure by using word-processing software to add some of the features listed above.

Sometimes more than one structure could be appropriate for a writer's purpose. However, in many cases, a particular type of structure is more **effective**, or successful in producing the desired result.

Directions: Read the passage below. Then write the answers to these questions: *What is the purpose of the passage? What text structure is used?*

> Earth's atmosphere includes billions and billions of gallons of evaporated water: in fact, water vapor is Earth's most abundant greenhouse gas. Like the stuffing in an insulated sleeping bag, water vapor absorbs heat radiating from the sun-warmed surface of the Earth. When water evaporates from oceans, rivers, or the leaves of plants, it cools the Earth's surface. When water vapor condenses into clouds or rain, it releases heat back into the atmosphere. As a result, the volume of water vapor—the specific humidity—plays a key role in setting Earth's surface temperature.
>
> —From "2012 State of the Climate: Humidity"
> by Susan Osborne and Rebecca Lindsey

The purpose of the passage is to explain the relationship between water vapor and Earth's climate. The terms *when* and *as a result* are clues that the authors have chosen a cause-and-effect structure, which is effective in conveying how the volume of water vapor (cause) influences Earth's temperature (effect).

Text Structure in Literary Passages

Like authors of informational texts, authors of literary works choose a text structure that fits their purpose. They may use one or more of the same structures found in informational texts. In addition, literary writers use some text structures that are not generally used in informational pieces.

Many literary texts have a general chronological structure. However, there may be more complex structures beneath the main structure. These include alternating viewpoints, flashback, and parallel plots.

Alternating viewpoints The story is told chronologically, but it is narrated by different characters or from different points of view.

> The house was magical, with its leaded windows and steep gables. I forced open the rusty gate and blazed a trail through the overgrown garden. Walking down the side of the house, I stopped at each window to peer in. At the back door, I took out the keys the lawyer had given me. "Susana Rios: Door keys," read the typed label. The aunt whose name I shared had left everything to me.
>
> "Who's that at the old Rios place?" Dad muttered. Pointing to a dark-haired girl in jeans trying each window in turn, he called 9-1-1 and said, "This is Bart Gregson. There's a prowler trying to break into the house across the street."

The author's purpose is to entertain. The two narrators—Susana and her neighbor—have different information about and perspectives on the same experience. Readers see the action from both viewpoints. This engages the audience and raises curiosity about how the situation will be resolved.

Flashback The author inserts an event or events from the past into the normal chronological order of a story. Flashbacks provide background information for current story events.

> Rachel stomped down the back stairs to the parking lot and let the door slam shut behind her. She watched as a white sedan rolled into the spot her father had used for so many years. When she'd joined her father on city council, she'd seen him engage in plenty of lively debates, but he'd never lost his cool.
>
> Rachel replayed the scene in her mind. She had stood at the lectern presenting the budget she'd spent two months crafting. She'd worked and reworked the figures and was prepared to convince the council that this budget was workable. But when she finished speaking, Frank Costella smirked and intoned, "Rejected." Suddenly Rachel was shaking with anger and shouting at him. Then she felt a hand on her arm. "Get some air," Linda Walker suggested.
>
> Now, Rachel thought about how her father would have handled this situation. With a deep breath, she opened the heavy door and climbed the stairs again.

In this passage, the author's purposes are to create dramatic tension and to provide background information that explains Rachel's actions. The author uses flashback to describe what preceded the scene in the parking lot. By placing the flashback in the middle of the passage, the author has time to build tension before revealing why Rachel is at first angry and then ashamed.

Parallel plots A parallel plot exists when main characters have separate but related story lines that occur at the same time. The plots can be linked by a common character or similar themes.

> Hector caught Maria's eye and glanced at his wrist. She shook her head and pointed with her fork to the molten chocolate cake on her plate. Bracing himself, Hector tipped his glass over, covering his lap with cold water. "Oh, I'm so clumsy!" he exclaimed. Maria rolled her eyes at her husband's latest ploy to leave a dinner party early.
>
> At his desk, Ramon glanced at the clock on his computer. He was supposed to be writing his research paper. If he didn't make serious headway tonight, he would lose car privileges for another week. But the videos he was watching were much more interesting. Besides, Mom had begged Dad to let her stay for dessert for once. There was time for a few more videos before they got home.

This author's purpose is to entertain readers and to create dramatic tension. The parallel plot creates tension because readers know that Ramon's parents may be coming home soon, but Ramon does not.

Think about Reading

Directions: Read each author's purpose below. Identify which literary device would be most appropriate for the purpose. Explain your reasoning.

1. to describe a crime as seen by the criminal, the victim, and the police
2. to explain the motivation for a crime
3. to describe two strangers preparing to audition for the same role

CORE SKILL

Determine Author's Purpose

Every writer has at least one general purpose (to inform, to persuade, or to entertain) and at least one specific purpose (for example, to inform about something in particular). Sometimes the structure of a passage helps readers determine the author's purpose for writing.

The same can be said of literary texts. Authors choose structures to accomplish certain goals.

With a partner, analyze and discuss how the structure of the three literary passages helps the authors convey their purpose.

Summary

Writers choose a structure that helps enhance and fulfill their purpose. Some structures are better suited for one purpose than for another. To identify the structure and purpose of a text, you can ask yourself these questions: *What is the relationship among the ideas in this text? What is the author's reason for writing? How does this structure help the author achieve his or her purpose?*

Vocabulary Review

Directions: Complete the sentences using the following key terms and vocabulary words.

determine **effective** **parallel plots** **problem-and-solution structure**

1. The author used a ____________________ in her article about dealing with water shortage during a drought.
2. She needed to ____________________ which text structure would be most ____________________ in making her point.
3. The novelist used ____________________ to describe two characters who grew up in the same family but lead very different lives.

Skill Review

Directions: Read the passage below. Then choose the best answer to each question.

On March 24, 1989, a 987-foot oil tanker named the *Exxon Valdez* crashed into a reef in Alaska. The ship was filled with oil. After the crash, approximately 11 million gallons of oil gushed out of the tanker into the Prince William Sound in Alaska. By the end of the week, an oil slick spread across a huge area of formerly pristine Alaskan coastline. The oil covered more than one thousand miles of shoreline and threatened to poison millions of animals living on the coast.

Because oil is lighter than water, it spreads over the water's surface and washes up on beaches. It poisons the fish, shellfish, land animals, and birds that come in contact with it. Rescuers in Alaska tried to help the otters and waterfowl that had been coated with oil. Despite the rescuers' tireless efforts, thousands of animals died.

1. What is the main structure of the passage?
   A. cause-and-effect
   B. compare-and-contrast
   C. description
   D. problem-and-solution

2. How does the structure help achieve the author's purpose for writing?
   A. It helps readers understand what caused the oil tanker to crash.
   B. It helps readers understand how the crash affected the oil industry.
   C. It helps readers understand why the crash was devastating to wildlife.
   D. It helps readers understand the difference between healthy beaches and polluted beaches.

Skill Practice

Directions: Read the passage below. Then complete the activities.

It was going to be fun taking care of the Clines's dog, cat, and lizard—and Juan was going to be paid $35 to be their pet sitter for two weeks. "Not bad for dishing out a little food and water and letting a dog in and out," he thought.

The first morning of his job, Juan was getting ready to shoot some hoops in the driveway when his mother called out, "Hey, Juan, aren't you forgetting something?" Her stern look made sure he wouldn't forget again.

When he got to the Clines's house, it took him less than thirty minutes to feed and water all the pets. The rest of the first week went without incident, but Juan thought that Dusty the golden retriever seemed lonely. So Juan decided to bring over his homework each night and keep the animals company.

On the ninth day, Juan began to realize just what a responsibility he had taken on. He had just removed the lizard, Mr. O'Malley, from his cage to spritz him with water when the phone rang. Dusty started to bark, which startled the cat, Felix. Felix took off like a shot with Dusty in hot pursuit. Juan quickly set the lizard down in the terrarium and wheeled around to head off the chase—but he was too late. He heard the shatter of the bedside lamp as the cat and dog bounded over the bed. When he went to the bedroom to survey the damage, he noticed something small and dark flash by the baseboard near the bed. Then he saw the cover of the terrarium on the floor and realized that the flash had been Mr. O'Malley! It took Juan twenty minutes to catch the lizard and return him to his cage.

When the Clines came home, Juan apologized for the broken lamp and told them to take its cost out of his fee, but they refused. Mr. Cline told Juan that they appreciated his hard work and the peace of mind they had knowing he was caring for their critters. Then he insisted that Juan take two twenty-dollar bills for all his trouble. Mrs. Cline asked Juan if he was available to pet sit again the following weekend, and he gladly accepted. This time, though, he knew it wouldn't be as easy it as it sounded.

1. What is the main purpose of the passage?

A. to explain to readers how best to take care of pets

B. to persuade readers that cats and dogs should not live together

C. to express the author's negative opinion about Juan's pet sitting ability

D. to entertain readers with the story of Juan's experience taking care of his neighbor's pets

2. The author uses a __________ structure to tell a(n) __________.

Writing Practice

Directions: Find a news article about a specific current event in a print or an online newspaper. Describe the content of the article, and identify the author's general and specific purposes. Then identify the overall structure and the structure of at least one smaller section of the article. Evaluate how effective you think these structures are. Be sure to cite evidence from the text to support your analysis.

LESSON 5.3 Infer Author's Purpose

LESSON OBJECTIVES

- Infer the author's purpose using details from the text
- Use prior knowledge of context to infer author's purpose

CORE SKILLS

- Use a Graphic Organizer
- Determine the Implicit Purpose in a Text

Key Terms

context
circumstances or conditions in which something exists or occurs

prior knowledge
familiarity or awareness you already have about a topic

Vocabulary

rhetoric
the art of effective or persuasive (speaking or) writing, especially using figures of speech and composition techniques

satire
humor that mocks a person, event, or situation

Key Concept

When an author does not explicitly state his or her purpose for writing a text, readers can use their prior knowledge and details from the text to infer the author's purpose.

Have you ever realized that someone was mad at you even though he or she didn't tell you in so many words? You may have guessed from a facial expression or a change in behavior. This is similar to the way you must infer an author's purpose for writing when he or she doesn't directly state it. You have to examine the text, think about the context of the passage, and use your prior knowledge about the topic to infer the author's purpose.

Inferring the Author's Purpose

Every author has a reason, or general purpose, for writing a text. The general purpose may be to entertain, to inform, or to persuade, or a combination of these purposes. You need to know what the author's purpose is so that you don't misinterpret what he or she is saying. For example, it is important to be able to distinguish between an article that is designed to inform you about a product and an advertisement that is designed to persuade you to buy the product.

In some cases, the author explicitly states his or her purpose. He or she includes a direct statement about the purpose in the title or the text. However, in many cases, the author does not explicitly present the purpose. The purpose is implicit, or suggested but not directly expressed.

Using Details in the Text to Infer Purpose

It is up to readers to examine details in a text that provide clues to the writer's purpose. A reader can then infer the purpose, or draw a conclusion based on evidence in the text. An author's choice of words and supporting details provide clues to his or her purpose.

Texts written to persuade the reader might include words such as *should* or *must* to tell readers explicitly what the author wants to convince them to do or to think. Other persuasive texts will include the subtle use of positive or negative language that reveals the author's bias, or personal judgment, on the subject.

When reading persuasive texts, it is important for readers to recognize implicit opinions and to understand that the author is expressing a personal point of view rather than a fact.

The art of effective speaking or writing is known as **rhetoric**. Writers who are skilled at rhetoric are able to achieve their purpose for writing and bring about a change in their readers or listeners (for example, persuading them or leading them to a new understanding). Rhetoric is used to persuade, to inform, and to entertain.

Texts written to entertain generally include vivid descriptions and figurative language such as metaphors or personification. Some entertaining texts might appear to be informative or persuasive. Readers need to use their **prior knowledge**, or what they already know about the subject, to infer that the author's purpose is to entertain rather than to inform or to persuade.

A special category of writing is **satire**, a type of humor that mocks a person, event, or situation. Satire is often seen in political cartoons and commentary. A well-known example is Jonathan Swift's 1729 essay "A Modest Proposal: For preventing the children of poor people in Ireland, from being a burden on their parents or country, and for making them beneficial to the publick." In it, Swift recommends that the poor in Ireland sell their children to the wealthy as food. He does not mean his proposal to be taken literally, but uses satire to point out the indifference of Ireland's government and upper classes toward the poor. Swift's implicit purpose is to alert the reader to a social problem.

No matter what type of text you are reading, keep in mind that the author's purpose may be implicit. For example, in the passage below, the author describes a car but does not state his or her purpose for writing about it.

Directions: Note the words and phrases the author uses to describe the car. Write two unstated purposes that the author has for writing and explain how you determined these purposes.

> The Bonanza is the best new car on the market. In addition to getting 32 miles to the gallon, the Bonanza provides the smoothest ride on the road. Its classic styling and elegant color choices make it the automobile for the discriminating driver. Interior temperature control, sport wheels, satellite radio, and leather seats are standard equipment on this affordable but upscale car. This car is one you will be proud to drive for years to come.

If you wrote that the unstated purposes are to inform readers about the car and to persuade people to buy the car, you have accurately inferred the writer's purposes. The author provides facts about the car's features to inform and uses positive words and phrases to convince readers of the benefits of owning the car.

Think about this sentence: "Interior temperature control, sport wheels, satellite radio, and leather seats are standard equipment on this affordable but upscale car." What prior knowledge do readers need in order to infer that the author is trying to persuade them that the car is a good bargain?

Readers need to know that sport wheels, satellite radio, and leather seats are usually features in expensive luxury cars. Readers might also use prior knowledge to infer that a purpose of ads is to persuade.

CORE SKILL

Use a Graphic Organizer

You can use a graphic organizer such as the one below to help you determine an author's implicit purpose. Follow this procedure:

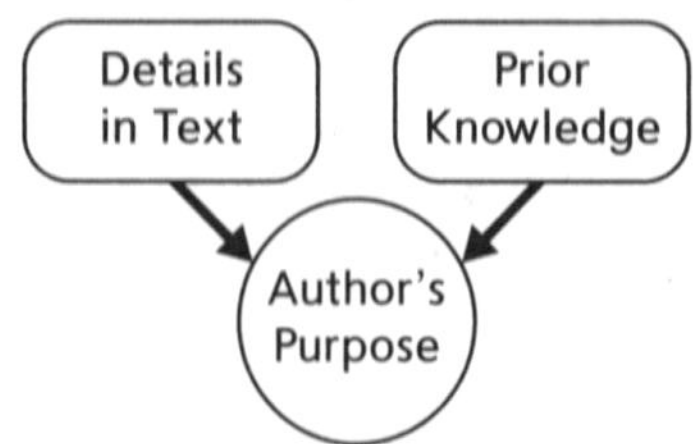

1. Read the entire text, and ask yourself: *What is this text about?*
2. Ask yourself: *What does the text say about this topic?* Note the details in the "Details in Text" section of your diagram.
3. Ask yourself: *What do I already know about this topic?* Note your prior knowledge about the topic in the appropriate section of your diagram.
4. Study the graphic organizer. Ask yourself: *What do these details tell me about the author's purpose for writing?* Use your notes to determine the author's purpose. Write the purpose in the bottom circle.

Find an advertisement online or in a magazine. Create a graphic organizer, and use the steps above to analyze the ad. What does your analysis reveal about the author's implied purpose? Which details in the ad and what prior knowledge helped you make that inference?

WRITE TO LEARN

Reread the passage about the Bonanza on page 155. Write a review of the Bonanza that is intended to discourage someone from buying the car. In the review, do not directly tell readers not to buy the car. Instead, use persuasive language, describing the car in such a way that it does not sound appealing.

TEST-TAKING SKILL

Use Prior Knowledge

When taking a test, you can use your prior knowledge to make inferences about a passage.

As you read, ask yourself:

1. *What do I already know about this topic?*
2. *What do I already know about the source of this text?*
3. *What do I already know about the author?*
4. *What information is the author including? What is being left out?*

As you read a text, use your prior knowledge to interpret the details and to infer the author's reason for including them. Use this information to write meaningful responses to test questions about a reading passage.

Create a checklist with the steps you should take to make inferences about a passage. Review it often so you are comfortable interpreting texts during tests.

Think about Reading

Directions: Read the phrases below from the passage about the Bonanza. For each phrase, underline the word or words that indicate that the author's purpose is to persuade readers to buy the Bonanza.

1. best new car on the market
2. smoothest ride on the road
3. classic styling and elegant color choices
4. automobile for the discriminating driver
5. standard equipment on this affordable but upscale car

Using Context to Infer Implicit Purpose

Another strategy readers use to infer an author's purpose is examining the **context** of the passage, or the circumstances in which it was written. Readers should consider who the author is and in which publication the passage appeared. Then they can use their prior knowledge about the author and about the general purpose of the publication to infer whether the author was writing to inform, to persuade, to entertain, or for more than one of these purposes. As you read, ask yourself:

- *Who is the author?* Is the author a comedian who is probably writing to entertain? A politician who is likely writing to persuade? A scientist who is probably writing to inform? If necessary, research the author's background.
- *In what part of the library or bookstore was this text located?* Most libraries and bookstores are organized to some extent by purpose. Did you find the text in the Fiction and Literature section? Travel? Humor? Biography? Science and Technology? Self-help? The way the text is categorized will give you a clue about at least one of its purposes. (There might be more than one.)
- *In what type of publication did the text appear, and who published it?* Was the text published in a fiction collection? A serious newspaper? A satirical newspaper? Was it published by a science publisher or an entertainment company? Keep in mind that many texts on the Internet come from sources other than where they appear. You may need to research the original source of the writing.
- *In what section of the newspaper or magazine did the text appear?* Did the article appear in the current events section, the humor section, the advertising section, or the opinion/editorial section? Keep in mind that magazines and newspapers generally include a mix of informational, persuasive, and entertaining articles.

Directions: Analyze the context of the following pieces related to the 2013 US government shutdown. Based on the title and what you know about the author or the publication, infer the author's main purpose for writing each article.

1. "Government Shuts Down in Budget Impasse" published in the politics section of *The New York Times*, September 30, 2013
2. "Let's Get Back to the Work of the American People" President Obama's Weekly Address, October 12, 2013
3. "How I Spent My Government Shutdown By John Boehner, Age 63" by Willie Muse

1. The first article is published in the Politics section of *The New York Times*, which is a serious newspaper. Based on the title and the publication, you can infer that the authors' purpose is to inform readers.
2. The second piece is a speech made by President Barack Obama. Politicians often want to persuade. You can infer from the title and context that the purpose of this speech is to convince people that the shutdown needs to end.
3. The title of the third piece suggests that it was written by John Boehner, Speaker of the House of Representatives when the article was written. However, the article was actually written by someone else. In addition, the title makes the article sound like a grade-school essay topic, "How I Spent My Summer Vacation." You can infer that the author's purpose is to entertain you with satire.

Directions: Read the excerpt about Wangari Maathai below. What is the implicit purpose of the piece? How do you know?

> Parts of Africa that were once forest were turning into desert for two reasons: forests were cleared and replaced with plantations, and wood was most families' only source of fuel for cooking and heating. A biologist named Wangari Maathai noticed the problem and came up with a solution.
>
> In 1977, Maathai started the Green Belt Movement. Local people began planting trees, and in less than thirty years, more than 30 million trees were planted. The trees provide fuel, food, shelter, and income for the poorest residents of Kenya's countryside, and they also improve soil and water quality. Maathai's work has spread successfully to many other African countries.

You can use the text details and the context of the passage to infer that the author's purpose is to inform and to persuade. The author includes details about the loss of forests in Africa to inform readers. The author also presents Wangari Maathai's accomplishments to persuade readers that she is an important figure.

Think about Reading

Directions: In a notebook, write your answers to the following questions.

1. Some companies distribute catalogs that include articles about certain products. Based on their context, what is the purpose of these articles?
2. What parts of a library or bookstore are most likely to include texts that are designed to entertain, rather than to inform or to persuade?

CORE SKILL

Determine the Implicit Purpose in a Text

Follow these steps to infer an author's implicit purpose:

1. Read the entire text.
2. Scan the text, and note the types of details the author includes. Ask yourself: *What is the author suggesting or implying by including these details?*
3. Then ask yourself: *Who is the author? Where did I find this text? Where was it first published?*
4. Finally, ask yourself: *Why did the author write this text? What is the author's intention?*

Read the list of articles about the government shutdown on this page. What would you infer to be the purpose of the article titled "Government Shuts Down in Budget Impasse" if it were published in a humorous or satirical magazine instead of a serious newspaper?

Summary

When you read, it is helpful to identify the author's purpose. Knowing whether the author intends to entertain, to inform, or to persuade helps you interpret the text. For example, the details in an entertaining or persuasive text may or may not be true, but the details in an informative text are likely to be factual. In many cases, an author's purpose is implicit. An implicit purpose is suggested rather than directly stated, and you must infer the author's reason for writing. You can use details from the text, your own prior knowledge, and your understanding of context to infer an author's purpose.

Vocabulary Review

Directions: Complete each sentence by unscrambling a key term or vocabulary word.

1. **rateis** ____________________ is often written to make fun of politicians.
2. **reciroth** A writer can use ____________________ to create text that changes a reader's opinion.
3. **noxtcet** The ____________________ of a written work includes the publication in which it appeared.
4. **riorp welnkedog** ____________________ is the information readers already have about a topic.

Skill Review

Directions: Read the passage below. Then choose the best answer to each question.

> The adjective *American* causes confusion and resentment. That is because many people have come to associate *American* exclusively with the United States. There are millions of Americans who are not citizens of the United States, and many of them take offense at being automatically linked with that country. Canadians and Mexicans in North America and the people of Central and South America are "Americans."

1. Which best describes an implicit purpose of the text?
   A. to explain why some people get offended when people use the term *American*
   B. to inform readers that the adjective *American* causes confusion and resentment
   C. to express the opinion that *American* should not refer only to citizens of the United States
   D. to remind readers that the people of Canada, Mexico, and Central and South America are also Americans

2. This passage is most likely to be published in which section of a newspaper?
   A. news
   B. opinion
   C. advertising
   D. entertainment

Skill Practice

Directions: Read the speech below. Then choose the best answer to each question.

Mr. President, the question before the Senate is . . . Shall a joint resolution providing for an amendment of the national Constitution, so that the right of citizens of the United States to vote shall not be denied . . . on account of sex . . . be submitted to the Legislatures . . . for ratification or rejection? . . .

Our form of government is founded [upon the] principle: . . . Every human being of mature powers . . . is entitled to all the rights and privileges which belong to any other such human being under the law.

The independence, equality, and dignity of all human souls is the fundamental assertion of those who believe in what we call human freedom. . . . But we are informed that infants, idiots, and women are represented by men. This cannot reasonably be claimed unless it [is] first shown that the consent of these classes has been given to such representation. . . . But the exclusion of these classes from participation in the Government deprives them of the power [to agree] to representation. . . . [To] say there can be representation which does not presuppose consent or authority on the part of the principal who is represented is to confound all reason. [Further, this claim] asserts . . . that all actual power, whether despotic or otherwise, is representative, and therefore free.

—From "The Debate on Woman Suffrage" by Henry W. Blair on December 8, 1886

1. Which phrase best describes an implicit purpose of the text?
   A. to express the opinion that women should be given the right to vote
   B. to ask the Senate whether or not the Constitution should be amended
   C. to persuade the Senate that women in the United States are more rational than men
   D. to inform the Senate that women are not allowed to vote because they are less independent than men

2. The author assumes his audience has prior knowledge that
   A. women were given the right to vote in 1920.
   B. giving women the right to vote is the right thing to do.
   C. giving women the right to vote is solely up to the president.
   D. giving women the right to vote requires a Constitutional amendment.

3. Which detail from the text most strongly suggests the implicit purpose of the speech?
   A. "Mr. President, the question before the Senate is"
   B. "we are informed that infants, idiots, and women are represented by men"
   C. "Every human being of mature powers . . . is entitled to all the rights and privileges which belong to any other such human being under the law."
   D. "Shall a joint resolution providing for an amendment of the national Constitution . . . be submitted to the Legislatures . . . for ratification or rejection?"

4. Which piece of contextual evidence LEAST helps the reader understand the implicit purpose of the text?
   A. The passage was written in 1886.
   B. The passage can be accessed on the Internet.
   C. The passage was addressed to the president and legislature.
   D. The passage is an excerpt from "The Debate on Woman Suffrage."

Writing Practice

Directions: In a print or online newspaper or magazine, find an article in which the author has an implicit purpose for writing. Identify the author's implicit purpose. Support your claim with details from the text and any prior knowledge you have about the topic, author, and context of the article.

LESSON 5.4 Analyze How Authors Differentiate Their Positions

LESSON OBJECTIVES

- Describe how authors use opposing positions to support their own position.
- Analyze and evaluate an author's support for his or her position.

CORE SKILLS

- Identify an Author's Position
- Evaluate Arguments

Key Terms

differentiate
distinguish

position
author's opinion or standpoint on a specific issue or question

Vocabulary

acknowledge
accept or note the existence of

conflicting
in opposition to

refute
claim, argue, or show as inaccurate or wrong

solidify
make stronger or more certain

Key Concept

Authors can strengthen their position by acknowledging viewpoints that differ from their own and by using evidence or reasoning to refute them.

Have you ever heard a politician describe an opponent's position on an issue? Many effective speakers point out the flaws in an opposing point of view while presenting their own position. Similarly, writers create effective persuasive texts by calling attention to conflicting positions in order to discredit those positions and strengthen their own.

Identifying an Author's Position

When writers present their **position** on a topic, they are stating an opinion or standpoint. To show that their position is reasonable, they have to support it with evidence. One way writers accomplish this is by including evidence to show that **conflicting**, or opposing, viewpoints are not reasonable.

Directions: Read the passage below. Underline the sentence that indicates the author's position, and circle the sentence that presents the opposing position.

> The outsider who claims that New York City is nothing but deafening chaos obviously has not been given a proper tour. Whatever your interests, New York can be a supreme site for relaxation and reflection. The jade expert can find an emperor's collection of carvings in the Jade Room of the Metropolitan Museum of Art. The artist can study at leisure a rare volume of William Blake's etchings in one of the specialized rooms of the main library or walk for years through the endless public and private galleries. The scientist can find a quiet spot before a diorama at the American Museum of Natural History. The reader can spend hours perusing books in one of the city's numerous independent bookstores. The philosopher can people-watch on a comfortable bench in Central Park.

The writer begins by presenting the opposing viewpoint that "New York City is nothing but deafening chaos" and then states his or her position that "New York can be a supreme site for relaxation and reflection." The rest of the passage consists of evidence that serves to support the writer's position and to **refute** the opposing viewpoint, or to show that it is inaccurate.

As the passage about New York illustrates, it is effective for a writer to **acknowledge**, or recognize the existence of, a conflicting viewpoint before defending his or her position. In this way, the writer can **differentiate**, or distinguish, his or her position from other positions on the topic.

Writers use a variety of techniques to indicate that they are acknowledging a conflicting position. For example, they might cite the source (the author or the publication) of the opposing opinion. They might also use text clues such as signal words indicating contrast (for example, *although, however, regardless*) to make it clear that they disagree with the position and are about to provide an alternative.

Directions: Read the passage below. Write the author's position and the conflicting position.

> Although Josie Vann claims in her latest *Cakemakers' Magazine* article that high-quality cake decorating requires extensive training, it's actually not too challenging. You just need to master a few basic techniques in order to frost like a pro. The first and most important step in cake decorating is leveling your cake so you'll have a flat surface to work on. Use a bread knife held horizontally to slice off any excess cake that may have domed up in the center of each layer. Once the layers are flat, putting them together and frosting the cake will be a breeze.

The first sentence serves the dual purpose of presenting the author's position on high-quality cake decorating—that it is not challenging—and the conflicting position—that it requires extensive training. Note that the author uses the word *although* to signal the opposing position. The author presents simple instructions that serve as supporting evidence for his or her claim that high-quality cake decorating can be easy.

Think about Reading

Directions: Each of the following statements is an author's position on a topic. To differentiate and support their own positions, the authors need to present an opposing position. Write an opposing position for each statement.

1. Salvador Dali was the most creative painter of the 20th century.
2. Without Malcolm X, the Civil Rights movement would have failed.
3. We are 95 percent certain that Earth's climate is changing in part as a result of human activities.

CORE SKILL

Identify an Author's Position

It is important for readers to differentiate between an author's position and conflicting positions that the author references for support. To identify the author's position, read the entire text. Then ask yourself: *What does the evidence tell me about how the author feels about this topic?* Your answer will help you distinguish the author's position from conflicting positions.

With a partner, read an article in the opinion/editorial section of a newspaper. Then discuss the following questions: *What is the topic of the article? What is the author's position? Does the author present an opposing viewpoint? If so, what is it?*

WRITE TO LEARN

Write a one- or two-paragraph essay in which you take a position on a current-events topic. Do some research to support your position with relevant evidence from more than one source. To strengthen your argument, acknowledge and refute a conflicting position.

CORE SKILL

Evaluate Arguments

One of the techniques writers use to strengthen an argument is to differentiate their position from opposing positions. Writers must also refute opposing arguments to defend their positions.

To evaluate an argument that uses this technique, follow this procedure:

1. Read the entire text.
2. Ask yourself: *What is the author's position on the topic?*
3. Then ask yourself: *What other viewpoints does the author present?*
4. Finally, consider the following: *Has the author proved that his or her viewpoint is reasonable by refuting others' viewpoints?*

Review the article you used for the Core Skill activity on page 161, and share it with a small group. Begin a group discussion based on the questions above. Finally, discuss the following questions: *Has the author sufficiently refuted the opposing position? Has the author persuaded you to agree with his or her opinion? What evidence do you think is most compelling? Why?*

Analyzing Support for an Author's Position

In a good persuasive text, the writer acknowledges other viewpoints, explains why he or she disagrees with those positions, and presents evidence against them. Doing this helps the author **solidify**, or strengthen, his or her position and present a balanced argument. If the author does not address a conflicting position, readers might think that the writer has not considered all perspectives on the issue and thus has not argued his or her position sufficiently.

When you read a text in which the author expresses a position, you should evaluate the text to decide whether you agree with that position. One way you can do this is by noting whether the author has acknowledged other viewpoints that you might consider valid. You should also determine whether the author has included details that support his or her position and refute the opposing position or positions.

Directions: Read the passage about animal emotions. Write the author's position and the opposing position. Then note any evidence that supports the author's position or refutes the opposing position.

> For centuries, many people denied that animals felt emotions. This gave them an excuse to mistreat animals. Some farmers worked horses to death. Hunters clubbed baby seals for their fur. Even today, there are still scientists who perform painful and unnecessary tests on animals—for example, blinding rabbits to test which mascara is most waterproof. But much evidence of animals' ability to feel has accumulated in recent years. In his book *When Elephants Weep*, psychologist Jeffrey Masson documents the emotions of many species. He describes a gorilla who did not like to be interrupted while listening to opera music, as well as a circus elephant who sobbed when her trainer hit her with a stick. Masson also relates the story of a peregrine falcon who mourned the death of his mate by emitting a plaintive screeching sound and perching motionless for an entire day in the last place he had seen her.

The author's position is clear: animals feel emotions. The reader can tell that this is the author's position from the evidence presented and from the way the author introduces the opposing viewpoint. Using the words "denied," "excuse," and "mistreat," which all have negative connotations, conveys that the author disagrees with the viewpoint that animals do not have the ability to feel emotions. The author includes a sufficient number of relevant examples to make a strong case that animals feel emotions and to effectively refute the opposing position.

Often writers will explicitly agree with one or two points made in an opposing argument and then refute the remainder of it. You have probably heard a politician say something like this: "My opponent is absolutely right. We need to create more jobs. But the legislation she is proposing will not achieve this goal." This tactic makes the speaker seem more reasonable and the argument seem more attractive than it would be if he or she dismissed the opposing argument completely. It is especially useful when writers are trying to convince readers who might agree with the opposing position.

Directions: Read the passage below. Underline the author's position, and circle the opposing position. Pay attention to similarities and differences between the two.

> Many people think that dangerous team sports such as football and soccer are the best way for children to stay fit and gain important team-building skills. Of course, it is true that children need physical exercise and opportunities to interact with others. However, dance is a better way to address these needs. Children who are involved in dance build tremendous strength, endurance, and flexibility in a calm and collaborative environment. In addition, they build their cognitive skills when memorizing choreography and team-building skills when performing in recitals.

Think about Reading

Directions: Answer the following questions about the above passage.

1. In what ways does the author agree with the opposing position? In what ways does the author disagree?
2. Does the author include details that not only support his or her own position, but also refute the opposing position? Explain.
3. Is the author's argument persuasive? Explain your reasoning.

Summary

Writers who present a position on a topic strengthen their argument by differentiating their position from those of others. To defend their position, effective writers refute opposing arguments in part or in full, using evidence that supports their position and discredits conflicting positions. Readers can assess an author's position by identifying the opposing viewpoint and evaluating the author's argument against it. Making this assessment helps readers clarify the author's position on a topic and determine whether the author's viewpoint is reasonable.

Vocabulary Review

Directions: Write one key term or vocabulary word in each space to complete the paragraph.

acknowledge	**conflicting**	**differentiate**
position	**refute**	**solidify**

To strengthen her argument that Pluto should be considered a planet, the astronomer first presented the ________ position that it should not be considered a planet. She decided to ________ this opposing viewpoint to ________ her ________ from others. She then went on to ________ the opposing argument to ________ her position.

21st CENTURY SKILL

Critical Thinking and Problem Solving

If you are having trouble confidently stating and defending your position on a topic, one way to solve the problem is to apply critical thinking—consider opposing positions and how you will refute them. Here is one strategy for writing an effective persuasive text.

1. Predict possible viewpoints that conflict with your position on a topic.
2. Analyze and gather information about those opposing viewpoints. Then choose ideas that your audience is most likely to agree with.
3. Conduct research to find evidence that you can use to disprove the opposing position, as well as evidence that supports your position. Some pieces of evidence accomplish both goals.
4. Brainstorm words and phrases with negative connotations that you can use when discussing the opposing position.

Follow the above procedure as you write a letter to the editor of a local newspaper. Attempt to persuade readers to agree with your position on a topic.

Skill Review

Directions: Read the passage below. Then choose the best answer to each question.

E-mail Message

From: Elena Santarpio

To: Janet Johnson

Subject: Ivan Chu – Recommendation for Promotion to Grill Cook

Dear Ms. Johnson,

I understand it is Seaside Café's policy that employees must have at least two years of kitchen experience in order to become a grill cook. However, even though Ivan Chu has worked in our restaurant for only one year, I believe that he should be promoted to the grill.

The rationale for the restaurant's policy is that grill cooks need two years to demonstrate they can keep up with the fast pace of the kitchen. However, Ivan has already proved that he can keep up. As shift supervisor at Seaside Café, I have had the opportunity to observe him in several jobs. He started delivering orders and then bused tables before deciding he wanted to learn to cook. After minimal instruction, he has proved himself to be a fast worker and an excellent fry cook.

Grill cooks are required to have a strong work ethic. Ivan fits the bill. He is always punctual, volunteers to cover his coworkers' shifts, and takes his job very seriously.

I strongly urge you to promote Ivan. He is a great asset to the café and will be even more valuable on the grill.

Sincerely,

Elena Santarpio

1. What is Elena Santarpio trying to persuade Janet Johnson to agree with?

A. Ivan Chu has a strong work ethic.

B. Ivan Chu should be promoted to grill cook.

C. Ivan Chu has worked at the restaurant for a year.

D. Ivan Chu is never late for work and takes his job seriously.

2. What is the opposing position that Elena Santarpio refutes to strengthen her position?

A. Grill cooks are required to have a strong work ethic.

B. Ivan Chu has already had too many positions in the restaurant.

C. Grill cooks need to demonstrate that they can keep up with the fast pace of the kitchen.

D. Employees must have at least two years of kitchen experience to become a grill cook.

Skill Practice

Directions: Read the passage written by Thomas Paine shortly before the start of the American Revolution. Then choose the best answer to each question.

> In the following pages I offer nothing more than simple facts, plain arguments, and common sense: and have no other preliminaries to settle with the reader, than that he will divest himself of prejudice and prepossession, and suffer his reason and his feelings to determine for themselves that he will put on, or rather that he will not put off, the true character of a man, and generously enlarge his views beyond the present day.
>
> Volumes have been written on the subject of the struggle between England and America. Men of all ranks have embarked in the controversy, from different motives, and with various designs; but all have been ineffectual, and the period of debate is closed. Arms as the last resource decide the contest; the appeal was the choice of the King, and the Continent has accepted the challenge.
>
> —From *Common Sense* by Thomas Paine, 1776

1. Which statement best represents Thomas Paine's position on the topic?

A. "Arms as the last resource decide the contest."

B. "Men of all ranks have embarked in the controversy."

C. "I offer nothing more than simple facts, plain arguments, and common sense."

D. "Volumes have been written on the subject of the struggle between England and America."

2. Which statement best represents the viewpoints that oppose Paine's?

A. "The Continent has accepted the challenge."

B. "[I] have no other preliminaries to settle with the reader."

C. "[The reader will] generously enlarge his views beyond the present day."

D. "Men of all ranks have embarked in the controversy, from different motives, and with various designs."

3. Which statement represents Paine's strongest refutation of opposing viewpoints?

A. "The appeal was the choice of the King."

B. "All have been ineffectual, and the period of debate is closed."

C. "[The reader] will divest himself of prejudice and prepossession."

D. "I offer nothing more than simple facts, plain arguments, and common sense."

Writing Practice

Directions: Write a paragraph about a controversial issue, incorporating research from at least two sources. Begin by introducing a position that conflicts with yours. Then indicate your understanding of that position, and explain how yours differs from it. Use evidence to support your position and to refute the opposing position.

LESSON 5.5 Analyze Author's Intention and Effect

LESSON OBJECTIVES

- Identify different types of rhetorical devices
- Connect the rhetorical devices used by the author with the purpose and intention of the text

CORE SKILLS

- Analyze Author's Purpose
- Determine Point of View

Key Terms

author's intention
what the writer hopes to accomplish

Vocabulary

analogy
a comparison of two things that are similar in some way

enumeration
listing or specifying one after another

rhetorical device
a language technique that writers or speakers use to create an effect

Key Concept

Authors use several types of rhetorical devices to communicate their position and to achieve their goals for writing.

When you tell a story, you most likely have a goal, or intention, such as making your friends laugh. You probably use storytelling techniques, such as comparing one thing to another, to create a humorous effect. Similarly, authors have an intention for their writing and use rhetorical devices, such as repetition or starting with a question, to produce a certain effect.

Identifying Rhetorical Devices

Authors use many different techniques to produce the result they want and to communicate their intentions. Among these techniques are **rhetorical devices**. Rhetoric is the art of speaking or writing effectively. A rhetorical device can make an opinion more convincing, an explanation clearer, or a narrative more compelling.

Below are some common rhetorical devices.

Analogy: When making an **analogy**, writers compare something they are describing to something familiar that readers can easily relate to. Analogies can make unknown, abstract, or complicated situations easier to understand.

- *Vanessa and Malika can't agree on who should have priority for using the company scanner. It's as though they are two children fighting over a ball.*

In this example, the author compares two adults using workplace equipment to two children fighting over a toy. This analogy effectively communicates the idea that Vanessa and Malika are acting childish.

Asking questions: Writers use this device to convey information. Asking a question prompts readers to consider an issue. The author then provides an answer that guides readers toward his or her way of thinking. Sometimes the author asks a question that is meant to engage the reader but isn't meant to be answered. This is known as a rhetorical question.

Enumeration: This technique involves listing a series of examples or details to explain or support a statement or position.

- *I love baseball. I love going to the stadium. I love sitting in the hard seats. I love watching the players. I love keeping statistics. I love the smell of pine tar.*

In this example, the writer makes a general statement about baseball. He or she follows with a list of details that helps the reader understand why and how much the writer loves baseball. This is a more effective way for the writer to communicate his or her message than simply stating, "I really love baseball."

Juxtaposition of opposites: With this rhetorical device, writers present two opposing ideas or situations.

- *In the same day, Winona lost her grandfather and learned that her sister had given birth to a baby girl.*

This device can also be used to differentiate an important point from an opposing point.

- *Although the taxpayers' association claims that the new plan will hike rates immediately, the plan actually ensures that rates stay flat for the next three years and increase only minimally in year four.*

Qualifying statements: A qualifying statement is extra information given to explain a previous statement.

- *Selena doesn't eat spinach. That is to say, she doesn't eat spinach unless it's part of a salad.*

Repetition and parallelism: Writers repeat phrases or ideas to strengthen their impact. Read this line from Abraham Lincoln's Gettysburg Address:

- *But, in a larger sense, we cannot dedicate—we cannot consecrate—we cannot hallow—this ground.*

Lincoln used repetition and parallelism by repeating the phrase *we cannot* three times. Notice the verbs that follow *we cannot.* Each one—*dedicate, consecrate, hallow*—means "to make a place special or sacred," and each verb increases in intensity. By using repetition and parallelism, Lincoln's sentiment is communicated with greater impact.

Directions: Read the passage about foxes. Then underline the rhetorical devices the author uses.

> You've probably heard the expression *sly as a fox.* How did the fox get its reputation for being a clever animal? The reputation may have begun with fox hunters. A hunter tries to catch a fox by chasing it on a horse. The hunter sends a pack of hound dogs ahead to find the fox, and the dogs pick up the fox's scent and chase it. Rather than slipping into the nearest thicket, the fox might continue running to keep the chase alive. If one of a pair of foxes is being chased, its mate might dash out of a hiding place and lead the pursuers in another direction. By crossing streams, running along the tops of fences, and darting through the woods, a pair of foxes can keep a pack of hounds totally confused—at least for a while.

CORE SKILL

Analyze Author's Purpose

An author's purpose is his or her reason for writing a piece. Identifying and analyzing the author's purpose will help you understand what the author wants you to take away from the text. When you read a text, ask yourself these questions:

- *Why did the author write this?*
- *What does the author want me to think or do after reading?*

Keep in mind that an author may have more than one overall purpose and different purposes for various parts of a text.

Review the passage about foxes. Write three or four sentences in which you identify the author's purpose or purposes and explain how the rhetorical devices helped you determine this purpose.

The author uses several rhetorical devices in the passage. Among them is asking and answering a question about the fox being clever. In addition, the writer ends with a qualifying statement. Most of the passage describes how foxes avoid being caught, but the writer does not want to leave the impression that foxes always evade capture. The qualifying statement *at least for a while* reminds readers that foxes are not always able to escape.

Think about Reading

Directions: Reread the passage about foxes. In a notebook, answer the questions below.

1. What type of rhetorical device is the writer using in the statement "Rather than slipping into the nearest thicket, the fox might continue running to keep the chase alive"?
2. How does the device help support the writer's point about foxes?

Identifying an Author's Intention and Effect

All authors have a reason, or purpose, for writing. The main purposes are to entertain, to inform, and to persuade. An **author's intention**, which incorporates his or her point of view and purpose, is what the author hopes to accomplish with the text. For example, an author's intention might be to make readers laugh, to clarify a difficult concept, or to change a reader's mind about an issue. Rhetorical devices help writers achieve these goals.

Directions: Read the passage below. Then answer these questions: *What is the author's purpose? What is his or her intention?*

> If you come to dinner with me instead of going to the movies, you'll have a better time. At the restaurant, they will give you a menu filled with tempting entrees, and you will be able to choose any that you desire. At the movies, you'll have to choose between overpriced popcorn with artificial butter flavoring and old candy in dusty boxes. Food at the restaurant will probably provide you with at least some nutrients, but popcorn will only leave you with pieces of kernels stuck between your teeth. You may be saying to yourself, "Yes, but what about the entertainment that the movie will provide me?" To this I say, "What could be more entertaining than my dazzling wit?"

The author's main purpose is to persuade. His or her intention is to convince a friend to skip the movies and go to dinner instead. The author clearly states his or her opinion and provides reasons to support it. Phrases such as *tempting entrees* and *any that you desire* make the restaurant seem more enjoyable than the movies. Likewise, the phrase *have to choose* makes the movies seem less appealing. The author juxtaposes attending the movie and going to dinner as a rhetorical device. The juxtaposition helps emphasize the positive aspects of going to dinner and makes the author's argument more effective.

LANGUAGE SKILLS

Participial Modifiers

A participle is a verb that acts as an adjective. It modifies nouns and pronouns and comes in two forms: present and past.

A present participial modifier is formed by adding *ing* to the end of a present-tense verb, such as *sparkle.* It can be placed before or after the word it modifies:

- I'd like a glass of sparkling water, please.
- The sea, sparkling and blue, rose to meet the jetty.

A past participial modifier is created by adding *ed* to the end of the present tense of the verb, such as *ruin.* It can also be placed before or after the word it modifies.

- The ruined castle stood stark against the gray sky.
- The trees, ruined and ragged after the storm, were chopped up and carted away.

Examine the text about going out to dinner and the memo about an office recycling program. List the participial modifiers in the passages, and determine which ones are present participles and which ones are past participles. Compare lists with a partner.

Directions: Read the memo below. Think about the writer's main intention and the effect that he hopes to have on readers. Then identify the rhetorical devices that help the author achieve his goals.

MEMO

To: All Employees
From: Carlos Stanford, Office Manager
Re: New Office Recycling Program

Did you know that...

- up to 77 percent of office paper waste is recyclable?
- a typical business wastes nearly 1.5 pounds of paper per employee daily?
- just one ton of recycled paper saves about six cubic yards of landfill space and 17 trees?

With these facts in mind, we have decided to implement a recycling program in our offices. We ask that you read through the enclosed flyer. We ask that you take a few minutes each week to participate in this effort. And we ask that you do your part to help the environment.

The flyer gives specific details about what materials can and cannot be recycled. As a general rule, almost all paper used in the office can be recycled, including letterhead, computer, notebook, and colored paper as well as magazines and newspapers. In addition, cardboard, aluminum cans, and plastic and glass bottles can also be recycled.

You will receive a small container for your daily recyclables. When your container is full, please empty it in one of the larger containers located in each work area. Bins will also be placed near photocopiers and in the cafeteria. Thank you for your participation. If you have any questions or concerns, please contact me at extension 342.

Think about Reading

Directions: Answer the questions below.

1. How do rhetorical devices help authors achieve their intention?
2. Why is it important for a writer to consider his or her intention when choosing specific words and phrases to use?

CORE SKILL

Determine Point of View

When you read a text, look for clues that help you identify how the author feels about the subject. Word choice and use of rhetorical devices are good indicators of the author's point of view.

Search online for a speech that uses at least two rhetorical devices. Write a paragraph in which you state the speaker's point of view and explain how the use of language and rhetorical devices helped you determine the point of view. Use details from the speech to support your claims.

WRITE TO LEARN

Review the passage about going to dinner versus going to the movies. Rewrite the passage with a different intention, such as to inform the reader about the health hazards of movie-theater food. Use language that helps you effectively communicate your point of view and purpose.

Summary

To communicate their intention, or what they hope to accomplish with a text, authors often use rhetorical devices. Rhetorical devices include analogy, enumeration, and repetition. These and other techniques help writers effectively convey their purpose and point of view while prompting a certain response from readers.

Vocabulary Review

Directions: Complete the paragraph using the following key terms and vocabulary words.

analogy **enumeration** **author's intention** **rhetorical device**

Because the essay was so poorly written, Tyrine was still unsure of the ________________, even after reading it three times. The essay was clearly supposed to be humorous, but the purpose was obscure. Tyrine provided a list, or an ________________ of the problems, including the inappropriate use of a(n)________________ by the writer. For example, the ________________ in which the writer compared a scalding cup of coffee to a piece of notebook paper made no sense at all.

Skill Review

Directions: Read the following excerpt from a speech by President John F. Kennedy, which he gave on September 12, 1962, before humans had been to the moon. Then choose the best answer to each question.

> No man can fully grasp how far and how fast we have come, but condense, if you will, the 50,000 years of man's recorded history in a time span of but a half-century. Stated in these terms, we know very little about the first 40 years, except at the end of them advanced man had learned to use the skins of animals to cover them. Then about 10 years ago, under this standard, man emerged from his caves to construct other kinds of shelter. Only five years ago man learned to write and use a cart with wheels. The printing press came this year, and then less than two months ago, during this whole 50-year span of human history, the steam engine provided a new source of power.
>
> Newton explored the meaning of gravity. Last month electric lights and telephones and automobiles and airplanes became available. Only last week did we develop penicillin and television and nuclear power, and now if America's new spacecraft succeeds in reaching Venus, we will have literally reached the stars before midnight tonight.
>
> This is a breathtaking pace, and such a pace cannot help but create new ills as it dispels old, new ignorance, new problems, new dangers. Surely the opening vistas of space promise high costs and hardships, as well as high reward.
>
> —From a speech by John F. Kennedy, September 12, 1962

1. What is the intention of Kennedy's speech?

A. to persuade readers that space exploration is costly and dangerous

B. to inform readers that America's new spacecraft has reached Venus

C. to persuade readers that space missions are an important human endeavor

D. to convince the audience that people have been on Earth for only 50,000 years

2. Which sentence best describes the effect of the speech?

A. It stimulates a tragic view of space exploration.

B. It prompts a sarcastic response from the audience.

C. It generates suspicion about recorded history.

D. It inspires the audience to share Kennedy's passion for the space program.

Skill Practice

Directions: Read the passage below. Then choose the best answer to each question.

Aren't your neighbors fascinating? They are not very sociable, but on a clear night you can glimpse them in the sky. Mars is sometimes as close as 55 million kilometers from your front door. It has a rocky, lifeless surface and a thin, oxygen-free atmosphere. Your other neighbor, Venus, has a thick atmosphere that would crush you instantly if your blood did not boil first. If you are invited for coffee on either planet, think twice before accepting.

1. The first sentence is an example of
   A. parallelism.
   B. a rhetorical question.
   C. a qualifying statement.
   D. juxtaposition of opposites.

2. Which best describes the author's intention?
   A. to persuade readers to stay away from Mars and Venus
   B. to convince readers that Mars and Venus are actually people
   C. to entertain readers while informing them about Mars and Venus
   D. to explain to readers why Mars and Venus are so different from each other

3. When comparing Mars and Venus to neighbors, the author is using a rhetorical device known as
   A. analogy.
   B. parallelism.
   C. enumeration.
   D. juxtaposition.

4. Which best describes the effect of the passage?
   A. It convinces readers that Mars and Venus are superior to other planets.
   B. It motivates readers to travel to outer space.
   C. It elicits skepticism from readers.
   D. It amuses and educates readers.

Writing Practice

Directions: Find the transcript of a recent political speech on a government website, such as the site of the White House, the US Senate, the US House of Representatives, or a local government website. Then write an essay in which you describe the topic of the speech and analyze the speaker's intention and effect. Describe at least two rhetorical devices the speaker uses, and explain how these devices help the speaker achieve his or her goals. Use evidence from the speech to support your analysis.

Directions: Read the following passage. Then choose the best answer to questions 1 through 3.

As an American, I want to speak for those women in my own country, women who are raising children on the minimum wage, women who can't afford health care or child care, women whose lives are threatened by violence, including violence in their own homes.

I want to speak up for mothers who are fighting for good schools, safe neighborhoods, clean air, and clean airwaves; for older women, some of them widows, who find that, after raising their families, their skills and life experiences are not valued in the marketplace; for women who are working all night as nurses, hotel clerks, or fast food chefs so that they can be at home during the day with their children; and for women everywhere who simply don't have time to do everything they are called upon to do each and every day.

Speaking to you today, I speak for them, just as each of us speaks for women around the world who are denied the chance to go to school, or see a doctor, or own property, or have a say about the direction of their lives, simply because they are women. The truth is that most women around the world work both inside and outside the home, usually by necessity.

We need to understand there is no one formula for how women should lead our lives. That is why we must respect the choices that each woman makes for herself and her family. Every woman deserves the chance to realize her own potential. But we must recognize that women will never gain full dignity until their human rights are respected and protected.

—From *Remarks to the UN 4th World Conference on Women Plenary Session, September 5, 1995, Beijing, China* by Hillary Rodham Clinton

1. What is the speaker's purpose for giving this speech?

A. to explain the increase in the number of women who stay at home

B. to describe a formula for how all women should lead their lives

C. to inform listeners that women's rights are respected worldwide

D. to persuade others that women's human rights should be protected

2. How does the use of repetition help communicate the author's point of view?

A. It allows her to present opposing ideas about women's rights.

B. It helps her compare similar occupations among women.

C. It emphasizes the multitude of women who deserve human rights.

D. It provides examples of successful women.

3. What is the main structure of the passage?

A. cause and effect

B. description

C. problem and solution

D. sequence

Directions: Read the following passage. Then choose the best answer to questions 4 through 7.

The Hard Facts on Helmet Laws

The tug-of-war between motorcycle safety and personal freedom has been going on for decades. As helmet laws were implemented in some states and repealed in others, researchers gathered numerous statistics on how the laws affected rider safety. For example:

- In 1997 Arkansas and Texas repealed helmet laws. As of May 1998, helmet use fell from 97 percent in both states to 52 percent in Arkansas and 66 percent in Texas. Motorcycle operator fatalities increased by 21 percent in Arkansas and 31 percent in Texas.

(Continued on page 173)

(Continued from page 172)

- In 1989 Nebraska enacted a helmet law and experienced 32 percent fewer fatalities to motorcyclists that year.
- In 1992 California required all motorcyclists to wear helmets, and that year there were 36 percent fewer motorcyclist deaths.

These numbers clearly illuminate the success of helmet laws in saving lives. People often argue that if riders choose not to wear helmets, they're only responsible to themselves. But injured riders affect all taxpayers because almost half of motorcycle crash victims don't have insurance that covers all their medical costs. It's a fact that helmets lower victims' medical costs, the length of time spent in the hospital, and the chance of long-term disability.

Another common argument against helmets is that they restrict people's vision and hearing, thus causing more crashes. However, a study done by the U.S. Department of Transportation showed that people wearing helmets could see and hear traffic nearly as well as people without helmets.

Who benefits from helmet laws? The statistics show that we all do. Helmet laws have been successful in saving motorcyclists' lives and taxpayers' money.

4. Which purpose belongs in the center circle of the concept web?

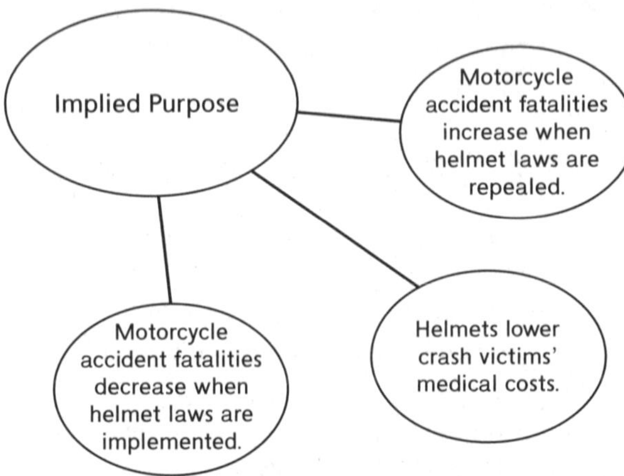

A. to persuade readers to wear helmets
B. to warn readers that their rights are being threatened
C. to inform readers about which states have helmet laws
D. to describe the serious injuries sustained in motorcycle accidents

5. What does the author accomplish by presenting information that refutes the opposing viewpoint?

A. The author offers an unstable outlook.
B. The author strengthens his or her own position.
C. The author provides a more biased discussion.
D. The author supports the opposing viewpoint.

6. Determine the author's point of view based on this sentence from the passage: "These numbers clearly illuminate the success of helmet laws."

A. The author has a positive point of view toward helmet laws.
B. The author has a positive point of view about statistics.
C. The author has a negative point of view toward helmet laws.
D. The author has a neutral point of view about helmet laws.

7. Which statement from the passage reflects the author's position on helmet laws?

A. "The tug-of-war between motorcycle safety and personal freedom has been going on for decades."
B. "[I]f riders choose not to wear helmets, they're only responsible to themselves."
C. "[H]elmets . . . restrict people's vision and hearing, thus causing more crashes."
D. "Helmet laws have been successful in saving motorcyclists' lives and taxpayers' money."

Directions: Read the following passage. Then choose the best answer to questions 8 through 10.

Building the Erie Canal

In 1817 DeWitt Clinton, the governor of New York, persuaded the state legislature to pass a bill allotting $7 million dollars to build a canal between the Hudson River and Lake Erie. The waterway would be 363 miles long, running from Albany, New York, which sat on the upper Hudson River, to Buffalo, New York, on the eastern shore of Lake Erie. Although the canal would expedite shipping between the Midwest and East, critics scoffed at the idea. They called it "Clinton's Folly" or "Clinton's Ditch," and said that it was a waste of time and tax dollars. They believed that no one would use the canal if it were built.

Despite all the criticism, for the next eight years, thousands of British, German, and Irish immigrants joined forces to dig the canal. It was a remarkable undertaking, considering that the United States didn't even have an engineering school yet.

By October of 1825, the Erie Canal was complete. DeWitt Clinton himself opened the canal by traveling via boat from Buffalo to Albany and then down to New York City. Along the length of the canal, 85 separate locks, like steps of a staircase, gradually lifted boats up the 500-foot rise in elevation between the Hudson River and Lake Erie. Boats weren't propelled by sails, oars, or engines. Instead, they were pulled by teams of horses, oxen, or mules from a path along the bank of the canal.

The canal immediately had the effect that Clinton had hoped for. Grains and produce were shipped more quickly and economically from the Midwest to the East. In addition, the canal allowed settlers to travel more easily into the areas of the Great Lakes and upper Midwest. New York City, at the mouth of the Hudson River, became the busiest port in America.

8. What is the author's purpose in the first paragraph of the passage?

A. to refute opposing views

B. to provide background information

C. to express the author's point of view

D. to explain the author's position

9. How does the author refute the position that building the canal was a waste of time and money?

A. by stating the good points in the opposing position

B. by explaining who the critics were who opposed the canal

C. by comparing the opposing position to his or her own position

D. by presenting information that contradicts the opposing position

10. Which of the following best describes an implied purpose of the text?

A. to explain that too much money was spent to build "Clinton's Folly"

B. to point out that more money should have been spent to complete the Erie Canal more quickly

C. to explain why the money spent to build the Erie Canal was a good investment

D. to suggest that the money spent on the Erie Canal could have been used more wisely

Check Your Understanding

On the following chart, circle the number of any item you answered incorrectly. In the third column, you will see the pages that you can review to study the content covered in the question. Pay particular attention to reviewing those lessons in which you missed half or more of the questions.

Lesson	Core Skill	Item Number(s)	Review Page(s)
Lesson 5.1 Determine Author's Purpose and Point of View	Determine Author's Purpose	1, 8	143
	Establish Point of View	2, 6	145
Lesson 5.2 Analyze How Author's Purpose Determines Structure	Analyze Text Structure	3	149
	Determine Author's Purpose	1, 8	151
Lesson 5.3 Infer Author's Purpose	Use a Graphic Organizer	4	155
	Determine the Implicit Purpose in a Text	4, 10	156
Lesson 5.4 Analyze How Authors Differentiate Their Positions	Identify an Author's Position	7	161
	Evaluate Arguments	5, 9	162
Lesson 5.5 Analyze Author's Intention and Effect	Analyze Author's Purpose	8	167
	Determine Point of View	2, 6	169

WRITE ABOUT Nixon's Resignation Speech

Read President Richard M. Nixon's resignation speech on page 312, and research its historical background. Then write an essay in which you

1. identify Nixon's audience and the purpose (or purposes) of his speech
2. describe the historical background of the speech
3. examine the language (tone and word choice) that Nixon used in his speech
4. assess whether or not the speech is effective. Be sure to cite specific evidence from the speech and from your research to support your claims.

BEFORE YOU WRITE Research the Historical Background

After you read Nixon's speech, find out more about why Nixon resigned and what was happening in the United States at the time, the early 1970s. Use a news article from a reliable source such as *The Washington Post* or *The New York Times*. You may want to use search terms such as "Watergate scandal," "Nixon hearings," and "Nixon resignation."

Use a two-column chart to take notes on the relationship between historical circumstances and parts of Nixon's speech. You can find an example of a two-column chart in the Graphic Organizer section at the back of the book. Label the left column "Historical Background" and the right column "Nixon's Speech." As you read the news article, record notes about the events leading up to Nixon's resignation in the left column. Then go back to Nixon's speech. In the right column of the chart, identify sections of the speech that relate to the events you noted in the left column.

When you have finished, review your chart. Ask yourself: *Who was Nixon's audience, and what was Nixon's purpose for giving the speech?* Use your answer to develop a topic sentence for your essay. Note that you can find clues about Nixon's audience early in his speech, in the way he addresses listeners. Also, keep in mind that speakers often have more than one purpose. In many cases, they do not state their purposes explicitly, or directly.

TIP Use Clear Pronoun References in Your Essay

Pronouns are words that are used in place of nouns. For example, *he, him, she, her, they,* and *them* are substitutes for peoples' names. *It, this, that, these,* and *those* are substitutes for the names of objects, places, ideas, or other nouns. Possessive pronouns such as *his* and *her* show ownership, or possession, of a noun.

In his speech, Nixon uses the pronoun *he* to refer to the vice president and the possessive pronoun *his* to refer to the vice president's shoulders.

> *In passing this office to the vice president, I also do so with the profound sense of the weight of responsibility that will fall on his shoulders tomorrow and, therefore, of the understanding, the patience, the cooperation he will need from all Americans.*

This sentence would have been awkward if Nixon had repeated the phrase *the vice president* instead of replacing it with pronouns. Writers use pronouns to make writing more interesting and less cumbersome.

Sometimes, however, pronouns can make writing confusing for the reader. For example,

> *Yesenia met Chantel for lunch. She gave her a sandwich.*

In this sentence, it is not clear who *she* and *her* refer to. Did Yesenia give Chantel a sandwich? Or did Chantel give Yesenia a sandwich? When using pronouns, make sure the reader knows who or what you are referring to. How might you change these sentences to make them less confusing? One option is to combine the sentences:

- Yesenia met Chantel for lunch and gave her a sandwich.

WHILE YOU WRITE Synthesize and Analyze Information

You have identified Nixon's audience and purpose or purposes for speaking. As you describe Nixon's audience and purpose, use information from the news article as well as details from the speech, such as quotations and paraphrases, to support your claims.

Use notes from the left side of your two-column chart to summarize what was happening in the United States at the time of Nixon's resignation. What was Nixon responding to? Think about the language that Nixon used in the speech. What words and phrases alert you to Nixon's audience and purpose? Explain how Nixon's audience and purpose influenced his tone and word choices.

In your conclusion, assess whether or not the speech was effective. Do you think the speech achieved each of the speaker's purposes that you identified? Support your claim with details from the speech, information from the news article, and your own reasoning.

TIP Be Sure to . . . Capitalize Properly

A proper noun is a noun that names a specific person, place, thing, or idea. Proper nouns generally begin with a capital letter. Common nouns begin with a lowercase letter, unless they begin a sentence.

Proper nouns include the following:

- Names of people, including their title
  Millions of people watched and listened to President Nixon's resignation speech.
- Names of places, such as countries, states, counties, cities, landforms, and specific buildings
  The White House is in Washington, DC.
- Names of specific events
  The Watergate scandal occurred while the United States was involved in the Vietnam War.
- Days and months, but not seasons
  Nixon resigned during the summer, on Thursday, August 8, 1974.

You should also capitalize the first word of a direct quotation that is a complete sentence.

Nixon said, "Therefore, I shall resign the presidency effective at noon tomorrow."

After you write, review your work to make sure that words are capitalized properly.

AFTER YOU WRITE Check Your Work

Reread the writing assignment. Then read your essay carefully three times.

The first time you read, ask yourself whether you have completed the writing assignment correctly. Have you (1) identified the speaker's purpose or purposes and audience, (2) described the historical context, or background, of the speech, (3) explained how the speaker's audience and purpose(s) influenced his tone and word choices; (4) assessed whether or not the speech was effective, and (5) used evidence from the speech and from your research to support your claims?

Then read the essay again. Did you use pronouns properly? Does each pronoun have a clear reference? Are the quotations accurate? Did you capitalize proper nouns and leave common nouns lowercase?

Reread the essay one last time. Did you use correct grammar, spelling, and punctuation? Do you see any errors? Did you type the words you meant to use?

Before submitting your essay, have another student read it and provide you with feedback.

Chapter 6

Evaluate Textual Evidence

You might not realize it, but arguments are happening all around you. Advertisements, blogs, and other types of persuasive texts contain an argument, or set of reasons that support an opinion or point of view. In an argument, the author states that something is true, or makes a claim, and then provides evidence and reasoning to support it. You can evaluate an argument by identifying the author's claim and determining how well it is supported.

Ingram Publishing

In this chapter you will study these topics:

Lesson 6.1

Identify Argument Development

Have you ever read a restaurant review? The author might be trying to convince you to eat at the restaurant or to stay away. A review is a kind of argument, and whatever the author's opinion is, it should be supported with reasons and evidence. Learn how writers construct their arguments.

Lesson 6.2

Identify Supporting Evidence

Have you ever watched a political debate on television? The speakers often make conflicting statements, and the audience has to decide whose argument makes the most sense. The strength of an argument comes from the evidence and reasons that are used to support it. Learn how to identify the supporting evidence in an argument.

Lesson 6.3

Evaluate Relevance and Sufficiency

Have you ever received an e-mail message that tried to convince you to buy a product or service? Authors of these messages and other types of persuasive documents must provide a sufficient amount of evidence that is related to their claim in order to be convincing. Learn how to evaluate the relevance and sufficiency of evidence in an argument.

Lesson 6.4

Evaluate Validity and Reasoning

How can you tell whether an author's argument is valid? Authors who are trying to convince you that their argument is reasonable must support their position with credible evidence that makes sense. Learn how to evaluate the validity and reasoning of an argument.

Lesson 6.5

Evaluate Logic and Identify Hidden Assumptions

Arguments are not always based on evidence alone. Sometimes an author starts with a fact or assumption, or unproven idea, and argues by drawing a series of logical conclusions from it. Learn how to evaluate arguments based on logical reasoning and how to identify stated and hidden assumptions.

Goal Setting

Has a writer or speaker ever tried to persuade you to buy something or change your point of view? Why was he or she successful or unsuccessful? How can these lessons improve the way you evaluate persuasive texts?

Why is it important to be able to evaluate the validity of an argument? How can this help you while shopping, voting, or making other decisions?

LESSON 6.1 Identify Argument Development

LESSON OBJECTIVES

- Explain the steps that a writer uses to build an argument
- Analyze texts to determine how authors build an argument

CORE SKILLS

- Understand the Relationship among Ideas
- Analyze Text Structure to Evaluate an Argument

Key Terms

argument
reasons given to persuade an audience

claim
a statement that something is true

evidence
details that support a claim

Vocabulary

proof
evidence establishing a fact

reiterate
repeat for emphasis or clarity

vague
unclear

Key Concept

The purpose of an argument is to persuade the reader that a claim is reasonable. A well-developed argument includes reasons and evidence that support the writer's claim.

Have you ever read a movie review? The author might be trying to convince you to see the movie or to avoid it. Whatever the author's opinion is, the review should include reasons and evidence that support it. Valid, relevant evidence is more likely to persuade readers to share the author's opinion.

Developing an Argument

When you read documents such as speeches, memos, letters, and even some instructional texts, you'll notice that the authors make a **claim**. A claim states the writer's opinion on a topic. Writers try to convince readers that the claim is true by presenting a set of persuasive reasons, or an **argument**. **Evidence**, details that support a claim, helps persuade an audience. To build an argument in any type of text, writers follow a series of steps that include stating a claim, supporting it with evidence, and finishing with a strong conclusion.

The Claim

Every argument starts with a claim that states the author's opinion on a topic. The claim might also state what the author wants readers to do or believe. It's important to begin an argument with a claim that can be supported by reasons and solid evidence in the form of facts and examples. As the writer develops the argument, he or she tries to persuade readers to think a certain way or to take some kind of action.

Directions: Read the passage and write down the claim that the author makes.

> The Great Wall of China was one of the most impressive engineering projects ever undertaken. The barrier, which was intended to protect central China from invaders, was begun around 403 BC. It stretches about 5,500 miles (8,851 km) from the Bo Gulf of the Yellow Sea to a point far inland. In some areas, the wall has fallen into ruin, but much of it is still standing today. The ruined areas don't detract from the greatness of the whole.

If you wrote that the claim in the passage on the previous page is that the Great Wall of China was one of the most impressive engineering projects ever undertaken, you understand what the author wants readers to believe.

The Evidence

Once a writer has made a claim, the work of persuading begins. To support the claim, a writer must provide convincing examples and **proof**, or evidence that establishes a fact. The supporting evidence should be accurate and relevant to the topic to prove that the claim is reasonable.

The Conclusion

The last step in developing an argument is to write a conclusion. The conclusion should **reiterate**, or repeat, the claim and summarize the supporting evidence. It might also include an appeal to the audience to accept the author's claim. The conclusion can even present a new idea that follows logically from the argument.

Look at how the concluding sentence in this passage reiterates the claim that some lead explorers were despised by their expedition crews:

> Some famous explorers were not very popular with their expedition crews. They probably inspired the anger of the people they managed because their job was to lead people into dangerous, uncomfortable places and situations. Henry Hudson, for example, was set adrift in the bay that bears his name by a disgruntled, hungry crew. It was Hudson's last voyage. The explorer La Salle was killed by a band of 20 explorers on the Gulf Coast in 1687, and his body was left to the buzzards. This dreadful act might be explained by the fact that the band of 20 was all that remained of the original force of 400. These crews were not subtle in demonstrating their contempt for their leaders.

Think about Reading

Directions: Read the following sentences. Place a checkmark beside the sentences that provide evidence to support the author's claim.

1. ________ Some famous explorers were not very popular with their expedition crews.
2. ________ Henry Hudson, for example, was set adrift in the bay that bears his name by a disgruntled, hungry crew.
3. ________ The explorer La Salle was killed by a band of 20 explorers on the Gulf Coast in 1687, and his body was left to the buzzards.
4. ________ This dreadful act might be explained by the fact that the band of 20 was all that remained of the original force of 400.

WRITE TO LEARN

Write a concluding paragraph that summarizes the evidence presented in the passage about the Great Wall of China. In your paragraph, include reasons why the evidence supports the claim. Make sure you reiterate the claim for emphasis and clarity.

CORE SKILL

Understand the Relationship among Ideas

To understand how facts and examples support an author's claim, follow this procedure:

1. Read the entire passage.
2. Ask yourself: *What is the author trying to convince me to believe or do?*
3. List the evidence that the author provides to support the claim.
4. Ask yourself: *Do the ideas in the passage connect to each other and support the claim?*

Find an opinion article that interests you in a print or online newspaper. With a partner, use the procedure above to identify the claim and the supporting evidence. Then write a paragraph describing the connection between the claim and the supporting evidence.

21st CENTURY SKILL

Civic Literacy

A good writer builds an argument with several pieces of evidence. In the passage on this page, the author poses an argument about the effect of Herbert Hoover's election and presidency. The time described is an economically difficult period in US history. Understanding the implications of civic decisions is an important part of being a responsible citizen.

Read the passage, and ask yourself the following questions:

- *What does the author want the reader to believe?*
- *What pieces of evidence does the author give to develop the argument?*

Then write a letter to the editor of a newspaper from the point of view of a citizen who lived during this time. State a claim about the impact of the economic crisis on your life. Give evidence to support your claim. Finish with a concluding sentence that reiterates your claim.

Analyzing Argument Development

Sometimes an author's claim is stated directly, and sometimes it is **vague**, or unclear. Analyzing an argument can help you gain a better understanding of the author's claim.

Identifying the Claim

To identify the author's claim, think about the idea that the author is presenting. Ask yourself: *What is the author asking me to believe? What is the author asking me to do, and why? What opinion is the author expressing?*

Directions: Read the passage below. Then write the opinion that the author is expressing.

> In the election of 1928, Herbert Hoover, a Republican, was elected President of the United States over Alfred E. Smith. It was one of the biggest mistakes Americans ever made. He was sworn in as president in March 1929, and just a few months later, in the fall of 1929, the New York Stock Exchange, America's largest stock market, crashed. Many investors lost money, and soon the United States dipped into an economic depression. It was the worst time in the country's history. During President Hoover's term of office (1929–1933), unemployment rose, national output declined, many factories were idle, and unemployed workers sank into despair. As president, Hoover was a poor leader and an even worse decision maker. Many people could not make their monthly mortgage payments, and families were evicted from their homes by the thousands. Shantytowns, sometimes called Hoovervilles, sprang up all over the country, created from old tin and salvaged wood.

You correctly identified the claim if you wrote that the author's opinion is that the election of Herbert Hoover was one of the biggest mistakes Americans ever made.

When you first read a text that presents an argument, it is helpful to think about the intended audience. Ask yourself: *Who is this author trying to persuade?* Answering this question provides clues about the author's goal and his or her expectations of the audience's interests and needs. It may also reveal why the author chose a particular structure for the argument. For example, evidence might be presented in order of importance. With this text structure, authors can emphasize the strongest point by placing it last in the text, where it will be most memorable to readers. Authors might also use cause and effect to develop an argument. This type of structure connects the reasons things happen to the potential consequences of the events. Authors choose the content and the structure that will have the greatest impact on the intended audience.

Directions: Read the following workplace memo. Write the claim that you, as a call center employee, will be stating to clients to convince them to refinance their mortgage loans.

MEMO

To: All Sales Associates
From: Lauren Block, Director of Marketing
Re: Mortgage Talking Points

To meet our goals for this quarter, we must increase the number of refinanced loans for existing clients. Use the following information to encourage callers to refinance their mortgage loan with us.

Mortgage interest rates are falling. Refinancing now can help you reduce the cost of borrowing money over the long term.

- Refinancing can reduce your monthly payment for a repayment term that is similar to your existing mortgage.
- Refinancing can reduce your repayment term while making a monthly payment that is similar to your existing mortgage.

Refinancing pays off your existing mortgage loan and starts a new loan. This is more helpful during the early years of your existing mortgage, when most of the payment is applied to the loan's interest. It makes less sense to refinance a loan later in the loan's life cycle when payments are applied primarily to the loan principal.

Think about Reading

Directions: Next to each statement, circle C if the statement is the claim in the letter or E if it is supporting evidence for the claim.

1. C E Refinancing can provide benefits that will help clients reduce the cost of borrowing money.
2. C E Refinancing can reduce monthly payments.
3. C E Refinancing can reduce the repayment term.

Summary

An argument starts with a claim, or a statement about a topic, that the author wants to persuade readers to believe. In a good argument, claims are supported by evidence such as facts and examples. The conclusion of an argument restates the author's claim and summarizes the evidence. When an argument is structured properly, there is a clear relationship among ideas and readers can easily understand the author's point of view.

CORE SKILL

Analyze Text Structure to Evaluate an Argument

In workplace memos, it can be difficult to identify the claim because there may be more than one. When you analyze the structure of the argument, you can clarify what the author of the memo wants to accomplish. The author may be asking a question and answering it, defining a problem and giving a solution, or presenting evidence in a particular order of importance.

Read the memo about mortgages on this page. Ask yourself: *What does the author state that she wants employees to do? What is the unstated claim the employees need to understand? What is the structure of the first paragraph? How is it different from the structure of rest of the memo? Why are the structures different?*

Write the answers to the questions above. Discuss your answers in a small group.

Vocabulary Review

Directions: Complete the sentences using the following key terms and vocabulary words.

argument **claim** **evidence** **proof** **reiterate** **vague**

1. A(n) ________________ can be structured as a problem and solution or as a question and answer.
2. Evidence establishing a fact is called ________________.
3. The author's ________________ that only girls like ballet is false.
4. I don't know what the author wants me to believe because her claim is ________________.
5. Facts, reasons, and examples are types of supporting ________________.
6. State a claim at the beginning of an argument and ________________ it in the conclusion.

Skill Review

Directions: Read the passage below. Then complete each activity.

Today, education is perhaps the most important function of state and local governments. Compulsory school attendance laws and the great expenditures for education both demonstrate our recognition of the importance of education to our democratic society. It is required in the performance of our most basic public responsibilities, even service in the armed forces. It is the very foundation of good citizenship. Today it is a principal instrument in awakening the child to cultural values, in preparing him for later professional training, and in helping him to adjust normally to his environment. In these days, it is doubtful that any child may reasonably be expected to succeed in life if he is denied the opportunity of an education. Such an opportunity, where the state has undertaken to provide it, is a right which must be made available to all on equal terms.

We come then to the question presented: Does segregation of children in public schools solely on the basis of race, even though the physical facilities and other "tangible" factors may be equal, deprive the children of the minority group of equal educational opportunities? We believe that it does.

. . . To separate [students] from others of similar age and qualifications solely because of their race generates a feeling of inferiority as to their status in the community that may affect their hearts and minds in a way unlikely ever to be undone . . .

We conclude that in the field of public education the doctrine of "separate but equal" has no place. Separate educational facilities are inherently unequal.

—From *Brown v. Board of Education Ruling* by the Supreme Court of the United States

1. What claim is made in the passage?
   A. Separate educational facilities are unequal.
   B. Separate educational facilities have the same resources.
   C. Separate educational facilities are the foundation of good citizenship.
   D. Separate educational facilities provide the same level of education.

2. How is this argument structured?
   A. Problem and solution
   B. Question and answer
   C. Evidence presented from least to most important
   D. Evidence presented from most to least important

3. The conclusion ________________ the claim and summarizes the points made in the argument.

4. The authors' intended audience for this argument is ________________.

Skill Practice

Directions: Read the passage below. Then choose the best answer to each question.

> That man over there says that women need to be helped into carriages, and lifted over ditches, and to have the best place everywhere. Nobody ever helps me into carriages, or over mud-puddles, or gives me any best place! And ain't I a woman? Look at me! Look at my arm! I have ploughed and planted, and gathered into barns, and no man could head me! And ain't I a woman? I could work as much and eat as much as a man—when I could get it—and bear the lash as well! And ain't I a woman? I have borne thirteen children, and seen most all sold off to slavery, and when I cried out with my mother's grief, none but Jesus heard me! And ain't I a woman?
>
> Then they talk about this thing in the head; what's this they call it? [member of audience whispers, "intellect"] That's it, honey. What's that got to do with women's rights or negroes' rights? If my cup won't hold but a pint, and yours holds a quart, wouldn't you be mean not to let me have my little half measure full?
>
> Then that little man in black there, he says women can't have as much rights as men, 'cause Christ wasn't a woman! Where did your Christ come from? Where did your Christ come from? From God and a woman! Man had nothing to do with Him.
>
> If the first woman God ever made was strong enough to turn the world upside down all alone, these women together ought to be able to turn it back, and get it right side up again! And now they is asking to do it, the men better let them.
>
> —From "Ain't I a Woman?" by Sojourner Truth

1. Which sentence best states the argument made in the passage?

A. Intellect should not determine who has rights and who does not.

B. Men think women are weak and need to be helped with heavy tasks.

C. Religious leaders think that women don't have as many rights as men.

D. Women are asking for rights, and men should stand aside and let them have those rights.

2. Which sentence describes evidence presented in the argument?

A. Women work, eat, and suffer like men.

B. Women should be given the same rights as men.

C. The preacher says that women don't have rights because Christ wasn't a woman.

D. Men say women need to be lifted over ditches and given the best place everywhere.

Writing Practice

Directions: Search the Internet for a historical document that presents an argument about an important political or social issue. Analyze the argument. First, write the claim or claims that the author makes. Then, list the evidence the author provides to support the claim. Finally, describe what the author wants the reader to believe or do.

LESSON 6.2 Identify Supporting Evidence

LESSON OBJECTIVES

- Identify supporting evidence for a claim
- Determine whether evidence supports a claim

CORE SKILLS

- Evaluate Arguments
- Cite Specific Evidence

Key Terms

logical evidence
clear and reasonable support for a claim

supporting evidence
facts, reasons, and examples that back up a claim

Vocabulary

connected
linked or joined together

faulty
not valid; ineffective

reasoning
process of thinking, understanding, and forming conclusions

Key Concept

Authors use various types of reasoning in developing an argument. Some types of reasoning are useful, but others are ineffective.

Have you ever watched a political debate on television? Politicians present conflicting claims, and the audience decides who has the better reasoning and the better argument. Reading persuasive text is like listening to a debate. You can identify and evaluate the reasons an author gives as supporting evidence to determine whether or not an argument is valid.

Supporting Evidence

Marketing materials such as advertisements and brochures are written to convince readers that they need what a particular company is selling. Political speeches are given to convince listeners that a candidate or an action is right. Authors of these communications present claims—what they want audiences to think or believe. Claims must be supported with evidence, or facts, reasons, and examples. Authors use this **supporting evidence** to back up a claim and to persuade you, the reader, that the claim is reasonable.

There are three types of supporting evidence. Facts are the most credible type of support. Good writers also give examples to show that a claim is reasonable. Thoughtful, well-founded opinions may also serve as supporting evidence. The more evidence a writer provides to support a claim, the more reasonable the claim will seem to the reader.

Logical Evidence

A claim should be backed up with **logical evidence**, or evidence that is clear and reasonable. In addition, the supporting evidence must reasonably lead to the claim. If it isn't **connected**, or linked in some way, to the claim, the evidence doesn't contribute to a logical argument.

Directions: Read the passage on the next page and write down logical evidence that supports the claim that "the discovery of the polio vaccine is one of the most thrilling stories in the history of medicine."

Pixtal/AGE Fotostock

> The discovery of the polio vaccine is one of the most thrilling stories in the history of medicine. In the ten years following the development of the polio vaccine, the reported cases of polio in the United States were cut by 80 percent. In New York City alone, cases dropped by 93 percent. One of the most dreaded diseases was brought under control by a simple vaccination.

Did you write that reported polio cases in the United States dropped by 80 percent within ten years of the vaccine's discovery and that in New York City the cases dropped by 93 percent? These details are logical evidence that support the author's claim and make the argument reasonable and valid.

Emotional Appeals and Faulty Logic

Sometimes the evidence an author provides is not legitimate. It may be an appeal to your emotions or a statement about a person's character.

Appeals to emotion are often used in politics and advertising. For example, an ad for a pharmaceutical company—a company that develops and produces medications—may show someone playing with a cute puppy or a loving couple enjoying a sunset together. However, these pictures have no real connection to the characteristics of the medication being advertised. The company's goal is for viewers to associate the product with pleasant images and emotions.

In addition, political speeches and advertising materials frequently use statements about character in place of valid evidence. Imagine a debate on the economy in which one candidate says, "Are we supposed to take this plan seriously? After all, my opponent failed math in high school!" By making this remark, the speaker hopes to cast doubt on the opponent's ability to deal with economic issues. In reality, this comment does not supply any analysis or prove that the other candidate's figures are wrong, so it is not valid supporting evidence.

Logical **reasoning**—thinking, understanding, and forming conclusions—is based on facts and relevant examples. Read the following book review for another example of logic that is **faulty**, or not valid.

> Everyone should read Baron Childs' new novel *Jumping to Conclusions*. The latest novel by my favorite author is about a man who decides to make a career of bungee jumping. I loved it, and I'm sure it will go on the bestseller list. Every book I've ever given a good review has gone on the bestseller list, so you should definitely buy the book. You'd be a fool not to like it, because it is sure to win awards, and you read about it here first! What are you waiting for? Enjoy!

Note the reviewer's claim that "you'd be a fool" not to like the book is a statement about character. In addition, the reviewer gives his or her prediction that the book will be a bestseller as evidence that you should buy the book. This is faulty logic.

CORE SKILL

Evaluate Arguments

To evaluate an argument based on its supporting evidence, follow this procedure:

1. Read the entire passage.
2. Ask yourself: *What is the author's claim? What does the author want readers to believe? What evidence does the author give to support the claim?*
3. List examples, facts, and well-founded opinions that the author provides to support the claim.
4. Consider whether the evidence persuades you to accept the author's claim. Ask yourself: *Do I still have questions about whether the claim is reasonable?*

In a print or an online source, find a transcript of a political debate. With a partner, identify each participant's claim and supporting evidence using the procedure above. Then decide whether each claim is reasonable based on the supporting evidence.

WRITE TO LEARN

Imagine that you have read *Jumping to Conclusions* by Baron Childs, the novel reviewed in the passage on the previous page. Write a book review in which you state a different claim from the one presented in the passage and include logical supporting evidence for or against reading the book. Make up examples from the book as evidence. Be sure to support your claim.

WORKPLACE SKILL

Evaluate Policy Documents

Employers often require staff to read workplace documents such as memos, written policies, and procedures manuals. When you read these documents, look for supporting evidence to help you understand the author's claim and what you should do with the information.

Read the passage about biological hazards in the workplace and ask yourself the following questions:

- *What is the author's claim?*
- *What evidence does the author provide to support the claim?*
- *What does the author want readers to do with the information?*

Then write an e-mail message to a fellow hospital employee who has not yet read the document. In it, explain the author's claim, the evidence provided to support the claim, and instructions for how to use the information.

Think about Reading

Directions: Read the following phrases. Decide whether each phrase is an example of logical or faulty evidence for a book reviewer's claim. Circle the L for logical or the F for faulty.

1. L F a detailed explanation of the book's plot
2. L F the reviewer's relationship to the book's author
3. L F humorous or vivid descriptions of scenes from the book
4. L F the reviewer's reputation as a writer

Connecting Claims and Evidence

The ability to evaluate supporting evidence is crucial to understanding writing in which authors try to convince readers to do something or to think a certain way. If the evidence does not support the author's claim, then the argument is not valid.

When reading a persuasive text, ask yourself whether the evidence is directly related to the claim. If the author provides valid supporting evidence that connects with his or her claim in a clear and logical way, then the claim is reasonable.

As you read the passage below, identify the author's claim and draw lines connecting the claim to the supporting evidence.

> Occupations that deal with plants or animals or their products or with food and food processing may expose workers to biological hazards. Laboratory and medical personnel also can be exposed to biological hazards. Any occupations that [involve] contact with bodily fluids pose a risk to workers from biological hazards.
>
> In occupations where animals are involved, biological hazards are dealt with by preventing and controlling diseases in the animal population. It is crucial to properly care for and handle infected animals. Also, effective personal hygiene helps keep worker risks to a minimum. It is particularly important to pay proper attention to minor cuts and scratches, especially on the hands and forearms.
>
> In occupations where there is potential exposure to biological hazards, workers should practice proper personal hygiene. Hand washing is particularly important. Hospitals should also provide proper ventilation and proper personal protective equipment, such as gloves and respirators. In addition, they should provide adequate infectious waste disposal systems and appropriate controls. This includes isolation in instances of particularly contagious diseases such as tuberculosis.
>
> —Adapted from *OSHA Office of Training and Education: Industrial Hygiene*

The supporting evidence explains the types of hazards workers encounter in various occupations in order to convince employers and workers that they should take measures to protect against those hazards. Your lines should connect the hazards (the evidence) with the means of protection (the claim).

Think about the advertising images mentioned previously. The pharmaceutical company hopes viewers will associate their product with emotionally appealing images. Moreover, images in pharmaceutical ads may be used to distract viewers from relevant facts and details about the medication, such as negative side effects. The images are not really connected with the claim and do not provide logical support.

Based on other evidence provided in the advertisement, the claim might still be valid. This evidence may include statistics (for example, "83% of migraine suffers who took this medication reported a noticeable decrease in symptoms within one hour"). It may also include other findings from medical studies, reports from users of the medication, and statements of opinion from medical professionals. All these examples connect directly with the claim and provide valid evidence.

Think about Reading

Directions: Reread the passage about exposure to biological hazards in the workplace. Then choose the sentence that directly connects the importance of hand washing with hazards encountered in working with animals.

A. It is crucial to properly care for and handle infected animals.

B. When working with animals, effective personal hygiene helps keep worker risks to a minimum.

C. Biological hazards are dealt with by preventing and controlling diseases in the animal population.

D. Any occupations that result in contact with bodily fluids pose a risk to workers from biological hazards.

Summary

When reading an argument, ask yourself: *What is the author's claim? What evidence does the author give to support the claim?* Use reasoning to evaluate the author's argument and to determine whether it is valid. If the supporting evidence is logical and you can cite specific evidence that connects directly to the author's claim, then you can safely say that the argument is valid and reasonable.

CORE SKILL

Cite Specific Evidence

To evaluate an argument, you must be able to cite specific text evidence that supports the author's claim.

Find an editorial in a print or online source. Read the editorial, then ask yourself:

- *What is the author's claim?*
- *What evidence does the author provide to support the claim?*
- *How does the evidence connect to the claim?*
- *Is the evidence convincing?*

Write the author's claim and the supporting evidence. Evaluate each piece of evidence and decide whether it supports the claim. If any evidence does not provide reasonable support, then note how it fails. Exchange papers, and discuss your answers with a partner.

Vocabulary Review

Directions: Draw a line to match each definition in the first column with a word in the second column.

1. not valid; ineffective
2. linked or joined together
3. elements used to back up a claim
4. supporting details that are clear and reasonable
5. the process of thinking, understanding, and forming conclusions

a. **supporting evidence**
b. **reasoning**
c. **logical evidence**
d. **connected**
e. **faulty**

Skill Review

Directions: Read the passage about working conditions in factories. Then complete the activities.

(1) One of the most important tasks for factory managers is to improve working conditions in their factories. (2) Cleaner working areas have been shown to improve workers' attitudes and their output. (3) In some factories, management has taken steps to make the work itself more interesting. (4) Interesting work, more than any other single factor, enables workers to take pride in what they do and obtain satisfaction from their jobs.

1. Which sentence states the claim in the paragraph?
   A. sentence 1
   B. sentence 2
   C. sentence 3
   D. sentence 4

2. The evidence provided in the passage directly connects to how ________ affect(s) factory workers.

Skill Practice

Directions: Read the passage about climate change. Then complete the activities.

Why Does Climate Science Literacy Matter?

- Over the 21st century, climate scientists expect Earth's temperature to continue increasing, very likely more than it did during the 20th century. Two anticipated results are rising global sea level and increasing frequency and intensity of heat waves, droughts, and floods. These changes will affect almost every aspect of human society. This includes economic prosperity, human and environmental health, and national security.
- Scientific observations and climate model results indicate that human activities are now the primary cause of most of the ongoing increase in Earth's globally averaged surface temperature.
- Climate change will bring economic and environmental challenges as well as opportunities, and citizens who have an understanding of climate science will be better prepared to respond to both.
- Society needs citizens who understand the climate system. Citizens need to know how to apply that knowledge in their careers and in their engagement as active members of their communities.
- Climate change will continue to be a significant element of public discourse. Understanding the essential principles of climate science will enable all people to assess news stories and contribute to their everyday conversations as informed citizens. [191 words; 1260L]

—From the U.S. Global Change Research Program

1. Which sentence describes supporting evidence presented in this passage?

A. Citizens need to understand climate change.

B. Citizens will benefit from knowledge about climate change.

C. The essential principles of climate science are important to know.

D. Climate change will affect almost every aspect of human society. ✓

2. The supporting evidence presented in this passage is connected to the claim in a _____ way.

Writing Practice

Directions: Find an online or a print editorial. Identify the claim in the text, and analyze the evidence given to support it. First, write the claim or claims that the author makes. Then list the evidence the author provides to support the claim. Finally, write a few sentences explaining how the evidence is connected to the claim and stating whether the claim is reasonable or not.

LESSON 6.3 Evaluate Relevance and Sufficiency

LESSON OBJECTIVES

- Explain relevance and sufficiency in terms of arguments
- Evaluate an argument for relevance and sufficiency of evidence

CORE SKILLS

- Identify Relevant Information
- Evaluate Arguments

Key Terms

relevant
related

sufficient
enough

Vocabulary

apply
be connected to

appropriate
especially suitable or proper for a particular circumstance

irrelevant
not related

support
confirm

Key Concept

To create a reasonable argument, an author must provide relevant and sufficient evidence for his or her claim.

Have you ever signed a petition to support a group's cause? Before signing, you probably read a paragraph about the cause that included evidence to support the group's argument. To inform and convince readers, authors make a claim and then provide relevant and sufficient supporting evidence to convince readers that the argument is reasonable.

Building a Case

Authors of targeted advertising campaigns know who their audience is, so they support their arguments with evidence that fits their audience's interests and needs. The evidence should be **relevant**, or related, not only to the audience, but also to the claim. In addition, writers must provide **sufficient**, or enough, evidence to build a case that is convincing.

Solid Evidence and Examples

Good writers do not simply state a claim in an argument. They must offer relevant evidence—proof in the form of examples, facts, or statistics that are related to the claim. In turn, good readers pay close attention to the details that are used to **support**, or confirm, the claim. Evaluating the evidence helps readers decide whether or not the writer's argument is valid.

Some arguments contain details that are **irrelevant**, or unrelated, to the claim. These details are not connected to the claim in a direct and reasonable way. As a reader, you must disregard details that are irrelevant to the claim and focus on the evidence that is relevant.

Directions: Read the radio advertisement. Then list the evidence that is relevant to the claim that River's End Books is the best independent bookstore on the seaboard.

Radio Advertisement

Voiceover:

(Continued on page 193)

(Continued from page 192)

River's End Books is the best independent bookstore on the seaboard. We have a large book selection with genres from mysteries to literary fiction, as well as everything from magazines to locally produced greeting cards and handcrafted gifts. Our well-read and fun-loving staff are here for you in a way that online retailers can't be, with a friendly smile and intelligent recommendations to assist customers wondering "What should I read next?" If we don't have the book you want in stock, we will have it shipped to you the very next day, so there's no reason to shop anywhere else!

If you wrote that the bookstore has a large selection of products, that the staff is helpful to customers, and that the bookstore will order any book they don't have, you understand that relevant evidence is related to the claim and supports the claim.

Sufficiency of Supporting Evidence

The supporting evidence a writer provides for a claim should **apply**, or be connected to, the claim. In addition, there should be enough supporting evidence to make the claim believable.

Good writers provide a sufficient amount of supporting evidence in the form of details, facts, reasons, or examples in order to persuade readers. A strong argument includes relevant evidence from a variety of credible sources. One or two examples from unreliable sources are not sufficient support.

Read the passage about television. The author's claim is that television was not invented, but developed over many years. Note the amount of evidence related to television technology the author presents to support this claim.

The Development of Television

Television was not really invented; it was developed over many years through the work of numerous scientists and engineers. The history of television began with the first experiments with electricity. In 1817 a Swedish chemist found and named the element *selenium*. It conducts electricity strongly when it is exposed to light. Work with selenium led to the photoelectric cell, which converts light into electrical impulses. A German engineer built a practical mechanical television in 1884. In the 1920s scientists combined radio-broadcasting techniques with the mechanical television. An American and an Englishman separately developed picture transmission by combining photography, optics, and radio. More efficient systems, based on the work of these early scientists, were soon built.

Think about Reading

Directions: Read the passage about the development of television. Then write the answers to the following questions in a notebook.

1. How is the text evidence relevant to the claim that television was not invented but developed?
2. Is there sufficient evidence related to the claim to support it? Explain.

CORE SKILL

Identify Relevant Information

To identify relevant information when you are reading an argument, follow this procedure:

1. Read the entire text.
2. Ask yourself: *What claim is the author making in this text?*
3. Search for details that support the claim.
4. Write any supporting details that are directly related to the claim.

In a print or online newspaper or magazine, find an opinion essay about a topic that interests you. With a partner, identify the claim and the relevant supporting evidence using the procedure above. Then discuss how each detail that supports the claim is relevant to the claim.

WRITE TO LEARN

Write a script for a radio advertisement about a product that you use. State a claim about the product. Then support your claim with sufficient relevant evidence to persuade listeners to buy the product.

TEST-TAKING SKILL

Eliminating Irrelevant Information

Some test questions require you to choose from among several possible answers. When answering this type of question, it is helpful to eliminate answer choices that are not relevant, or related to the question.

Read the following test question, and eliminate the answer choices that are not relevant to the question.

Which of the following describes common fairy tale characters?

A. The animals can speak.

B. There is a royal ball.

C. A problem is resolved by magic.

D. The setting is a forest.

Answer choice A is correct because it describes characters that are commonly found in fairy tales. The other answer choices are not relevant to the question because they describe plot and setting. By eliminating them, you can isolate the correct answer to the question.

Evaluating Evidence in Various Texts

As you evaluate the support for an argument in a text, you need to determine whether the evidence is relevant and sufficient.

Evaluating Relevance

When you evaluate the evidence in a text, you look for **appropriate**—or especially suitable—details, reasons, and examples that support the author's claim. Appropriate evidence must be relevant to the topic. It should also be relevant to the audience's interests.

How can you tell whether evidence is relevant? Ask yourself: *Is the evidence connected to the topic in a meaningful way? Does the evidence provide more information about the topic? Will it help the audience understand the text?*

Directions: Read the passage about businesses in Thomas Jefferson's day. Then write a two or three sentences describing the author's claim and the relevance of the evidence. Note whether the evidence is connected to the topic, who the intended audience is, and whether the evidence is relevant to that audience.

Business in Thomas Jefferson's Day

Back in Thomas Jefferson's day, the United States was a nation of farmers and merchants, and the boss of each farm or store was the owner. Some worked hard, were cruel, and enjoyed prosperity. Some worked hard, were fair, and prospered even more because they attracted loyal workers who didn't need as much expensive supervision. Some were lazy, and they failed. In any event, it was their business, and they were entitled to run their business any way they saw fit, free from the meddlesome government that today's businesses must deal with.

The author's claim is that in Jefferson's day, business owners could run their farm or store however they wanted, without government interference. The examples of different approaches bosses took to running a business provide evidence that is connected to the topic. The intended audience may be a history class or modern-day bosses. If you wrote that the evidence about successful and failed businesses shows that owners could do what they wanted, you understand evidence that is relevant to the audience and the topic.

Evaluating Sufficiency

When you evaluate the evidence for a claim in an argument, you consider more than just its relevance. You also check to see whether there is sufficient evidence to support the claim.

Sufficiency refers to the amount and the strength of the evidence. A few strong examples are more persuasive than many weak examples. A single example, however, is usually not sufficient to support a claim.

Directions: Reread the passage about business in Thomas Jefferson's day. Is there enough evidence to support the claim that bosses in that time period could run their business however they wanted? How strong is the evidence? Write two or three sentences explaining whether or not the passage contains sufficient evidence to support the author's claim.

When you evaluate evidence for sufficiency, remember that there must be more than one example of evidence, and it must be strongly connected to the topic.

Think about Reading

Directions: Read the question and choose the best answer.

Which of the following sentences accurately describes how to evaluate the relevance and sufficiency of evidence in a text?

A. Look for several examples of evidence that are related to the topic and appeal to the audience.

B. Look for at least one example of evidence that is related to the topic and appeals to the audience.

C. Look for at least one example of evidence that is related to the topic and appeals to the author.

D. Look for several examples of evidence that are related to the topic and appeal to the author.

Summary

To convince readers that a claim is reasonable, writers must provide evidence that is relevant to the claim and to the readers. In addition, there must be sufficient evidence to support the claim. One piece of evidence or a few weak reasons and examples do not provide sufficient support for a claim. To evaluate an argument, determine whether there is relevant and sufficient supporting evidence. With both, a claim is more likely to be reasonable.

CORE SKILL

Evaluate Arguments

To evaluate an author's argument for relevance and sufficiency:

1. Read the entire text.
2. Ask yourself: *What evidence has the author given to support the claim?*
3. Think about relevance. Ask yourself: *Is the evidence well-connected to the claim? Will the audience find it interesting? Will the audience understand it?*
4. Think about sufficiency. Ask yourself: *Has the author provided enough evidence to support the claim?*

Search the Internet for an example of a cover letter for a job application. List the evidence the applicant gives for why he or she should be hired. Label each piece of evidence "Relevant" or "Irrelevant." Then decide whether there is sufficient relevant evidence to support the claim. Exchange your letter, and list your evaluations with a partner and discuss them.

Vocabulary Review

Directions: Draw a line to match each definition in the first column with a word in the second column.

1. related	a. **sufficient**
2. confirm	b. **appropriate**
3. be connected to	c. **relevant**
4. not related	d. **apply**
5. enough	e. **irrelevant**
6. suitable or proper for a particular circumstance	f. **support**

Skill Review

Directions: Read the passage below. Then complete the activities.

A Day Without Space

To say that space has become a victim of its own success is a huge understatement. Because our space systems work so well today, they have become transparent to the end users and are simply taken for granted. As the saying goes, out of sight, out of mind. It is only on those rare occasions when satellite services are interrupted that we realize the full extent of our dependence on them.

If you think it is hard to get work done when your Internet connection goes out at the office, imagine losing that plus your cell phone, TV, radio, ATM access, credit cards, and possibly even your electricity.

—From "A Day Without Space," Edward Morris, Director,
U.S. Office of Space Commercialization

1. Which phrase is most strongly related to the claim that our space systems are taken for granted?

A. our space systems work so well

B. success is a huge understatement

C. satellite services are interrupted

D. we realize the full extent of our dependence

2. The author provides a(n) __________ amount of evidence to support the claim that space is a victim of its own success.

3. The phrase "losing your Internet connection . . . plus your cell phone, TV, radio" is evidence that is __________ to the claim in this passage.

Skill Practice

Directions: Read the letter below. Then complete the activities.

July 21, 2014

National Manufacturing–Human Resources Department
Attn: Sherrie Archambeault, Ombudsman
10 National Circle
Springville, MD 24716

Dear Ms. Archambeault,

I have been a line inspector at National Manufacturing since 2004. I am writing to you to request that our company add a flu-shot clinic to our already excellent range of employee services.

Influenza is a public health issue. It can bring down whole departments for days at a time. Because influenza's negative effects on a workforce are well-documented, I feel that it is necessary for our company to take a proactive stance.

To prevent income loss for our employees and profit loss for National Manufacturing, employees need access to free flu shots. Many of our employees who are working first shift find it difficult to schedule doctor's appointments outside of working hours. Also, given our somewhat remote location in the industrial district of Springville, employees can't take advantage of the daytime flu-shot clinics offered at pharmacies in town. In addition, workers on rotating shifts find it particularly difficult to schedule this important component of their health care.

I know that the health and safety of its employees is important to National Manufacturing. I look forward to hearing from you about plans to start a flu-shot program at our facility before the next flu season begins. Please contact me if I can be of further assistance.

Sincerely,

Jamila Grafton

1. Which sentence is irrelevant to the author's claim in this passage?

A. I have been a line inspector at National Manufacturing since 2004.

B. Influenza is a public health issue.

C. Employees can't get to daytime clinics for flu shots.

D. The negative effects of influenza are well documented.

2. The fact that the author has provided several examples to support her claim shows that there is __________ evidence for the claim in this passage.

Writing Practice

Directions: Write a cover letter applying for a job that interests you. First, write a claim that you are the best candidate for the job. Then provide sufficient and relevant evidence to support your claim.

LESSON 6.4 Evaluate Validity and Reasoning

LESSON OBJECTIVES

- Describe validity and reason in terms of an argument
- Evaluate the validity and reason used in an author's argument

CORE SKILLS

- Cite Specific Evidence
- Evaluate Arguments

Key Terms

validity
the quality of being logically or factually reliable

Vocabulary

biased
showing unreasoned judgment or prejudice

contradictory
inconsistent; suggesting the opposite

sound
error-free; logical; based on thorough knowledge or experience

verifiable
capable of being confirmed as accurate

Key Concept

Readers can use logical tests to determine whether the reasoning authors use in their arguments is valid.

Have you ever wanted something very badly and found reasons to justify getting it? Have you ever been told your reasons weren't good enough? If you have, then you might not have presented a valid argument. A valid argument contains points that relate to each other logically and support the intended claim. Biased statements and fallacious reasoning are signs that an argument is not valid. These are things to look for when evaluating an argument.

Understanding Validity and Reasoning

The **validity** of an argument—the degree to which it is logically or factually reliable—depends upon the evidence and reasons, or explanations, that a writer presents. A strong argument is supported with evidence that is **sound**, or sensible. The points a writer makes in an argument should be connected in a reasonable way to the claim and to each other. In addition, the evidence must logically lead to a reasonable conclusion about the claim.

What makes an argument invalid? If an author is **biased**, he or she shows unreasoned judgment or prejudice. This kind of poor reasoning makes the author's argument invalid. Evidence that is **contradictory**, or inconsistent, also makes an argument invalid. The pieces of evidence in an argument should jointly relate to and support the claim.

Directions: Read the passage below. Write the details that the author gives to support the claim that household pesticides should not be considered hazardous. Then identify the contradictory evidence.

> The local recycling facility sent out a flyer saying hazardous household waste must be brought to their facility. It defined hazardous household waste as any product or chemical used in the home that contains toxic or corrosive ingredients. It gave examples such as leftover house paints, gasoline, motor oil, and old batteries. It also mentioned products used to control insects and pests.
>
> *(Continued on page 199)*

Hero Images/Getty Images

(Continued from page 198)

I don't think pesticides are hazardous. We spray pesticides in our homes and gardens to protect our plants from destruction and ourselves from being bitten. We spread them on the ground to make our lawns look lush. Because we are spraying pesticides in the air and sprinkling them on the soil, we come into contact with them every day. Some wildlife has been poisoned by pesticides, but they still have certain benefits. There is no need to dispose of pesticides at the hazardous waste facility. Leftover household pesticides should be placed in the regular trash.

If you wrote that the author gives examples of the benefits of pesticides, you understand how to identify supporting evidence. If you wrote that the example of wildlife being poisoned does not support the argument, you understand how to spot contradictory evidence.

When you evaluate the validity and reasoning of an argument, you should cite specific evidence to support your assessment. Remember to be on the lookout for fallacious, or false, evidence. Facts and expert opinions used as evidence must be **verifiable** to support a valid argument. That is, readers must be able to confirm, or verify, their accuracy using well-known and trustworthy resources. If you can't verify that examples are factual and expert opinions are based on solid evidence, the writer's argument probably is not valid.

Directions: Read the passage below. Identify the author's claim and the evidence that she presents. Decide whether the evidence contributes to a valid argument. Explain your answer. Keep in mind that valid evidence is sound, logically connected, and verifiable.

Although white and colored teachers are under the same Board of Education and the system for the children of both races is said to be uniform, prejudice against the colored teachers in the public schools is manifested in a variety of ways. From 1870 to 1900, there was a colored superintendent at the head of the colored schools. During all that time the directors of the cooking, sewing, physical culture, manual training, music and art departments were colored people. Six years ago, a change was inaugurated. The colored superintendent was legislated out of office, and the directorships . . . were taken from colored teachers and given to the whites. Now, no matter how competent or superior the colored teachers in our public schools may be, they know that they can never rise to the height of a directorship. [They] can never hope to be more than an assistant and receive the meager salary . . . unless the present regime is radically changed. . . .

—Speech by Mary E. Church Terrell to the United Women's Club in Washington, D.C., October 10, 1906

CORE SKILL

Cite Specific Evidence

To cite specific evidence that supports or invalidates a claim, use the following procedure:

1. Read the entire text.
2. Ask yourself: *What evidence and reasons does the author present to support the claim? Is the evidence relevant, sufficient, and verifiable?*
3. Then ask yourself: *Which pieces of evidence do not support the claim? Do any pieces of evidence make the claim invalid?*
4. Accurately cite specific supporting points from the text that you have confirmed to be sound and accurate or unreasonable and invalid.

Choose a persuasive text from an online or print source. Use the above procedure to identify and analyze the evidence that the author presents. Research examples or expert opinions to check whether they are verifiable. Then list the evidence that supports or invalidates the claim.

Exchange texts and lists with a partner. Examine your partner's text and list. Decide whether there is any evidence missing from the list or points that have been incorrectly analyzed. Work together to complete your lists of cited evidence.

CORE SKILL

Evaluate Arguments

To evaluate an argument for validity and reasoning, do the following:

1. Read the entire text.
2. Ask yourself: *Has the author presented valid and verifiable evidence to support the claim? Has the author given sound reasons to support the claim?*
3. Then ask yourself: *Does the author present any evidence that is not verifiable? Does the author show bias? Does the author contradict himself or herself? Does this argument make logical sense?*

Evaluate the letter to a customer service representative. Write two or three sentences explaining whether the customer's argument is valid and how you would improve the supporting evidence in terms of validity and reasoning.

You should have identified the author's claim that there is prejudice against colored teachers in public schools and the evidence presented to support it—that "colored" superintendents and directors were replaced by whites due to a change in the law. To decide whether the evidence helps make a valid argument, check its accuracy. Research shows that in 1900 Congress passed a law changing the governance of schools in the District of Columbia and placing all of them, both white and "colored," under one superintendent. The evidence is verifiable and logically connected to the claim, and it supports the author's argument.

Think about Reading

Directions: Refer to the passage at the bottom of page 199. Write a check mark next to the methods the author uses to present a valid argument.

A. _______ verifiable facts

B. _______ logical points

C. _______ expert opinions

D. _______ sound reasoning

Evaluating Validity and Reasoning in Texts

Supporting details that are credible and verifiable are valid evidence. If the details do not relate to or fully support the claim, then the argument's reasoning is not sound.

To evaluate an argument for validity, check whether the evidence is accurate, relates to the claim, and helps build a logical argument.

Directions: Read the passage below. Write two or three sentences explaining how the evidence in the passage relates to and supports the customer's claim.

Dear Customer Service Representative:

Recently I returned a DVD that I had purchased from your website. I received a reply from your department saying that, as stated in your general returns policy, no refunds would be made for any item that had been removed from its packaging.

However, as I explained in the form that accompanied the return, the DVD you sent was faulty and would not play more than the first five minutes of the movie. Obviously, I only discovered this after removing the disc from its packaging and inserting it into my DVD player.

Because I needed the DVD for a certain event, I replaced it at a higher cost from a brick-and-mortar store near my home. (Please see the enclosed copy of my receipt.) Consequently, I do not want a replacement.

What I want is a full refund for the price of the DVD and complete reimbursement for all shipping costs. I should not have to bear any costs for an unusable product.

Please send me a check by return mail. Thank you.

Miko Asturian

The letter includes valid evidence that the customer should get a refund. The evidence relates to and supports the claim because it explains that the only way to know that the product was faulty was to open it and use it.

Sound reasoning that results from logically related evidence is another aspect of a valid argument. To evaluate for sound reasoning, make sure that the evidence progresses in a logical order, makes sense all together, and supports the author's claim.

Remember that an argument is not valid if it contains false evidence or illogical reasoning. In addition, if the author presents contradictory evidence or shows bias, the argument is most likely invalid.

Sometimes an author will present contradictory evidence that does not invalidate the argument as a whole but negates one part of the argument. Check for these instances as well, and decide how they affect the main claim of the argument.

Think about Reading

Directions: Read the customer's letter about returning a DVD. Choose the best word to complete each sentence below.

logically **related** **sound** **validity**

The evidence in this passage is (1.) ________ to the claim that customers should be able to get a refund if a product is faulty. The reasoning is (2.) ________ connected to the author's claim, and the pieces of evidence build on each other. Together, the (3.) ________ reasoning and the evidence presented ensure the (4.) ________ of the author's argument.

Summary

When you evaluate an argument for validity and reasoning, look for points in the argument that connect to each other logically and that support the intended claim. A valid, reasonable argument has facts that are usually verifiable, and examples that make sense. In an argument that is invalid or unreasonable, the author might show bias, or prejudice. Also look for evidence that is false or incorrectly stated. Be aware of weaknesses in the argument, such as instances in which the author contradicts himself or herself or the supporting points don't connect logically.

21st CENTURY SKILL

Flexibility and Adaptability

Flexibility and adaptability are skills you use in the workplace and in your daily life. *Flexibility* is the willingness to try new methods and an openness to different ways of thinking. *Adaptability* is the ability to successfully change for specific situations.

Write a paragraph explaining why flexibility and adaptability are necessary for success in the workplace. Provide evidence for a valid argument to support your claim. Exchange paragraphs with a partner and discuss ways to improve each argument.

WRITE TO LEARN

Write a letter in which you ask a supervisor to change a work policy, such as being able to wear casual clothes or to work from home. Be sure to provide sufficient evidence to support your claim and to build an argument that is logical and reasonable. Exchange letters with a partner, and evaluate the validity of each other's argument. Suggest ways to ensure that your partner's argument is valid.

Vocabulary Review

Directions: Draw a line to match each definition in the first column with a word in the second column.

1. free from mistakes and showing good judgment	a. **biased**
2. showing unreasoned judgment or prejudice	b. **verifiable**
3. capable of being confirmed as accurate	c. **validity**
4. inconsistent; suggesting the opposite	d. **sound**
5. the quality of being logically or factually reliable	e. **contradictory**

Skill Review

Directions: Read the passage below. Then choose the best answer to each question.

Ever since the existence of the White House taping system was first made known last summer, I have tried vigorously to guard the privacy of the tapes. I have been well aware that my effort to protect the confidentiality of presidential conversations has heightened the sense of mystery about Watergate and, in fact, has caused increased suspicions of the president. Many people assume that the tapes must incriminate the president, or that otherwise, he would not insist on their privacy.

But the problem I confronted was this: Unless a president can protect the privacy of the advice he gets, he cannot get the advice he needs.

This principle is recognized in the constitutional doctrine of executive privilege, which has been defended and maintained by every president since Washington and which has been recognized by the courts, whenever tested, as inherent in the presidency. I consider it to be my constitutional responsibility to defend this principle. . . .

—From Richard Nixon's Address to the Nation on Presidential Tape Recordings (April 29, 1974)

1. Which statement is not verifiable?

A. Nixon instituted a taping system in the White House.

B. Nixon recorded private conversations.

C. Nixon's efforts to guard privacy caused increased suspicions of the president.

D. Nixon expected a greater degree of privacy than other presidents.

2. What reason supports Nixon's claim that he must "vigorously guard the privacy of the tapes"?

A. The White House taping system has only been in place since summer, and that is not long enough to have recorded useful information.

B. The contents of the tapes are private, so they would cause increased suspicion of the president.

C. The constitution provides Nixon the privilege to keep the tapes secret, so he is going to keep their content private.

D. If the president cannot keep what his advisors tell him secret, then they will not give him the advice he needs.

Skill Practice

Directions: Read the passage. Then complete the activities.

E-mail Message

From: Luisa Patrick, Director of Human Resources

To: Geraldo Gonzales, Vice President, Operations

Subject: Dress code change during move

Dear Geraldo,

As you know, over the next couple of weeks, we will be cleaning out our offices and packing them up. Because this will be a fairly labor-intensive process, employees are asking that the dress code be modified.

Normally, our dress code is business casual, and jeans are permitted only on Fridays. However, during the moving process, it seems reasonable to permit jeans on a daily basis. Employees will be more comfortable and productive during the move if they are not concerned about damaging their nicer attire. Once the move has been completed, we would return to our usual dress code.

Please let me know whether you approve this temporary change in policy.

Thank you,

Luisa

1. Which word best describes the evidence the author presents for her decision?

A. logical

B. factual

C. unreasonable

D. invalid

2. Choose the best word to complete each sentence below.

reasoning **related** **support** **valid**

The author of this memo presents evidence to (A.) __________ her claim that the dress code should be temporarily changed. Her request follows from her sound (B.) __________, and the evidence is (C.) __________ to the claim, making this a (D.) __________ argument.

Writing Practice

Directions: Think of an issue that interests you. Search the Internet for a persuasive text that makes an argument related to that issue. Write a paragraph identifying the supporting evidence and evaluating its validity. Then assess the author's argument and determine whether it is reasonable. Remember to verify information presented as facts, research expert opinions, and check for sufficiency and relevance of the evidence.

LESSON 6.5 Evaluate Logic and Identify Hidden Assumptions

LESSON OBJECTIVES

- Describe assumptions supporting an argument based on logical reasoning
- Infer hidden assumptions and assess how they affect an argument

CORE SKILLS

- Identify Stated Assumptions
- Infer Hidden Assumptions

Key Terms

assumption
a statement or idea that is accepted as true

underlying
supporting, forming the foundation of (an idea, process, etc.)

Vocabulary

deductions
conclusions reached through logical reasoning

scrutiny
close examination

suppositions
ideas or theories believed to be true even though there is no proof of them

Key Concept

Authors may support their claims with arguments based on logical reasoning.

You might have heard a small child continually ask a parent, "Why?" until the parent finally stops explaining and says something like "Because that's just how it is." This situation resembles that in which a writer's argument is not based on tangible evidence or expert opinion, but on a series of logical conclusions. The conclusions are accepted as true because "that's just how it is."

Arguments Founded on Logical Reasoning

Writers often support their claims using evidence such as facts, examples, and expert opinion. However, in some cases this type of evidence is not available or appropriate. In these cases, writers might support their claims with logical reasoning.

To build an argument based on logical reasoning, the writer begins by making a statement that is true or is assumed to be true. This statement is called an **assumption**. The rest of the argument is built on that foundation of truth through a series of **deductions**, or conclusions based on logical reasoning.

Directions: Read the passage below and on the next page. In a notebook, write answers to the following questions: What is the writer's claim? What assumptions does she make? How does she use deductions to build a logical argument?

> We have discovered that two of the dyes used for our new line of textiles (R8BN3 and R8BN7) may be having adverse health effects on some workers. This is a serious situation, and we must act immediately and decisively in response.
>
> Toxic dyes represent a threat to line workers who come into contact with them during the dying process. If the dyes release toxins into the air, they also pose a risk to workers who enter the production area. We must also consider the possible adverse effects to workers, distributors, and customers who subsequently handle the dyed cloth.
>
> (Continued on page 205)

©Rob Daly/age fotostock

(Continued from page 204)

Moreover, the company might be held liable for any severe or long-term adverse effects of the dyes on workers or others. Of course, before their use was implemented, government regulators studied these substances. Neither was listed as poisonous. This should mitigate any liability on our part up until we became aware of the problem; however, now that we are aware of it, we must act quickly to ward off possible legal action against us.

We have decided to conduct our own toxicological tests. We are currently analyzing the dyes to determine which toxins might be present and in what amounts. We should have results in about two weeks, at which time we will be able to determine the actual risk, if any, to employees, distributors, and customers and advise you on any necessary production changes, including removal of the dyes from use.

In the meantime, it is imperative that we take steps to protect our workforce and to guard against increased liability on our part. My recommendations for precautions are as follows, to be implemented immediately:

- All line workers must wear protective clothing covering all exposed skin.
- Workers entering the production area must wear a facemask at all times.
- Workers who become ill should inform management immediately, leave the premises, and seek medical care.

For further information, contact:

Kayla Salcedo, Materials Director

If you wrote that the writer's claim is that the company must take immediate action because of potentially toxic dyes, you understand how she begins her argument. If you wrote that she assumes the dyes could be toxic and the company could be sued, you understand the assumptions on which the argument is based. If you wrote that the writer recommended precautions based on her assumptions, you correctly identified the deductions used to create a logical argument.

Think about Reading

Directions: Refer to the passage above. Use the words below to complete the sentence that follows.

assumptions **deductions** **logical**

The author's argument is based on ________ reasoning because she makes ________ based on ________ that certain things are true.

CORE SKILL

Identify Stated Assumptions

To identify the **underlying** assumptions of a logical argument—those that form the foundation of the argument—look for clues in the words the author uses. Words such as *assume, true,* and *possible* are clues that an assumption might follow.

Find a copy of the Declaration of Independence online. Read the first three paragraphs after "We hold these truths to be self-evident." List all the stated assumptions.

Exchange lists with a partner, and compare the assumptions each of you identified.

CORE SKILL

Infer Hidden Assumptions

To infer the hidden assumptions in an argument, follow these steps:

1. Read the entire text.
2. Ask yourself: *What argument is the author making?*
3. Identify the stated assumptions and evidence in the argument.
4. Ask yourself: *What assumption is presumed to be true but is not stated?*

Evaluate the passage about wages for police officers on page 207. Write a sentence describing the argument the author is making. Then write the assumptions that are presumed to be true but are not stated.

WRITE TO LEARN

Write a paragraph making a claim about something that you feel is obviously true, without stating that assumption. Exchange paragraphs with a partner, and try to identify each other's hidden assumptions. Discuss how you each reached your conclusion.

Evaluating Arguments Based on Hidden Assumptions

When you evaluate an argument, you look for the author's claim and the supporting evidence used to build the argument. You know to look for **suppositions** that the author makes—ideas that he or she presents as true even without proof. Suppositions, or assumptions, may be stated or unstated, valid or invalid. The validity of a writer's suppositions affects the validity of the argument as a whole.

Finding an unstated, or "hidden," assumption can be tricky. First, ask yourself whether an idea that supports the claim is missing from the argument. Then think about the reasoning in the argument. Does it depend on the reader accepting an idea that is not explicitly stated? If it does, then that idea is a "hidden" assumption.

Directions: Read the passage below. Then write two or three sentences explaining what the hidden assumption is, how you identified it, and why the author did not state it.

Policies and Procedures

Your business, like all others, has formal and informal policies, practices, and procedures that keep it running smoothly. However, sometimes your policies or procedures can inadvertently make it difficult or impossible for a customer with a disability to access your goods and services. That is why the Americans with Disabilities Act (ADA) requires businesses to make "reasonable modifications" to their usual ways of doing things when serving people with disabilities. Most modifications involve only minor adjustments in policies. For example, . . . a clothing store must modify its policy of permitting only one person at a time in a dressing room because a person with a disability might need a companion's assistance to try on clothes. . . .

Customers with disabilities might need different types of assistance to access your goods and services. For example, a grocery store clerk is expected to assist a customer using a mobility device by retrieving merchandise from high shelves. A person who is blind might need assistance maneuvering through a store's aisles. A customer with an intellectual disability may need assistance in reading product labels and instructions. Usually the customer will tell you up front whether he or she needs assistance, although some customers might wait to be offered help. When only one staff person is on duty, it might not be possible for him or her to assist a customer with a disability. The business owner or manager should advise the staff person to assess whether he or she can provide the assistance that is needed without jeopardizing the safe operation of the business.

As evidence for the claim that businesses must accommodate people with disabilities, the author describes problems faced by people with disabilities and the changes required to help them. This evidence indicates a hidden assumption: disabled people are entitled to the same access to goods and services as able-bodied customers. The writer might not have stated this assumption because it is obvious. Remember, to infer hidden assumptions, look for an idea on which the claim depends.

Writers often think that readers share their assumptions. This is one reason an underlying assumption might not be stated. Another is that the writer simply forgets to mention it or wants to avoid the assumption coming under **scrutiny**, or close examination. When readers scrutinize an assumption, they might discover that it is not reasonable.

Directions: Read the passage below. Write the assumptions that the author makes, and examine them to see if they are valid. Write two or three sentences explaining how the validity of the assumptions affects the overall argument.

To the Editor:

I am writing to raise awareness about a problem in our community: pay practices in public services discriminate against women.

The police department recently hired two new officers, and they are both members of my family. They went to the Police Academy together and have very similar educational and work backgrounds. However, my cousin, who is female, was hired at a salary that is one third lower than that of my brother, who was hired the same day as my cousin.

Female officers work just as hard as male officers do and must pass the same physical exams as the male officers to graduate from the Police Academy. Female officers should earn just as much as male officers earn.

Sincerely,

Madison Matthews

Remember that if you discover that the assumptions an author makes are invalid, then the argument is also invalid. If this author's assumptions about her community's wage policies are wrong, then her claim is not valid.

Think about Reading

Directions: Reread the passage above. Put a check mark next to the phrase that describes a hidden assumption in the passage.

A. __________ Women work as hard as men.

B. __________ Female officers must pass the same exams as male officers.

C. __________ The cousin and brother have been hired to do the same job.

D. __________ Pay practices in public services discriminate against women.

LANGUAGE SKILLS

Passive and Active Verbs

Verbs can convey actions in a passive or an active way. If the subject names the person or thing performing the action, then the verb is active. However, if the subject names the person or thing receiving the action, then the verb is passive.

Every passive verb consists of the past participle of a main verb and a form of *to be*. The performer of the action may appear elsewhere in the sentence or not be mentioned at all.

- Test pilots have flown this experimental plane many times. (active)
- This experimental plane has only been flown by test pilots. (passive)
- The model's maneuverability pleases the pilots. (active)
- The pilots are pleased by the model's maneuverability. (passive)
- The plane will be sold to the public soon. (passive)

Read the second paragraph of the letter to the editor. Identify each verb as active or passive. Ask yourself: *Who is each sentence about? Who is performing the action?* Discuss with a partner how the action changes within the paragraph.

Summary

Authors sometimes build an argument through logical reasoning. An argument developed in this way is based on assumptions, or ideas that are assumed to be true. These may be stated outright, or they may be hidden assumptions. Hidden assumptions must be inferred from text evidence in the argument. When assumptions are invalid, they invalidate the argument as a whole.

Vocabulary Review

Directions: Draw a line to match each phrase in the first column with the word it defines in the second column.

1. conclusions reached through logical reasoning	**a. underlying**
2. close examination	**b. assumption**
3. a statement or idea that is accepted as true	**c. deductions**
4. ideas or theories that are believed to be true even though there is no proof that they are	**d. scrutiny**
5. supporting or forming the foundation of (an idea, process, etc.)	**e. suppositions**

Skill Review

Directions: Read the passage below. Then complete the activities.

> Slavery, like all other great systems of wrong, [was] founded in the depths of human selfishness. . . . It has steadily exerted an influence upon all around it favorable to its own continuance. And to-day it is so strong that it could exist, not only without law, but even against law. Custom, manners, morals, religion, are all on its side everywhere in the South. . . . [W]hen you add the ignorance and servility of the ex-slave to the intelligence and accustomed authority of the master, you have the conditions, not out of which slavery will again grow, but under which it is impossible for the Federal government to wholly destroy it. . . . The true way and the easiest way is to make our government entirely consistent with itself, and give to every loyal citizen the elective franchise. . . . [This is] a right and power which will be ever present, and will form a wall of fire for his protection.
>
> —from "Reconstruction" by Frederick Douglass

1. Write the following words in the blanks to complete the sentence: *hidden, right, skin color,* and *vote.*

The __________ assumption in this passage is that it is the __________ of every citizen, regardless of __________, to __________.

2. Which statement is consistent with the unstated assumption in the passage?

A. Voting is an ever present right and power.

B. Slavery is a system of wrong.

C. The master is used to dominating the slave.

D. Ex-slaves are not given the opportunity for knowledge.

Skill Practice

Directions: Read the passage. Then complete the activities.

A ship lost at sea for many days suddenly sighted a friendly vessel. From the mast of the unfortunate vessel was seen a signal, "Water, water; we die of thirst!" The answer from the friendly vessel at once came back, "Cast down your bucket where you are. . . . The captain of the distressed vessel . . . cast down his bucket, and it came up full of fresh, sparkling water from the mouth of the Amazon River. To those of my race . . . who underestimate the importance of cultivating friendly relations with the Southern white man, who is their next-door neighbor, I would say: "Cast down your bucket where you are"—cast it down in making friends in every manly way of the people of all races by whom we are surrounded. . . .

Our greatest danger is that in the great leap from slavery to freedom we may overlook the fact that the masses of us are to live by the productions of our hands. . . . It is at the bottom of life we must begin, and not at the top.

—From *Up from Slavery* by Booker T. Washington

1. Which word or phrase best describes the idea of freed slaves having unreasonably high expectations?

A. stated assumption

B. logical argument

C. hidden assumption

D. valid evidence

2. Write the following words in the blanks to complete the sentence: *hidden, scrutiny.*

The argument in this passage is based on two __________ assumptions that did not pass __________ with other writers, such as Frederick Douglass.

Writing Practice

Directions: Find a copy of the Bill of Rights online, and choose one amendment. Write a paragraph identifying the claim, the assumptions that the authors of the document make, and whether those assumptions are stated or unstated. Evaluate the logic of the claim as related to the assumptions. Remember to establish whether the assumptions are valid or invalid and how they affect the claim.

Directions: Read the following passage. Then complete activities 1 through 3.

Marriage is one of the "basic civil rights of man, fundamental to our very existence and survival. Skinner v. Oklahoma, 316 U.S. 535, 541 (1942). See also Maynard v. Hill, 125 U.S. 190 (1888). To deny this fundamental freedom on so unsupportable a basis as the racial classifications embodied in these statutes, classifications so directly subversive of the principle of equality at the heart of the Fourteenth Amendment, is surely to deprive all the State s citizens of liberty without due process of law. The Fourteenth Amendment requires that the freedom of choice to marry not be restricted by invidious racial discriminations. Under our Constitution, the freedom to marry, or not marry, a person of another race resides with the individual, and cannot be infringed by the State.

These convictions must be reversed.

It is so ordered.

—From *Loving* v. *Virginia*, Opinion of the Court by Chief Justice Earl Warren, June 12, 1967

1. Chief Justice Warren's underlying assumption is that marriage is a __________ __________.

2. What is Chief Justice Warren's claim?

A. The Fourteenth Amendment is about marriage.

B. The freedom of choice to marry must not be restricted.

C. Denying the right to marry because of race is part of the constitution.

D. Having the freedom to marry a person of another race is unsupportable.

3. Chief Justice Warren supports his claim by presenting

A. expert opinions.

B. verifiable facts.

C. testimonials from witnesses.

D. a series of logical deductions.

Directions: Read the following passage. Then choose the best answer to questions 4 and 5.

Q. Robert Richards, Copley Press: Mr. President, would you mind commenting on the strategic importance of Indochina to the free World? I think there has been, across the country, some lack of understanding on just what it means to us.

THE PRESIDENT. You have, of course, both the specific and the general when you talk about such things.

First of all, you have the specific value of a locality in its production of materials that the world needs.

Then you have the possibility that many human beings pass under a dictatorship that is inimical to the free world.

Finally, you have broader considerations that might follow what you would call the "falling domino" principle. You have a row of dominoes set up, you knock over the first one, and what will happen to the last one is the certainty that it will go over very quickly. So you could have a beginning of a disintegration that would have the most profound influences.

Now, with respect to the first one, two of the items from this particular area that the world uses are tin and tungsten. They are very important. There are others, of course, the rubber plantations and so on.

(Continued on page 211)

(Continued from page 210)

Then, with respect to more people passing under this domination, Asia, after all, has already lost some 450 million of its peoples to the Communist dictatorship, and we simply can't afford greater losses.

But when we come to the possible sequence of events, the loss of Indochina, of Burma, of Thailand, of the Peninsula, and Indonesia following, now you begin to talk about areas that not only multiply the disadvantages that you would suffer through loss of materials, sources of materials, but now you are talking really about millions and millions and millions of people.

Finally, the geographical position achieved thereby does many things. It turns the so-called island defensive chain of Japan, Formosa, of the Philippines and to the southward; it moves in to threaten Australia and New Zealand.

It takes away, in its economic aspects, that region that Japan must have as a trading area or Japan, in turn, will have only one place in the world to go—that is, toward the Communist areas in order to live.

So the possible consequences of the loss are just incalculable to the free world.

—Excerpt from President Eisenhower's News Conference, April 7, 1954

4. What supporting evidence does President Eisenhower present that is relevant to his claim?

A. explanations and justifications

B. expert opinions

C. logical deductions

D. verifiable facts

5. Which statement describes the validity of Eisenhower's argument?

A. The argument is valid because every piece of evidence is verifiable.

B. The argument is not valid because some of his evidence is not verifiable.

C. The argument is valid because all his explanations are logical.

D. The argument is not valid because none of his justifications are logical.

Directions: Read the following passage. Then complete activities 6 and 7.

I long to hear that you have declared an independency—and by the way in the new Code of Laws which I suppose it will be necessary for you to make I desire you would Remember the Ladies, and be more generous and favourable to them than your ancestors. Do not put such unlimited power into the hands of the Husbands. Remember all Men would be tyrants if they could. If particular care and attention is not paid to the Ladies we are determined to foment a Rebellion, and will not hold ourselves bound by any Laws in which we have no voice, or Representation.

That your Sex are Naturally Tyrannical is a Truth so thoroughly established as to admit of no dispute, but such of you as wish to be happy willingly give up the harsh title of Master for the more tender and endearing one of Friend. Why then, not put it out of the power of the vicious and the Lawless to use us with cruelty and indignity with impunity. Men of Sense in all Ages abhor those customs which treat us only as the vassals of your Sex. Regard us then as Beings placed by providence under your protection and in imitation of the Supreme Being make use of that power only for our happiness.

—From Letter from Abigail Adams to John Adams, 31 March–5 April 1776

6. Which part of an argument's structure could Abigail Adams have used to make her argument stronger?

   A. a claim

   B. a conclusion

   C. supporting evidence

   D. an introduction

7. In Abigail Adams's letter, the hidden assumption is that women deserve to have _________ if they are bound by laws.

Directions: Read the following passage. Then complete activities 8 through 10.

So far as I am aware, the Fair Labor Standards Act is the only statute under which coverage depends upon the work of the individual employee. The supposed constitutional justification no longer exists. Accordingly, the committee bill puts coverage upon an establishment basis, as under other labor legislation.

The change will greatly simplify enforcement of the statute. Employers and the officials of the Wage and Hour Division will be able to determine the status of all employees in an establishment without checking the individual work of every employee. The inequity between employees in the same establishment will be abolished.

The justification for applying the proposed new minimum wage to the newly covered employees is the same as the reasoning which supports the increase in the minimum. The employees have the same needs. Their wages have fallen behind average hourly earnings to the same, and possibly a greater, extent than the wages of employees earning the statutory minimum. They are equally entitled to share in economic progress.

The fiscal burden of an inadequate minimum wage law lies upon the community, and thus upon every taxpayer. In New York City, 44 percent of the families to whom relief is extended include those who are wage earners but whose incomes are inadequate. An economic burden also lies upon competitors whose ability to pay a just wage is frustrated by unfair, low-wage competition. But the burden which should concern us most lies upon the American conscience. We can no longer tolerate growing patches of poverty and injustice in America—substandard wages, unemployment, city slums, inadequate medical care, inferior education and the sad plight of migratory workers. The enactment of this bill is only one step, but an essential step forward, as we cross this frontier to grasp the high opportunities which face the Nation.

—From "Speech in Senate on Fair Labor Standards Act, 10 August 1960" by John F. Kennedy

8. Senator Kennedy's statement that the _________ between employees in the same company will be _________ is supporting evidence for his claim that the Fair Labor Standards Act should be passed.

9. Which statement best describes the evidence that Senator Kennedy uses to support his claim?

   A. sufficient and relevant evidence

   B. insufficient and irrelevant evidence

   C. insufficient but relevant evidence

   D. sufficient but irrelevant evidence

10. Senator Kennedy states the underlying assumption that _________ have the same needs as a reason for increasing the minimum wage.

Check Your Understanding

On the following chart, circle the number of any item you answered incorrectly. In the third column, you will see the pages that you can review to study the content covered in the question. Pay particular attention to reviewing those lessons in which you missed half or more of the questions.

Lesson	Core Skill	Item Number(s)	Review Page(s)
Lesson 6.1 Identify Argument Development	Understand the Relationship among Ideas	2, 4, 7	180–181
	Analyze Text Structure to Evaluate an Argument	3, 6	182–183
Lesson 6.2 Identify Supporting Evidence	Evaluate Arguments	5, 6, 9	186–187
	Cite Specific Evidence	8	188–189
Lesson 6.3 Evaluate Relevance and Sufficiency	Identify Relevant Information	3, 4, 9	192–193
	Evaluate Arguments	5, 6, 9	194–195
Lesson 6.4 Evaluate Validity and Reasoning	Cite Specific Evidence	8	198–199
	Evaluate Arguments	5, 6, 9	200–201
Lesson 6.5 Evaluate Logic and Identify Hidden Assumptions	Identify Stated Assumptions	1, 10	204–205
	Infer Hidden Assumptions	7	206–207

WRITE ABOUT The Third McCain-Obama Presidential Debate

Read the excerpt from *The Third McCain-Obama Presidential Debate* on page 313. Write an analysis of the debate in which you

1. research the evidence each candidate presents to support his argument
2. assess the relevance and validity of the supporting evidence
3. evaluate the logic of each candidate's argument based on your analysis and research.

BEFORE YOU WRITE Research Supporting Evidence Online

Use a two-column chart to take notes on each candidate's argument so you can compare them side by side. You can find an example of a two-column chart in the Graphic Organizer section at the back of the book. Use the question that the moderator asks as the title for your chart. Label each column with a candidate's name. Begin each column by writing the claims the candidate makes in his argument. Below the claims, write the supporting evidence each candidate presents.

Then go online to research the validity of the supporting evidence presented by each candidate. Remember that facts are details that can be proved. Opinions are personal beliefs or judgments that cannot be proved. In the chart, note whether each candidate's evidence is related to the topic, accurate, and convincing.

When you have finished, review your chart. Ask yourself: *Is the evidence each candidate presents accurate, relevant, and valid? Does each candidate use mostly facts or opinions to support his claim?* Use your answers to develop an opening sentence for your analysis of the two arguments.

TIP Use Subject-Verb Agreement in Your Analysis

When you write a sentence, if the subject of your sentence is singular, the verb must also be singular; if the subject is plural, the verb must be plural. This is called subject-verb agreement.

The singular form of a verb is almost always its base form plus *-s* or *-es*. This form is used only with a third-person singular subject. (Any subject that can be replaced with *he, she,* or *it* is third-person singular.) For example:

> The moderator watches the clock and asks questions.

The subject, *moderator*, is singular. The verbs, *watches* and *asks*, are singular.

Usually, the plural form of a verb is its present-tense form. For example:

> The two candidates prepare their arguments.

The subject, *candidates*, is plural, and the verb, *prepare*, is also plural.

The singular subject pronouns *I* and *you* are exceptions. Use the plural form of a verb with *I* and *you* as well as with plural nouns and pronouns.

> I agree with what you think about this issue.
>
> They agree with you as well.

As you write your essay, be sure to use a singular verb with a singular subject and a plural verb with a plural subject, with the exception of when you use *I* or *you*.

WHILE YOU WRITE Evaluate Arguments and Logic

Now that you have identified the candidates' claims and assessed their supporting evidence, you can evaluate the logic of each candidate's argument.

First, look at your two-column chart again. Use the information from your chart to evaluate how well each candidate defends his position. Ask yourself: *Is the candidate's argument based more on fact or opinion? Is the evidence valid and relevant to the argument? Is each argument reasonable, given the evidence presented?* Use your answers to these questions to evaluate the logic of each candidate's argument. Include quotes and paraphrases from your online research about the evidence.

Finally, write two or three sentences summarizing your evaluation of each candidate's argument. Be sure to use your research to justify your evaluation.

TIP Watch Out for . . . Title Formatting

When you cite sources of information in your analysis, make sure you correctly format the titles. Titles of longer works appear in italics, while titles of shorter works (which often appear within longer works) appear in quotation marks.

The names of books, newspapers, and websites are italicized; the names of chapters, articles, and essays are placed in quotation marks and not italicized. Here's an example.

> In his article "U.S. Rivals Spar in First TV Debate" on the *BBC News* website, BBC reporter Jude Sheerin provides a running commentary on the debate.

Note, however, that names of organizations, such as the BBC, are not italicized or placed in quotation marks.

AFTER YOU WRITE Check Your Work

Reread the writing assignment. Then read your analysis carefully three times.

The first time you read, ask yourself whether you have completed the writing assignment correctly. Have you (1) researched the evidence that each candidate presents for his argument, (2) assessed the relevance and validity of the evidence, and (3) evaluated the logic of each candidate's argument based on your analysis and research?

Then read your analysis again. Do your sentences demonstrate subject-verb agreement? Did you correctly format titles of the sources you used to do you research?

Reread the analysis one last time. Did you use correct grammar, spelling, and punctuation? Do you see any errors? Did you type the words you meant to use?

Before submitting your analysis, have another student read it and provide you with feedback.

Chapter 7

Analyze Structure across Texts

Today's world provides more ways to communicate ideas than ever—movies and web TV, short stories and graphic novels, letters and e-mail, theater performances that are simulcast around the country, and more.

To get the full meaning and a deep understanding of a topic, you need to be able to understand information presented in many ways. You must also be able to analyze, compare, and evaluate the medium and the message.

U.S. Air Force photo by Master Sgt. Val Gempis

In this chapter you will study these topics:

Lesson 7.1

Compare Similar Topics in Different Formats

Even if two texts address the same topic or theme, they can differ in many ways. One may be fiction, while the other is an informational text. One may rely on images, while the other does not. Explore how and why authors choose to use different types of texts and images in different formats to convey their messages.

Lesson 7.2

Compare Similar Genres

Have you ever read a novel and then seen a movie that tells the same story? Even though they are presented in different media, novels and movies can be very similar. Yet, they often affect their audiences in dissimilar ways. Learn about the characteristics of different genres and acquire strategies for comparing their structures, content, and effect.

Lesson 7.3

Analyze Two Arguments

When you hear politicians or advertisers presenting an argument, can you identify the claims they are making and evaluate the evidence that is used to support each claim? Learn how to apply criteria to assess and compare the validity and reliability of arguments and to decide which ones are more convincing and why.

Lesson 7.4

Evaluate Impact of Genre and Format

Why does one author write a poem about a subject while another creates a photo essay on the same topic? Why does one author write a play and another a history book about the same event? Their choices are determined by the topic, purpose, and intended audience. Learn how to evaluate the relative effectiveness of using different genres and formats and how to assess their impact.

Goal Setting

What different types of communication do you come into contact with in your everyday life? In your notebook, list the types of communication you encounter at home, at work, on the street, in shops, and in other places you go.

How would it help you if you could analyze the messages, characteristics, and impact of each of these forms of communication? How would it help you if you could assess the authors' reasons for choosing a particular means of communication? Write your ideas about how these skills will help you in class, at work, and in everyday life in your notebook.

LESSON 7.1 Compare Similar Topics in Different Formats

LESSON OBJECTIVES

- Compare two texts on similar topics
- Compare texts in different formats that address a similar topic
- Compare fictional and nonfictional accounts of the same event

CORE SKILLS

- Compare Two Texts in Different Formats
- Compare Fiction and Nonfiction

Key Terms

format
order and form in which a text is arranged or presented

topic
subject

Vocabulary

characteristics
features that identify something

similar
alike but not identical

Key Concept

Different writers can present similar information in different formats. Each format fits the message the writer wants to convey.

Have you ever looked at an instruction manual for setting up a television or computer? The instructions are usually given in diagrams and in words. Looking at the same or similar information in different formats helps the reader understand the information. The same is true in other types of texts.

Comparing Texts on Similar Topics

Context, the circumstances under which the writer is creating a text, can exert influence on how the writer presents a **topic**, or subject, to his or her audience. That context may be personal, as in an e-mail to a friend. The context may be professional, as in a work report. In other cases, the context is much broader; for instance, an editorial in a newspaper may reach an international audience.

Directions: Read the passage below and the passage at the top of the next page, and write one similarity between the two topics. Then describe how the contexts are different.

Transcript of President John F. Kennedy's Inaugural Address (1961)

Vice President Johnson, Mr. Speaker, Mr. Chief Justice, President Eisenhower, Vice President Nixon, President Truman, Reverend Clergy, fellow citizens:

. . . Since this country was founded, each generation of Americans has been summoned to give testimony to its national loyalty. The graves of young Americans who answered the call to service surround the globe. . . . And so, my fellow Americans: ask not what your country can do for you—ask what you can do for your country. My fellow citizens of the world: ask not what America will do for you, but what together we can do for the freedom of man.

(Continued on page 219)

©Paul Bradbury/age fotostock

(Continued from page 218)

Transcript of President Abraham Lincoln's Second Inaugural Address (1865)

Fellow Countrymen:

. . . With malice toward none; with charity for all; with firmness in the right, as God gives us to see the right, let us strive on to finish the work we are in; to bind up the nation's wounds; to care for him who shall have borne the battle, and for his widow, and his orphan—to do all which may achieve and cherish a just, and a lasting peace, among ourselves, and with all nations.

If you wrote that the topic for both texts is how the country needs to move forward, but the ways in which each author wants the country to move forward are affected by the events occurring in each historical period, then you understand how context can shape the way a writer presents a topic.

The two passages above are **similar**, or alike. They share a goal—to inspire the American people—but the historical context changes what each writer urges his audience to do.

Texts on similar topics may present the topics differently. The two passages below are business letters. The context for each is different, and the presentation of the topic is different. How do these letters differ in context and presentation?

To Whom It May Concern:

I've noticed that there have been some billing irregularities since I accepted the new insurance. Please take some time to review the new insurance forms. Note that the new insurance company demands a code for each part of an exam I do. Most other companies don't have this requirement. I've indicated each separate procedure involved in an exam on the patient chart. Please find the code for each and bill for all of them.

I do understand that the new policy can be confusing. Many thanks, and keep up the good work!

Dr. Williams

Dear Customer Service Manager:

I am writing to complain about a bad experience with one of your products. I bought your combination TV/ DVD player for my daughter. There was no coaxial cable in the box, to start. Then we discovered that the remote control uses the same button for Stop and Eject. This means that instead of just stopping when you press the button, the DVD ejects. We tried to return it to the store, but they refused to take it back. This is an outrage. If you want our business ever again, you'll fix this problem. I expect you to take back this piece of junk and refund our money.

Frustratedly yours,

Jenna Yablonsky

Both letters address a problem or complaint. However, the tone of each letter is very different, reflecting the difference in context.

WORKPLACE SKILL

Interpret Business Letters

It is important for people in the workplace to pay close attention to their business communications. Procedure clarifications, complaints, or other issues may arise that need to be handled in a professional way. Carefully read the business letters on this page. How does their tone differ? How does their context differ?

Write a business memo to a supervisor, addressing a complaint you have. Consider the context—a letter to the person for whom you work—and use a professional tone.

Then exchange letters with a partner. Examine your partner's letter and decide whether the tone fits the context. Decide whether the letter suggests a positive approach to the problem.

Work through the letters together to make any changes needed to improve the tone.

CORE SKILL

Compare Two Texts in Different Formats

Similar information can be arranged in different formats. Formats such as tables and charts show information in different ways than text. Tables and chart are often suitable for organization data or other numerical-based information. To compare different formats, ask yourself questions about similarities and differences in the type, organization, length, and purpose.

With a partner, find a table or chart in print or online that gives data about a topic that interests you. One of you will write a factual description about what the table or chart shows. The other will write a list of points the table or chart makes about the topic

Which format do you find easier to understand—the table or chart, the list, or the factual description? Discuss your answers with your partner.

Think about Reading

Directions: Place a checkmark beside the phrases that tell you the second business letter does not approach the problem with a positive tone.

1. ________ we tried to return it to the store
2. ________ this is an outrage
3. ________ if you want our business ever again
4. ________ take back this piece of junk

Exploring Formats

The **format**—the order and form in which a text is arranged or presented—of a text is an important part of the writer's message. Writers choose the format of a text, such as an article or speech that communicates his or her point best. They may also use a visual format, such as a chart, graph, or cartoon, to present their ideas. Sometimes, they use a combination of formats.

To explore formats effectively, first identify the type of format used for texts on similar topics.Then ask questions as you read each format that deals with the topic. *What information is common to them? What is my response to each?*

Directions: Read the two passages below. Identify the format of each passage, and write a compare-and-contrast sentence about the two formats.

Graduated Driver Licensing for Safe Teen Driving

In some states, the completion of driver education qualifies a teen for full driving privileges. The National Safety Council believes this is not a wise approach. Research shows that significant hours of behind-the-wheel experience are necessary to reduce crash risk. Parent involvement and Graduated Driver Licensing play important roles in developing skills.

—From the National Safety Council

Elements of an Effective GDL

Studies show that graduated driver licensing significantly decreases the risk of fatal teen crashes among 16- to 17-year-old drivers. Research funded by the National Institutes of Health found that the most effective legislation had at least five of the following seven key elements:

- A minimum age of 16 for a learner's permit
- A mandatory waiting period of at least six months before a driver can apply for an intermediate license
- A requirement for 50 to 100 hours of supervised driving before testing for an intermediate license
- A minimum age of 17 for an intermediate license
- Restrictions on nighttime driving
- A limit on the number of teenaged passengers allowed in the car
- A minimum age of 18 for a full license

—From the Centers for Disease Control and Prevention Public Health Law Program

 **Think about Reading**

Directions: In a notebook write a short paragraph explaining which of the two formats presents the topic in the more detailed way.

Fiction versus Nonfiction

Because fiction is often rooted in fact, it is not always easy to distinguish between fiction and nonfiction. However, a text's **characteristics**—the features that identify it—can help you tell the difference. Different types of texts vary in context, purpose, and tone. Historical fiction, for example, treats the same events very differently from news articles. Even when a poem or play is based a factual event, the format alone is a clue to the fictional nature of the text.

Directions: Read the fictional and nonfictional accounts of Cleopatra's death. Then look again at the dialogue in the excerpt from *Antony and Cleopatra*. Write a sentence or two explaining how you know the content is fictional.

> **Cleopatra:** Peace, peace!
> Dost thou not see my baby at my breast,
> That sucks the nurse asleep?
>
> —William Shakespeare, *Antony and Cleopatra*, Act V, Scene 2
>
> The story of Cleopatra's suicide is not without its detractors. While classical historians believed that she died from the bite of an asp, later scholars thought it more likely that her death came from the bite of a cobra. More recently, historians have challenged the notion that she committed suicide at all, suggesting instead that she was murdered by her enemy, Octavian.

The use of metaphor in the play is a clue. Shakespeare often based his plays on historical events, but the metaphor of the snake as a baby would never appear in a factual account of her suicide.

 **Think about Reading**

Directions: Place a checkmark beside the statement that differentiates the nonfictional from the fictional approach to Cleopatra's death.

A. ________ topic

B. ________ historical era

C. ________ analysis of facts

D. ________ main character

Summary

Many texts may address similar topics, especially topics of general interest. However, not all these texts have the same purpose or adopt the same tone. Writers choose the way they present and arrange information (the format) to suit their purpose and address their intended audience. The writer's choice of format can affect the reader's or viewer's understanding of the content. Nonfictional texts as well as fictional texts, for example, may be based in fact. However, each has different characteristics that affect how these texts interpret and present the facts, as well as how the reader understands them.

CORE SKILL

Compare Fiction and Nonfiction

Fiction and nonfiction differ in the objective or fact-based nature of their content. Look for strictly factual reports of time, place, names, and actions based on a real story in nonfiction passages. Compare this with the imaginary or creative points of view found in fiction that are not solely based on fact.

Choose an event in American history, and find a poem or story about that event. Then find a nonfiction description of the event.

Compare how the authors use different types of factual or imaginary content to write about the same topic. Write a compare-and-contrast sentence describing the differences between the two texts.

WRITE TO LEARN

Think of an event in history that has happened in your lifetime. Write a factual description of that event. Then write a short scene in a play, with lines of dialogue between two people involved in this historical event. How does your style of writing change?

Vocabulary Review

Directions: Read the sentences. For each sentence, fill in the blank using a word from the word bank below.

topic **similar** **characteristics** **format**

1. The writer chooses the ________________ that best suits the ideas he or she is presenting.
2. The ________________ of this essay is the inauguration of President Abraham Lincoln.
3. Some of the ________________ that help you identify poetry are use of metaphor and lines of verse.
4. These essays are ________________ in that both address the idea of buying locally grown food.

Skill Review

Directions: Read the passages below. One is a nonfictional account of a historical event. The other is an excerpt from a novel about the same event. Then choose the best answer to each question.

Chickamauga

After the Tullahoma Campaign, Rosecrans renewed his offensive, aiming to force the Confederates out of Chattanooga. The three army corps comprising Rosecrans's army split and set out for Chattanooga by separate routes. In early September, Rosecrans consolidated his forces scattered in Tennessee and Georgia and forced Bragg's army out of Chattanooga, heading south. The Union troops followed it and brushed with it at Davis' Cross Roads.

Bragg was determined to reoccupy Chattanooga and decided to meet a part of Rosecrans's army, defeat them, and then move back into the city. On the 17th he headed north, intending to meet and beat the XXI Army Corps.

As Bragg marched north on the 18th, his cavalry and infantry fought with Union cavalry and mounted infantry which were armed with Spencer repeating rifles. Fighting began in earnest on the morning of the 19th, and Bragg's men hammered but did not break the Union line.

—from "Battle Summaries: Chickamauga Campaign (1863)," National Park Service

The Rock of Chickamauga

". . . . the Southern leaders poured their troops continually upon [Union General] Thomas. If they could break that wing, cut it off in fact, and rush in at the gap, they would be between Rosecrans and Chattanooga and the Northern army would be doomed. They made gigantic efforts. The cavalry charged again and again. Huge masses of infantry hurled themselves upon the brigades of Thomas, and every gun that could be brought into action poured shot and shell into his lines.

Many of the young as well as the old officers in Thomas' corps felt the terrible nature of the crisis. Dick knew . . . that the fortunes of the Union were swinging in the balance there among those Tennessee hills and valleys. If Thomas were shattered the turn of Grant farther south would come next. Vicksburg would have been won in vain and the Union would be broken in the West.

—from *The Rock Of Chickamauga: A Story Of The Western Crisis* by Joseph A. Altsheler

1. Which sentence best describes a difference between the two passages?
   A. The fictional account describes more experiences and emotions than the nonfictional account.
   B. The fictional account presents more facts than the nonfictional account.
   C. The fictional account presents the event using straight facts, but the nonfiction account includes people's feelings.
   D. The fictional account presents the event in less detail than the nonfictional account.

2. Which sentence best describes the author's purpose in the nonfictional account?

   A. The author's purpose is to make the reader empathize with the characters.

   B. The author's purpose is to reveal the emotions of the soldiers.

   C. The author's purpose is to present verifiable facts about the event.

   D. The author's purpose is to develop the main character to engage the reader.

Skill Practice

Directions: Read the passages below. Then complete the activities.

The next day, Bragg continued his assault on the Union line on the left, and in late morning, Rosecrans was informed that he had a gap in his line. In moving units to shore up the supposed gap, Rosecrans created one, and James Longstreet's men promptly exploited it, driving one-third of the Union army, including Rosecrans himself, from the field. George H. Thomas took over command and began consolidating forces on Horseshoe Ridge and Snodgrass Hill. Although the Rebels launched determined assaults on these forces, they held until after dark. Thomas then led these men from the field leaving it to the Confederates. The Union retired to Chattanooga while the Rebels occupied the surrounding heights.

—from "Battle Summaries: Chickamauga Campaign (1863)," National Park Service

Order and cohesion were lost among many of the regiments, but the men stood firm. They re-formed without orders and fought continuously against overwhelming might. Ground and guns were lost, but . . . the slow retreat never became a panic.

"We're going back," shouted Warner in Dick's ear. "Yes, we're going back, but we'll come forward again. They'll never crush the old man."

The Winchester regiment in its new position was still among the gullies and bushes, and they were thankful for such shelter. Although veterans now, most were lads, and they did not scorn to take cover whenever they could. For a little while they did not reply to the enemy's fire, but lay waiting and seeking to get back the breath which seemed to be driven from their bodies by the very violence of the concussion. . . .

—from *The Rock Of Chickamauga: A Story Of The Western Crisis*, by Joseph A. Altsheler

1. Which option below best expresses the contrast between the two accounts of the battle?

   A. general vs. specific

   B. historical vs. modern

   C. emotions vs. facts

   D. detailed vs. simple

2. The passages are __________ in that both are about __________.

3. The two passages are different in that the nonfictional account gives only the __________ about the battle, but the fictional account is told from the perspective of a fictional character, revealing his __________ about it.

Writing Practice

Directions: Think of a topic that interests you. Search the Internet for two texts in different formats that address this topic. The formats can be fictional or nonfictional, poetry or prose, in list format or a chart, an essay or a blog, as long as they are two different formats. Write a paragraph analyzing the similarities and differences in the way the two formats present the topic. Remember to include information about the tone the author uses, how easy or difficult each format is to understand, and each author's purpose and reason for choosing each format.

LESSON 7.2 Compare Similar Genres

LESSON OBJECTIVES

- Compare different genres
- Compare and contrast texts from similar genres

CORE SKILLS

- Determine Genre
- Compare Similar Genres

Key Terms

genre
category of writing with certain identifiable characteristics

literary techniques
methods authors use to convey their messages

Vocabulary

approach
how an author presents a subject

convey
express; communicate

symbolism
the use of objects or actions to represent something else

Key Concept

Authors may use similar genres to address common themes or ideas.

What is your favorite kind of book? As you walk through a bookstore or browse an online bookstore, you probably head for a particular section of books, organized by genre, to look for your favorite types of books. For example, if you're looking for a collection of essays, you look in the nonfiction section; fantasy novels are a fiction genre. Authors choose to use different genres, or types of writing, depending on the effect they want their writing to have and on the point they are making.

Identifying Genre

A **genre** is a category of writing with certain identifiable characteristics. Literary genres include poetry, fiction, drama, and folktales. Poetry explores feelings and experiences in lines of rhymed or unrhymed verse. Fiction, which includes various subgenres, or categories within the genre, and formats such as novels and short stories tell of imaginary events and characters, using narration and dialogue. Drama, which includes plays, depicts events occurring to characters in stage directions and dialogue and is meant to be performed. Folktales are imaginary stories passed down through a culture, which often feature **symbolism**, or objects or actions representing something else, to teach lessons.

Nonfiction genres include essays, biographies, and autobiographies. Essays are about real people or events and are meant to inform or persuade the audience. Biographies tell the story of real people's lives; autobiographies do the same, but they are written by the people they are about.

Directions: Read the passage at the top of the next page. Write characteristics that help you identify the genre. Then name the genre of the passage.

Advice to Young Men

To have a trust-worthy wife, you must begin by showing her, even before you are married, that you have no suspicions, no fears, no doubts, with regard to her. Many a man has been discarded by a virtuous girl, merely on account of his querulous conduct. All women despise jealous men; and, if they marry such their motive is other than that of affection. Therefore, begin by proofs of unlimited confidence.

—from *Advice to Young Men* by William Cobbett

If you wrote that the author is trying to inform or persuade using an essay, you understand how certain details help you identify a genre.

Same Genre, Different Approach

Texts in the same genre may take a very different **approach** to similar topics; that is, they may present the same topic differently. The two passages below are from autobiographies, but one is personal and serious, and the other is humorous. How can you tell that they are from the same genre, despite their differences?

My father, Theodore Roosevelt, was the best man I ever knew. He combined strength and courage with gentleness, tenderness, and great unselfishness. He would not tolerate in us children selfishness or cruelty, idleness, cowardice, or untruthfulness. . . . With great love and patience, and the most understanding sympathy and consideration, he combined insistence on discipline. He never physically punished me but once, but he was the only man of whom I was ever really afraid. I do not mean that it was a wrong fear, for he was entirely just, and we children adored him.

—From *Theodore Roosevelt: An Autobiography* by Theodore Roosevelt

Back of the Virginia Clemenses is a dim procession of ancestors stretching back to Noah's time. According to tradition, some of them were pirates. . . . But this is no discredit to them, for so were Drake and Hawkins and the others. It was a respectable trade, then, and monarchs were partners in it. . . . Later, according to tradition, one of the procession was Ambassador to Spain . . . and married there and sent down a strain of Spanish blood to warm us up. . . . I have not examined into these traditions myself, partly because I was indolent, and partly because I was so busy polishing up this end of the line and trying to make it showy. . . .

—From *Chapters from My Autobiography* by Mark Twain

Roosevelt takes a personal, serious approach, and Mark Twain takes an impersonal, humorous approach. However, you can tell that both texts are autobiographies because the authors are writing about their own lives.

CORE SKILL

Determine Genre

To determine the genre of a text, follow this procedure:

1. Read the entire text.
2. Examine its physical appearance as well as its content.
3. Ask yourself: *How is the physical text divided? Are there paragraphs? Dialogue? Pictures?*
4. Read two or three random sentences in the text. Ask yourself: *Do they report facts? Do they narrate events or try to persuade the reader? Do the sentences describe people or actions? Are the sentences written in the first or third person?* Use the description of genres in this lesson to determine the genre.

Choose a text from an online or a print source. Use the procedure to determine its genre. Take notes on the details that helped you make this determination.

Then exchange texts with a partner. Examine your partner's text, and determine its genre.

Check your work with your partner to see whether you agree. Resolve any differences by working through the questions in the procedure together.

Think about Reading

Directions: Read the texts by Roosevelt and Twain on the previous page. What are the details in each text that help you identify their genre? Explain. Write your answer and explanation in your notebook.

Comparing Texts from Similar Genres

Many authors write about similar themes. You have probably read novels and seen a play about themes such as growing up responsibly or good versus evil. A moral or social theme can be addressed in an essay or a speech. Despite some differences, novels and plays share many characteristics, just as essays and speeches are similar genres.

To compare similar genres, you must first identify the genres and then look at specific similarities and differences in the texts.

Science fiction, a subgenre of fiction, imagines the effects of existing or future science on people and events. A closely related subgenre is fantasy, which tells about things that happen in an imaginary world. Each of the following excerpts relates to the discovery of a hidden world. In the early science fiction novel *20,000 Leagues Under the Sea*, a newly invented submarine takes a group of people to the ocean floor. In Arthur Conan Doyle's fantasy *The Lost World*, the author imagines a group of travelers happening upon a prehistoric Amazon basin. The themes are similar, but the word choices show that the narrators of each text have different attitudes.

Directions: Read the two passages below. How do the authors convey the attitudes of the protagonists through word choice? Write a sentence explaining how the word choices shows these feelings. Then write a sentence comparing how the two narrators feel.

> A thousand specks of light glittered in . . . the gloom. They were the eyes of gigantic crustaceans crouching in their lairs, . . . titanic crabs aiming their bodies like cannon . . . , and hideous devilfish [with] tentacles like . . . writhing snakes.
>
> —From *20,000 Leagues Under the Sea* by Jules Verne
>
> . . . [S]uddenly out of the darkness, . . . there swooped something with a swish like an aeroplane. The whole group of us were covered for an instant by a canopy of leathery wings, and I had a momentary vision of a long, snake-like neck, a fierce, red, greedy eye, and a great snapping beak. . . . The next instant it was gone—and so was our dinner. . . .
>
> —From *The Lost World* by Arthur Conan Doyle

The word choices in each passage show that the narrators feel differently about the amazing creatures they encounter. In the first passage, the narrator is afraid. Words and phrases like "gloom," "crouching in their lairs," "aiming their bodies like cannon," "hideous," and "writhing snakes" impart a sense that there is half-hidden danger all around and show that he feels threatened. In the second passage, in contrast, the narrator is fascinated by his encounter.

WRITE TO LEARN

Think of an event in your life, and write an autobiographical paragraph or two about it. Then write a poem about the same event. How does the way you express your ideas in the text change when you change genres?

CORE SKILL

Compare Similar Genres

To compare similar genres, identify the genres, and then look at specific similarities and differences in the texts.

One point of comparison is **literary techniques**, the methods by which writers **convey**, or express, their messages. Literary techniques include characterization, figurative language, and symbolism. You might also compare literary elements, such as character, mood, plot, setting, theme, and tone. Examine the moods conveyed by Jules Verne and Arthur Conan Doyle. Verne's undersea world is frightening, and Conan Doyle's is exciting.

Think of two stories or novels you have read in similar genres. Compare how the authors use literary techniques and elements. Write one or two paragraphs focusing on at least two points of comparison or contrast.

Expressions such as "swish like an aeroplane," "canopy of leathery wings," and "fierce, greedy eye" are descriptive but not threatening; especially combined with the outcome of the encounter—"The next instant it was gone—and so was our dinner"—they convey adventure but not threat.

Directions: Determine whether the following passages are from the same genre. Write a sentence or two explaining your decision.

[The king announced,] "I will hang up the flower of a banana plant, which will represent the heart of my daughter. The one who shoots it in the middle with an arrow shall be my daughter's husband and [inherit] my kingdom."

The first to shoot was Pedro, whose arrow passed directly through the middle of the banana flower. Juan shot second, and his arrow passed through the same hole Pedro's arrow had made. Now came Pablo's turn, but he refused to shoot, saying that if the banana flower represented the heart of the princess, he could not shoot it, for he loved her too dearly.

When the king heard this answer, he said, "Since Pablo really loves my daughter, while Pedro and Juan do not, for they shot at the flower that represents her heart, Pablo shall marry the princess." And so Pablo married the king's daughter, and in time became king of that country.

—From "Pablo and the Princess"

Young Alistair, exhausted, barely managed to stumble into the throne room and hold the dragon's head high for the princess to see. The princess clapped her hands in glee and spoke to him. "So you have slain the dragon, driven away the giant, found the lost treasure… I think that's enough. You have proved yourself worthy, so let the wedding preparations begin!"

The lad finally caught his breath. "I'm afraid, Princess, that there will be no wedding. As I performed my labors, the thought of you sustained me. Soon, I will marry her, I thought, and all will be well. But now my eyes are opened. You have set me impossible tasks because watching people suffer amuses you. There is no love in your heart, Princess, nor is there any left in mine. Farewell." And Alistair turned on his heel and walked out of the throne room.

—From "Alistair and the Princess"

Think about Reading

Directions: Place a checkmark beside the literary technique that differentiates the genres in the two stories above.

A. ________ character

B. ________ plot

C. ________ symbolism

D. ________ theme

TECHNOLOGY SKILL

Apply Technology to a Task

Technology offers many ways to present text. Newspapers can be delivered to our door or to our e-reader. At work, we still send and receive letters, but most correspondence takes place through e-mail. Reports and presentations may be delivered in person or online.

Similarly, you can buy a paperback novel in a bookstore located in a building, but you may prefer to download an e-book to your tablet. Drama can be viewed in a live theater or watched in a movie theater via live satellite stream. Print books are turned into audio books and can be downloaded to a mobile device so you can enjoy them while driving or jogging. Even how we watch TV has become a multimedia experience. Not only has the script been translated from the page to the small screen, but viewers can use phones and other mobile devices to access related features and chat online with stars during the show.

Think about different genres and subgenres. In a small group, discuss which delivery modes best fit specific genres and subgenres, such as fiction, poetry, biography, drama, advertising, news reports, company policies, and political statements. Do you agree with one another? Discuss the reasons for any differences of opinion.

Summary

Genres or types of writing can be identified by characteristics such as physical layout, content, or purpose. To compare texts, examine words and phrases as well as literary techniques to see how authors use genres to affect content, approach, and effect on the audience.

Vocabulary Review

Directions: Read each sentence in the first column. Then draw a line to the word that it defines.

1. type of writing with certain identifiable characteristics	**a. approach**
2. express or communicate	**b. symbolism**
3. how an author presents a subject	**c. genre**
4. methods authors use to convey their messages	**d. literary techniques**
5. the use of objects or actions to represent something else	**e. convey**

Skill Review

Directions: Read the passages below. One is young adult fiction, and the other is historical fiction. Then complete the activities.

There were six young colts in the meadow besides me. . . . We used to gallop all together round and round the field as hard as we could go. Sometimes we had rather rough play, for they would frequently bite and kick as well as gallop.

—From *Black Beauty* by Anna Sewell

Various veterans had told him tales. Some talked of gray, bewhiskered hordes who were advancing with relentless curses and chewing tobacco with unspeakable valor; tremendous bodies of fierce soldiery who were sweeping along like the Huns. Others spoke of tattered and eternally hungry men who fired despondent powders. . . . From the stories, the youth imagined the red, live bones sticking out through slits in the faded uniforms.

—From *The Red Badge of Courage* by Stephen Crane

1. Which sentence best describes a similarity between the two short passages?

A. They tell stories about things that really happened.

B. They tell stories about events that are based on history.

C. They tell stories from the perspective of a human being.

D. They tell stories about fictional characters.

2. These two passages belong to different __________ of fiction.

3. Another difference is that the main __________ in the first is a __________ and in the second is a __________.

Skill Practice

Directions: Read the passages. Then complete the activities.

It was clear that the sleigh from Weymore had not come; and the shivering young traveller from Boston, who had counted on jumping into it when he left the train at Northridge Junction, found himself standing alone on the open platform, exposed to the full assault of night-fall and winter.

The blast that swept him came off New Hampshire snow-fields and ice-hung forests. It seemed to have traversed interminable leagues of frozen silence . . . searching and sword-like, it alternately muffled and harried its victim . . . Faxon saw himself under the necessity of plodding through several feet of snow.

He understood well enough what had happened: his hostess had forgotten that he was coming.

—From "The Triumph of Night" by Edith Wharton

The cramped atmosphere of neglect oppressed Phatik so much that he felt that he could hardly breathe. He wanted to go out into the open country and fill his lungs with fresh air. . . . Surrounded on all sides by Calcutta houses and walls, he would dream night after night of his village home and long to be back there. He remembered the glorious meadow where he used to fly his kite all day long; . . . and, above all, the memory of that tyrant mother of his, who had such a prejudice against him. . . .

—From "The Homecoming" by Rabindranath Tagore

1. What is the genre of these two passages?

A. autobiography

B. essay

C. folktale

D. short story

2. What is one major difference between these two passages?

A. the main character

B. the level of description

C. the setting

D. the genre

3. The two passages are similar in that both use __________ language.

Writing Practice

Directions: Think of a topic that interests you. Search the Internet for a poem or short story that addresses the topic and an essay that does the same. Write a paragraph analyzing the similarities and differences in the way the two genres treat the topic. Remember to state the specific characteristics of the genre to which each text belongs to support your analysis.

LESSON 7.3 Analyze Two Arguments

LESSON OBJECTIVES

- Compare and contrast two arguments expressing opposing views of the same topic
- Analyze the evidence used by authors expressing opposing views of the same topic

CORE SKILLS

- Compare Arguments
- Evaluate Evidence in Opposing Arguments

Key Terms

contestable
disputable; subject to differences of opinion

Vocabulary

criteria
measures used to evaluate something

dispute
debate; call into question

hearsay
rumor; information based on another's statement

opinion
statement of the reasons and principles upon which a legal decision is based

proponents
people who argue in favor of something

Key Concept

In order to choose which side of an argument to support, a reader must evaluate the evidence and logic used by each side.

Every day people try to convince you of something: this car will use less fuel; that candidate will do more for citizens; doing this will save the planet. Not all arguments for a claim are equal, however. How can you decide which claims are valid? Recognizing whether or not a claim is supported by evidence is a necessary skill for making good decisions.

Comparing and Contrasting Two Arguments

Because people have differing opinions, they often create arguments to support those opinions. You have probably seen political candidates in debates or heard people in meetings offering different opinions about the next step for the country or for the company. When this happens, it may be up to you as a voter or coworker to decide which argument is more convincing.

An argument has two main parts: the claim and the evidence that supports the claim. A claim is the statement the arguer wants his or her audience to agree with. The evidence consists of facts, expert opinions, and logical statements that back up or prove the claim.

For an argument to occur, a claim must be **contestable**. This means that people must have differences of opinion about it and be able to **dispute**, or debate, the truth of another's claim.

We see examples of this on television all the time. In a legal drama, for instance, the prosecutors build their case to support a claim of guilt. The defense team disputes that claim and presents evidence to discredit it. It is the jury's job to decide which group has presented the more convincing argument.

In some situations, more than two claims may be made regarding a topic. You may be familiar with this from watching television. In crime dramas, detectives may disagree about the perpetrator of a crime and assemble evidence to support their varying claims about the identity of the culprit. To make a convincing argument, they must provide evidence to support their claims.

Brand X Pictures

These three statements are in favor of banning smoking, and the reason is the same in each case. Yet each claim is different.

Multiple Claims About One Topic

1. Smoking should be prohibited because it damages the health of anyone who inhales the smoke.
2. Smoking should be prohibited in all public places because it damages the health of anyone who inhales the smoke.
3. Smoking should be prohibited in public indoor areas because it damages the health of anyone who inhales the smoke.

Analyze Opposing Arguments

You have probably heard or read about criminal trials in which the defendant is accused of multiple counts of a crime or crimes. Each count is a claim and must be proved individually by the evidence the prosecutors present.

This is equally true of civil cases. Below are two passages taken from the majority **opinion** (a statement of the reasons and principles upon which a legal decision is based) written by Justice Hugo Black after the US Supreme Court heard a case brought by Sears, Roebuck, and Co. against Stiffel Co. in 1964. The Court found in favor of Sears.

Directions: Read the excerpts, and identify evidence each side used to support its claim.

Sears v. Stiffel Majority Opinion 1964

The Argument for Stiffel

The respondent, Stiffel Company, secured . . . patents on a "pole lamp"—a vertical tube . . . lamp . . . that . . . will stand upright between the floor and ceiling of a room. Pole lamps proved a . . . commercial success, and soon after Stiffel brought them on the market Sears, Roebuck & Company put [out] a substantially identical lamp, which it sold more cheaply . . . Stiffel then brought this action against Sears . . . claiming in its first count that by copying its design Sears had infringed Stiffel's patents and in its second count that by selling copies of Stiffel's lamp Sears had caused confusion . . . as to the source of the lamps and had thereby engaged in unfair competition under Illinois law.

The District Court, after holding the patents invalid . . . went on to find as a fact that Sears' lamp was "a[n] . . . exact copy" of Stiffel's and that the two lamps were so much alike . . . "that confusion between them . . . has already occurred."

The Argument for Sears

In the present case the "pole lamp" sold by Stiffel has been held not to be entitled to the protection of . . . a . . . patent. An unpatentable article . . . is in the public domain and may be made and sold by whoever chooses to do so. . . . Of course there could be "confusion". . . . But mere inability of the public to tell two . . . articles apart is not enough to support an injunction against copying or an award of damages.

CORE SKILL

Compare Arguments

To compare two arguments, the first thing you need to do is identify the claim made by the **proponents** for, or people in favor of, each side of the argument. Remember that the claim is the statement that the arguer wants you to agree with.

Reread the three statements about prohibiting smoking.

Work with a partner to identify differences between the three claims. Together, write a sentence or two explaining how they differ.

WRITE TO LEARN

Select one of the statements about smoking, and develop a paragraph supporting the claim made in the statement. When you are finished, find someone who has developed an argument supporting one of the other claims. How are your arguments alike? How are they different?

CORE SKILL

Evaluate Evidence in Opposing Arguments

To evaluate the evidence in opposing arguments, read the arguments. Then ask yourself

- Is the evidence relevant, accurate, and sufficient?
- Is the argument based on fact or opinion?
- Are the sources credible?

Reread "Children and Secondhand Smoke." As you read, write the answers to the questions above. Discuss your answers with a partner.

Think about Reading

Directions: What was the main issue being contested in *Sears* v. *Stiffel*? What claims did each party make? Write your answers in a notebook.

Analyzing Evidence in Two Arguments

In courtroom trials, the goal of the prosecution and the defense is to provide enough evidence to convince the jury that their side is right. The jury then has to evaluate this evidence and come to a decision. As in courtroom trials, when you are confronted with an argument, it is up to you to evaluate the evidence presented to support each claim.

Evaluating Evidence

An argument can't be judged just by looking at the claim. There is no way of telling whether a claim such as "In two years our city will be bankrupt" is valid without evaluating the evidence.

These are some of the **criteria**, or measures for evaluation, on which evidence should be judged:

- Is it relevant? Does the evidence actually relate to the claim?
- Is it accurate? Is the evidence factual?
- Is it sufficient? Is there enough evidence to prove the claim?

Directions: Read the passage about children and secondhand smoke. The claim, stated at the end, is that people should protect their children by not smoking in their homes and cars. What evidence is used to support this claim?

Children and Secondhand Smoke

Breathing secondhand smoke can be harmful to children's health. [It has been linked to] asthma, Sudden Infant Death Syndrome (SIDS), bronchitis and pneumonia, and ear infections.

Children's exposure to secondhand smoke is responsible for

1. increases in the number of asthma attacks and severity of symptoms in 200,000 to 1 million children with asthma;
2. between 150,000 and 300,000 lower respiratory tract infections (for children under 18 months of age); and
3. respiratory tract infections resulting in 7,500 to 15,000 hospitalizations each year.

The developing lungs of young children are severely affected by exposure to secondhand smoke for several reasons including that children are still developing physically, have higher breathing rates than adults, and have little control over their indoor environments. Children receiving high doses of secondhand smoke, such as those with smoking [parents], run the greatest risk of damaging health effects.

Join the millions of people who are protecting their children from secondhand smoke. You can become a child's hero by keeping a smoke-free home and car.

—from the U.S Environmental Protection Agency

Evidence in Opposing Arguments

Evidence can come from many sources. These sources include scientific research and analysis, witness statements, records of events, and legal codes and documents. All these sources tend to provide factual evidence.

Of course, evidence that appears to be factual might not be. If information does not come from a reliable source, it might be **hearsay**, or rumor; it might be a mistake; or it might be a deliberate attempt to mislead the reader or listener.

Another type of evidence is expert opinion. An expert's experience with and knowledge about a topic makes his or her judgment or estimation credible. This is true in the case of a crime scene investigator, just as it is in the case of a medical scientist who has spent years studying the effects of secondhand smoke.

In addition to evidence, an argument can be based on logic. To support its claim, an argument based on logic starts with a fact or assumption (an idea thought to be true) and draws a series of conclusions, or deductions. Such an argument is valid as long as the assumption and reasoning are valid.

Directions: Read the letter below. As you read, examine the evidence given. Is it fact? Is it opinion? Is it logical? Is the source of the information credible?

A Letter to the Editor

The move toward smoke-free apartment buildings is discriminatory. While it may be true that secondhand smoke is dangerous, there is no justification for telling people what they can or cannot do in their own homes. As long as people are not smoking in a public place, they are harming no one but themselves. Since taxes on cigarettes go toward funding the treatment of smoking-related diseases, smokers are also contributing to their own healthcare costs. Until cigarettes are banned entirely, smoking is legal, and the rights of smokers to enjoy a cigarette in their own homes must be protected!

Think about Reading

Directions: In a notebook, create a two-column chart. You can find an example of a two-column chart in the Graphic Organizer section at the back of the book. Label the columns "Valid Argument" and "Invalid Argument." List the elements of a valid argument in the first column and those of an invalid argument in the second.

Summary

When comparing two arguments, first identify the claim made in each argument and the evidence that supports the claim. Next, apply criteria to determine the validity of the evidence used to support the claim in each argument. These criteria include accuracy, relevance, and sufficiency. Determine the reliability of the evidence by identifying its source and assessing whether it is based on fact, logic, or expert opinion or on unreliable opinion, hearsay, or false assumptions.

21st CENTURY SKILL

Health Literacy

Television, e-mail, and the Internet offer us many opportunities to learn about the latest research on medicines, treatments, and supplements. Not all this information is reliable.

The methods of evaluating arguments can also be applied when you are confronted with advertising about the latest drug, herbal cure, or quick-and-easy office procedure to cure what ails you.

Read or listen to the advertisement carefully. Then ask yourself:

- *Is the evidence relevant, accurate, and sufficient?*
- *Is the information based on fact or opinion?*
- *Is the reasoning logical?*
- *Is the source credible?*

After you answer these questions, you will have a better idea of whether you really want to invest in the product being offered.

Find an advertisement, an article, or a press release about a new health product online or in a magazine, and evaluate it using the criteria above. Share your findings with a partner.

Vocabulary Review

Directions: Draw a line from each word to its definition.

1. contestable	**a.** statement of the reasons and principles upon which a legal decision is based
2. dispute	**b.** disputable; subject to differences of opinion
3. proponents	**c.** rumor; information based on another's statement
4. opinion	**d.** measures used to evaluate something
5. criteria	**e.** debate; call into question
6. hearsay	**f.** people who argue in favor of something

Skill Review

Directions: Read the two passages about colonists' rights in colonial America. Then fill in the blanks to complete the sentences that follow.

The Loyalists' Argument (1774)

The position that we are bound by no laws to which we have not consented . . . is a novel position, unsupported by any authoritative record of the British constitution. . . . It is republican in its very nature and tends to the utter subversion of the English monarchy. . . .

This position has arisen from an artful change of terms. To say that an Englishman is not bound by any laws but those to which the representatives of the nation have given their consent is . . . true. But to say that an Englishman is bound by no laws but those to which he ha[s] consented in person or by his representative . . . never was true and never can be true. A great part of the people in England have no vote in the choice of representatives and therefore are governed by laws to which they never consented. . . .

The right of colonists to exercise a legislative power is no natural right. They derive it not from nature but from the . . . parent state, whose subjects they were when the colony was settled and by whose permission and assistance they made the settlement.

—From *Letters of a Westchester Farmer* by Samuel Seabury

The Patriots' Argument (1775)

The origin of all civil government . . . must be a voluntary compact between the rulers and the ruled. [It] must be liable to such limitations as are necessary [to secure] the absolute rights of the latter, for what [right] can any man or set of men have to govern others except their own consent? To [assume power] over a people, . . . or to grasp at a more extensive power than they are willing to entrust, is to violate that law of nature which gives every man a right to his personal liberty. [To do so] can, therefore, confer no obligation to obedience.

If we examine the pretensions of parliament by this criterion, . . . we shall . . . detect their injustice. First, they are subversive of our natural liberty because an authority is assumed over us which we by no means assent to. . . . Secondly, they divest us of that moral security for our lives and properties which we are entitled to and which it is the [main purpose] of society to bestow. For such security can never exist while we have no part in making the laws that are to bind us—and while it may [benefit] our . . . legislators to oppress us as much as possible.

—From *The Farmer Refuted* by Alexander Hamilton

1. Seabury supports his claim with an argument based mainly on ____________________.

2. Hamilton supports his claim with an argument based mainly on ____________________.

Skill Practice

Directions: Read the two passages about the position of freed slaves after the Civil War. Then choose the best answer to each question.

Washington's Argument

A ship lost at sea for many days suddenly sighted a friendly vessel. From the mast of the unfortunate vessel was seen a signal, "Water, water; we die of thirst!" The answer from the friendly vessel at once came back, "Cast down your bucket where you are." . . . The captain of the distressed vessel . . . cast down his bucket, and it came up full of fresh, sparkling water from the mouth of the Amazon River. To those of my race . . . I would say: "Cast down your bucket where you are"—cast it down in making friends . . . of the people of all races by whom we are surrounded. . . .

Our greatest danger is that in the great leap from slavery to freedom we may overlook the fact that the masses of us are to live by the productions of our hands . . . It is at the bottom of life we must begin, and not at the top.

—From *Up from Slavery* by Booker T. Washington

Du Bois' Argument

Mr. Washington distinctly asks that black people give up, at least for the present, three things,—

First, political power,
Second, insistence on civil rights,
Third, higher education of Negro youth,—

and concentrate all their energies on industrial education, the accumulation of wealth, and the conciliation of the South. This policy has been courageously and insistently advocated for over fifteen years. . . . As a result of this tender of the palm-branch, what has been the return? In these years there have occurred:

1. The disfranchisement of the Negro.
2. The legal creation of a distinct status of civil inferiority for the Negro.
3. The steady withdrawal of aid from institutions for the higher training of the Negro.

—From *The Souls of Black Folk* by W.E.B. DuBois

1. Which of the following best paraphrases Washington's claim?

A. Sailing is a dangerous occupation.
B. Fresh water can be found at the mouth of a river.
C. Freed slaves are only prepared to do manual labor.
D. Free slaves need to work slowly toward equal rights.

2. Which of the following best paraphrases DuBois's claim?

A. It is time for freed slaves to insist on their rights.
B. It has taken courage for freed slaves to be patient.
C. Freed slaves need to concentrate on Southern reconciliation.
D. Because of Washington's advice, freed slaves are disenfranchised.

Writing Practice

Directions: Reread the arguments posed by Booker T. Washington and W.E.B. DuBois. Which one is more convincing? Write a paragraph that states and explains your opinion. Use evidence from the passages to support your statement.

LESSON 7.4 Evaluate the Impact of Genre and Format

LESSON OBJECTIVES

- Assess the scope and impact of visual and textual formats
- Evaluate the impact of genre on text

CORE SKILLS

- Compare Text and Image
- Compare Textual Genres

Key Terms

textual
consisting of words

visual
consisting of images

Vocabulary

audience
group of people who will read, see, or hear something

impact
effect or impression

scope
breadth; area covered

Key Concept

By comparing genres that present similar ideas, readers can identify differences in scope, impact, purpose, and intended audience.

Think about an article you have read about a current event and a photo you have seen of the same event. Each probably conveyed different information and affected you differently. Authors and artists of all kinds present their ideas in genres. A genre may be represented as a text, but it may also be shown through a picture, a movie, or some other aural or visual genre. The genre and format chosen by authors and other artists influence how their message comes across.

Comparing Textual and Visual Genres

A writer or artist chooses a specific genre in a specific format for a number of reasons. One is the **impact**, or effect, that the format will have. Some formats are **textual**—they consist of words—and others are **visual**—they consist of images. A text describing, for example, a forest fire, makes one kind of impact on the **audience**—the people who will read it—because it uses words to describe events. A photo of the fire makes another kind of impact because the visual image evokes emotions immediately in the viewer.

Genre, the category of the presentation of ideas, and the format also expand or limit **scope**, or the breadth of information. In the forest fire example, a news report can have a greater scope than a photograph because the format allows it to offer more information. An in-depth online interview with a firefighter on the scene might have a broader, more up-to-date scope than a short film clip with a voiceover by a news anchor.

Impact and scope are two important factors writers and visual artists have to consider when choosing the genre and format in which they will present their ideas. In many cases, textual and visual formats work together to create the maximum impact and to broaden the scope.

Directions: Look at the cartoon about the sinking of the passenger ship the *Titanic*, which was on its first voyage, and read the passage about the tragedy. Write a sentence describing the impact and scope of the picture. Then write a sentence describing the impact and scope of the passage.

Note: In 1912, when the *Titanic* sank, it was considered a man's duty to help women and children escape from danger before saving himself. Because there were not enough lifeboats for everyone, many men stayed aboard the ill-fated ship while their wives and children were rowed to safety.

Eyewitness Account of the Sinking of the *Titanic*, Elizabeth Shutes, Aged 40

Our lifeboat, with thirty-six in it, began lowering to the sea. . . . [O]nly one side of the ropes worked [and] it seemed we must capsize in mid-air. At last the ropes worked together, and we drew nearer and nearer the black, oily water. The first touch of our lifeboat on that black sea came to me as a last good-bye to life. . .

The first wish on the part of all was to stay near the Titanic [as] we all felt so much safer near the ship. Surely such a vessel could not sink. . . . But . . . [t]he bow of the boat was getting black. Light after light was disappearing, and now those rough seamen put to their oars . . . Every place was empty. There was no water . . . Not a biscuit—nothing to keep us alive . . .

—From *The Truth about the* Titanic by Archibald Gracie

If you wrote that the viewer of the cartoon instantly sees an image that conveys emotion and danger while the passage connects readers to that emotion and danger through the story of a real person and includes factual details of the tragedy and its impact on the victims, which gives it a broader scope, then you understand how different formats can have different impact and scope.

The sinking of the *Titanic* was a terrible tragedy that has inspired books, films, artwork, and compilations of eyewitness accounts. Survivor Elizabeth Shutes' account is just one format that addresses the tragedy from one perspective. The artist's drawing portrays the same event in a different way.

When you assess the impact and scope of different formats that address the same event, think about what each format conveys compared to other formats. In addition, think about how each portrayal of the event affects the reader or the viewer.

CORE SKILL

Compare Text and Image

When looking at a text and an image about the same event, ask yourself these questions:

- *What information is conveyed in both?*
- *Is there information that is conveyed only in the text or only in the image? If so, what is it?*
- *What elements of each format, such as word choice or the people the cartoonist chooses to portray, are used to have the greatest impact or scope?*

Choose a text from an online or print source that includes an image that accompanies the text. Use the procedure above to compare the text and the image. Take notes on the information that is conveyed by each format, and decide which format has the greater impact.

Then exchange your notes with a partner. Examine your partner's notes, and see whether there are details about impact and scope that you can add to your partner's notes. Discuss how you reached your conclusions about the impact of each format with your partner.

WRITE TO LEARN

Write a short essay about someone in your life who had an influence on who you are today. Be sure to describe that person and his or her influence on you in as much detail as you can. Then write a bulleted list of ways in which this person influenced you. Share your essay and list with a partner, and have your partner answer the following questions: How are the two genres different? What is the difference in impact and scope?

CORE SKILL

Compare Textual Genres

When evaluating two texts from different genres that focus on the same subject, follow this procedure:

- Identify the topic and genre of each text.
- Identify each author's purpose and audience.

Then ask yourself:

- *Does the genre fit the subject? Does the genre make the subject matter clear without distraction?*
- *Does the genre convey the author's purpose?*
- *Does the genre have the desired impact on the audience?*

Choose a poem or story that you like. Find another short text on the same topic. It can be a nonfiction text such as an essay or blog entry or a literary text that is not in the same genre as the first text you picked. Use the procedure above to identify the topic and the genres. Then write your answers to the questions about each text in your notebook.

Share your answers with a partner, and discuss the impact each genre has on the audience.

Think about Reading

Directions: Look at the cartoon and reread the passage about the *Titanic* tragedy. What does the passage convey that the picture cannot? What can the picture convey that the text cannot? Which one has a greater impact, and why? Explain.

Evaluating Differences between Textual Genres

There are variations in format between textual and visual genres, but different textual genres also employ different formats. For example, when examining two different literary genres, such as a poem and a play, it is easy to see the differences in physical format and scope.

Poems are different from most other forms of writing. The familiar structure of sentences and paragraphs are not present in a poem. Poetry presents thoughts and feelings of the writer, as well as images that can make a strong impression on the audience, using lines of text, metaphor, and poetic language.

Plays, in contrast, are written in dialogue, or lines delivered by actors, that are meant to be performed in front of an audience. Like poems, they can use highly charged, or intense, language to appeal to the audience's emotions. However, plays are meant to be heard and seen in person, as well as read.

As with literature, informational texts can be presented in a wide variety of genres and formats. Think of the many types of informational texts you have read. They may include news reports, procedural guidelines, historical documents, memos, essays, and textbooks. In some cases, the subject, purpose, and target audience for a range of informational genres will be the same. In other cases, the writers' purposes and target audiences might differ.

Directions: Read the passage below and the passage on the next page. Both cover the same topic. Write a sentence stating the purpose of each passage. Then write a sentence describing the intended audience for each passage.

Quagga Mussels

Native to Eastern Europe, these mussels have invaded waterways throughout the United States. Most recently the Quagga mussels have been moving westward and were identified in Lake Mead. These mussels have several significant impacts on the water bodies they invade. [They] deplete plankton levels, reducing food supply for native aquatic organisms. Quagga also attach to and damage infrastructure such as water intake pipes, docks, and boats.

DON'T MOVE A MUSSEL!

Invasive mussels are here! Quagga mussels have been found in Lakes Mead and Mohave. Mud, plants, and animals that may be lurking on your watercraft, your trailer, or your vehicle will cause the spread of invasive mussels. Invasive mussels cause millions of dollars of damage to boat and water systems by clogging pipes and engines. They also impact the native ecosystem and sport fisheries.

Clean Your Boat and Your Equipment!

Every time you leave the water:

- Remove any visible mud, plants, fish, or animals before transporting equipment;
- Eliminate water from equipment before transporting;
- Clean, drain, and dry anything that comes in contact with water (boats, trailers, vehicles, equipment, clothing, dogs, etc.).

Contact a Lake Mead or Lake Mohave marina to obtain a boat wash.

The purpose of both texts is to inform the audience about Quagga mussels and how invasive a species they are. However, the audiences are different, so the reason for informing these audiences is somewhat different as well. The second not only seeks to inform its audience, but also uses a different format—a bulleted list—to motivate them to take certain actions.

Keep the following in mind: Even when the topic is the same in informational texts, the author's purpose and the intended audience determine the format in which the information is presented and affect how the author's purpose is achieved. The impact and scope of each of these passages is different because of who is being reached and why they are being informed.

Think about Reading

Directions: Place a checkmark beside the audiences that the first and second passages, in that order, try to reach.

A. ________ the general public; boat and equipment owners using these lakes

B. ________ boat and equipment owners using these lakes; vacationers to these lakes

C. ________ vacationers to these lakes; boat owners across the country

D. ________ boat owners across the country; the general public

TECHNOLOGY SKILL

Work Effectively with Tools and Technology

When conducting an Internet search, you can make your search more effective by using Boolean operators. Boolean operators are words that help narrow and define your search. The most common Boolean operators are AND, OR, and NOT.

- Use AND to limit your results to ones that contain both search terms.
- Use OR to find results that contain one or the other of the terms.
- Use NOT if you want to keep the word after NOT from appearing in your search results. For example, if you wanted to learn about building a fence, you might enter "fencing NOT sword" as your search terms.

Research other invasive species on the Internet to find textual and visual resources. Think of two search terms you can use. Search using your search terms and the Boolean operators above. Write a sentence for each search, describing how effective the search is in returning useful information on your topic. Share your search results with a partner and discuss them. What would you change to improve your search results?

Summary

Different genres and formats can vary in impact and scope. Authors and visual artists use various genres to convey their ideas, and they choose the genre and format that will best suit their purposes. When you evaluate genres, examine them carefully to see how similarities and differences affect the subject matter and the reader's reaction to it. When comparing two passages, identify the authors' purpose and target audience. These factors influence choices such as genre, format, and content.

Vocabulary Review

Directions: Complete the following sentences by adding the appropriate key terms or vocabulary words from the lesson.

audience **impact** **scope** **textual** **visual**

1. A format consisting of images is ________________.
2. The area covered by a text is its ________________.
3. An author chooses a particular genre to reach his or her ________________.
4. The effect or impression a passage has on the reader is its ________________ on the reader.
5. A format consisting of words is ________________.

Skill Review

Directions: Read the passages below. Then choose the best answer to each question.

Diagnosing Alzheimer's Disease

Alzheimer's disease can be . . . diagnosed only after death . . . with an examination of brain tissue . . . in an autopsy. But doctors now have several methods and tools to help them determine fairly accurately whether a person who is having memory problems has Alzheimer's. . . . Early . . . diagnosis is beneficial for several reasons. It can tell people whether their symptoms are from Alzheimer's . . . or another cause. . . . Conditions may be treatable and possibly reversible. Beginning treatment early on in the disease process can help preserve function for some time. . . . Having an early diagnosis also helps families plan for the future [when the disease is more advanced].

What are the signs of Alzheimer's disease?

Early signs

- finding it hard to remember things
- asking the same questions over and over
- having trouble paying bills or solving simple math problems
- getting lost
- losing things or putting them in odd places

Later signs

- forgetting how to brush your teeth or comb your hair
- being confused about time, people, or places
- forgetting the names of common things
- wandering away from home

1. Which text was written to provide information about recognizing symptoms of Alzheimer's disease?
   A. Diagnosing Alzheimer's disease
   B. What are the signs of Alzheimer's disease?
   C. both texts
   D. neither text

2. What do the formats of the two passages have in common?
   A. Both use bulleted lists.
   B. Both have dialogue.
   C. Both are visual.
   D. Both are textual.

Skill Practice

Directions: Read the passage, and look at the image. Then complete the activities.

At about noon today, a forest fire broke out north of the mountain community of Whitewater. Despite firefighters' efforts, the blaze continued to grow, fanned by strong winds and feeding on dry brush and timber in the area. Residents in northern sections of Whitewater have been told to prepare to evacuate. Current containment is 20 percent.

1. Which sentence best expresses the scope of the passage compared with the scope of the image?
   A. The image has a broader scope than the passage.
   B. The passage has a broader scope than the image.
   C. The image and the passage have an equally broad scope.
   D. The image and the passage have an equally limited scope.

2. The passage and the photo are similar in that they address the same __________, but they are in different __________ and have a different __________ on the reader and the viewer.

Writing Practice

Directions: Think of a topic, such as an activity you do in your free time, that interests you. Search the Internet for an essay and a FAQ that address the topic. Write a paragraph evaluating the impact and scope of each text. Then compare and contrast the two genres in terms of audience and purpose.

Directions: Read the following passages. Then complete activities 1 through 4.

. . . Sometimes they seemed to me, like what the police call them, "street-rats" who gnawed at the foundations of society, and scampered away when light was brought near them. Their life was, of course, a painfully hard one. To sleep in boxes, or under stairways, or in hay-barges on the coldest winter-nights, for a mere child, was hard enough; but often to have no food, to be kicked and cuffed by the older ruffians, and shoved about by the police, standing barefooted and in rags under doorways as the winter-storm raged, and to know that in all the great city there was not a single door open with welcome to the little rover—this was harder. . . .

Yet, with all this, a more light-hearted youngster than the street-boy is not to be found. He is always ready to make fun of his own sufferings, and to "chaff" others. His face is old from exposure and his sharp "struggle for existence;" his clothes flutter in the breeze and his bare feet peep out from the broken boots. Yet he is merry as a clown, and always ready for the smallest joke, and quick to take "a point" or to return a repartee. . . . Yet he has his code; he will not get drunk; he pays his debts to other boys, and thinks it dishonorable to sell papers on their beat, and, if they come on his, he administers summary justice by "punching;" he is generous to a fault, and will always divide his last sixpence with a poorer boy. Life is a "strife" with him, and money its reward; and, as bankruptcy means to the street-boy a night on the door-steps without supper, he is sharp and reckless, if he can only earn or get enough to keep him above water. . . .

The choice of these lads of a night's resting-place is sometimes almost as remarkable as was Gavroche's in "Les Miserables." Two little newsboys slept one winter in the iron tube of the bridge at Harlem; two others made their bed in a burned-out safe in Wall Street. Sometimes they ensconced themselves in the cabin of a ferry-boat, and thus spent the night. Old boilers, barges, steps, and, above all, steam-gratings, were their favorite beds.

In those days the writer would frequently see ten or a dozen of them, piled together to keep one another warm, under the stairs of the printing-offices.

—From *The Dangerous Classes of New York, and Twenty Year's Work Among Them* by Charles Loring Brace

At first none of the other newsboys paid any attention to him, perhaps because they were too busy; but as trade began to grow dull they commenced to gather around Paul, until he was thoroughly alarmed at some of the demonstrations they made.

One boy, considerably larger than he was, insisted that if he wanted to sell papers he should go somewhere else to do it, because that particular portion of the city was under the immediate control of himself and his friends. Paul made no reply . . . and he remained silent, which caused his tormentors to think—exactly what was the true state of the case—that he was afraid of them.

One boy, the same who had first spoken, began pushing him aside, and poor Paul, seeing at least a dozen boys, nearly all of them larger than he was, standing in threatening attitudes, looked around in vain for his two friends, who had promised to care for him.

"[Y]ou don't want to show your nose 'round here agin," said the largest member of the party, as he pushed Paul rudely aside with one hand, and with the other attempted to take his papers from him.

It was this, more than anything else, which made Paul resist; for even if he had no right on that particular spot, they surely had no right to take his papers from him; and besides, they were Johnny's property, not his. Therefore he felt he should defend them all the more strongly.

—From *Left Behind or, Ten Days as a Newsboy* by James Otis

1. The second passage portrays a scene unfolding in a single _________, and the first passage describes details about events that occur in different places.

2. What are the genres of these two passages?
   A. The first passage is a fictional story; the second is a nonfiction article.
   B. Both passages are fictional stories.
   C. Both passages are nonfiction articles.
   D. The first passage is a nonfiction article; the second is a fictional story.

3. How does the second passage differ from the first?
   A. It describes people who once lived.
   B. It describes what characters are thinking.
   C. It includes a setting that resembles an actual city.
   D. It includes dialogue from real people who live in a city.

4. The _________ of these passages is the same, but the genre affects the way the narrative is presented in that the first passage presents _________ and the second passage tells _________.

Directions: Read the following passages. Then complete activities 5 through 7.

NORA: Sit down here, Torvald. You and I have much to say to one another.

HELMER: *[sits down at the opposite side of the table]* You alarm me, Nora! —and I don't understand you.

NORA: No, that is just it. You don't understand me, and I have never understood you either—before tonight. No, you mustn't interrupt me. You must simply listen to what I say. Torvald, this is a settling of accounts.

HELMER: What do you mean by that?

NORA: *[after a short silence]* We have been married now eight years. Does it not occur to you that this is the first time we two, you and I, husband and wife, have had a serious conversation?

HELMER: . . . Was it likely that I would be continually and forever telling you about worries that you could not help me to bear?

NORA: That is just it; you have never understood me. I have been greatly wronged, Torvald—first by papa and then by you.

HELMER: What! By us two—by us two, who have loved you better than anyone else in the world?

NORA: *[shaking her head]*. You have never loved me. You have only thought it pleasant to be in love with me.

HELMER: Nora, what do I hear you saying?

NORA: It is perfectly true, Torvald. When I was at home with papa, he told me his opinion about everything, and so I had the same opinions; and if I differed from him I concealed the fact, because he would not have liked it. He called me his doll-child, and he played with me just as I used to play with my dolls. And when I came to live with you—

HELMER: What sort of an expression is that to use about our marriage?

NORA: *[undisturbed]* I mean that I was simply transferred from papa's hands into yours. You arranged everything according to your own taste, and so I got the same tastes as you or else I pretended to, I am really not quite sure which—I think sometimes the one and sometimes the other. When I look back on it, it seems to me as if I had been living here like a poor woman—just from hand to mouth. I have existed merely to perform tricks for you, Torvald. But you would have it so. You and papa have committed a great sin against me. It is your fault that I have made nothing of my life.

(Continued on page 244)

(Continued from page 243)

HELMER: How unreasonable and ungrateful you are, Nora! Have you not been happy here?

NORA: . . . No, only merry . . . our home has been nothing but a playroom. I have been your dollwife, just as at home I was papa's doll-child; . . . that is what our marriage has been, Torvald.

HELMER: There is some truth in what you say—exaggerated as your view of it is. But playtime shall be over, and lesson-time shall begin.

NORA: Whose lessons? Mine, or the children's?

HELMER: Both yours and the children's, my darling Nora.

NORA: Alas, Torvald, you are not the man to educate me into being a proper wife for you.

HELMER: And you can say that!

NORA: And I—how am I fitted to bring up the children?

HELMER: Nora!

—From *A Doll's House* by Henrik Ibsen

LIZA: How do you do, Professor Higgins? Are you quite well?

HIGGINS: *[choking]* Am I . . . *[He can say no more].*

LIZA: But of course you are: you are never ill. . . .

HIGGINS: Don't you dare try this game on me. I taught it to you; and it doesn't take me in. Get up and come home; and don't be a fool.

MRS. HIGGINS: Very nicely put, indeed, Henry. No woman could resist such an invitation.

HIGGINS: You let her alone, mother. . . . You will jolly soon see whether she has an idea that I haven't put into her head or a word that I haven t put into her mouth. . . .

LIZA: *[to Pickering . . .]* . . . It was from you that I learnt really nice manners; and that is what makes one a lady, isn't it? You see it was so very difficult for me with the example of Professor Higgins always before me. . . . Do you know what began my real education? . . . Your calling me Miss Doolittle that day when I first came to Wimpole Street. That was the beginning of self-respect for me. . . .

PICKERING: Oh, that was nothing.

LIZA: . . . that showed you thought and felt about me as if I were something better than a scullery-maid; though of course I know you would have been just the same to a scullery-maid if she had been let in the drawing-room. . . .

PICKERING: You mustn't mind . . . Higgins. . . .

LIZA: . . . I am not blaming him. It is his way, isn't it? . . . the difference between a lady and a flower girl is not how she behaves, but how she's treated. I shall always be a flower girl to Professor Higgins, because he always treats me as a flower girl, and always will; but I know I can be a lady to you, because you always treat me as a lady, and always will.

PICKERING: . . . you're coming back to Wimpole Street, aren't you? You'll forgive Higgins?

HIGGINS: *[rising]* Forgive! Will she, by George! Let her go. Let her find out how she can get on without us. . . . If you come back I shall treat you just as I have always treated you. I don't intend to change my manners. My manners are exactly the same as Colonel Pickering's.

LIZA: That's not true. He treats a flower girl as if she was a duchess.

(Continued on page 245)

(Continued from page 244)

HIGGINS: And I treat a duchess as if she was a flower girl. . . . The great secret, Eliza, is not having bad manners or good manners, but having the same manner for all human souls.

LIZA: *[with sudden sincerity]* . . . I don't care how you treat me. But . . . I won't be passed over.

HIGGINS: Then get out of my way; for I won't stop for you. You talk about me as if I were a motor bus.

LIZA: So you are a motor bus: all bounce and go, and no consideration for anyone. But I can do without you: don't think I can't. . . .

HIGGINS: Eliza, you're an idiot. . . . So you can come back or go to the devil: which you please.

LIZA: Oh! If I only COULD go back to my flower basket! I should be independent . . . ! Why did you take my independence from me? Why did I give it up? . . .

HIGGINS: Very well: be off with you to the sort of people you like . . . if you can't appreciate what you've got, you'd better get what you can appreciate. . . .

LIZA: If I can't have kindness, I'll have independence. . . . I'll go and be a teacher.

HIGGINS: What'll you teach, in heaven's name?

LIZA: What you taught me. I'll teach phonetics.

HIGGINS: Ha! Ha! Ha!

LIZA: . . . What a fool I was not to think of it before! You can't take away the knowledge you gave me. . . . Now I don't care that [snapping her fingers] for your bullying and your big talk. . . . when I think . . . all the time I had only to lift up my finger to be as good as you, I could just kick myself.

HIGGINS: *[rising]* By George, Eliza. . . . I like you like this.

—From *Pygmalion* by George Bernard Shaw

5. These passages are from the _________ genre.

6. How do the arguments each main character makes differ from each other?

A. Nora has children involved; Liza does not.

B. Nora states her case calmly; Liza is clearly angry.

C. Nora is married to Torvald; Liza is not married to Higgins.

D. Nora learned nothing from Torvald; Liza learned from Higgins.

7. How does Shaw's approach to the topic differ from Ibsen's?

A. Shaw uses comedic devices to create his characters; Ibsen does not.

B. Shaw includes characters who disagree more than Ibsen does.

C. Shaw introduces other characters; Ibsen does not.

D. Shaw uses a different setting than Ibsen uses.

Directions: Read the following passage, and look at the chart. Then complete activities 8 through 10.

The Relationship among Energy, Wavelength, and Frequency

The electromagnetic spectrum can be expressed in terms of *energy, wavelength,* or *frequency.* Each way of thinking about the EM spectrum is related to the others in a precise mathematical way. Scientists represent wavelength and frequency by the Greek letters lambda (λ) and nu (ν). Using those symbols, the relationships between energy, wavelength, and frequency can be written as:

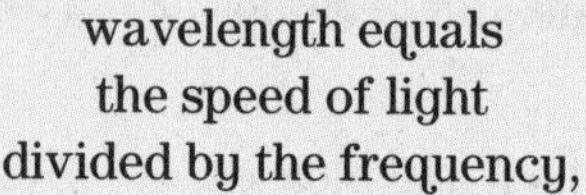

wavelength equals the speed of light divided by the frequency,

or

$\lambda = c/\nu$

and

energy equals Planck's constant times the frequency,

or

$E = h \times \nu$

where:

- λ is the wavelength
- ν is the frequency
- E is the energy
- c is the speed of light, c = 299,792,458 m/s (186,212 miles/second)
- h is Planck's constant, $h = 6.626 \times 10^{-27}$ erg-seconds

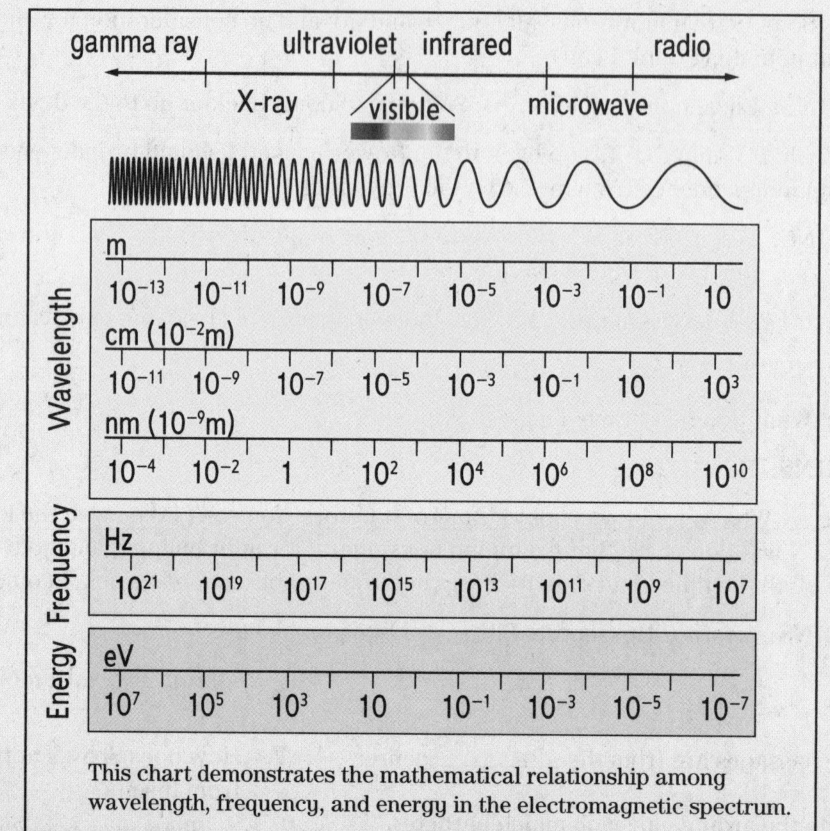

This chart demonstrates the mathematical relationship among wavelength, frequency, and energy in the electromagnetic spectrum.

Both the speed of light and Planck's constant are constant—they never change in value.

—From "The Electromagnetic Spectrum" by NASA

8. Into which format does the chart fall?

A. dramatic

B. fictional

C. textual

D. visual

9. The __________ of the chart is instant, but the text requires a full reading to understand the explanation of the electromagnetic spectrum

10. Which statement best describes the difference in the information provided by the passage compared to the chart?

A. The passage visually shows information about the electromagnetic spectrum.

B. The passage explains the concepts of the electromagnetic spectrum in detail.

C. The passage shows that energy, wavelength, and frequency have a mathematical connection.

D. The passage shows how the wavelength changes across the spectrum.

Check Your Understanding

On the following chart, circle the number of any item you answered incorrectly. In the third column, you will see the pages that you can review to study the content covered in the question. Pay particular attention to reviewing those lessons in which you missed half or more of the questions.

Lesson	Core Skill	Item Number(s)	Review Page(s)
Lesson 1: Compare Similar Topics in Different Formats	Compare Two Texts in Different Formats	9, 10	218–220
	Compare Fiction and Nonfiction	1, 2, 3, 4	220–221
Lesson 2: Compare Similar Genres	Determine Genre	2, 5	224–225
	Compare Similar Genres	6, 7	225–226
Lesson 3: Analyze Two Arguments	Compare Arguments	6	230–231
	Evaluate Evidence in Opposing Arguments	6	232–233
Lesson 4: Evaluate The Impact of Genre and Format	Compare Text and Image	8, 9, 10	236–237
	Compare Textual Genres	1, 2, 3, 4	238–239

WRITE ABOUT The Milky Way

Read the article and the story, both titled "The Milky Way," on pages 315 and 317. Examine the photograph of a nebula on page 316, a cloud of gas and dust that is part of the Milky Way. Then write an essay in which you integrate the information from all three sources to gain a better understanding of how human beings think of the Milky Way. Identify similarities and differences among the passages and the photograph to support a thesis, or main idea, for your essay that combines various aspects of the sources.

As you read each passage or look at the photo, think about its source, format, and reliability. Ask yourself: *Who wrote this, or where did this photo come from? What is the author's purpose for writing each text? Why was the photograph taken? What does the photograph show? Who is the intended audience for the passage or the photo? What information does each author emphasize? What impression does the photo make on the viewer? Why?*

BEFORE YOU WRITE Determine Similarities and Differences

Use a 3-circle Venn diagram like the one below to compare and contrast the passages and photo.

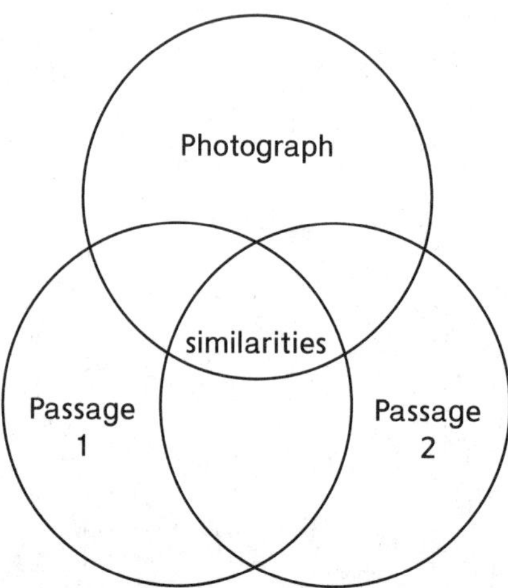

The diagram will help you organize your thoughts on the similarities and differences among the three items. As you read, use the Venn diagram to take notes on facts, details, and ideas that are unique to each item or that are common to two or to all three of them. Remember the points of comparison—source, format, reliability, emphasis, purpose, and intended audience.

TIP Use Terms and Sentence Structure to Compare and Contrast

There are many terms that signal comparison and contrast. Sentence structure can also indicate these relationships. Look at these sentences.

- Both pairs of jeans are the same price. (The words *both* and *same* signal similarity.)
- This pair of jeans is smaller than that one. (The phrase *is smaller than* signals contrast.)
- This pair of jeans is too small; that pair of jeans is too large. (The semicolon indicates that these clauses are closely related. Here the relationship is a contrast.)
- This pair of jeans is too small; that pair of jeans is too large, though. (The semicolon indicates a close relationship between the clauses and the signal word *though* indicates contrast.)
- This pair of jeans, as well as that one, costs less than $30. (The commas and signal words *as well as* indicate similarity.)

As you write, use words, phrases, and sentence structures to indicate comparison and contrast.

WHILE YOU WRITE Use Comparison-and-Contrast Organization

Look at your Venn diagram. Ask yourself: *On what points are the passages and image similar? On what points are they different? In what way?* Then consider these questions: *How do these items relate to the human desire to examine the heavens? How do they relate to the human need to explain things? How do they relate to the idea of science versus myth?* Use your answers to these questions to decide what you want to say in your essay. Create a sentence that states the claim you will make in your essay—a thesis statement. To construct the statement, examine information from all the sources and form a new idea based on the combination of information. The new idea is your thesis. Then organize your essay in a comparison-and-contrast structure to support this idea.

There are two ways to organize a comparison-and-contrast essay. One is using a point-by-point pattern. This means writing one point and comparing all three items on that point and then doing the same with the other points.

The other type of comparison-and-contrast organization is the whole-to-whole pattern. To use the whole-to-whole pattern, write about one item listing all the points of comparison for that item. Then list all the points for the second item, followed by all the points for the third item.

Look at the information in your Venn diagram, and think about your thesis statement. Decide which of the two structures you think would work best for your essay. Use the structure you have chosen consistently.

Use evidence from the passages and the photograph to support your thesis. Make sure you use organization, sentence structure, and signal words and phrases to indicate comparison and contrast.

At the end of your essay, summarize the conclusions you drew about your thesis based on evidence.

TIP Watch Out for . . . Spelling Errors and Typos

Check carefully to make sure that your words are spelled correctly. Watch for homophones—words that sound the same, but have different spellings (such as *their, there, they're; to, too, two; write, right*). Make sure that any words taken directly from the passages match the spelling used in the original.

It's a good idea to use the spell checker in your word processing program. However, the spell checker may suggest the wrong word, so choose carefully from the list it offers. Remember: Even if a word is correctly spelled, it might not have the meaning you intended.

AFTER YOU WRITE Check Your Work

Reread the writing assignment. Then read your essay carefully three times.

The first time you read, ask yourself whether you have completed the writing assignment correctly. Have you compared and contrasted the sources on the points you identified? Do all the paragraphs connect to the thesis statement? Do they lead logically to the conclusion?

Then read your essay again. Did you use appropriate comparison-and-contrast terms and sentence structure? Did you use one type of comparison-and-contrast organization consistently?

Reread the essay one last time. Did you use correct grammar, spelling, and punctuation? Do you see any errors? Did you type the words you meant to use?

Before submitting your essay, have another student read it and provide you with feedback.

Directions: Read the following passage. Then choose the best answer to questions 1 through 6.

(1) It was a cold morning of the early spring, and we sat after breakfast on either side of a cheery fire in the old room at Baker Street. A thick fog rolled down between the lines of dun-coloured houses, and the opposing windows loomed like dark, shapeless blurs through the heavy yellow wreaths. Our gas was lit and shone on the white cloth and glimmer of china and metal, for the table had not been cleared yet. Sherlock Holmes had been silent all the morning, dipping continuously into the advertisement columns of a succession of papers until at last, having apparently given up his search, he had emerged in no very sweet temper . . . .

(2) . . . "the days of the great cases are past. Man, or at least criminal man, has lost all enterprise and originality. As to my own little practice, it seems to be degenerating into an agency for recovering lost lead pencils and giving advice to young ladies from boarding-schools. I think that I have touched bottom at last, however. This note I had this morning marks my zero-point, I fancy. Read it!" He tossed a crumpled letter across to me.

(3) It was dated from Montague Place upon the preceding evening, and ran thus:

DEAR MR. HOLMES: I am very anxious to consult you as to whether I should or should not accept a situation which has been offered to me as governess. I shall call at half-past ten tomorrow if I do not inconvenience you.

Yours faithfully, VIOLET HUNTER.

(4) "Do you know the young lady?" I asked.

(5) "Not I."

(6) "It is half-past ten now."

(7) "Yes, and I have no doubt that is her ring."

(8) "It may turn out to be of more interest than you think. You remember that the affair of the blue carbuncle, which appeared to be a mere whim at first, developed into a serious investigation. It may be so in this case, also."

(9) "Well, let us hope so. But our doubts will very soon be solved, for here, unless I am much mistaken, is the person in question."

(10) As he spoke the door opened and a young lady entered the room. She was plainly but neatly dressed, with a bright, quick face, freckled like a plover's egg, and with the brisk manner of a woman who has had her own way to make in the world.

(11) "You will excuse my troubling you, I am sure," said she, as my companion rose to greet her, "but I have had a very strange experience, and as I have no parents or relations of any sort from whom I could ask advice, I thought that perhaps you would be kind enough to tell me what I should do."

—From *The Adventure of the Copper Beeches* by Sir Arthur Conan Doyle

1. When was the note to Mr. Holmes written?

A. while Sherlock Holmes read advertisement columns

B. at half-past ten

C. the night before his meeting with Violet Hunter

D. on a cold morning in early spring

2. Read this text from the passage: *"You will excuse my troubling you, I am sure," said she, as my companion rose to greet her . . ."*

To whom does the term "my companion" refer?

A. Violet Hunter

B. Doctor Watson

C. Sherlock Holmes

D. Arthur Conan Doyle

3. Read this sentence from the passage: *Man, or at least criminal man, has lost all enterprise and originality.*

   The sentence includes an example of which rhetorical device?

   A. analogy
   B. enumeration
   C. juxtaposition
   D. qualifying statement

4. Which of the following is NOT a characteristic of complex text found in this passage?

   A. The topic is an abstract concept.
   B. The sentences are long and elaborate.
   C. The speaker is not always identified.
   D. Readers need prior knowledge of what a plover is.

5. What is the relationship between paragraphs 10 and 11?

   A. The event in paragraph 10 happens after the event in paragraph 11.
   B. Paragraph 10 introduces the character who speaks in paragraph 11.
   C. Paragraph 10 introduces Holmes, who helps the girl in paragraph 11.
   D. Paragraph 11 explains what happened before the event in paragraph 10.

6. What can you infer from Holmes's statement "I think that I have touched bottom at last, however."?

   A. He is eager to meet Violet Hunter.
   B. He knows Violet Hunter's father and mother.
   C. He is not looking forward to meeting Violet Hunter.
   D. He thinks his next case will be the most exciting he has ever had.

Directions: Read the following passages. Then choose the best answer to questions 7 through 13.

Blog: Cooking with Cathy

Spinach Dip á la Jane

I owe this one to my Aunt Jane. She is a great all-around cook, but party food is her specialty, and her spinach dip is my favorite.

I remember the last time Aunt Jane made this dip. It was a hot, sweaty summer night, and my mother decided to get the family together for an impromptu barbecue. With Jane and her brood, my uncle and his girlfriend, and our houseful, there were well over a dozen people. We dug a fire pit not far from the water's edge, chopped some vegetables, and marinated some chicken, beef, and shrimp for kebabs. Uncle Johnny brought a cooler full of drinks, and Jane brought her famous dip. As soon as they arrived, the kids headed for the lake. While they splashed in the water, the rest of us set up the tables and chairs. Then Mom turned on the outdoor speakers, and the party ticked up a few notches. People who felt famished skewered their own kebabs and, while impatiently waiting for the meat to cook over the fire, they pigged out on corn chips and spinach dip. The kebabs were tasty, but the spinach dip was the runaway hit of the evening. So I asked Jane for her recipe . . . and here it is.

Put two cups of sour cream (use low fat if you wish) into a large bowl. Add a cup of mayonnaise (I prefer creamy salad dressing). You're going to need some chopped green onions and chopped water chestnuts (one can), so you might want to get the chopping done first. Also, you'll need to thaw out a package of chopped spinach in advance. After you've finished chopping, squeeze all the water out of the spinach (or almost all—it's probably impossible to get the spinach completely dry). Throw everything into the bowl with one packet of dry vegetable soup mix, and beat with an electric mixer. Don't go any higher than medium speed, though, or those water chestnuts will lose their crunchiness! When the texture of the dip is right, cover the bowl and put it in the fridge for a couple of hours (overnight if you're the plan-ahead type). Enjoy with your favorite chips.

Thanks, Jane!

Aunt Jane's Spinach Dip

Ingredients

- 2 c. sour cream
- 1 c. mayonnaise
- 1 pkg. (1.25 oz.) dry vegetable soup mix
- 1 can (8 oz.) water chestnuts, drained and chopped
- 3 green onions, chopped
- 1 pkg. (8 oz.) frozen chopped spinach, thawed

Directions

1. Combine sour cream and mayonnaise in a large bowl.
2. Stir in soup mix, water chestnuts, and green onions.
3. Squeeze excess water from thawed spinach with your hands, or use a spoon and a strainer.
4. Add dried spinach to other ingredients in bowl.
5. Blend with electric mixer at medium speed.
6. Chill and enjoy.

7. How are the two texts similar?

A. Both entertain readers with interesting details.
B. Both inform readers about various uses for spinach.
C. Both explain how to make a dip.
D. Both persuade readers to eat more vegetables.

8. Which of the following is a hidden assumption that BOTH authors make?

A. Their readers like barbecues.
B. Their readers can operate an electric mixer.
C. Their readers will know to use a dry soup mix.
D. Their readers know that water chestnuts come in cans.

9. Read the following sentence from Cathy's blog entry: *The kebabs were tasty, but the spinach dip was the runaway hit of the evening.* What relationship does the word *but* signal?

A. a solution to the problem of messy kebabs
B. an effect caused by eating too much spinach dip
C. a contrast between Aunt Jane's everyday cooking and her party food
D. a comparison of Aunt Jane's dish to other food served at the barbecue

10. Which text feature does *Aunt Jane's Spinach Dip* recipe NOT use to help readers?

A. subheads
B. bulleted list
C. boldface words
D. italicized words

11. Read the following sentence from the blog: *Uncle Johnny brought a cooler full of drinks, and Jane brought her famous dip.* Why is a comma used in this sentence?

A. to separate items in a series
B. to separate an introductory clause
C. to separate independent ideas
D. to separate a pronoun and antecedent

12. Which of the following has the same denotation, or literal meaning, but a less negative connotation than the phrase *pigged out on*, as used in Cathy's blog entry?

A. abstained from
B. devoured
C. gorged themselves on
D. picked at

13. Which sentence most accurately compares the impact of the blog entry and the recipe on a reader intending to make the dip?

A. The blog has a greater impact because it is on the Internet.
B. The recipe has a greater impact because it covers many topics at one time.
C. The recipe has a greater impact because it lists exactly what readers should do to make the dip.
D. The blog has a greater impact because readers find out about the writer's family.

Directions: Read the following passage. Then choose the best answer to questions 14 through 20.

The Wicked Gravedigger

A Traditional German Tale Retold

The wife of a wealthy merchant suddenly died. Overcome by grief, the husband had her buried in her most beautiful gown, wearing the large diamond ring he had given her on their wedding day.

Everyone in town heard about the priceless ring, including the local gravedigger. He waited impatiently for the curtain of night to fall, and when the clock struck midnight, he crept back to the graveyard. He quickly dug up the dirt around the coffin and, reaching down with quivering fingers, opened the lid. There, shining in the moonlight, was the diamond ring. As the gravedigger tried to pull the ring off the woman's finger, she sat up and screamed.

The gravedigger fell to the ground, unconscious from fright. The poor woman, having woken from a trance, climbed from her grave and walked home as fast as her weakened legs would take her. "It's me," she told the servant who answered the door. "Go tell my husband that I am back from the dead."

The terrified servant ran to his master and blurted out the strange news. The husband shook his head and muttered, "My wife returning from the dead is as unbelievable as my horse coming in here to speak to me!"

Suddenly he heard a clip-clopping sound as his horse trotted in and said, "Good evening, master." Then the grief-stricken husband knew it must be true. He dashed downstairs to find his wife waiting for him. They embraced and lived happily together for many years.

14. What is the genre of the passage?

A. essay
B. folktale
C. science fiction
D. autobiography

15. Which of the following best describes the overall structure of this passage?

A. cause and effect
B. compare and contrast
C. problem and solution
D. sequence

16. How does the author use personification?

A. by describing the gravedigger creeping
B. by having the ring shine in the moonlight
C. by making the merchant's horse talk like a human
D. by making the gravedigger fall unconscious from fright

17. How does the setting of the story contribute to the plot?

A. The graveyard is necessary because the horse lives there.
B. The graveyard is necessary because someone is buried there.
C. The road to the graveyard is necessary because the plot involves a wagon on the road.
D. The gravedigger's house is necessary because he runs there as fast as he can.

18. Which statement best states the theme of the story?

A. Anything is possible.
B. Hard work is honorable.
C. It is better to give than to receive.
D. It is wise to trust your instincts.

19. Identify the type of figurative language used in the following phrase: *He waited impatiently for the curtain of night to fall.*

A. connotation
B. metaphor
C. personification
D. simile

20. Read the following sentence from the passage: *The terrified servant ran to his master and blurted out the strange news.* What is another way to write the sentence correctly?

A. The servant ran to his master and blurted out the strange, terrified news.
B. The servant ran to his terrified master and blurted out the strange news.
C. The terrifying servant ran to his master and blurted out the strange news.
D. Terrified, the servant ran to his master and blurted out the strange news.

Directions: Read the following passage. Then choose the best answer to questions 21 through 25.

Frostbite

Winter will soon be here, and many areas of the country will see sub-zero temperatures. Along with the bitter cold comes a threat to life and limb—the danger of frostbite. Overexposure to extreme cold can cause frostbite. Ice crystals form in the body's tissues and impede blood flow to affected areas. Most frequently, frostbite affects the toes, fingers, cheeks, chin, nose, and ears—areas of the body that are not adequately covered up and protected from the elements. You can tell that someone has frostbite if skin on an exposed area turns exceedingly pallid or grayish-blue. Initially, the cold body part is painful when touched, but it eventually becomes numb. It is important to restore circulation and warmth to the frostbitten area as quickly as possible. Use of hot water bottles or heating pads should be avoided because the temperature change will be too extreme. Instead, the affected area should be gently soaked in warm water (102°F to 105°F), then wrapped in soft gauze or cloth before being loosely bandaged. For serious frostbite, immediate medical attention is recommended to avoid extensive tissue damage. Frostbite can permanently damage the body, and severe cases can lead to amputation.

21. What is the main idea of the passage?

A. Frostbitten skin begins to fall off.
B. Frostbite is a dangerous condition.
C. Frostbite most frequently affects the toes and fingers.
D. Frostbitten skin should be soaked in warm water.

22. Which type of supporting details does the author use to support the main idea?

A. facts and descriptions
B. statistics and questions
C. descriptions and opinions
D. questions and reasons

23. Which option best describes an implicit purpose of the text?

A. to persuade readers to send in questions about frostbite
B. to entertain readers with a story about surviving frostbite
C. to persuade readers not to expose vulnerable body parts to extreme cold
D. to inform readers how to seek help if they have a temperature over 105°F

24. What is the tone of the passage?

A. hostile
B. serious
C. humorous
D. threatening

25. Which text structure best describes the way this passage is organized?

A. cause and effect
B. chronological
C. compare and contrast
D. order of importance

Directions: Read the following passages. Then choose the best answer to questions 26 through 32.

Dear Editor:

The local recycling facility sent out a flyer saying hazardous household waste must be brought to their facility. It defined hazardous household waste as any product or chemical used in the home that contains toxic or corrosive ingredients. It gave examples such as leftover house paints, gasoline, motor oil, and old batteries. It also mentioned products used to control insects and pests. I don't think pesticides are hazardous. We spray pesticides in our homes and gardens to protect our plants from destruction and ourselves from being bitten. We spread them on the ground to make our lawns look lush. Because we are spraying pesticides in the air and sprinkling them on the soil, we come into contact with them every day. Some wildlife has been poisoned by pesticides, but they still have certain benefits. There is no need to dispose of pesticides at the hazardous waste facility. Leftover household pesticides should be placed in the regular trash.

Marsha Smith

To Residents:

The local recycling facility has asked us to post the following guidelines regarding disposal of pesticides. Your compliance is of utmost importance in maintaining a safe and healthy environment in our apartment community.

ALL leftover pesticides, as well as the containers in which they were packaged, are considered to be hazardous waste and MUST be brought to the recycling facility. Items include:

- weed killers
- animal repellents
- insecticides
- fungicides

Be sure to place these items in bins for delivery to the recycling center. Do NOT place these items in the regular trash, and do NOT pour them down sinks, toilets, or street drains. Pesticides might pollute waterways and cause serious harm to fish, plants, and other wildlife.

Your immediate cooperation is appreciated.

The Management Office

26. On what subject do the two passages disagree?

A. whether or not pesticides protect plants
B. whether or not pesticides are hazardous waste
C. whether or not light weed killers should be used
D. whether or not the recycling facility should pick up hazardous waste

27. Which statement expresses the author's claim in the letter to the editor?

A. The local recycling facility sent out a flyer.
B. Some wildlife has been poisoned by pesticides.
C. There is no need to dispose of pesticides at the hazardous waste facility.
D. Hazardous household waste is any product or chemical that contains toxic or corrosive ingredients.

28. What does the author of the letter to the editor accomplish by presenting an idea that contradicts her viewpoint?

A. She strengthens her position.
B. She offers a more balanced position.
C. She strengthens the opposing viewpoint.
D. She offers sufficient, sound, and relevant evidence.

29. Which sentence is a valid inference that readers could make after reading both arguments?

A. The apartment building has a new manager.
B. A new recycling plant has just opened in town.
C. Some tenants in the apartment building are producing too much trash.
D. Some people in town are not properly disposing of hazardous household waste.

30. Which statement best describes the effect of the apartment management's memo?

A. It amuses residents.
B. It offends residents by its bossy tone.
C. It convinces residents that recycling is not important.
D. It motivates residents to follow the recycling rules closely.

31. In what way are the two texts similar?

A. Both are persuasive texts that try to bring about change.
B. Both are literary texts with an environmental theme.
C. Both are informational texts focused on the subject of wildlife.
D. Both are descriptive texts that explain the purpose of pesticides.

32. Which relevant detail does Marsha Smith include in her letter to support the idea that pesticides are helpful?

A. The local recycling facility sent out a flyer.
B. Some wildlife has been poisoned by pesticides.
C. We use pesticides to protect us from insect bites.
D. The recycling facility gave examples such as leftover paint and old batteries.

Directions: Read the following passage. Then choose the best answer to questions 33 through 38.

Invasion of the Plant and Animal Snatchers

Across the landscape they silently creep, powerful forces that are almost impossible to overcome. They aggressively conquer bubbling ponds and streams, destroy pastoral meadows, invade neighborhood canals . . . and maybe your backyard. They are invasive species, aggressive predators that dine on native plants and feast on helpless fish and wildlife, creating a growing ecological nightmare.

The first nonnative plants and animals were brought to this country by colonists. Today exotic animals can be purchased from pet stores or through a growing Internet market. Invasive species can also arrive through the ballast ejected from oceangoing ships, or as innocent seeds wedged in the shoes of oblivious international travelers.

According to the U.S. Fish and Wildlife Service, approximately 50,000 of these nonnative species have been documented, though most experts indicate that the figure will go much higher as more species are discovered and identified.

One of the more popular nonnative species is the Burmese python. All too often, python owners will discover that their exotic pet has outgrown its enclosure and sometimes the owner's interests. Sadly, they choose an imperfect solution—they release the python into the wild where it quickly hunts and devours native rabbits, raccoons, and rats, upsetting the natural ecosystem balance.

Though native to the South Pacific, lionfish have established an aggressive presence along the southeastern coast of the United States since they were first sighted in the 1980s. As nonnatives, they have few natural predators. One favorite meal of the lionfish is the native parrotfish, which thrives on algae. Without the parrotfish, algae become a health hazard, particularly to fragile coral reefs.

(Continued on page 257)

(Continued from page 256)

In 1890, the American Acclimatization Society released European starlings into New York's Central Park in an effort to populate the landscape with birds referenced by Shakespeare (*Henry IV*, Part I). Today starlings cause more than $800 million per year in damage to agriculture and $6 million in damage to aircraft. The starlings move together in droves, taking over the nests of other birds, eating their eggs and any weaker wildlife that might get in their way.

33. Which of the following describes the main idea of the passage?

A. Nonnative species change all ecosystems for the better.
B. Native species control any invasion by nonnative species.
C. Native species threaten the natural balance of an ecosystem.
D. Nonnative species upset the natural balance in an ecosystem.

34. Which detail could you eliminate without losing a supporting detail for that main idea?

A. Burmese pythons eat small native animals such as rabbits.
B. The first invasive species were brought over by colonists.
C. Nonnative starlings cause millions of dollars in damage to agriculture each year.
D. Nonnative lionfish eat parrotfish, which keep algae under control.

35. Which of the following best summarizes the information in the passage?

A. Lionfish from the South Pacific now live in other regions where they eat the native fish. The native fish help control algae.
B. Invasive plant and animal species first came to America with the colonists. Now nonnative species are found throughout the country.
C. Thousands of nonnative plants and animals have invaded North America. They eat local species and damage natural resources that are needed to provide a balanced ecosystem.
D. Some people keep nonnative Burmese pythons as pets. Unfortunately, many owners release their "pets" into the wild, where they eat small native animals, such as rabbits and raccoons.

36. How does the use of enumeration in the first paragraph help the author achieve his or her intention?

A. It enables the author to contrast similar ideas.
B. It allows the author to present opposing ideas.
C. It strengthens the impact of what the author is saying.
D. It provides extra information as a solution to a problem.

37. What is the author's purpose?

A. to persuade readers to buy nonnative species as pets
B. to amuse readers with a story about a lost Burmese python
C. to inform readers that nonnative species are a danger to the environment
D. to convince readers that local parks and waterways are safe from nonnative species

38. Based on the information in the passage, what is the author's point of view?

A. The author has a neutral point of view toward native species.
B. The author has a negative point of view toward native species.
C. The author has a positive point of view toward nonnative species.
D. The author has a negative point of view toward nonnative species.

Directions: Read the following passage. Then choose the best answer to questions 39 through 42.

For many days we had been tempest-tossed. Six times had the darkness closed over a wild and terrific scene, and returning light as often brought but renewed distress, for the raging storm increased in fury until on the seventh day all hope was lost.

We were driven completely out of our course; no conjecture could be formed as to our whereabouts.

The crew had lost heart, and were utterly exhausted by incessant labour. The riven masts had gone by the board, leaks had been sprung in every direction, and the water, which rushed in, gained upon us rapidly. . . .

My heart sank as I looked round upon my family in the midst of these horrors. Our four young sons were overpowered by terror. 'Dear children,' said I, 'if the Lord will, He can save us even from this fearful peril; if not, let us calmly yield our lives into His hand, and think of the joy and blessedness of finding ourselves for ever and ever united in that happy home above. Even death is not too bitter, when it does not separate those who love one another.'

At these words my weeping wife looked bravely up, and, as the boys clustered round her, she began to cheer and encourage them with calm and loving words. I rejoiced to see her fortitude, though my heart was ready to break as I gazed on my dear ones. . . .

Amid the roar of the thundering waves I suddenly heard the cry of 'Land! land!', while at the same instant the ship struck with a frightful shock, which threw everyone to the deck, and seemed to threaten her immediate destruction. Dreadful sounds betokened the breaking up of the ship, and the roaring waters poured in on all sides.

Then the voice of the captain was heard above the tumult, shouting, 'Lower away the boats! We are lost!'

'Lost!' I exclaimed, and the word went like a dagger to my heart; but seeing my children's terror renewed, I composed myself, calling out cheerfully, 'Take courage, my boys! We are all above water yet. There is the land not far off, let us do our best to reach it. . . . Remain with your mother, while I go on deck to see what is best to be done now.' With that, I left them and went on deck.

A wave instantly threw me down; another followed, and then another, as I contrived to find my footing. The ship was shattered on all directions, and on one side there was a large hole in the hull.

Forgetting the passengers, the ship's company crowded into the lifeboats, and the last who entered cut the davit ropes to cast each boat into the sea.

What was my horror when through the foam and spray I beheld the last remaining boat leave the ship, the last of the seamen spring into her and push off, regardless of my cries and entreaties that we might be allowed to share their slender chance of preserving their lives. My voice was drowned in the howling of the blast, and even had the crew wished it, the return of the boat was impossible, for the waves were mountain-high.

Casting my eyes despairingly around, I became gradually aware that our position was by no means hopeless, inasmuch as the stern of the ship containing our cabin was jammed between two high rocks, and was partly raised from among the breakers which dashed the fore-part to pieces. As the clouds of mist and rain drove past, I could make out, through rents in the vaporous curtain, a line of rocky coast, and, rugged as it was, my heart bounded towards it as a sign of help in the hour of need.

Yet the sense of our lonely and forsaken condition weighed heavily upon me as I returned to my family, constraining myself to say with a smile, 'Courage, dear ones! Although our good ship will never sail more, she is so placed that our cabin will remain above water, and tomorrow, if the wind and waves abate, I see no reason why we should not be able to get ashore.'

—From *The Swiss Family Robinson* by Johann David Wyss

39. Which word best describes the character of the father in the story?

A. jealous
B. frantic
C. unreasonable
D. determined

40. Which word or phrase best states the theme of the passage?

A. perseverance
B. the importance of community
C. the beauty of nature
D. faithfulness

41. What is the major conflict in this story?

A. an internal conflict of a woman with her fear
B. an external conflict of humans against nature
C. an external conflict of a man against his children
D. an internal conflict of sailors about whether to abandon shipmates

42. Which word best describes the mood that the author creates?

A. anxious
B. giddy
C. hostile
D. indifferent

Directions: Read the following passage, and study the chart. Then choose the best answer to questions 43 through 46.

George Washington, First President

In 1732, George Washington was born into a family of Virginia tobacco planters. At the age of 16, he was off to help survey the lands of Shenandoah, Virginia's western territory through which pioneers would travel as they headed West. In 1754, he fought in the first conflicts that escalated into the French and Indian War, a fight over control of frontier lands. The British, aided by their Indian allies, defended Virginia's and Britain's claims on the lands against the French. At the age of only 22, Washington commanded troops that were successful in defeating French forces.

From 1759 to the outbreak of the American Revolution in 1775, Washington managed his lands around Mount Vernon, his family home in Virginia, and served in Virginia's legislature, the House of Burgesses. He devoted himself to his home and his wife, Martha Dandridge Custis.

In 1775, the Second Continental Congress assembled in Philadelphia and drafted the Declaration of Independence. Washington attended the gathering as a delegate from Virginia. He was elected Commander in Chief of the new Continental Army, and in 1781 he forced the surrender of British General Charles Cornwallis at Yorktown, Virginia, successfully ending the War for Independence.

Washington longed to retire to his fields at Mount Vernon. But in 1787, he was persuaded to be a Virginia delegate to the Constitutional Convention in Philadelphia, where he was chosen to lead the group as its president. After the new US Constitution was ratified, Washington was unanimously elected president the country. He retired at the end of his second term in office and returned to Mount Vernon. There, he died of a throat infection in 1799.

A Look at George Washington			
1732	Born: Westmoreland County, Virginia	**1776**	Wins the Battle of Trenton
1749	Official surveyor for Virginia	**1783**	Resigns army commission; heads home to Mount Vernon
1753	Sent to Ohio during French and Indian War	**1787**	Elected President of the Constitutional Convention
1755	French and Indian War ends; Washington saves troops	**1789**	Unanimously elected first president of the United States
1759	Marries widow Martha Dandridge Custis	**1793**	Reelected US president
1774	Delegate to the First Continental Congress	**1797**	Returns to Mount Vernon
1775	Appointed commander-in-chief of Continental Army	**1799**	Dies at Mount Vernon

43. Into which category of formats does the time line belong?

A. dramatic
B. fictional
C. graphic
D. textual

44. Which statement best compares information in the passage with information in the time line?

A. The time line presents important dates and information in a shorter form.
B. The time line compares and contrasts more events in Washington's life.
C. The passage features more important dates in Washington's life.
D. The passage includes fewer details about Washington's life.

45. Which detail best supports the inference that Washington was a brave leader?

A. He was the official surveyor for Virginia.
B. He longed to retire to his fields at Mount Vernon.
C. He was a delegate to the First Continental Congress.
D. He was only 22 years old when he successfully led troops in battle.

46. What is the purpose of the first sentence in the passage?

A. to present an opposing view
B. to provide background information
C. to express the author's point of view
D. to express the author's purpose for writing

Directions: Read the following passages. Then choose the best answer to questions 47 through 50.

I heartily accept the motto, "That government is best which governs least"; and I should like to see it acted up to more rapidly and systematically. Carried out, it finally amounts to this, which also I believe—"That government is best which governs not at all". . . . Government is at best but an expedient; but most governments are usually, and all governments are sometimes, inexpedient. . . .

This American government—what is it but a tradition, though a recent one, endeavoring to transmit itself unimpaired to posterity, but each instant losing some of its integrity? . . . Yet this government never of itself furthered any enterprise, but by the alacrity with which it got out of its way. It does not keep the country free. It does not settle the West. It does not educate. The character inherent in the American people has done all that has been accomplished; and it would have done somewhat more, if the government had not sometimes got in its way.

—From *On the Duty of Civil Disobedience* by Henry David Thoreau

Some writers have so confounded society with government, as to leave little or no distinction between them; whereas they are not only different, but have different origins. Society is produced by our wants, and government by our wickedness; the former promotes our happiness POSITIVELY by uniting our affections, the latter NEGATIVELY by restraining our vices. . . . The first is a patron, the last a punisher.

Society in every state is a blessing, but government even in its best state, is but a necessary evil; in its worst state an intolerable one: for when we suffer, or are exposed to the same miseries BY A GOVERNMENT, which we might expect in a country WITHOUT GOVERNMENT, our calamity is heightened by reflecting that we furnish the means by which we suffer. Government, like dress, is the badge of lost innocence; the palaces of kings are built on the ruins of the bowers of paradise.

—From *Common Sense* by Thomas Paine

47. What point of view do the two authors share?

A. They share a negative point of view about society.

B. They share a neutral point of view about government.

C. They share a neutral point of view about society.

D. They share a negative point of view about government.

48. Why does Thomas Paine write some words in all capital letters?

A. Each is the first word in a sentence.

B. He wants to emphasize the words for effect.

C. They are part of an abbreviation or acronym.

D. He wants to emphasize that the words are proper nouns.

49. In the second paragraph, how does repetition of the phrase "It does not" help Thoreau achieve his implied intention?

A. It strengthens the support of opposing viewpoints.

B. It allows him to compare the governments of two similar nations.

C. It reinforces the argument that only a central government can do great things.

D. It helps him persuade citizens that they can do great things without a government.

50. What effect is created by Paine's choice of the words *patron* and *punisher*?

A. It explains the origins of society and government.

B. It helps readers envision a country without government.

C. It emphasizes the benefits of society and disadvantages of government.

D. It describes the similarities between society and government.

Extended Response Activity

Directions: Read the following quotation.

"A house without books is like a room without windows."

—Horace Mann, American educator, 1796–1859

Some people believe that traditional, print books should be replaced by e-books. Do you agree? Write your view on the topic as persuasively as you can. Remember to provide evidence, reasons, and examples that support your view in order to convince readers.

ANSWER KEY

Pretest

1. **D** The author's purpose is to inform readers, not to persuade or to entertain them. The author identifies some jobs held by ancient Egyptians, but only to explain the country's hierarchical class structure.

2. **B** The word *while* signals a contrast, or sets information apart. It does not introduce a cause, a solution, or the next step in a process.

3. **D** Choice D rephrases the main idea and key details. It does not change the focus of the text (A). And it does not use exact phrases from the text (B) or leave out important details while mentioning less significant ones (C).

4. **B** Although this passage describes the structure of Egyptian society, it does not use descriptions to support the main idea. It uses examples, such as "scribes and doctors." It does not present reasons or statistics.

5. **B** The passage contains a flashback to an event in the past, when the narrator's girlfriend was killed by a lightning strike. The passage is told only from the narrator's point of view, no future events are foreshadowed, and there is only one plot line.

6. **B** In the last two sentences, the words "to the left" provide a spatial description of the tree and the factory. The text structure does not indicate chronology, degrees of importance, or a cause and effect.

7. **C** Although there are traces of hope and threat in the flashback, the overall tone of the passage is melancholy. Years have passed since Mi-Na's death, and Jong-Kyu's thoughts do not indicate anger.

8. **A** At the end of paragraph 1, the narrator mentions his "greatest loss." The third paragraph goes back in time to tell about that loss. Paragraph 1 does not explain the cause of Mi-Na's death or introduce her character, and the events in Paragraph 3 happened prior to Paragraph 1.

9. **D** The idea that Jong-Kyu has to "let" himself recall Mi-Na's face shows that losing her still has a powerful effect on him. The other statements are not directly related to how that loss still affects him.

10. **D** The author explains the preferred method for attaching files because the intention is to prevent further errors in employees' e-mail messages. Although the author explains a problem with attachments, the intention is not to send an attachment or to explain or describe how to do so.

11. **D** The text first describes a problem and then provides the solution. The description includes an explanation of cause and effect, but this is not the overall structure of the text. Neither comparison nor order of importance is used.

12. **A** The writer does not mention the amount of attachments users send but wants to enable users to attach files to e-mail messages using the Attach File button and not by dragging them to the body of the e-mail message. The latter method causes text to disappear from e-mail messages.

13. **C** The text has a businesslike tone. None of the words or phrases expresses anger, apology, or optimism.

14. C The main idea of the paragraph is that denying women the right to vote violates the US Constitution. The other three ideas are stated or implied in the passage, but none is the main idea.

15. A The passage is an example of a complex text. It contains technical legal vocabulary; it includes long, elaborate sentences; and it requires the reader to recognize the reference to the Preamble to the US Constitution in the first paragraph. It is not an example of historical fiction (B), literary nonfiction (C), or a rhetorical device (D).

16. B The phrase "downright mockery" has a negative connation with angry overtones. The other phrases are neutral ("the male citizens" and "supreme law of the land") or positive ("the blessings of liberty").

17. A The last line of the first paragraph says that "the ballot" (voting) is the only way to secure "the blessings of liberty." The other concepts are mentioned in the passage, but the author does not say that these things will ensure one's liberty.

18. A The phrase *of course* introduces a statement of agreement with the opposing argument. It does not introduce a statement of disagreement, the author's assumption, or evidence.

19. B All the evidence offered relates to how children can improve their fitness and team-building skills through dance; therefore, it is relevant to the claim. Because it supports all aspects of the claim and meets reasonable expectations of readers' prior knowledge, it is also sufficient. No sources are cited.

20. A The signal word *however* indicates that the author is about to make a statement that contrasts two ideas. The phrase *in addition* indicates that more information will follow, *of course* indicates agreement, and *when* indicates time or order.

21. B The author says explicitly that team sports are dangerous for children and then recommends dance as a better alternative. The main argument for preferring dance over team sports is implicit—that dance is not dangerous. The author openly acknowledges that dance is active, builds strength, and requires cooperation.

22. D Because the graveyard is secluded, anyone who strayed there would be alone with the spectre with little chance of escape. The idea that the dead are the only other people there might scare characters and readers even more. Since the horseman came at night, the churchyard would not be sunny, but dark. It is not said that the horseman is buried in the churchyard. The other stories mentioned are set elsewhere in the area.

23. C Fiction and nonfiction are written in paragraphs, they may use chronological order, and they frequently include many details. Only fiction tells stories about imaginary events and characters.

24. A The introductory paragraphs provide background information for a story about the Headless Horseman. The other answer choices are supporting details that contribute to a story featuring the Headless Horseman.

25. A A concept web would be best for recording the characteristics of the Headless Horseman. A time line (B) is used for recording a series of events. Two-column charts (C) and Venn diagrams (D) are good for comparing and contrasting, but not for recording the characteristics of only one character.

26. D The first paragraph introduces the ghost stories told at Van Tassel's, and the second paragraph identifies the subject of most of those stories: the Headless Horseman. The phrase "the chief part of the stories" makes the transition clear. Answer choices A and B do not address transition, and choice C is incorrect because the transition does not involve opposing topics.

27. C The paragraph describes cowboys' equipment. It does not tell a story, explain cowboys' jobs, or introduce any characters.

28. D Although the photo's impact is immediate, its setting is not dramatic and its impact is not as great as the text's impact. This is because the text provides deeper insight into how and why cowboys use their equipment. The text does not use dramatic language.

29. B The pronoun *they* refers to the antecedent *leggings*, which appears at the beginning of the same sentence. The word *spurs* (A) appears in an earlier sentence. The words *outfit* and *herd* are in sentence 7, too, but they are singular.

30. C Spurs with dull rowels would not hurt the horses as much as sharp rowels, and the text states explicitly that using ropes on cattle is more humane that using whips. None of the other details support the notion that cowboys did not want to hurt the animals.

31. C The numbered list provides statistics showing a dramatic increase in the incidence of asthma and respiratory infections among children as a result of exposure to secondhand smoke. It does not describe a specific illness, explain how smoking can affect adults' health, or identify three specific groups of children.

32. C The argument hinges on the belief that parents want to protect their children's health. Given that assumption, the author explicitly states that secondhand smoke can damage children's health. The argument is not based on the assumption that all parents smoke or that children imitate their parents.

33. B The author's argument is valid because it is based on relevant, verifiable facts. There is no contradictory evidence or statement of biased opinion. The argument is developed from an underlying assumption but not from unsound reasoning.

34. A The author states his or her assumption that people have the right to smoke in their homes because it is legal to do so. The author does not state that second-hand smoke is illegal or that smokers' healthcare costs are higher. That people pay taxes on cigarettes is a fact stated in the text.

35. D The EPA supports its argument with facts and statistics about the biology and health of children. The argument presented in the letter is based on opinion. It is the letter that expresses a negative bias and an emotional tone. Both state their claims explicitly.

36. C Choice C maintains the meaning of the original sentence while changing from passive to active voice. The phrasing of choice A suggests that children smoke, and choices B and D are written in passive voice.

37. A It is typical of drama that the character's name is indicated before the text he or she speaks. In fiction and essays, both of which are written in paragraphs, this generally does not occur. Nor does it typically occur in poems, which are written in stanzas.

38. D This paragraph states its evidence in time order, starting with early scholarship and finishing with recent scholarship. It does not use the other structures mentioned.

39. B Cleopatra refers to the asp as a baby, which is a metaphor. A simile (A) would use a comparison word such as *like* or *as*. Cleopatra's death is understated rather than exaggerated (C). Repetition (D) is not a type of figurative language; it is a rhetorical device.

40. D The metaphor that Shakespeare uses reflects the belief of early scholars that Cleopatra died from a snake bite. The play is a work of fiction and, therefore, not a factual account or a reliable reference source. The play does not contradict the belief that Cleopatra died from a snake bite.

Check Your Understanding

On the following chart, circle the number of any question you answered incorrectly. In the third column, you will see the pages that address the content covered in the question.

Lesson	Item Number(s)	Review Page(s)
1.1: Determine the Main Idea	3, 14, 26	13–17
1.2: Identify Supporting Details	3, 4, 9, 30	21–23
1.3: Identify Direct and Implied Main Ideas	3, 14, 30	27–29
1.4: Summarize Details	3	33–35
1.5: Identify a Theme	9, 26	39–41
2.1: Sequence Events	5, 8, 31, 38	52–55
2.2: Infer Relationships between Events, People, and Ideas	4, 22, 24	58–61
2.3: Analyze Relationships between Ideas	22, 23, 25	64–67
2.4: Determine Implicit Relationships between Ideas	18, 24	70–73
2.5: Analyze the Role of Details in Complex Texts	8, 15, 27, 29, 30, 39	76–78
3.1: Determine Connotative and Figurative Meanings	16, 39	90–93
3.2: Analyze Tone	7, 13, 16	96–99
3.3: Analyze Word Choice	16, 18	102–105
4.1: Analyze the Development of Ideas	4, 5, 8, 38	116–119
4.2: Analyze How Structure Impacts Key Ideas	6, 8, 11, 31	122–125
4.3: Analyze the Effect of Transitional and Signal Words	2, 8, 18, 20, 26	128–131
5.1: Determine Author's Point of View	10, 16	143–145
5.2: Analyze How Author's Purpose Determines Structure	10, 11, 27	148–151
5.3: Infer Author's Purpose	1, 10, 25	154–157
5.4: Analyze How Authors Differentiate Their Positions	14, 18, 21	160–163
5.5: Analyze Author's Intention and Effect	10, 12, 16, 18, 27	166–169
6.1: Identify Argument Development	18, 20, 31, 32, 34	180–183
6.2: Identify Supporting Evidence	17, 31, 33	186–189
6.3: Evaluate Relevance and Sufficiency	19, 21	192–195
6.4: Evaluate Validity and Reasoning	33	198–201
6.5: Evaluate Logic and Identify Hidden Assumptions	21, 32, 33, 34, 36	204–207
7.1: Compare Similar Topics in Different Formats	40	218–221
7.2: Compare Similar Genres	23, 37	224–226
7.3: Analyze Two Arguments	35	230–233
7.4: Evaluate the Impact of Genre and Format	23, 28	236–239

Lesson 1.1

Think about Reading, page 14

1. C
2. B
3. C
4. A

Think about Reading, page 16

1. The first sentence introduces the topic of the cowboys' equipment and states the main idea that each cowboy had to provide his own equipment.
2. The rest of the passage gives examples of the equipment that the cowboys carried.
3. Answers will vary. Sample answers: the indispensable slickers; spurs were a matter of taste; if a rider carried a quirt, he usually dispensed with spurs.

Think about Reading, page 17

1. **F** Literary and informational text can contain topic sentences.
2. **T** Literary texts can be imaginary or about a real event or person.
3. **T** Workplace texts often use headings so the reader can identify what the text is about.

Vocabulary Review, page 18

1. identify
2. literary text
3. main idea; topic sentence
4. supporting details
5. informational text

Skill Review, page 18

1. **C** All the sentences in the passage are about the ways people are expressing their worry about Tom and Becky being missing. Answers A, B, and D are incorrect because the passage does not say anything about people worrying about the church, the questioning of the children, or the way Mrs. Thatcher and Aunt Polly are behaving.
2. **D** The terms "boding uneasiness" and "anxiously" illustrate a tense environment, which worried people can create. None of the other terms are related to tension.
3. **A** All the events indicate that people are concerned. They are not related to any of the other answer choices.
4. **D** There is no topic sentence stating a main idea, but all the sentences in the passage are details that support a main idea.

Skill Practice, page 19

1. **C** Adams writes many details supporting the main idea that people in Boston are suffering. These details include people being treated like slaves and trying to leave the city.
2. **B** The details in the paragraph support the statement that prisoners live in poor conditions. Details about the price of fish, the death of wounded prisoners, and where they slept the first night after being captured are details that support this main idea.
3. **D** Putting people in jail for no reason is an example of the unfair treatment of Bostonians. The posting of handbills, the bringing of prisoners to Long Wharf, and the difficulty of procuring fish are details that do not show unfair treatment.
4. **A** People were placed in jail.

Writing Practice, page 19

The summary should include a topic sentence stating the main idea of the article and summarize the key supporting details. All the details in the summary should clearly support the main idea.

Sample answer: People around the world are celebrating the birth of the Duchess of Cambridge's first child. The baby will one day become the King of England. People in England and in many other countries are fascinated with the royal family, so the child will be in the public eye all his life.

Lesson 1.2

Think about Reading, page 21

1. fact
2. description
3. reasons or facts

Think about Reading, page 22

Answers will vary. Sample answers:

"storm clouds darkened the sky" (description)

"the water level crept up in the city" (description)

"winds of the hurricane rose to 135 miles per hour—a category 4 storm" (fact)

Think about Reading, page 23

1. An excess of nutrients in water can result in hypoxic or dead zones.
2. The decomposition of large amounts of algae depletes the supply available to marine life.
3. Without enough oxygen, marine life leaves the area or dies.
4. Habitats become biological deserts.

Explanation of *dead zones*: *Dead zones* are areas in the ocean that are devoid of life because excess algal growth has used up all the available oxygen.

Vocabulary Review, page 24

1. visualize
2. generalization
3. observe
4. description

Skill Review, page 24

1. B The other responses can be determined to be untrue from the supporting details, or they only address one detail.

2. A After an atomic bomb was dropped on Hiroshima, Japan in 1945, people observed a similar phenomenon.

B Experts estimate that the force of the Tunguska explosion was 1,000 times stronger than the atomic bomb dropped on Hiroshima.

Skill Practice, page 25

1. A All the other details support this main idea.

2. D The sentence gives one reason why it is necessary for human rights to be broadened globally. The sentence does not give a description, a fact, or an example.

Writing Practice, page 25

Answers will vary. Your paragraph should use a variety of details to describe an event you found interesting or significant. The paragraph should combine at least three of the following types of details: description, facts, reasons, or examples.

Sample paragraph: It was the start of the baseball game. There was a storm brewing in the sky, but I was determined that our team would win and the game wouldn't be rained out. We were first at bat, and all three of our batters struck out. Our pitcher was strong, however, and struck out the other team's batters. Back and forth we went, without a single score for eight innings. It was almost as if we were playing in fast motion to finish before the rain. Finally, I got up to bat and hit the ball over the fence. A home run! It was the only score that inning, and in the top of the ninth, the other team failed to score. Just as my teammate caught the ball for the last out, there was a wild crack of thunder and the storm broke. We won!

Lesson 1.3

Think about Reading, page 28

Sentences 3 and 4 should be checked. Both sentences suggest the main idea of the paragraph.

Think about Reading, page 29

1. They are coworkers.
2. friends
3. Sentence 3

Vocabulary Review, page 30

1. implied: expressed indirectly
2. deduce: figure out
3. emphasize: stress or highlight
4. collaboration: the act of working together

Skill Review, page 31

1. **B** It is the only sentence that ties all the ideas in the passage together. A, C, and D contain details that relate to the main idea but do not completely express it.
2. **C** Only C is a detail in the passage showing how much Della values her hair. A is a statement of the main idea, and B and D are hypothetical: the queen does not live across the airshaft.
3. **D** Only D is a detail in the passage showing how much Jim values his watch. A is a statement of the main idea, and B and C are hypothetical: King Solomon is not the janitor.

Skill Practice, page 32

1. **C** The passage has an implied main idea. The reader needs to tie all the supporting details together to come up with a main idea such as "Veterans told very different stories about their war experiences."
2. **A** The details in the sentence support the statement that veterans are brave with its description of acts of valor.
3. **B** The details from the stories (such as "fierce soldiery," "eternally hungry men," "despondent powders," and "hell's fire and brimstone") and from the youth's image in the last sentence ("red, live bones sticking out through slits in the faded uniforms") portray war as frightening.

Writing Practice, page 32

There should be two responses to this question—one response for a passage with a direct main idea and one for a passage with an indirect main idea.

A The direct main idea response should have the main idea sentence followed by one or two sentences describing how the details relate to the main idea.

B The implied main idea response should have a main idea stated in your own words, followed by one or two sentences describing how these ideas support the main idea.

Sample answers:

A Directly stated main idea response: "The evening altogether passed off pleasantly to the whole family." The rest of the passage includes details about the Bingley daughters being admired and everyone enjoying the dancing and the company.

B Implied main idea response: Elizabeth is not impressed by Mr. Bennet's manners. The passage provides details of Elizabeth's attempts to converse with Mr. Bennet and his rebuffs of her topics of conversation. The narrator describes his rudeness.

Lesson 1.4

Think about Reading, page 33

1. A "[Many] were surprised, astounded, and frequently dismayed by the tens of thousands of buffaloes they observed, avoided, or escaped from."

   B "they frequently stopped boats in the rivers [and] threatened to overwhelm travelers on the plains"

   C "[they] derailed locomotives and cars,"

2. B Paraphrases A, C, and D relate to another category of details, or they represent conclusions that cannot be drawn from the passage.

Think about Reading, page 35

1, 2, 3, and 4 should be checked as they are the text features in the memo that give information relevant to summarizing the passage.

Vocabulary Review, page 36

1. summarize
2. concise
3. skim
4. paraphrase
5. comprehensive

Skill Review, page 36

1. F The passage has an implied main idea, not a direct one.
2. T The sentence describes the process for summarizing a passage.
3. T The sentence encompasses the main idea of all the paragraphs.
4. F Trudy's use of the crawl stroke is a minor detail.

Skills Practice, page 37

1. A Choices B, C, and D do not tell what the passage is mainly about.
2. B Choices A, C, and D are do not provide key information in supporting the main idea, or they are not true, according to the passage.

Writing Practice, page 37

The summary should include a statement paraphrasing the main idea of the passage and sentences summarizing the key supporting details. All the details in the summary should clearly support the main idea.

Sample summary: The race for city mayor includes a diverse body of candidates. Five of the eight candidates are women, two candidates are Hispanic, three are African-American, and one is Asian American. Each candidate comes from a different neighborhood in the city and brings a range of innovative ideas to the election.

Lesson 1.5

Think about Reading, page 40

The sentence "I guess it goes to show how surfaces can be deceiving" describes the tension between the narrator's past and present. This sentence states the theme emphasized in this passage.

Think about Reading, page 41

Answers may vary but should contain the following ideas.

1. Spitz knows he is weaker than Buck but he continues to fight.
2. The stronger Buck defeats Spitz and becomes dominant.
3. The strongest and fittest survive by conquering the weak.

Vocabulary Review, page 42

1. conflict
2. synthesize
3. theme
4. perspective

Skill Review, page 42

1. **A** theme

   B Answers will vary. Sample answers: suicidal, angry, depressed

   C agree

2. Answers will vary. Sample answers:

   A "Whenever I find myself growing grim about the mouth . . . I account it high time to get to sea as soon as I can."

   B "all men in their degree, some time or other, cherish very nearly the same feelings towards the ocean with me"

Skill Practice, page 43

1. **C** The passage is mostly about Jo's dream of striving for something heroic, versus Meg's dream of contentment, which is portrayed as less noble in comparison.
2. **A** Jo believes that having a "splendid, wise, good husband" is her sister Meg's dream, not hers. The narrator tells us that Jo "scorned romance" and had no "tender fancies."

Writing Practice, page 43

Answers will vary. The completed story should include the following:

1. A beginning, a middle, and an end.
2. A different main idea for each paragraph.
3. A theme that is stated in the story or implied.
4. Details that clearly support your theme.

Sample story: When I was a little girl, I used to go with my father to visit my grandmother in a nursing home. She was blind and starting to lose her memory. Sometimes she knew who I was and greeted me by name; other times, she mistook me for one of my cousins or for someone else. One thing we had in common, though, was that we both loved to play the piano. No matter what else she forgot, she always remembered that I played the piano.

One day, we brought my grandmother a surprise. My father had arranged to donate my grandmother's piano to the nursing home. The piano at the home was very old, and a number of the keys stuck. When we played together, we used to laugh about the stuck keys and sing the missing notes to fill in the gaps.

We led my grandmother down the corridor to the lounge where the piano was kept. But that day, the old piano had been replaced by my grandmother's piano, which was in excellent shape. As soon as she sat down, she seemed to feel that something was different. Her hands found the keys, and she played for several minutes without stopping. Then she exclaimed, "Robert! This is my piano, isn't it? I can feel how lovely it plays. Come on up, Ariel, and let's play our duet together." She had remembered everything! That day I learned how memory can be triggered and strengthened when a person is reconnected with a familiar passion, and since then I have seen it happen again and again in my work as a doctor.

Chapter 1 Review

1. D The other statements are not supported by the details in the text.

2. C The author uses examples and facts but does not use reasons or questions to support this statement.

3. B This statement best tells what the whole passage is mainly about.

4. A text

B Boston

C main idea

5. A Choices B and C summarize only a part of the information presented in the paragraph, and Choice D summarizes information in the fourth paragraph, not the second.

6. A opinion

B Harriet

C Miss Woodhouse

D marriage

7. D Miss Woodhouse strongly disapproved of Harriet's marriage to Mr. Martin, even though she could see that Harriet was unsure and liked Mr. Martin.

8. A happiness

B friendship

C society

D character

E marry

9. A The main character never mentions that she wishes that Tom Canty is her son; on the contrary, she suggests that it might be a relief to find out that he was not.

10. C The passage suggests that the mother suspects that Tom Canty is not her son even though he looks like the son. She figures out the one definable difference that will distinguish them.

Lesson 2.1

Think about Reading, page 53

1. Then, When
2. Jong-Kyu lies down and listens to his heartbeat get slower.
3. The author explains how Jong-Kyu lost Mi-na.
4. Jong-Kyu opens his eyes, and the narrative returns to the present.
5. Mi-Na sprinted away and called for Jong-Kyu to follow her.

Think about Reading, page 55

1. You should throw it down somewhere in the center of the lot or barn and walk off to one side.
2. He will cautiously stretch out his neck as far as he can reach and touch the blanket with his nose.
3. He will play with it.

Vocabulary Review, page 56

1. d
2. f
3. e
4. a
5. c
6. b

Skill Review, page 56

1. **C** Before Onoda went to Lubang, he attended the Japanese Imperial Army Intelligence School. Although the other events are mentioned in the passage, none of them happened before Onoda was sent to Lubang.
2. **D** Onoda surrendered in 1974. The other dates are mentioned in the passage, but none of them are the date that Onoda surrendered.
3. **B** Paragraph 2 interrupts the chronological order of the passage because it goes back in time to address what happened prior to the main events in this passage.

Skill Practice, page 57

1. **A** The word *as* helps readers understand that Helen's teacher spelled the word water at the same time as the water flowed over Helen's hand.
2. **B** When Helen understands what "w-a-t-e-r" means, she also starts to understand language. She does not learn to draw water. The other details are mentioned in the passage, but they do not directly relate to this event.
3. **A** Helen tells about the day in sequence to show how one event leads to another. Sequence is not used to compare things or to explain causes and effects.
4. **C** Helen says that her soul is set free because of the day's events. The other events might be true of Helen's life at a later time, but only choice C explains how the day's events directly affect Helen.

Writing Practice, page 57

Your paragraph should be written in time order and use sequence words such as *first, next, then,* and *finally* to make the order of events clear. If a flashback is used, be sure to use words that indicate the events are taking place in the past.

Sample answer: Even though I had heard many times about the dangers of texting and driving, I never really thought anything bad would happen to me. Two weeks ago, my friend texted me to tell me she had just bought a smoothie from our favorite smoothie store. As I was texting her back, my car drifted into the other lane. A red truck honked loudly at me, and I just managed to avoid an accident. My heart was racing, and I put down my phone immediately. I decided my text wasn't that important. Since that day, I don't text and drive.

Lesson 2.2

Think about Reading, page 60, top

1. **D** The physical description of Jethro in D as "spluttering and turning red" when talking with others demonstrates his embarrassment. Answers A and B refer to reading, which Jethro enjoys, and C says that he does not like going to the store but does not say why.

2. **B** The only mention of farming in the paragraph tells readers that Jethro considers it "drudgery" and that he enjoys escaping through books.

Think about Reading, page 60, bottom

1. opinion
2. example
3. fact

Think about Reading, page 61

Answers will vary. Sample answer: The passage explains that Nobel regretted dynamite's use as a tool of aggression. Immediately after that, it says that he left his money to endow prizes for people who work in many fields, including those who promote peace. This implies that he was trying to make up for the aggressive uses of his invention.

Vocabulary Review, page 62

1. explicit
2. valid
3. cite
4. infer
5. imply

Skill Review, page 62

1. **C** The text states that the people waited until the kittens were rescued, which implies that they cared about the welfare of the animals. The fact that the system was shut down, that the kittens were on the tracks, or that the trains ran again does not support an inference of sympathy.

2. **A** The text says that the engineers were worried that the kittens would get run over or electrocuted. It does not mention anything about the number of cats living in subway tunnels or about skyscrapers in New York City. The text also points out that some subway riders waited patiently; you can infer that not everyone was happy to wait.

3. **D** Kittens on the subway tracks caused riders to be delayed. The other choices do not show a relationship between events in the passage.

Skill Practice, page 63

1. d
2. a
3. b
4. c

Writing Practice, page 63

Responses will vary. You should explain your inference and cite details in the text that clearly support your inference.

Sample answer: *Laura looked up as the door opened. A soaked Marco slipped inside and hung up his coat. As he crossed the room, his shoes made a squishy, squeaking sound. "What a day!" he groaned as he plopped into a chair and grabbed a menu.*

The author did not say where the people were or what the weather was like, but clues in the text help me infer that because Marco is soaked and his shoes make a squishy sound, it is a very rainy day. Because Marco sits down and grabs a menu, I can infer that he is meeting Laura in a restaurant.

Lesson 2.3

Think about Reading, page 66

1. The lady does not have a close relationship with any of the other characters. People in the town do not know her name and call her simply "the lady with the dog." Gurov is curious about and interested in the lady.
2. Gurov's conflict is that he wants to meet the lady with the dog, but he is unsure whether it is the right thing to do because no one knows her and, therefore, no one can introduce them. This is an internal conflict.

Think about Reading, page 67

1. Carrie is in a public place, but she doesn't want anyone to see her applying for a job. When she realizes that she has been observed on the busy sidewalk, she flees.
2. Carrie has never had to look for work before, and it makes her nervous to be in the busy city where she is observed by others. She is probably used to a comfortable, quiet life and being provided for.
3. Answers will vary. Sample answers: It takes courage to do something for the first time; it is easier to retreat than to show courage.

Vocabulary Review, page 68

1. e
2. d
3. b
4. a
5. c

Skill Review, page 68

1. **B** A dynamic character changes. When Edna married, she expected to be disappointed and to have given up romance; however, she grew fond of her husband. The other choices do not show change.
2. plot; happy/stable
3. **D** Edna's thoughts and actions demonstrate the unpredictability of humans' emotions. She decided to marry Leonce because she thought that they had similar ideas and tastes and because she wanted to spite her family, who were opposed to the marriage. Eventually, Edna surprises even herself by realizing she has a true affection for her husband. The passage does not address loneliness, ignorance, or a battle between good and evil.

Skill Practice, page 69

1. **D** The author reveals something about Mary's personality by stating that she believes in Magic. The other choices do not describe a specific character.
2. **B** Colin screamed and bit his pillow while he was in a bed, not in the garden, which is the setting of the passage. The other choices do take place in the garden.
3. **D** The author communicates the idea that the beauty and wonder of nature have the power to transform people. In the garden, Colin was changed from a "crazy creature" who didn't look well to a calm boy with a "faint glow of color." The other choices might be true, but they are not the author's theme, or underlying message.

Writing Practice, page 69

Answers will vary. Summaries should identify the character, setting, conflict, and theme and include a brief explanation of how the setting affects the plot.

Sample answer: In Frank O'Connor's "Guests of the Nation," two English soldiers are being held hostage by a small group of IRA fighters in a small cottage in the Irish bogs. The conflict reaches a climax when the IRA fighters are ordered to execute the two British soldiers. Themes of the story include betrayal and the senselessness of war.

The setting of an isolated cottage in the bleak bogs makes the events of the story possible. Because of the remote location, the characters do not have constant reminders that they should be enemies. This allows a friendly relationship to develop among them. The isolation also means that the execution can occur without hope of rescue.

Lesson 2.4

Think about Reading, page 72

replaced; because; faster than

Think about Reading, page 73

Answers will vary. Sample answer: Humans killed millions of sea otters for their pelts, oil spills come from human activities such as drilling for oil and shipping oil, and humans who work at factories dump industrial chemicals into oceans. All these details imply a relationship between human actions and threats to sea otters.

Vocabulary Review, page 74

1. predict
2. proximity
3. outcome
4. inference

Skill Review, page 74

1. **C** Chemical-free food is more healthful for consumers. The writer did not say organic foods were lower in fat; higher prices do not make the foods more healthful; and the fact that organic apples look like standard ones does not prove that they are more healthful.

2. **B** You can logically predict that cows on organic farms get more exercise because the passage states that "livestock roam free." You cannot predict that they will be taller or live longer; in fact, the passage states that cows on standard farms might be given chemicals to make them bigger. Because the animals on organic farms roam free, it is illogical to predict that cows are kept in large barns.

Skill Practice, page 75

1. **B** The writer implies that because New Jersey teens get a license when they are older, they have fewer accidents. The other choices do not imply a relationship between teen driving and safety.

2. **C** The writer implies that the number of teen deaths would be reduced if teens practiced driving more before they got a license. They would be better drivers and have fewer accidents. The other choices do not imply that relationship.

Writing Practice, page 75

Responses will vary. Your writing should show relationships between ideas, including a relationship that allows readers to predict an outcome based on evidence in the text.

Sample answer: I really like to cook, not just for myself but also for others. Yesterday I tried to make banana bread, so I looked up a recipe. The bread smelled great baking in the oven. It didn't look as great because it stuck to the pan when I tried to take it out. It didn't taste that great either. I must have left something out. Oh, well, I suppose I shouldn't just look at a recipe—I should actually follow it. Maybe I'll try baking again tomorrow.

Lesson 2.5

Think about Reading, page 77

Answers will vary. Sample answer: The sentence structure and vocabulary make the passage complex. Also, the topic is the abstract idea that government cannot exist without the consent of the governed.

Think about Reading, page 78

Answers will vary. Sample answer: The phrase "a cultural achievement without parallel" means something made by humans that has no equal and is unlike anything else.

Vocabulary Review, page 80

1. b
2. d
3. a
4. c

Skill Review, page 80

1. **B** The author states that the woman in white "haunted the dark glen . . . and was often heard to shriek on winter nights before a storm, having perished there in the snow." No mention was made of her marriage, seeing the Headless Horseman, or being on the bridge.

2. **C** The author said that the air "breathed forth an atmosphere of dreams and fancies"; he did not mention it being unfriendly, cheerful, or enthusiastic.

3. **B** The Headless Horseman was described as "the favorite spectre of Sleepy Hollow," and the author is talking about troubled spirits, such as the dead woman in white, so you can assume that *spectre* means "ghost." No mention was made that the horseman was a hero, a dancer, or a soldier.

Skill Practice, page 81

1. **D** In the fourth paragraph, the author states that Lionfish are native to, or originate in, the South Pacific.

2. **C** The author's message is that invasive species are creating an ecological disaster and the fact that invasive pythons eat native animals upsets the ecosystem. Although the other choices refer to invasive species, they do not stress how these species affect ecosystems.

Writing Practice, page 81

Responses will vary. Your written piece should include technical terms or advanced vocabulary, compound or complex sentences, abstract ideas, or an unusual text structure. Your writing might also be about a subject that is unfamiliar to many readers.

Sample answer: Have you ever watched a figure skater spin so fast that his or her body became a blur? Although the effect is quite impressive, this is a relatively easy maneuver. To perform a scratch spin, propel yourself forward on your left skate, with your arms straight out to the side. Then put your right leg out to the side and begin to rotate on the blade, up near the toe-pick, as you lift and hold your right foot over your left boot and slowly bring your arms in toward your chest. You will begin to spin at an accelerated rate. Lowering your right skate on the outside edge of the left boot, almost touching the ice, makes your body straighter and causes you to rotate even faster. To stop, extend your hands and feet outward at the same time, step onto your right blade, and stretch your left leg straight behind you.

Chapter 2 Review

1. **C** The young man states that he brings the Captain's sword and cross of honor "to his widow," so he is probably at Captain Leclere's family home. Choices A and B are settings where events took place before the action in this passage, and choice D was never mentioned.

2. **D** Readers could infer that the young man took over as captain when Leclere died because the young man tells about the burial ceremony and has come to see the family. There are no details to support an inference that the young man is from Naples or that he is the captain's son, and he mentions fighting the British, so he is not likely to be British.

3. **A** The owner's statement that "the old must make way for the young" implies the theme—the circle of life. There was no mention of power or honesty in the passage, and although it is wise to always believe in yourself, that is not the theme of the passage.

4. **B** The author tells events in chronological order except for a brief flashback when Harjanti first sees the doves. Events are not compared or ranked by importance, and although Harjanti has a problem, the organization for the majority of the passage is not problem and solution.

5. **D** We never find out whether Harjanti will go to the market to sell her cinnamon bark. The other events are mentioned in the story.

6. **C** Harjanti has an inner conflict—should she help her sister or go to the market because this may be her last chance to go there for several months? The other conflicts do not apply to the end of the story.

7. **C** The author uses a bulleted list to highlight some important details. There are no subheads, italic type, or boldfaced words in the passage.

8. **A** You can logically infer that someone has reported possible harassment and, in turn, has caused Human Resources to write the memo. There is no information in the text to imply the other conclusions.

9. **D** The speaker's proceeding in the direction he judges as right foreshadows his error. He is in fact going in the wrong direction and will get lost. The other story events do not foreshadow any particular action.

10. **C** Because the creature spoke the word "No!" you can logically predict that when the narrator finally meets the creature, it will be a human, too. The other choices might happen because the future is unsure, but you cannot logically predict them based on information from the passage.

Lesson 3.1

Think about Reading, page 92

1.

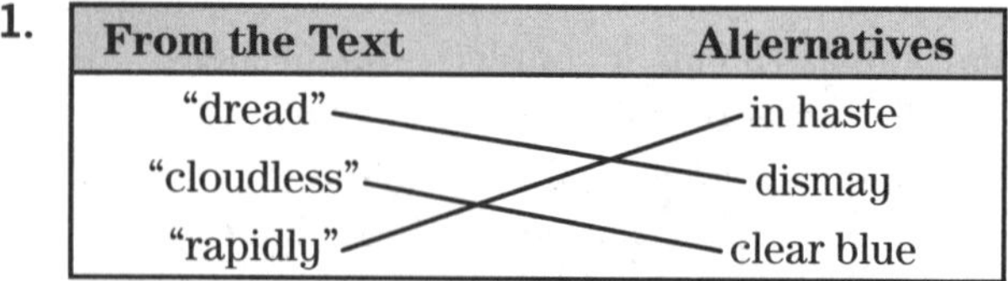

2. Answers may vary. Sample answers: foreboding, tense, serious, scary

Think about Reading, page 93

1. Personification; the phrase attributes to clouds the human ability to scowl.
2. **A** It helps readers visualize the setting with the black clouds looming ominously over the airfield. Choice B is incorrect because the simile describes the clouds, not the planes. Choice C is incorrect because the author does not define *dew-infested*, which would mean "very humid with drops of moisture."
3. The author uses a simile to compare the Naval training planes on the ramp to ghosts. He or she says that the planes look "like gray ghosts," and a simile compares things using the word *as* or *like*.

Vocabulary Review, page 94

1. connotative
2. context
3. tone; mood
4. homophones
5. figurative

Skill Review, page 94

1. **B** The author is hopeful that the team will begin a winning streak again. None of the other choices reflect the author's attitude.
2. **B** The coach is described as "thin as a rail," a simile comparing a person to a thin handrail or the width of one rail of a train track, using the word as. Sentences 2, 7, and 9 do not make a comparison using the word *like* or *as*.
3. **C** *Demanded* is a command like *insisted*. None of the other choices have the same connotation as *insisted*.
4. **C** The author compares the coach to a guiding light without using the word *like* or *as*. Choices A and D are only descriptions. Choice B is a simile, comparing things using the word as.

Skill Practice, page 95

1. **B** *Jalopy* is a negative word that conjures up visions of an old wreck of a car with dents and scratches. Choices A, C, and D are neutral types of vehicles.
2. **C** The author compares Jana's body taking in the salty air at the beach to a sponge soaking up liquid, but does not use the word *as* or the word *like*. Choices A, B, and D just describe some of Jana's actions.
3. **D** The author's attitude toward Jana and her excursion to the shore is excited and delighted. The author is not fearful, sarcastic, or indifferent about Jana's trip.

Writing Practice, page 95

Answers will vary. In the rewrite, you should have changed neutral words to words that have positive or negative connotations, and you should have used figurative language that enhances the positive or negative impact of the writing.

Sample answer: Today's city council meeting devolved into civil war when the members chose sides over Councilwoman Marion Davies' proposal that the city build an electric tram system to connect the train station with the downtown area. Mayor Jamie Watkins dragged out the tired old argument that the city's budget can't possibly fund a project of this magnitude. Councilwoman Davies diagnosed the mayor as shortsighted and regurgitated her claim that the measure will ultimately increase income for the city because it will provide better access to downtown shops and businesses. The council members lined up behind the two ringleaders, and no one would budge in the budgetary tug of war. In the end, they agreed on one thing: to postpone the next skirmish for another month.

Lesson 3.2

Think about Reading, page 98

Answers will vary. Sample answer: The author's tone is critical and judgmental. The author stresses that Emmett is confident to the point of being obnoxious. The following words and phrases help me identify the author's tone: "making no effort to be quiet"; "disturbing the other students"; "strolled"; "smiling to himself contentedly"; "certain he would get an A"; "think faster"; and "quicker meant better."

Think about Reading, page 99

1. scared, interested, indifferent, relaxed
2. Answers will vary. Sample answer: to entertain or thrill readers with a scary scene
3. Answers will vary. Sample answer: The author writes about hearing footsteps approach, a scary situation for someone who doesn't know who is coming near. Then the author mentions a shadow in a short sentence that makes the reader stop short and think that something bad is coming, creating a feeling of suspense that fits the author's purpose for writing.
4. **C** The topic emphasizes the way people helped others after the fire. Words such as *kindly, concerned, generously,* and *amazing* set an admiring tone. None of the words indicate an attitude of anger, embarrassment, or worry on the part of the writer. Although the fire might have been a cause for worry when it occurred, the writer of this text is emphasizing positive rather than negative feelings.
5. Answers will vary. Sample answer: to inform readers about an upcoming community action segment on a TV news show
6. Answers will vary. Sample answer: The author writes briefly about the fire and then in more detail about good things people did. The author tries to persuade people to tune in and watch the show using emotional language.

Vocabulary Review, page 100

1. c
2. d
3. b
4. a

Skill Review, page 100

1. **D** The passage uses professional terms such as "held positions" and "respectfully." Rema is not trying to amuse the potential employer, and she is optimistic, not pessimistic, about getting the job. Finally, a casual tone would have included informal language, which the letter does not contain.
2. **A** Sentence 1 states that the author wants the job that is available at Sunny Days Senior Home. Sentences 2 and 4 list the author's experience, and sentence 7 thanks Ms. Moreno for reading the letter.
3. **C** Phrases such as "I would appreciate," "discuss my qualifications," and "mutually convenient time" add to the professional tone of the letter. They do not show anger. To be casual or friendly, the author would have used informal language.

Skill Practice, page 101

1. **B** The author's tone is serious because she wants employees to understand that they must follow the directions or they will be locked out of the system. The author is not hostile (unpleasant) or flippant (joking) about the change. She is not desperate (frantic) when telling employees that they have a month to comply with the new rule.
2. **D** The phrase "you must log on" achieves the purpose of telling employees about a mandatory policy that they must follow. Getting an e-mail, being prompted, or being told you "may reset" your password do not transmit the importance of the mandate.

Writing Practice, page 101

Responses will vary. Your purpose for writing and your tone should be apparent from your word choices and sentence structure.

Sample answer: I love the movie *The Gift of the Magi*, based on the story by O. Henry. It's about a married couple, Jim and Della, who have no money to buy gifts at Christmas time. Della sells her beautiful long hair to buy a chain for Jim's gold watch, not knowing that he has sold the watch to buy combs for her hair. Of course, she can't use the combs and he can't use the chain, but Della and Jim are happy because they each gave up something special for the person they loved. (Purpose: to inform readers about a movie; Tone: personal and sentimental)

Lesson 3.3

Think about Reading, page 103

Answers will vary. Sample answer: The word gives the e-mail a very formal, businesslike tone.

Think about Reading, page 105

1. *bleak, expectant* should be circled; the author's words do not convey a sense of hope (*hopeful*) or stability (*stable*).
2. **B** The author's words do not encourage readers to build new homes or lead readers to worry about their own homes.
3. Answers will vary. Sample answer: The author conveys Hurricane Ivan's strength by stating that it is "the worst hurricane Grenada had experienced in almost ten years." The author also uses words such as "devastated" and "rubble" and details such as "140-mile-per-hour winds" to describe the hurricane's strength.

Vocabulary Review, page 106

1. e
2. d
3. f
4. a
5. c
6. b

Skill Review, page 106

1. nervous; the other words do not describe the tone of the passage.
2. prompt; *prompt* has the same meaning as *punctual.*
3. unhelpful; the other words do not convey Rosalind's personality as the author implies it in the passage.

Skill Practice, page 107

1. **D** Choices A, B, and C do not convey the thrill and excitement described in the passage.
2. **C** Choices A, B, and D describe actions and conditions of the flight but not what it was like.
3. **A** Choices B, C, and D are elements that are included in the author's style.

Writing Practice, page 107

The passage should include a description of a specific event, a clearly identifiable mood, actions described by verbs, and descriptive words. Every sentence should be related to the event.

Answers will vary. Sample answer: A kerfuffle erupted at this year's PTA Members party. More than a hundred teachers, administrators, and parents had grabbed up raffle tickets. The prizes ranged from a Date Night dinner-and-movie package to the grand prize, an expensive weekend trip to the Hidden Woods Hotel and Resort. When the grand prize ticket was announced, an excited winner shrieked. A moment later, so did another winner, and then one more, and another one. Two teachers, one parent, and a principal waved their winning tickets in the air. And then they rushed the stage! Over the winners' shouts and audience chatter, the emcee announced that everything would be straightened out. She signaled the band to start playing. A moment later, the strains of a John Philip Sousa march was increasing the din.

Chapter 3 Review

1. **B** The author's purpose for writing the passage was to inform people who might come to Philadelphia which parts of the city are nice and which are not. The author warns readers to stay away from one section of the city, especially in the summer. The author's purpose is not to persuade local leaders that they should clean up, to get people to visit the city, or to tell a funny story about the city.

2. **D** The author's tone is judgmental, or critical, about the conditions of the city. The author's tone is not bitter or ashamed, and it is definitely not admiring.

3. **B** *Aroma* has the same denotation, or literal meaning, as *stench* (a smell in the air), but it does not have a negative connotation; the word *aroma* has a positive connotation, and it is used in reference to pleasant smells. *Color, texture,* and *consistency* do not relate to smell.

4. **D** The author uses the words "spacious" and "elegant neatness" to help readers visualize some of the good features of Philadelphia. Those words do not contrast Philadelphia and New York or describe the Delaware River or Water Street.

5. **D** *Myriad* means "countless or numerous." The author uses this word to emphasize the great degree of diversity. *Myriad* does not indicate that anything is lacking, and the author does not use this word to make a plea or to define another term.

6. **B** The author's tone, created through word choices in the speech, sets a hopeful mood. It expresses hope that, together, the President and the citizens will work for change. Clinton expresses disappointment at some actions in the past, but the overall mood is positive and hopeful.

7. **B** A *metaphor* makes a comparison saying that one thing is like another, but does not use the word *as* or *like*. In the phrase given, the result of freedom is compared to sunshine. A simile does use *as* or *like*, connotation is the added meaning of a word, and *personification* endows a non-human object or animal with human qualities.

8. **C** The animals have the human quality of speech. Mowgli is a human, and the yams and river display natural, not human, qualities.

9. **B** The tone is whimsical, or fanciful, not making fun (mocking), sad (depressing), or ashamed (embarrassed).

10. **C** Mowgli is the man-cub (note the clue "a boy" in the second paragraph). Baloo is afraid that if he and Mowgli move to a new hunting ground, Mowgli might get hurt as the animals fight over food. The other choices do not make sense.

Lesson 4.1

Think about Reading, page 118, top

1. cause and effect
2. description
3. compare and contrast
4. sequence

Think about Reading, page 118, bottom

Answers will vary. Sample answer: In the example of slow pacing, there is no movement or passage of time; the text describes in great detail what can be seen in a room. In the example of fast pacing, more than three hours pass; there are very few details until the narrator reaches the plane.

Think about Reading, page 119

1. "Finally, all parties and all other social events must be reviewed by the property management staff one week before the event."
2. There have been several noise complaints in the apartment community in recent weeks.
3. The author included the third paragraph to show the consequences (effects) if residents violate the listed policies (cause).

Vocabulary Review, page 120

1. contrast
2. organization
3. compare
4. text structure

Skill Review, page 120

1. **D** Anthony wants to contrast the principles of freedom that are important in the history of the United States to the reality of the actual treatment of women, who make up half of all people.
2. **D** The second paragraph compares denying women the right to vote with passing a bill of attainder, or a law, that removes rights from half of the population. Therefore, it compares denying women the right to vote with violating the law of the land.

Skill Practice, page 121

1. **C** The first paragraph provides descriptions about how Rosalia experiences her first snowfall, including how she notices individual snowflakes. Therefore, the passage is describing how Rosalia is experiencing her first snowfall.
2. **C** The word "Finally" is a clue that putting on a scarf is the last step in Rosalia's process.
3. **A** The word "like" is a clue that this sentence is a comparison. The sentence compares snowflakes and fingerprints.

Writing Practice, page 121

Your cause-and-effect paragraph should include two to three sentences that show the causes of the environmental problem. Then it should include some effects of that problem. Words that signal cause and effect, such as *because, so, therefore, since,* and *as a result* should be used.

Sample answer: Agricultural runoff can enter nearby rivers, lakes, and other bodies of water. Similarly, industries near water sometimes introduce harmful chemicals. Such events lead to water pollution. As a result of water pollution, fish gills can become clogged, causing their death. Birds that rely on the plants and animals living in the water for food may be poisoned. Yet another effect is a contaminated drinking-water supply.

Lesson 4.2

Think about Reading, page 124

The answer is 2, order of importance. Structures 3 to 6 are also present, but they are not the dominant structure.

Think about Reading, page 125

1. The market is very noisy; the bookstalls are quiet, which is a solace.
2. Answers will vary. Sample answer: The writer uses description, placing descriptive details in the order the narrator perceives them while walking through the market to the bookstalls. The last sentence reveals a compare-and-contrast structure as well. The author uses many descriptive words that relate to loud sounds, such as *noise, calls,* and *clamor*, to emphasize the key idea of the noisiness of the market. The last sentence quickly describes the bookstalls by stating the opposite, quiet; this description of the bookstalls and its placement at the end of the paragraph emphasize the key idea of the bookstalls as an escape from the noise of the market.

Vocabulary Review, page 126

1. d
2. e
3. a
4. b
5. c

Skill Review, page 126

1. **D** The first paragraph introduces the fact that Georgia and Sheila are from military families and move a lot. The second paragraph expands on this idea by showing an event that happens when Georgia learns that her family is moving again.
2. **B** The first paragraph contains information about Georgia and Sheila (characters), Sun Valley High School in California (setting), and Sheila and Georgia's friendship and struggles at school (plot). Therefore, character, setting, and plot is the correct answer.
3. **A** The passage is told in a sequence starting with the first day of tenth grade for Sheila and Georgia and ending a few months into their relationship with Sheila's response to Georgia's announcement. There are details about their past, but these are presented within the content of the time order in the main story.

Skill Practice, page 127

1. **A** Since the second paragraph is about Alexie's writing accomplishments, this information connects to the first paragraph which is about Alexie's early life before he became a writer. The other answer choices do not show this relationship.
2. **C** The first paragraph starts with Alexie's early life, and each sentence moves forward in time order up to Alexie's current life. The other answer choices do not reflect this relationship.

Writing Practice, page 127

Your paragraph should identify the problem and three different ideas that could solve the problem. The text structure of the paragraph should be problem and solution. Also, the sentences should lead into one another.

Sample Answer: The rising cost of a college education is a major problem in the nation. To solve this problem, schools, loan agencies, and the government should work together. First, schools should try to lower tuition by 2 percent every year. Second, the government should offer more needs-based scholarships for students to attend college. Finally, the government should create a program where low-income students are allowed to pay tuition on a sliding scale based on what they can afford.

Lesson 4.3

Think about Reading, page 130

1. Reading the paragraph below will answer some of your questions.
2. Three days after the flood, the family was allowed back in the house.
3. Low humidity, high temperatures, and strong winds can cause forest fires.
4. Caffeine can be found in many beverages, including coffee, tea, and cola.

Think about Reading, page 131

1. Answers will vary: Sample answer: The first sentence of the first paragraph contains the signal words "when" and "immediately." Both words indicate a time relationship between the ideas in the sentence.
2. The signal word "unlike" at the beginning of the second paragraph emphasizes the contrast—also indicated by "but" in the middle of the first paragraph—between the memorials mentioned at the beginning of the first paragraph and Maya Lin's memorial.

Vocabulary Review, page 132

1. d
2. c
3. a
4. b

Skill Review, page 133

1. **C** The signal phrase "in conclusion" reveals a conclusion or the end of someone's points. In this paragraph, the signal phrase shows that Sarah is finishing her points, and the rest of the paragraph restates her qualities.
2. Since

Skill Practice, page 133

1. time order; contrast
2. **D** The word "finally" is the signal word in this sentence. "Finally" introduces the concluding step in the jury duty process.

Writing Practice, page 133

The paragraph should include five important events that led to the war. They should be listed in chronological order, and include transitions between sentences that show time relationships.

Sample answer: From 1946 to 1954, France fought a losing battle to maintain control of Laos, Cambodia, and Vietnam. These three countries were part of French Indochina. During this time, President Truman began providing economic and military assistance to the French. The first American military advisors arrived in French Indochina in 1950. In 1954, the Vietnamese Nationalist Army (which was Communist) defeated the French in a battle at Dien Bien Phu. After this defeat, the French were forced to agree to the creation of a Communist North Vietnam and a non-Communist South Vietnam. However, the United States refused to accept the creation of the Communist North Vietnam. President Eisenhower worried that Communism would spread to South Vietnam, so he pledged continuing support for the new government of South Vietnam. As the war between North and South escalated, so did American involvement.

Chapter 4 Review

1. **B** The third paragraph provides information about Inouye's later achievements, including being on the 442md Regimental Combat Team. The rest of the paragraph describes the early successes that led to these achievements.

2. **A** The sentence "Inouye sensed the depth of this injustice" shows the cause that led to Daniel Inouye petitioning the White House to change its policy. This information helps the reader understand what ultimately led Inouye to help make a change.

3. **C** The transition word *like* shows a comparison. In this sentence, Inouye's grandparents' reason for emigrating from Japan to Hawaii is compared to other immigrants' reasons for emigrating from Japan to Hawaii.

4. **B** Compare and contrast and description; the writer uses description to present pictures of Benjamin Franklin and compare and contrast to show similarities and differences between Franklin and Lincoln and between Franklin and Washington.

5. **B** The second paragraph compares and contrasts Franklin's appearance and abilities as a young and older man. The first part of the paragraph compares and contrasts his appearance, and the second half of the paragraph compares and contrasts his abilities.

6. **B** In the first and second stanzas, the speaker asks "Why in my neighbour's garden . . . ?" to compare the neighbour's garden to his or her own. The stanzas are not about a cause and effect, events in order, or a problem and its solution.

7. **D** The poet uses the question "Why in my neighbour's garden . . . ?" to describe the neighbour's garden, which reveals the reasons for the speaker's envy.

8. **A** The signal word *immediately* reveals a transition in time. It shows how the events of the third paragraph reveal a change in time from the events of the second paragraph.

9. **A.** In the sixth paragraph, the writer uses the word *soon* to signal that support came after only a short period of time and the phrase *in addition* to signal that another accomplishment follows.

10. The text structure of this piece is sequence. Any of the following words that are specific to its text structure could be used: *next*, *before*, *finally*, *immediately*, *meanwhile*, and *subsequently*.

Lesson 5.1

Think about Reading, page 143

1. **P** The word "greatest" reveals the author's opinion about Magellan, and the phrase "should be known" indicates that the author believes that readers should agree with him or her. If the sentence were written to inform, the author might have written that many people consider Magellan to be the greatest navigator.
2. **I** The sentence is straightforward and factual. If the sentence were written to persuade, it would express an opinion, either implicitly or explicitly, and provide reasons for the reader to agree with that opinion.
3. **P** The words "most important" indicate the author's attitude toward Magellan's voyage. If the passage were written strictly to inform, it would be more neutral.

Think about Reading, page 145

1. The author's point of view is that Choconana cereal should be advertised on the Internet rather than on television.
2. The author's point of view is explicit—he states it directly at the beginning of the second paragraph.

Vocabulary Review, page 146

1. point of view
2. neutral
3. author's purpose
4. implicitly

Skill Review, page 146

1. **B** The author presents facts to inform readers about the risks posed to American sailors in 1793. The author also expresses a negative opinion of the French and British at the time by using negative language to describe their actions.
2. **A** The expression "preyed on" provides the strongest clue to the author's negative point of view toward the French and British. The other choices are factual, with mostly neutral language.

Skill Practice, page 147

1. **C** One of the author's purposes is to inform readers how to start running without getting injured. The article is fairly straightforward and is not intended to be humorous. It does not try to persuade readers that running is the best form of exercise or that running is difficult and dangerous.
2. **C** The second sentence explicitly states the author's point of view that running is an easy way to exercise. The author uses language such as "benefits of running" to reinforce this positive attitude. The author is positive about physical activity in general. He or she is neutral toward the CDC guidelines for activity and strength training, mentioning them only as an introduction to the topic of running.

Writing Practice, page 147

Answers will vary. Your response should include a brief summary of an article, identify the author's purpose and point of view, and explain whether the point of view is implicit or explicit. Claims should be supported with evidence from the text.

Sample answer: The article "Royal Mother, Royal Treatment," by DeShawn Rillman, describes a day in the life of the Duchess of Cambridge and her infant son. The purpose of the article is to inform, entertain, and persuade. Rillman's point of view toward the Duchess is implicitly negative. Without stating his point of view outright, he provides facts about the Duchess's activities—including a "sumptuous three-course lunch" and a fitting for "her next designer frock"—to inform readers and to persuade them that she is overprivileged. Details such as the Duchess "gaz[ing] at the baby on the video monitor as she receives her leisurely royal pedicure" lend an understated humor that entertains the reader.

Lesson 5.2

Think about Reading, page 149

Answers will vary. Sample answers:

1. A compare-and-contrast structure would probably be most appropriate to persuade readers that dogs are better than cats. This structure would allow the writer to highlight the positive qualities of dogs against the negative qualities of cats.
2. A problem-and-solution structure would probably be most appropriate to explain why telephones were invented. Inventions come about in response to problems. In this case, the problem was the inability to communicate quickly and easily over long distances. Another possible structure is description.
3. A chronological sequence structure would probably be most appropriate to describe what happened in a movie. Readers can more easily follow the plot if events are described in the order in which they occurred.

Other structures may be appropriate for each of the examples above, as long as the choice is well justified.

Think about Reading, page 151

1. An alternating viewpoint would be the most appropriate device for describing a crime from several points of view. This would allow the reader to understand the crime from different characters' perspectives.
2. Flashback would be the appropriate device for explaining the motivation for a crime. The author could explain how events from the past influenced the criminal.
3. A parallel plot structure would be appropriate for describing two actors who are preparing to audition for the same role. The actors have separate lives, but their story lines are related because they are preparing for the same event.

Vocabulary Review, page 152

1. problem-and-solution structure
2. determine; effective
3. parallel plots

Skill Review, page 152

1. **A** The main structure of the passage is cause and effect. The passage describes the effects of the crash of the *Exxon Valdez* oil tanker.
2. **C** The structure helps readers understand the negative effects of the crash on wildlife.

Skill Practice, page 153

1. **D** The main purpose of the passage is to entertain readers with the story of Juan's experience taking care of his neighbor's pets. It does not explain how to take care of pets, it is not trying to persuade readers of anything, and it does not express a negative opinion about Juan.
2. sequence/chronology/time order; story/series of events

Writing Practice, page 153

Your response should describe the article's content as well as identify the general and specific purposes of the article, the overall structure of the article, and the structure of a smaller portion (such as a paragraph) of the article. It should also evaluate how the structure or structures affect readers' understanding and support the author's purpose.

Sample answer: The article "US Government Shutdown—It's Not Just Government Employees Who Are Hurting," by Katherine Baniker (*Baltimore Post*, October 10, 2013), describes the effects of the 2013 shutdown of the U.S. federal government on the service industry. The general purpose is to inform, and the specific purpose is to inform readers about negative effects of the government shutdown. The overall structure of the article is cause and effect. This structure helps readers understand how the shutdown (the cause) hurt businesses such as cafés, restaurants, and office-supply stores (the effect). The article also includes a few paragraphs with a problem-and-solution structure. For example, Dave's Café lost 75 percent of its lunchtime patrons and is addressing the problem in various ways, such as handing out coupons. The text structures in the article support the author's purpose of informing readers by clearly explaining the relationships between causes and effects and problems and solutions related to the government shutdown.

Lesson 5.3

Think about Reading, page 156

1. best new car on the market
2. smoothest ride on the road
3. classic styling and elegant color choices
4. automobile for the discriminating driver
5. standard equipment on this affordable but upscale car

Think about Reading, page 157

1. You can infer from their context that articles published in catalogs are designed to persuade readers to buy something that the company makes or distributes. They may also be designed to inform readers about the merits of the products.
2. Texts that are written solely for entertainment are likely to be found in the fiction, literature, and humor sections of a library or bookstore.

Vocabulary Review, page 158

1. satire
2. rhetoric
3. context
4. prior knowledge

Skill Review, page 158

1. **C** Without stating it explicitly, the author implies that the word *American* should not be used only to refer to citizens of the United States.
2. **B** This passage expresses an opinion and would most likely be published in the op/ed (Opinion/Editorial) section of a newspaper.

Skill Practice, page 159

1. **A** An implicit, unstated purpose of the text is to express the author's opinion that women should be given the right to vote. The text is designed to support this opinion, but it does not state the opinion directly.
2. **D** The author (Henry Blair) assumes that the audience knows that giving women the right to vote requires a Constitutional amendment. In the first sentence, he mentions "a joint resolution providing for an amendment of the national Constitution."
3. **C** This detail expresses the author's opinion that women should have the right to vote. The author's purpose was to persuade readers to share this opinion.
4. **B** Because the Internet provides access to a wide variety of texts with many purposes, knowing that the passage can be accessed on the Internet does not help the reader infer the purpose. Knowing when the passage was published, who the direct audience was, and the source of the speech can help a reader infer the purpose.

Writing Practice, page 159

Answers will vary. The response should include a brief summary of an article that has an implicit purpose. You should identify the purpose and support your inference with details from the text as well as prior knowledge about the author, subject, and context of the article.

Sample answer: The implicit purpose of the article "What Everyone Should Know about Football," by James Ross, is to discourage parents from letting their young children play football. The article, which Ross published in his blog *BanHighSchoolSportsNow*, includes phrases such as "senseless violence" and "avoidable injury" to imply that children should not play football and to persuade readers to agree. I used these details along with my prior knowledge of what happens during a football game to infer the author's implicit purpose. The title of the author's blog provides context that is also helpful for inferring that the author's purpose is to persuade.

Lesson 5.4

Think about Reading, page 161

Answers will vary. Sample answers:

1. "One art critic said Salvador Dali's work is overrated."
2. "Malcolm X played a minor role in the Civil Rights movement."
3. "Some people think climate change is unrelated to human activity."

Think about Reading, page 163

Answers will vary. Sample answers:

1. The author agrees with the opposing position that children need exercise and socialization. The author disagrees that team sports are the best way to accomplish these goals.
2. The author supports his or her position by using negative language about the opposing opinion and by presenting evidence to support the position that dance is good for children. However, the author neglects to provide evidence that refutes the opposing position.
3. The author's argument is not persuasive. Although readers might gain a better understanding of how dance can benefit children, they will not necessarily be persuaded that it is better than team sports, because the author did not include any evidence to refute the opposing position.

Vocabulary Review, page 163

To strengthen her argument that Pluto should be considered a planet, the astronomer first presented the conflicting position that it should not be considered a planet. She decided to acknowledge this opposing viewpoint to differentiate her position from others. She then went on to refute the opposing argument to solidify her position.

Skill Review, page 164

1. **B** Elena Santarpio's position is stated in the second sentence: "Even though Ivan Chu has worked in our restaurant for only a year, I believe that he should be promoted to the grill." The other choices are true, but they are details that support the writer's position.
2. **D** The opposing position is stated in the first sentence: "It is Seaside Café's policy that employees must have at least two years of kitchen experience in order to become a grill cook." Choices A and C are elements of the opposing position that the writer highlights to make her case for Ivan Chu's promotion. Choice B is not stated in the letter, although Elena Santarpio mentions several positions Ivan Chu has held in the restaurant.

Skill Practice, page 165

1. **A** Paine's position is that the only way to solve the conflict between England and America is to fight. The other statements are written to persuade readers to side with his position.
2. **D** Paine's position is in opposition to numerous other possible solutions.
3. **B** Paine argues that all the other measures taken to solve the conflicts have been unsuccessful.

Writing Practice, page 165

Your response should identify an issue and acknowledge at least one opposing viewpoint. It should differentiate your position from the opposing one through the use of connotative language, signal words that indicate contrast, and evidence that supports your position while refuting the opposing one.

Sample answer: There are those in the US corporate world today who say that American adults need to sleep less and work longer hours so the country can keep pace with other nations. Although it might be true that American companies need to find more competitive strategies, trading on the health of their workers is not an effective one. Recent studies have shown that getting too little sleep can lead to headaches, heart disease, diabetes, depression, attention lapses, and memory loss. Surveys indicate that American workers already sleep too little. In fact, in her article "Sleep More, Work Less," B.K. Lierman estimates that American productivity would increase if adults got an average of 1.75 hours *more* sleep per night.

Lesson 5.5

Think about Reading, page 168

1. The rhetorical device used is juxtaposition of opposites. "Rather than slipping into the nearest thicket" is juxtaposed with, or placed next to, the opposite fact "the fox may continue running."

2. The device serves to emphasize the fox's slyness and to support the author's argument that foxes are clever—the fox keeps running to try to confuse or elude the dogs.

Think about Reading, page 169

Answers will vary. Sample answers:

1. Rhetorical devices strengthen the impact of an author's message. Authors are more likely to achieve their intention when they communicate their message successfully.

2. It is important for a writer to consider his or her intention when choosing specific words or phrases because those words and phrases influence the effect of the piece. They can make an author successful or unsuccessful in achieving his or her goal for writing.

Vocabulary Review, page 170

Because the essay was so poorly written, Tyrine was still unsure of the <u>author's intention</u> even after reading it three times. The essay was clearly supposed to be humorous, but the purpose was obscure. Tyrine provided a list, or an <u>enumeration</u>, of the problems, including the inappropriate use of a <u>rhetorical device</u> by the writer. For example, the <u>analogy</u> in which the writer compared a scalding cup of coffee to a piece of notebook paper made no sense at all.

Skill Review, page 170

1. **C** Kennedy's intention was to persuade his audience that space missions were the next step in human achievement. He acknowledges that space exploration is expensive and dangerous, but his intent is not to convince the American people that the cost and danger are worth it. He is not informing readers that the new spacecraft has reached Venus; in fact, he says "*if* the new spacecraft succeeds in reaching Venus." He is not trying to convince the audience that people have been on Earth for only 50,000 years. Rather, he refers to 50,000 years of humans' *recorded* history.

2. **D** The grand scale of events that Kennedy refers to, as well as his use of words and phrases such as "breathtaking" and "how far and how fast we have come," inspires the audience to share his passion for the space program. The effect of the speech is not likely to be a tragic view of space exploration, a sarcastic response from the audience, or a suspicion about recorded history.

Skill Practice, page 171

1. **B** The first sentence is a question that is intended to engage the audience but is not meant to be answered. It is not an example of parallelism because no repetition is involved. It is not a qualifying statement because no extra information is given to explain a previous statement. Nor is it a juxtaposition of opposites, because only one idea is presented instead of two.

2. **C** The author's intention is to inform readers about Mars and Venus in a humorous, entertaining way. The author does describe the inhospitable environments of Venus and Mars, but the intention is not to persuade readers to stay away. The author also attributes some human qualities to the planets ("your neighbors," "invited for coffee"), but this is meant to make the passage more engaging. While the author presents the characteristics of each planet, he or she does not call attention to their differences.

3. **A** A comparison of Mars and Venus to neighbors is a form of analogy. The writer uses this analogy in the first and last sentences. Parallelism involves the repetition of a text structure, which is not the case in this passage. The author does not list, or enumerate, any examples. And although the two planets are different from human neighbors, the author does not contrast or juxtapose the planets and human neighbors.

4. **D** The passage's effect is to amuse and to educate readers. The effect is not likely to be that readers are convinced about the superiority of Mars and Venus, motivated to travel to outer space, or prompted to feel skeptical.

Writing Practice, page 171

Your essay should analyze a recent speech by a politician and should include the following: a description of the topic, analysis of the author's intention and effect, and a description of at least two rhetorical devices and an explanation of how these devices help the speaker achieve his or her goals.

Sample answer: Police Commissioner Brown's April 13th speech to the city was intended to persuade residents that the recent increase in crime is a result of policies put in place before he became commissioner and that changing these policies is crucial for the safety of the city. Commissioner Brown uses a number of rhetorical devices, including enumeration and juxtaposition of opposites, to make his point. He enumerates the policies that he claims have led to the increase in crime. For example, he states that "crime went up when prison sentences became shorter, when furloughs increased, when parole was granted to nearly all prisoners. . . ." Commissioner Brown also juxtaposes his own new policies with his predecessor's. Both of these devices are effective in convincing readers and listeners that new policies must be put in place immediately.

Chapter 5 Review

1. **D** Clinton's purpose is summarized in the last sentence of the passage. She wants to persuade others that women's human rights must be respected and protected.

2. **C** The author's point of view is that women deserve human rights. The author uses repetition to emphasize the challenges that many women face and their need for equal rights.

3. **B** The passage describes women in a wide variety of circumstances in the United States and around the world. Although the speaker acknowledges the problem that many women are denied equal rights and suggests a solution—respecting and protecting women's rights—problem and solution is not the main structure of the passage.

4. **A** In addition to the stated purpose of explaining the benefits of helmet laws, the author hopes to persuade readers to wear helmets. Information about states' helmet laws and motorcycle injuries provide support for the author's implied purpose.

5. **B** By addressing the opposing viewpoint and presenting statistics that refute it, the author strengthens his or her own position.

6. **A** The excerpt expresses the author's positive point of view toward helmet laws.

7. **D** The author states his or her position in the final sentence of the passage. Choice A is an introductory statement, and choices B and C state arguments for the opposing position.

8. **B** The first paragraph introduces the topic and establishes context; therefore, the author's purpose is to provide background information. The first paragraph does not address opposing views or express the author's point of view or position.

9. **D** To successfully refute an opposing viewpoint, an author must present information that contradicts it. In this excerpt, the author presents information that refutes the opposing opinion that the canal was a waste of money because people would not use it.

10. **C** An implicit, unstated purpose of the text is to explain why the $7 million spent to build the Erie Canal was a good investment. The text supports this opinion but does not state it directly.

Lesson 6.1

Think about Reading, page 181

Sentences 2, 3, and 4 should be checked.

Think about Reading, page 183

1. C
2. E
3. E

Vocabulary Review, page 184

1. argument
2. proof
3. claim
4. vague
5. evidence
6. reiterate

Skill Review, page 184

1. **A** The Supreme Court's opinion is that separate educational facilities are inherently unequal. The other answer choices do not state claims made by the Supreme Court.
2. **B** The structure of this argument is to ask a question and answer it with a claim, providing evidence that supports the claim.
3. Possible answers: restates, reiterates, repeats
4. Possible answers: the American people, citizens of the United States

Skill Practice, page 185

1. **D** The argument is that women are asking for rights and should be given those rights. The other statements are related to the evidence provided for the argument.
2. **A** The author gives evidence of the strength and capability of women, which is equal to that of men. This is evidence supporting her argument that women should have the same rights as men. The other statements are the claim itself, or they are related to arguments against it.

Writing Practice, page 185

The analysis should contain the claim, the evidence, and the purpose of the argument.

Sample answer: Thomas Paine claimed that the colonists should declare independence from England. He supported his claim with examples of ways in which the King of England deprived the colonists of their rights, such as taxing them without their permission. Paine wanted colonists to fight for their independence.

Lesson 6.2

Think about Reading, page 188

1. L
2. F
3. L
4. F

Think about Reading, page 189

B Personal hygiene includes hand washing, which is crucial for maintaining safety when working with animals. Choices A, C, and D are related to the issue but do not directly connect with the importance of hand washing.

Vocabulary Review, page 190

1. e
2. d
3. a
4. c
5. b

Skill Review, page 190

1. **A** The first sentence states the claim that it is important for factory managers to improve working conditions in their factories. The other sentences offer evidence to support this claim.
2. working conditions

Skill Practice, page 191

1. **D** Climate change will affect human society on several levels, which supports the claim that literacy on the topic is important to everyone. The sentences in Choices A, B, and C are variations of the claim that climate science literacy matters.
2. logical

Writing Practice, page 191

Your analysis should state the claim, give examples of supporting evidence, and explain how the evidence is connected to the claim. It should also state whether or not the claim is reasonable based on the evidence given.

Sample answer: The author of this editorial claims that access to education is important for everyone, regardless of gender or ethnicity. The evidence presented shows that in countries where access to equal education has been denied—such as Afghanistan, where girls have been denied the right to an education—basic human rights are also ignored and the effect is detrimental to society as a whole. The argument is reasonable because the evidence is logically connected to the claim.

Lesson 6.3

Think about Reading, page 193

1. Answers will vary. Sample answer: The text evidence is relevant to the claim because it presents the steps of television's development.
2. Answers will vary. Sample answer: There is sufficient evidence to support the claim because the author provides several strong examples that appear to be factual.

Think about Reading, page 195

A To evaluate the evidence in a text for relevance and sufficiency, you must look for several examples of evidence that are related to the topic and appeal to the audience. One example is not sufficient support, and evidence that appeals only to the author is not relevant.

Vocabulary Review, page 196

1. c
2. f
3. d
4. e
5. a
6. b

Skill Review, page 196

1. **D** The phrase "we realize the full extent of our dependence" is most relevant to the claim that our space systems are taken for granted. This phrase expresses the idea that people expect satellite services to always be available. Choices A, B, and C are not directly related to the claim.
2. sufficient
3. relevant

Skill Practice, page 197

1. **A** The fact that the author has been working at this company since 2004 is not relevant to her claim that the company should provide employees with flu shots. The other statements are examples of evidence that support her claim.
2. sufficient

Writing Practice, page 197

Answers will vary. The letter should make the claim that the author is not only qualified for the position but is the best person for the job. The letter should include several relevant details that support the claim.

Sample answer: I am the best candidate for the position of paramedic at Northern City Hospital that you will find. To begin with, I am a certified First Aid First Responder and EMT. I have worked for the ambulance service in my hometown for three years, so I am highly qualified for the paramedic position. In addition, I recently passed the Wilderness First Aid Responder certification exam. As a result, I am fully prepared to reach and respond to patients in the isolated country community that your hospital serves, no matter how difficult the terrain might be.

Lesson 6.4

Think about Reading, page 200

Choices A, B, and D should have a check mark. Choice C is evidence that can be used to back up a claim, but it is not specifically used in this passage.

Think about Reading, page 201

1. related
2. logically
3. sound
4. validity

Vocabulary Review, page 202

1. d
2. a
3. b
4. e
5. c

Skill Review, page 202

1. **D** It is not possible to verify what degree of privacy other presidents expected. All the other responses are verifiable.
2. **D** As Nixon explains, if he cannot ensure that his conversations are private, people will not give him the advice and information that he needs.

Skill Practice, page 203

1. **A** The author presents logical reasons for temporarily changing the dress code. She does not present facts, but her reasons are valid, and her argument is reasonable.
2. A support

   B reasoning

   C related

   D valid

Writing Practice, page 203

Your paragraph should list and evaluate the evidence presented in the text you chose, and it should evaluate the argument in terms of validity and reasoning.

Sample answer: In John Forti's essay on local food, he presents facts about financial gains for farmers that make communities economically stronger. He also presents verifiable evidence that food grown locally takes less of a toll on the environment and that food grown organically is less likely to have adverse effects on people's health. He presents sufficient evidence to support the reasonable argument that buying locally and organically produced food is a better all-around choice for everyone in the long run.

Lesson 6.5

Think about Reading, page 205

logical, deductions, assumptions

Think about Reading, page 207

C The writer assumes that her cousin and her brother were hired for exactly the same job. The first two answer choices are evidence that support the author's argument, and the last answer choice is her claim.

Vocabulary Review, page 208

1. c
2. d
3. b
4. e
5. a

Skill Review, page 208

1. hidden, right, skin color, vote
2. **A** The idea that voting is an ever present right and power supports the assumption that every citizen has a right to vote. The rest of the statements do not support the assumption.

Skill Practice, page 209

1. **C** The idea that freed slaves have unreasonably high expectations is a hidden assumption, not a logical argument, stated assumption, or piece of valid evidence.
2. hidden, scrutiny

Writing Practice, page 209

Your paragraph should identify the claim in the amendment, any assumptions made, and whether those assumptions are valid or not.

Sample answer: In the First Amendment of the Bill of Rights, the authors claim that there are rights that Congress cannot prohibit. The unstated assumptions are that every citizen of the United States has inalienable rights and that those rights should be protected from laws that would disallow them. These assumptions are valid because they are true, supporting the argument that there should be no laws taking these rights away.

Chapter 6 Review

1. civil right

2. **B** Chief Justice Warren claims that the convictions to deny marriage due to race should be reversed. The other statements are falsehoods about marriage rights.

3. **D** Chief Justice Warren presents a series of logical deductions based on his assumption. He does not present expert opinions, verifiable facts, or testimonials.

4. **A** Eisenhower presents explanations and justifications. Not all of his facts are verifiable, and he does not present logical deductions or expert opinions.

5. **C** The argument is valid because Eisenhower's explanations are logical. Not every piece of evidence is verifiable because Eisenhower presents the "possibility" of certain events happening. However, some of the evidence is verifiable, and Eisenhower's justifications are logical.

6. **C** Abigail Adams could have provided more supporting evidence to make her argument stronger. She provides a claim (women should be included in the new laws) and a conclusion. An introduction is not part of an argument's structure.

7. representation/a voice

8. inequity, abolished

9. **A** Senator Kennedy has presented several verifiable facts and reasons directly related to his claim, so he has presented sufficient and relevant evidence.

10. employees/workers

Lesson 7.1

Think about Reading, page 220

A checkmark should appear next to phrases 2, 3, and 4.

Think about Reading, page 221, top

Answers will vary. Sample answer: The second passage presents the information in a more detailed way because it states the specific recommended qualifications for receiving a graduated driver's license.

Think about Reading, page 221, bottom

C The nonfiction description of what historians believe about Cleopatra's death analyzes the facts related to her death. The other options are characteristics of the fictional and the nonfictional accounts.

Vocabulary Review, page 222

1. format
2. topic
3. characteristics
4. similar

Skill Review, page 222

1. **A** The fictional account presents the emotions and experiences of the soldiers. The nonfictional account only presents verifiable facts and battle details.
2. **C** The author's purpose in the nonfictional account is to present the facts about the historical event, not the emotions or experiences of any of the soldiers in the battle.

Skill Practice, page 223

1. **C** Both passages address the same historical event, but the difference between the two presentations is emotions versus facts. Fictional accounts of events make the reader feel a certain way and identify with a character's emotions through the development of the character in a situation, and nonfictional accounts have the primary purpose of presenting the factual details of the events.
2. similar; the Battle of Chickamauga
3. facts; feelings/emotions

Writing Practice, page 223

Your paragraph should describe the similarities and differences between the two formats being compared.

Sample answer: The chart presenting the large amount of money spent on the military versus the small amount of money spent on education, health care, and social services gives a clear idea of the government's priorities. The essay on spending cuts in education, however, shows the actual effect on specific programs that will no longer be able to serve their communities because their funding has been reallocated. The chart is easier to read, but the essay connects the data with real life in a clearer way.

Lesson 7.2

Think about Reading, page 226

Answers will vary. Sample answer: The text by Roosevelt tells a story from his childhood about how he and his father interacted. The text by Twain describes his ancestors and the characteristics they brought to his family line. These details refer to the life and families of the authors and are written in the first person, which identifies the texts as autobiographies.

Think about Reading, page 227

B Comparison reveals that the themes are similar, in that both stories show that love requires a kind heart. The characters involved are also typical of folktales—a king, a princess, and a hero. Both use symbolism—the banana flower representing the princess's heart in the first and the dragon's head representing the hero's success in the second. The plot of the second story abruptly differs from that of a folktale—the hero decides that the actions of the princess don't show love at all, so he refuses to marry the princess (his reward) even though he has performed all the actions required of him.

Vocabulary Review, page 228

1. c

2. e

3. a

4. d

5. b

Skill Review, page 228

1. D Both tell stories about fictional characters. The other statements are true for only one or the other of the texts.

2. subgenres

3. character; colt/horse; youth/human

Skill Practice, page 229

1. D Both passages are short stories. The other genres are structured differently, either in terms of physical structure or in terms of how content is treated.

2. C The setting in the first passage is in the winter in New Hampshire, and the setting in the second is in hot, humid Calcutta. The main characters are young men, the levels of description are equally vivid, and the genres are the same.

3. figurative

Writing Practice, page 229

Your paragraph should describe the similarities and differences between the two genres being compared.

Sample answer: Mary Oliver describes the natural world in her collection of poems, *A Thousand Mornings*. Her poems are in lines and stanzas, and do not rhyme. They give vivid descriptions of animals, plants, and the places where the poet wanders. They also describe the feelings that the natural world evokes and how we are losing our connection with the natural world through various types of human activity that destroy it. By contrast, Al Gore's essays in *An Inconvenient Truth* describe the destruction of the natural world and the impact of human activity on our climate. He writes in an informative style in paragraphs and cites facts and data to back up his claims. Both texts deal with the impact of human activity on Earth but in different ways and with different techniques.

Lesson 7.3

Think about Reading, page 232

The main issue being contested in *Sears* v. *Stiffel* was Sears's right to sell pole lamps similar to the ones Stiffel designed. Stiffel claimed that Sears had infringed on Stiffel's patents by producing a lamp with the same design and that this had confused customers, amounting to unfair competition. Sears claimed that the lamp-on-a-pole design was unpatentable and therefore in the public domain and that public confusion was not enough to warrant an injunction or damages.

Think about Reading, page 233

Answers may vary. Sample answer:

Valid Argument	Invalid Argument
evidence from reliable sources	unreliable sources
factual evidence	hearsay
expert opinion	false evidence or lies
valid assumption	invalid assumption
logical deductions	illogical deductions

Vocabulary Review, page 234

1. b
2. e
3. f
4. a
5. d
6. c

Skill Review, page 234

1. legal codes and documents; Seabury bases his argument primarily on the British constitution, British law, and other legal evidence.
2. logic; Hamilton states the assumption that "all civil government . . . must be a voluntary compact between the rulers and the ruled." He then makes a series of logical deductions founded on the assumed truth of this statement.

Skill Practice, page 235

1. **D** Washington believes that freed slaves will not be able to progress if they take an assertive stance. Instead he feels they should be patient, cultivate good relations with their communities, and do jobs that they are already qualified to do.
2. **A** Du Bois feels that Negros have followed Washington's advice for 15 years with the result that their situation is worse than it was. His implied claim is that it is time for them to stop being patient and to insist that they be given equal rights. These rights include not only the vote, but complete civil equality and the right to higher education.

Writing Practice, page 235

Paragraphs should state an opinion about which argument is more convincing and support it with evidence from the passages. Evidence may include paraphrases, short quotations, prior knowledge, and inferences.

Sample answer: Washington's argument is more convincing because he is a true expert on the difficulties facing freed slaves. He was born into slavery and succeeded in education and society, so he knows what it takes. Du Bois, in contrast, does not know what it is like to be a slave or to be confronted with freedom in hostile surroundings. He lists facts, but has no experience or real understanding of the day-to-day realties that underlie the facts.

Lesson 7.4

Think about Reading, page 238

Answers will vary. Sample answer: The image conveys emotions that may not come across as clearly in the text, such as the sadness shown on the faces of the women and children as they leave the men behind. The text conveys details about the actual event that are not shown in the image. I think the image has a greater impact because you immediately see how awful the tragedy was.

Think about Reading, page 239

A The first passage is directed toward the general public, to inform them about an invasive species, and the second passage instructs boat and equipment owners on how to avoid spreading the growth of this invasive species.

Vocabulary Review, page 241

1. visual
2. scope
3. audience
4. impact
5. textual

Skill Review, page 240

1. **B** The other text informs the reader about diagnosis and treatment.
2. **D** Both texts use words to convey information. Only one uses a bulleted list, and neither is visual or contains dialogue.

Skill Practice, page 241

1. **B** The passage has a broader scope than the image because it provides information about several aspects of the fire, including why it is growing and its effects, which the image does not provide.
2. topic; formats; impact

Writing Practice, page 241

Your paragraph should describe the similarities and differences between the impact and scope of the two texts being compared. It should also describe the similarities and differences between the audience and the author's purpose for choosing each genre.

Sample answer: The essay on learning to run for beginners has a greater impact than the FAQ because it has a conversational tone and is easier to read than the FAQ. Also, the ideas are linked together. The FAQ feels a little more random in its organization, although all the points addressed are questions that are commonly asked by beginning runners about the sport. The audience for each is the same, but the FAQ's purpose is to directly address and answer the reader's possible questions. The essay's purpose is to teach readers how to participate in the sport at the entry level.

Chapter 7 Review

1. setting
2. **D** The first passage, which lists facts about actual people, is a nonfictional article, and the second passage, a fictional story, tells the story of a fictional character and relates his emotions.
3. **B** The second fictional passage includes descriptions of what characters are thinking. The first passage is merely descriptive and cannot have access to the thoughts of any of the people described.
4. topic/format, facts, a (made-up) story
5. drama
6. **D** Nora and Liza want to leave the men in their lives; however, Nora does not believe she has learned anything from Torvald, whereas Liza acknowledges that she has learned from Higgins. The other statements are differences in details of the women's lives but not differences in their arguments.
7. **A** Shaw's characters express their feelings in a comedic fashion, but Ibsen's characters express their feelings in a serious and dramatic way. The other statements are not different approaches to the topic of how the women in these plays are treated and how they feel about it.
8. **D** The chart is in a visual format because it uses an image to express an idea. The other categories describe genres or formats that are textual and use words.
9. impact
10. **B** The passage explains in detail the concept of the electromagnetic spectrum. The rest of the responses describe the information presented by the chart.

1. C The words "the preceding evening" indicate that the letter was written the night before Holmes met with Violet Hunter. The other choices are mentioned in the story, but do not correctly identify when the note was written.

2. C The mention of Sherlock Holmes in the first paragraph serves as a clue that the narrator (who is Doctor Watson) is referring to his "companion" Holmes. Doyle, the author of the story, and the young lady would not be considered "companions" of Watson.

3. D The author qualifies the word *man*, explaining that he refers only to criminals. An analogy makes a comparison, enumeration provides a list of items, and juxtaposition of opposites is placing contrasting ideas near each other to emphasize their differences.

4. A The topic is not an abstract concept such as "hope" or "democracy"; receiving a visitor is an everyday occurrence. The passage does include long sentences, presents dialogue without telling who is speaking, and requires prior knowledge that some readers might not have. Those characteristics do make the text complex.

5. B Paragraph 10 introduces Violet Hunter, the character who speaks in paragraph 11. The other answer choices do not accurately describe a relationship between the paragraphs.

6. C Holmes has no interesting case to investigate and assumes that he has hit a low point, so he is not looking forward to meeting Miss Hunter, whose case he's assuming will be unimportant. He definitely is not eager to meet her, there is no evidence to suggest that he knows her parents, and he does not think the case will be exciting.

7. C The blog and recipe card, in different forms, explain how to make spinach dip. The other choices do not reflect the purpose of the passages.

8. B The blog and the recipe specify using an electric mixer, something the authors assume that their readers can operate. The other choices are not assumptions made by either author.

9. D *But* is a signal word that connects two related ideas; in this case it compares Aunt Jane's spinach dip to kebabs, another food served at the barbecue. *But* does not signal a problem/solution or cause/effect relationship, and Aunt Jane's dip is not contrasted with her everyday cooking.

10. D There are no italicized words in the recipe, but there are subheads (*Ingredients/ Directions*), a bulleted list, and boldface words.

11. C A comma is used to separate two independent ideas in the sentence. There is no series of items or an introductory clause, and a comma is not used to separate a pronoun and its antecedent.

12. B *Devoured* has a less negative connotation than *pigged out on* when talking about people eating. The expressions *abstain from* (hold back) and *pick at* do not have the same meaning; *gorged themselves on* has a very negative connotation.

13. C Because the recipe gives step-by-step instructions, it has a greater impact. The blog presented the steps out of order, which made the recipe confusing. The other answer choices do not state valid reasons why either text would have greater impact.

14. B The story is a folktale—a fictional story that has been passed down through generations. It is not an essay, a work of science fiction, or an autobiography.

15. D The story presents the sequence of events as they happen. A cause and effect of the gravedigger's fright are included, but this is not the overall structure. The passage does not compare and contrast ideas or present a problem and solution.

16. C Personification means to give human qualities to nonhumans, and the horse speaks like a human. The other choices are incorrect because the gravedigger is human, and the shining ring does not exhibit a quality of a human.

17. B The plot involves a burial, so a graveyard is a necessary part of the story. The text does not say where the horse or the gravedigger live, and a wagon is not mentioned.

18. A The story is about an unbelievable event—someone who is buried comes back to life—so the theme is that anything is possible. The other answer choices are not addressed in the passage.

19. B A metaphor compares two things without using the word *as* or *like*. Here, the author compares the darkness of night to a curtain. Connotation is an impression of a word, personification is giving human qualities to animals or objects, and a simile makes a comparison using *as* or *like*.

20. D The sentence is correctly rewritten in choice D. Choices A and B are incorrect because the modifier is misplaced. Choice C is incorrect because the meaning of the modifier was changed from *terrified* to *terrifying*.

21. B The author explains the dangers associated with frostbite. The other choices are supporting details or are untrue.

22. A The author provides facts and descriptions in the discussion of frostbite. Questions and opinions are not presented as evidence.

23. C From information in the passage, readers can infer that the author's purpose is to persuade people not to expose vulnerable body parts to extreme cold and risk getting frostbite. The author did not intend to persuade readers to send questions, to entertain with a story, or to inform about high temperatures.

24. B The author's tone is serious, which is appropriate for addressing an important medical problem. The tone is not hostile (argumentative), humorous (joking), or threatening.

25. A The author tells what causes frostbite and explains the effects of it. The author does present some steps to take, but the whole passage is not organized in sequence. The text also does not compare and contrast information or rank it by importance.

26. B The letter writer does not think pesticides should be considered hazardous waste; the recycling plant argues that leftover pesticides do need to be treated as hazardous. The other choices were not argued in the passages.

27. C The letter writer's claim is that pesticides can be disposed of like any other trash. The other choices are merely details from the passage; the author does not try to build an argument to defend them.

28. C By including the statement that pesticides *do* harm some animals, the author strengthens the opposing view that pesticides are hazardous. The other choices don't describe the effect of presenting contradictory evidence in the letter.

29. D Because the recycling plant has issued the guidelines about hazardous materials, a reader can infer that some people in town have not been disposing of waste properly. The text does not offer clues to warrant an inference that the apartment manager or recycling plant are new or that tenants are producing too much trash.

30. D The manager's memo will most likely motivate residents to follow the rules. The memo does not intend to amuse, and the manager's tone is authoritative but not bossy. It is most unlikely that the memo would convince residents that recycling is unimportant.

31. A Both are persuasive texts that seek to make a change. They are not literary texts, and although each text mentions wildlife, that is not the main focus. Only the letter writer explains the purpose of pesticides.

32. C The fact that pesticides protect us from insect bites supports the idea that pesticides are helpful; the other choices do not support that idea.

33. D The main idea is that invasive, nonnative animals and plants threaten the natural balance of an ecosystem. The other choices do not describe the main idea.

34. B The fact that some animals and plants were brought to America by colonists does not support the main idea. The other answer choices do support the idea that invasive species threaten the environment.

35. C. This summary recaps the most important information in a few sentences. Each of the other choices includes a detail that does not summarize the entire passage.

36. C Enumerating the places that nonnative species are invading helps strengthen the impact of the author's message. None of the other choices relate to the author's intention.

37. C The writer wants to inform readers about the problem. He or she is not trying to persuade or amuse readers.

38. D. The author has a negative point of view toward nonnative species, as evidenced by the information in the passage. The author does not focus on species that are native to America.

39. D The father is determined to make the best of the situation for his children. He is not jealous, frantic, or unreasonable.

40. A The mother and father's efforts to encourage their children in a desperate situation reflect a theme of perseverance. While some of the other choices are touched on in the passage, they do not represent the overall theme.

41. B The family—especially the father— has an external conflict with nature in the form of a raging sea. The other conflicts are not mentioned.

42. A The dramatic events described in the passage create a mood of anxiety. The passage is not likely to make a reader feel giddy (silly), hostile (violent), or indifferent (uncaring).

43. C Although the timeline contains text, it is a graphic feature. It does not belong in the dramatic or fictional genres.

44. A The time line presents important dates and information in a shorter form than the passage. The time line does not compare and contrast information, and the passage does not include more important dates or fewer details than the time line.

45. D The passage includes the fact that when he was only 22 years old, Washington led his troops to victory. The other choices are details about Washington's life, but they do not imply brave leadership.

46. B The first sentence gives the reader some background information about Washington's childhood. It does not indicate an opposing view, the author's point of view, or the author's purpose.

47. D Thoreau and Paine share a very negative point of view about government. They were not negative or neutral about society, and they were not neutral about government.

48. B Paine uses capital letters to emphasize the words for effect. The words are not capitalized for any of the other reasons given.

49. D The list of what the government does not do (but which the people do) helps Thoreau persuade readers that they can do great things on their own, without a government. It does not strengthen the opposing viewpoint, make a comparison between nations, or make an argument for a central government.

50. C Paine uses the word *patron* to emphasize the benefits of society and the word *punisher* to emphasize the disadvantages of government. The other answer choices do not reflect the effect of Paine's words.

Extended Response Activity

Your opinion essay should include the following:

- an introduction that includes a statement of your claim
- two to four paragraphs—each with one central idea—providing evidence that supports your claim
- evidence that is relevant, sufficient, and valid
- a variety of specific supporting details, including examples and reasons
- words and phrases that signal relationships between ideas, sentences, and paragraphs
- an appropriate concluding paragraph that restates your claim and the main points of your argument

You may also include researched information, such as facts and statistics, to enhance your argument.

Check Your Understanding

On the following chart, circle the number of any question you answered incorrectly. In the third column, you will see the pages that address the content covered in the question.

Lesson	Item Number(s)	Review Page(s)
1.1: Determine the Main Idea	11, 21, 33	13–17
1.2: Identify Supporting Details	2, 22, 32, 34, 45	20–23
1.3: Identify Direct and Implied Main Ideas	22, 33	27–29
1.4: Summarize Details	10, 35	33–35
1.5: Identify a Theme	18, 40	38–41
2.1: Sequence Events	1, 5	52–55
2.2: Infer Relationships between Events, People, and Ideas	2, 5, 6, 29	58–61
2.3: Analyze Relationships between Ideas	5, 15, 17, 39, 41, 50	64–67
2.4: Determine Implicit Relationships between Ideas	5, 6, 45	70–73
2.5: Analyze the Role of Details in Complex Texts	4	76–79
3.1: Determine Connotative and Figurative Meanings	12, 16, 19	90–93
3.2: Analyze Tone	24, 42	96–99
3.3: Analyze Word Choice	3, 42, 50	102–105
4.1: Analyze the Development of Ideas	1, 9, 13, 15, 25	116–119
4.2: Analyze How Structure Impacts Key Ideas	1, 5, 46	122–125
4.3: Analyze the Effect of Transitional and Signal Words	1, 9, 25	128–131
5.1: Determine Author's Point of View	23, 37, 38, 47	143–145
5.2: Analyze How Author's Purpose Determines Structure	23, 49	148–151
5.3: Infer Author's Purpose	3, 23, 37	154–157
5.4: Analyze How Authors Differentiate Their Positions	28, 47	160–163
5.5: Analyze Author's Intention and Effect	13, 20, 30, 36, 37, 49	166–169
6.1: Identify Argument Development	26, 27, 28	180–183
6.2: Identify Supporting Evidence	32	186–189
6.3: Evaluate Relevance and Sufficiency	32, 34	192–195
6.4: Evaluate Validity and Reasoning	28	198–201
6.5: Evaluate Logic and Identify Hidden Assumptions	8	204–207
7.1: Compare Similar Topics in Different Formats	7, 31, 44	218–221
7.2: Compare Similar Genres	14, 31, 47	224–227
7.3: Analyze Two Arguments	26, 47	230–233
7.4: Evaluate the Impact of Genre and Format	13, 43, 44, 48	236–239

Excerpt from "The Gift of the Magi"

"Jim, darling," she cried, "don't look at me that way. I had my hair cut off and sold because I couldn't have lived through Christmas without giving you a present. It'll grow out again—you won't mind, will you? I just had to do it. My hair grows awfully fast. Say 'Merry Christmas!' Jim, and let's be happy. You don't know what a nice—what a beautiful, nice gift I've got for you."

"You've cut off your hair?" asked Jim, laboriously, as if he had not arrived at that patent fact yet even after the hardest mental labor.

"Cut it off and sold it," said Della. "Don't you like me just as well, anyhow? I'm me without my hair, ain't I?"

Jim looked about the room curiously.

"You say your hair is gone?" he said, with an air almost of idiocy.

"You needn't look for it," said Della. "It's sold, I tell you—sold and gone, too. It's Christmas Eve, boy. Be good to me, for it went for you. Maybe the hairs of my head were numbered," she went on with sudden serious sweetness, "but nobody could ever count my love for you. Shall I put the chops on, Jim?"

Out of his trance Jim seemed quickly to wake. He enfolded his Della. For ten seconds let us regard with discreet scrutiny some inconsequential object in the other direction. Eight dollars a week or a million a year—what is the difference? A mathematician or a wit would give you the wrong answer. The magi brought valuable gifts, but that was not among them. This dark assertion will be illuminated later on.

Jim drew a package from his overcoat pocket and threw it upon the table.

"Don't make any mistake, Dell," he said, "about me. I don't think there's anything in the way of a haircut or a shave or a shampoo that could make me like my girl any less. But if you'll unwrap that package you may see why you had me going a while at first."

White fingers and nimble tore at the string and paper. And then an ecstatic scream of joy; and then, alas! a quick feminine change to hysterical tears and wails, necessitating the immediate employment of all the comforting powers of the lord of the flat.

For there lay The Combs–the set of combs, side and back, that Della had worshipped long in a Broadway window. Beautiful combs, pure tortoise shell, with jewelled rims—just the shade to wear in the beautiful vanished hair. They were expensive combs, she knew, and her heart had simply craved and yearned over them without the least hope of possession. And now, they were hers, but the tresses that should have adorned the coveted adornments were gone.

But she hugged them to her bosom, and at length she was able to look up with dim eyes and a smile and say: "My hair grows so fast, Jim!"

And them Della leaped up like a little singed cat and cried, "Oh, oh!"

Jim had not yet seen his beautiful present. She held it out to him eagerly upon her open palm. The dull precious metal seemed to flash with a reflection of her bright and ardent spirit.

"Isn't it a dandy, Jim? I hunted all over town to find it. You'll have to look at the time a hundred times a day now. Give me your watch. I want to see how it looks on it."

Instead of obeying, Jim tumbled down on the couch and put his hands under the back of his head and smiled.

(continued)

"Dell," said he, "let's put our Christmas presents away and keep 'em a while. They're too nice to use just at present. I sold the watch to get the money to buy your combs. And now suppose you put the chops on."

The magi, as you know, were wise men—wonderfully wise men—who brought gifts to the Babe in the manger. They invented the art of giving Christmas presents. Being wise, their gifts were no doubt wise ones, possibly bearing the privilege of exchange in case of duplication. And here I have lamely related to you the uneventful chronicle of two foolish children in a flat who most unwisely sacrificed for each other the greatest treasures of their house. But in a last word to the wise of these days let it be said that of all who give gifts these two were the wisest. O all who give and receive gifts, such as they are wisest. Everywhere they are wisest. They are the magi.

—O. Henry

Fall Injuries Prevention in the Workplace

Falls are a hazard found in all [workplace] settings. A fall can occur during the simple acts of walking or climbing a ladder to change a light fixture. [It may also result from] a complex series of events affecting an ironworker 80 feet above the ground. . . .

The highest frequency of fall-related fatalities was experienced by the construction industry. . . . [The] highest counts of nonfatal fall injuries [are] associated with the health services and the wholesale and retail industries. Healthcare support, building . . . maintenance, transportation . . . , and construction and extraction occupations are particularly at risk of fall injuries.

Circumstances associated with fall incidents in the work environment frequently involve slippery, cluttered, or unstable walking/working surfaces. [Other risks are] unprotected edges; floor holes and wall openings; unsafely positioned ladders; and misused fall protection. Federal regulations and industry . . . standards provide specific measures and . . . recommendations for fall prevention and protection. However, persistent unsafe practices and low safety culture across many industries define steady fall injury rates year after year.

Fall injuries [are] a considerable financial burden: workers' compensation and medical costs associated with [workplace] fall incidents have been estimated at approximately $70 billion annually in the United States [NSC 2002]. Many countries are facing the same challenges as the United States on fall injury in the workplace. The . . . public health community has a strong interest in developing strategies to reduce the toll of fall injuries.

Successful reduction of fall injury and fatality rates requires continued concerted efforts . . . in enhancing the work environment. [It requires] implementing new effective fall prevention and protection technologies and improving the work safety culture through continuous education of the workforce.

Source: NSC [2002]. *Report on injuries in America 2002.* Itasca, IL: National Safety Council.

What It Means to Be Colored in the Capital of the United States

Washington, D.C., has been called *The Colored Man's Paradise*. . . .

It is certain that it would be difficult to find a worse misnomer for Washington. . . . For fifteen years I have resided in Washington. [W]hile it was far from being a paradise for colored people when I first touched these shores, it has been doing its level best ever since to make conditions for us intolerable. . . .

As a colored woman I may walk from the Capitol to the White House, ravenously hungry and abundantly supplied with money with which to purchase a meal. [But I will not find] a single restaurant in which I would be permitted to take a morsel of food, if it was patronized by white people, unless I were willing to sit behind a screen. . . .

Unless I am willing to engage in a few menial occupations, in which the pay for my services would be very poor, there is no way for me to earn an honest living, if I am not a trained nurse or a dressmaker or can secure a position as teacher in the public schools, which is exceedingly difficult to do. It matters not what my intellectual attainments may be or how great is the need [for] the services of a competent person. [I]f I try to enter many of the numerous vocations in which my white sisters are allowed to engage, the door is shut in my face. . . .

Some time ago a young woman who had already attracted some attention in the literary world by her volume of short stories answered an advertisement which appeared in a Washington newspaper. [It] called for the services of a skilled stenographer and expert typewriter. The applicants were requested to send specimens of their work and answer certain questions concerning their experience and their speed before they called in person. In reply to her application, the young colored woman received a letter from the firm, stating that her references and experience were the most satisfactory that had been sent and requesting her to call. When she presented herself, there was some doubt in the mind of the man to whom she was directed concerning her racial pedigree. [H]e asked her point-blank whether she was colored or white. When she confessed the truth, the merchant expressed deep regret that he could not avail himself of the services of so competent a person. [He] frankly admitted that employing a colored woman in his establishment in any except a menial position was simply out of the question. . . .

Although white and colored teachers are under the same Board of Education and the system for the children of both races is said to be uniform, prejudice against the colored teachers in the public schools is manifested in a variety of ways. From 1870 to 1900, there was a colored superintendent at the head of the colored schools. During all that time the directors of the cooking, sewing, physical culture, manual training, music and art departments were colored people. Six years ago, a change was inaugurated. The colored superintendent was legislated out of office and the directorships, without a single exception, were taken from colored teachers and given to the whites. Now, no matter how competent or superior the colored teachers in our public schools may be, they know that they can never rise to the height of a directorship. [They] can never hope to be more than an assistant and receive the meager salary therefore, unless the present regime is radically changed. . . .

(Continued)

The colored laborer's path to a decent livelihood is by no means smooth. Into some of the trade unions here he is admitted, while from others he is excluded altogether. By the union men this is denied, although I am personally acquainted with skilled workmen who tell me they are not admitted into the unions because they are colored. But even when they are allowed to join the unions they frequently derive little benefit, owing to certain tricks of the trade. When the word passes round that help is needed and colored laborers apply, they are often told by the union officials that they have secured all the men they needed . . . [T]he places are reserved for white men, until they have been provided with jobs, and colored men must remain idle, unless the supply of white men is too small.

And so I might go on citing instance after instance to show the variety of ways in which our people are sacrificed on the altar of prejudice in the [c]apital of the United States and how almost insurmountable are the obstacles which block [our] path to success.

It is impossible for any white person in the United States, no matter how sympathetic and broad, to realize what life would mean to him if his incentive to effort were suddenly snatched away. To the lack of incentive to effort, which is the awful shadow under which we live, may be traced the wreck and ruin of score[s] of colored youth. And surely nowhere in the world do oppression and persecution based solely on the color of the skin appear more hateful and hideous than in the capital of the United States . . . [T]he chasm between the principles upon which this Government was founded, in which it still professes to believe, and those which are daily practiced under the protection of the flag, yawns so wide and deep.

—Speech by Mary E. Church Terrell to the United Women's Club in Washington, D.C., October 10, 1906

Richard Nixon, resignation speech, August 8, 1974

Good evening.

This is the 37th time I have spoken to you from this office, where so many decisions have been made that shaped the history of this nation. Each time I have done so to discuss with you some matter that I believe affected the national interest.

In all the decisions I have made in my public life, I have always tried to do what was best for the nation. Throughout the long and difficult period of Watergate, I have felt it was my duty to persevere, to make every possible effort to complete the term of office to which you elected me.

In the past few days, however, it has become evident to me that I no longer have a strong enough political base in the Congress to justify continuing that effort.

But with the disappearance of that base, I now believe that the Constitutional purpose has been served, and there is no longer a need for the process to be prolonged.

I would have preferred to carry through to the finish whatever the personal agony it would have involved, and my family unanimously urged me to do so. But the interest of the nation must always come before any personal considerations.

I have never been a quitter. To leave office before my term is completed is abhorrent to every instinct in my body. But as president, I must put the interest of America first. America needs a full-time president and a full-time Congress, particularly at this time with problems we face at home and abroad.

To continue to fight through the months ahead for my personal vindication would almost totally absorb the time and attention of both the president and the Congress in a period when our entire focus should be on the great issues of peace abroad and prosperity without inflation at home.

Therefore, I shall resign the presidency effective at noon tomorrow. Vice President Ford will be sworn in as president at that hour in this office.

In passing this office to the vice president, I also do so with the profound sense of the weight of responsibility that will fall on his shoulders tomorrow and, therefore, of the understanding, the patience, the cooperation he will need from all Americans.

I regret deeply any injuries that may have been done in the course of the events that led to this decision. I would say only that if some of my judgments were wrong, and some were wrong, they were made in what I believed at the time to be the best interest of the nation.

To those who have stood with me during these past difficult months, to my family, my friends, to many others who joined in supporting my cause because they believed it was right, I will be eternally grateful for your support.

And to those who have not felt able to give me your support, let me say I leave with no bitterness toward those who have opposed me, because all of us, in the final analysis, have been concerned with the good of the country, however our judgments might differ.

So, let us all now join together in affirming that common commitment and in helping our new president succeed for the benefit of all Americans.

The Third McCain-Obama Presidential Debate, Hofstra University, Hempstead, NY October 15, 2008

BOB SCHIEFFER, MODERATOR:

By now, we've heard all the talking points, so let's try to tell the people tonight some things that they—they haven't heard. Let's get to it.

Another very bad day on Wall Street, as both of you know. Both of you proposed new plans this week to address the economic crisis.

Senator McCain, you proposed a $52 billion plan that includes new tax cuts on capital gains, tax breaks for seniors, write-offs for stock losses, among other things.

Senator Obama, you proposed $60 billion in tax cuts for middle-income and lower-income people, more tax breaks to create jobs, new spending for public works projects to create jobs.

I will ask both of you: Why is your plan better than his?

U.S. SENATOR JOHN MCCAIN (AZ)
REPUBLICAN PRESIDENTIAL NOMINEE:

. . . Americans are hurting right now, and they're angry. They're hurting, and they're angry. They're innocent victims of greed and excess on Wall Street and as well as Washington, D.C. And they're angry, and they have every reason to be angry.

And they want this country to go in a new direction. And there are elements of my proposal that you just outlined which I won't repeat.

But we also have to have a short-term fix, in my view, and long-term fixes.

Let me just talk to you about one of the short-term fixes.

The catalyst for this housing crisis was the Fannie and Freddie Mae [federal loan programs for mortgages] that caused [a] subprime lending situation that now caused the housing market in America to collapse.

I am convinced that, until we reverse this continued decline in home ownership and put a floor under it, and so that people have not only the hope and belief they can stay in their homes and realize the American dream, but that value will come up.

Now, we have allocated $750 billion. Let's take 300 of that billion and go in and buy those home loan mortgages and negotiate with those people in their homes, 11 million homes or more, so that they can afford to pay the mortgage, stay in their home.

Now, I know the criticism of this.

Well, what about the citizen that stayed in their homes? That paid their mortgage payments? It doesn't help that person in their home if the next door neighbor's house is abandoned. And so we've got to reverse this. We ought to put the homeowners first. And I am disappointed that Secretary Paulson and others have not made that their first priority.

SCHIEFFER: All right. Senator Obama?

(Continued)

U. S. SENATOR BARACK OBAMA (IL)
DEMOCRATIC PRESIDENTIAL NOMINEE:

. . . I think everybody understands at this point that we are experiencing the worst financial crisis since the Great Depression. And the financial rescue plan that Senator McCain and I supported is an important first step. And I pushed for some core principles: making sure that taxpayers can get their money back if they're putting money up. Making sure that CEOs are not enriching themselves through this process.

And I think that it's going to take some time to work itself out. But what we haven't yet seen is a rescue package for the middle class. Because the fundamentals of the economy were weak even before this latest crisis. So I've proposed four specific things that I think can help.

Number one, let's focus on jobs. I want to end the tax breaks for companies that are shipping jobs overseas and provide a tax credit for every company that's creating a job right here in America.

Number two, let's help families right away by providing them a tax cut—a middle-class tax cut for people making less than $200,000, and let's allow them to access their IRA accounts without penalty if they're experiencing a crisis.

Now Senator McCain and I agree with your idea that we've got to help homeowners. That's why we included in the financial package a proposal to get homeowners in a position where they can renegotiate their mortgages.

I disagree with Senator McCain in how to do it, because the way Senator McCain has designed his plan, it could be a giveaway to banks if we're buying full price for mortgages that now are worth a lot less. And we don't want to waste taxpayer money. And we've got to get the financial package working much quicker than it has been working.

Last point I want to make, though. We've got some long-term challenges in this economy that have to be dealt with. We've got to fix our energy policy that's giving our wealth away. We've got to fix our health care system and we've got to invest in our education system for every young person to be able to learn.

Passage 1

"The Milky Way" a Russian Folk Tale

Soon after the world was made, God created a beautiful maiden. Her name was Lindu, and her father's name was Uko. . . .

[Many of the Great Lights wished to take her for a wife. The North Star, the Moon and the Sun all wooed her, but she rejected them all because they did not ever change their courses in the sky.]

"You always stay in one place, and cannot stir from it," said she. "Go back to your watch-tower." . . .

At length the Northern Light came from his home in the midnight land in a diamond coach. . . . He was so grand that Lindu . . . loved this bright suitor at once.

"You do not travel the same path all the time like the others. You set out when you wish and rest when it pleases you. . . . You shall be my bridegroom."

And Lindu's choice was made.

. . . It was agreed that the wedding should be when the birds flew south. Back to his home in the midnight land went the Northern Light, knowing that Lindu loved him best.

The torrent which fell half a thousand feet over the mountain side sent Lindu her bridal veil. The Frost King sent her laces so fine that a breath of summer air would have destroyed them, and they were stored away in a block of ice for safe keeping. . . .

Spring passed away. Summer came and went. The birds flew south, and Lindu waited for the Northern Light's return. Snow sparkled on the earth, but no hoof-beat of his . . . white horses broke the stillness of the midnight air. Spring came, but never the Northern Light.

Then Lindu began to weep. . . . At last Uko heard [her] . . . and then saw his daughter's grief. . . . He ordered the Four Winds to lift her gently and bring her to him in his sky palace.

She dressed herself in her bridal veil [and] her frosted laces, and . . . with her white . . . veil streaming far out on the air . . . , Lindu sailed across the sky to Uko's palace. There she lives now, happy as her father Uko. Her white veil spreads from one end of the heavens to the other, and whoever lifts his eyes to the Milky Way beholds the maiden in her bridal robes.

Photo 1

The Rosette Nebula in the Monoceros, or Unicorn, constellation, in the Milky Way galaxy

A nebula is a huge cloud of dust and gas in space in which stars form. The Rosette nebula, also called NGC 2237, is about 5,000 light years from Earth in another part of our own Milky Way galaxy— the Monoceros, or Unicorn, constellation.

©Digital Vision/PunchStock

Passage 2

NASA'S Spitzer Sees Milky Way's Blooming Countryside

We live in a spiral collection of stars that is mostly flat, like a vinyl record, but it has a slight warp. Our solar system is located about two-thirds of the way out from the Milky Way's center. [We are located] in the Orion Spur, an offshoot of the Perseus spiral arm. Spitzer's infrared observations are allowing researchers to map the shape of the galaxy and its warp with the most precision yet.

. . . Spitzer and other telescopes have created mosaics of the galaxy's plane looking in the direction of its center before. The region behind us, with its sparse stars and dark skies, is less charted.

"We sometimes call this flyover country," said Barbara Whitney, an astronomer from the University of Wisconsin at Madison. She uses Spitzer to study young stars. "We are finding all sorts of new star formation in the lesser-known areas at the outer edges of the galaxy."

—Whitney Clavin and J.D. Harrington

Source: NASA. [2013] *Spitzer: Studying the Universe in Infrared.* www. nasa.gov

Directions: Use this rubric to guide your writing and to evaluate your finished work on a 1 to 4 scale. A score of 4 indicates a mastery of the element; a score of 1 indicates a need for extensive revision.

4	3	2	1
Development of Ideas/Organizational Structure			
Main Idea There is one fully developed main idea.	**Main Idea** There is one mostly developed main idea.	**Main Idea** There is a partially developed main idea.	**Main Idea** There is no main idea.
Details Accurate and directly relevant details support the main idea.	**Details** Accurate and mostly relevant details support the main idea.	**Details** Some of the details are accurate and relevant to the main idea.	**Details** There are no details relevant to the main idea.
Structure The writing has an introduction, a body, and a conclusion. The introduction states the main idea. The body presents information that is clearly relevant to the main idea. The conclusion restates or summarizes the main idea. Paragraph and text structures are clear and appropriate to the topic and purpose.	**Structure** The writing has an introduction, a body, and a conclusion. The introduction states the main idea. The body presents information that is mostly relevant to the main idea. The conclusion restates or summarizes the main idea. Paragraph and text structures are mostly clear and relevant to the topic and purpose.	**Structure** The writing has an introduction and a body. The introduction states the main idea. The body presents some information relevant to the main idea. There is no conclusion. An attempt is made to use paragraph and text structures that support the topic and purpose.	**Structure** The writing does not introduce a main idea. The purpose of the content in the body is unclear. There is no conclusion. Paragraph and text structures are not clear or appropriate to the topic and purpose.
Author's Purpose, Analysis of Arguments, and/or Use of Evidence			
Purpose The purpose for writing is clear. The writer has full knowledge of the topic and provides thorough supporting evidence. The writer uses appropriate techniques to connect to the audience.	**Purpose** The purpose for writing is somewhat clear. The writer has some knowledge of the topic and provides some supporting evidence. The writer makes some effort to connect to the audience.	**Purpose** The purpose for writing is unclear. The writer has little knowledge of the topic and provides some supporting evidence. The writer makes some effort to connect to the audience.	**Purpose** The purpose for writing is unclear. The writer has no knowledge of the topic and provides no supporting evidence. There is no attempt to connect to the audience.
Arguments/Evidence The writer develops a logical argument that includes a clearly stated claim related to the prompt and cites sufficient evidence from texts and other sources that is specific and relevant. If appropriate, the writer analyzes and evaluates the logic and validity of arguments in source texts.	**Arguments/Evidence** The writer's argument is generally logical; the claim is clear and relevant to the prompt; evidence is provided from texts and other sources but is not specific, sufficient, or relevant. If appropriate, the writer attempts to analyze and evaluate the logic and validity of arguments in source texts.	**Arguments/Evidence** The writer's argument contains logical flaws; the claim is stated, but does not relate directly to the prompt; some relevant evidence is provided. If appropriate, the writer mentions arguments in source texts, but the analysis/evaluation of them is incomplete, superficial, or incorrect.	**Arguments/Evidence** The writer does not develop an argument, or the argument is not logical; no claim is stated, or the stated claim is irrelevant to the prompt; little or no relevant evidence is provided. If appropriate, the writer may mention arguments in source texts, but fails to analyze or evaluate them.

4	3	2	1
English Conventions and Clarity			
Clarity The writer makes varied word choices that help readers visualize the content. Words and phrases are vivid, powerful, and engaging. Sentences are varied in style and length and read naturally. Relationships between ideas, sentences, and paragraphs are clear and frequently reinforced by signal words and phrases.	**Clarity** The writer makes some varied word choices that help readers visualize the content. The language is frequently engaging. Sentences exhibit some variety in style and length and are generally fluent. Relationships between ideas, sentences, and paragraphs are usually clear and sometimes reinforced by signal words and phrases.	**Clarity** The writer makes limited word choices that minimally help readers visualize the content. Few words and phrases engage readers. Sentences have little variety in style or length and at times read awkwardly. Relationships between ideas, sentences, and paragraphs are sometimes clear and occasionally reinforced by signal words and phrases.	**Clarity** The writer makes repetitive word choices, often incorrectly. Words and phrases do not engage readers. Sentences show little or no variety in style or length; the text does not flow naturally. Relationships between ideas, sentences, and paragraphs are unclear and are not reinforced by signal words and phrases.
Conventions All sentences are well constructed. There are no errors in spelling, grammar, or mechanics.	**Conventions** Most sentences are well constructed. There are almost no errors in spelling, grammar, or mechanics. Any errors do not affect comprehension.	**Conventions** Some sentences are well constructed. There are several errors in spelling, grammar, and mechanics. It is sometimes hard to understand what the writer means to say.	**Conventions** Sentences are poorly constructed. There are many errors in spelling, grammar, and mechanics. It is often hard to understand what the writer means to say.

Name ____________________ Date ____________ Class ____________

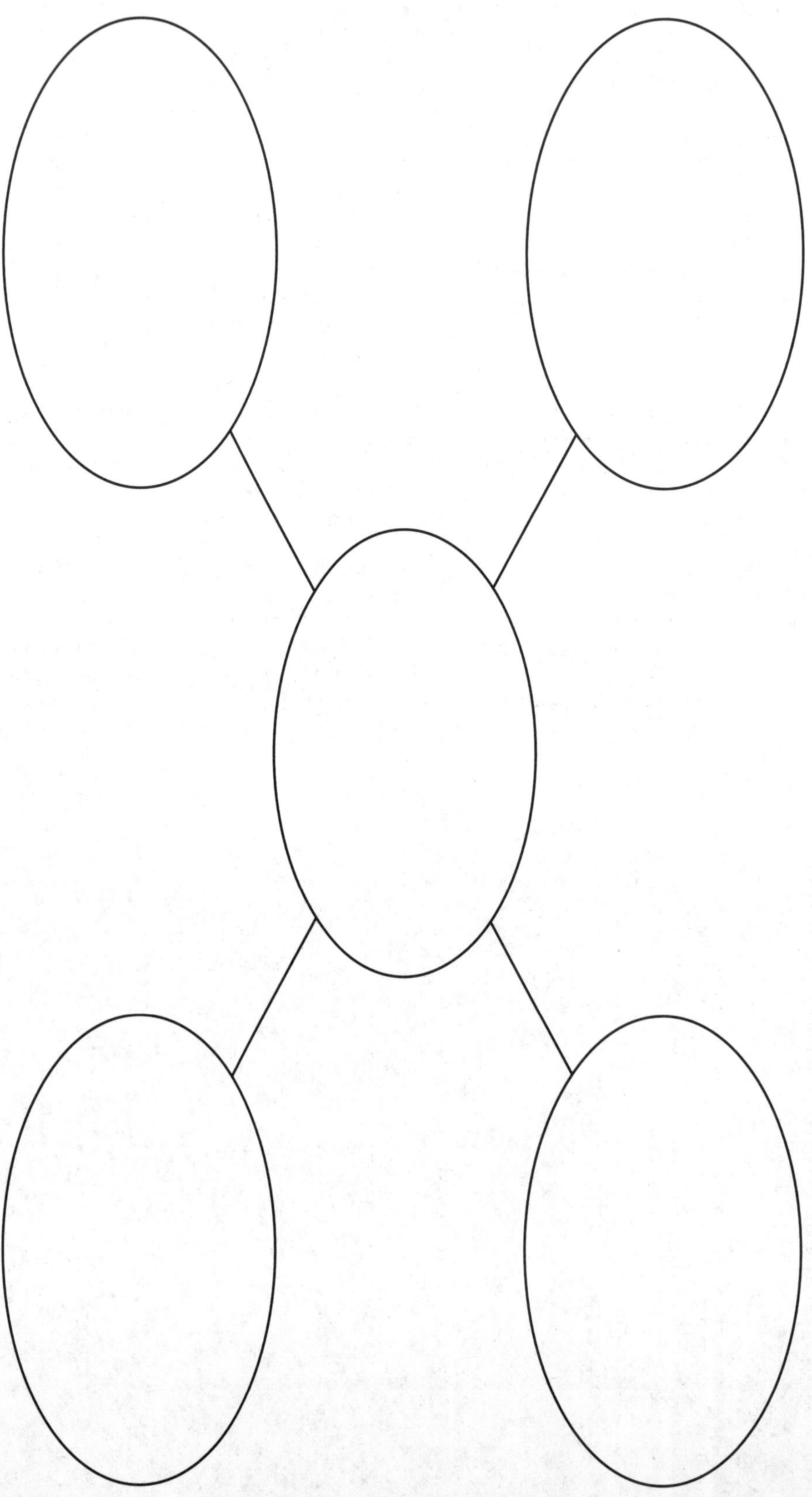

FLOW CHART

Name ______________________ Date ____________ Class ____________

Name ________________ Date ________ Class ________

TWO-COLUMN CHART

Name ________________ Date ________ Class ________

Name ______________________ Date ____________ Class ____________

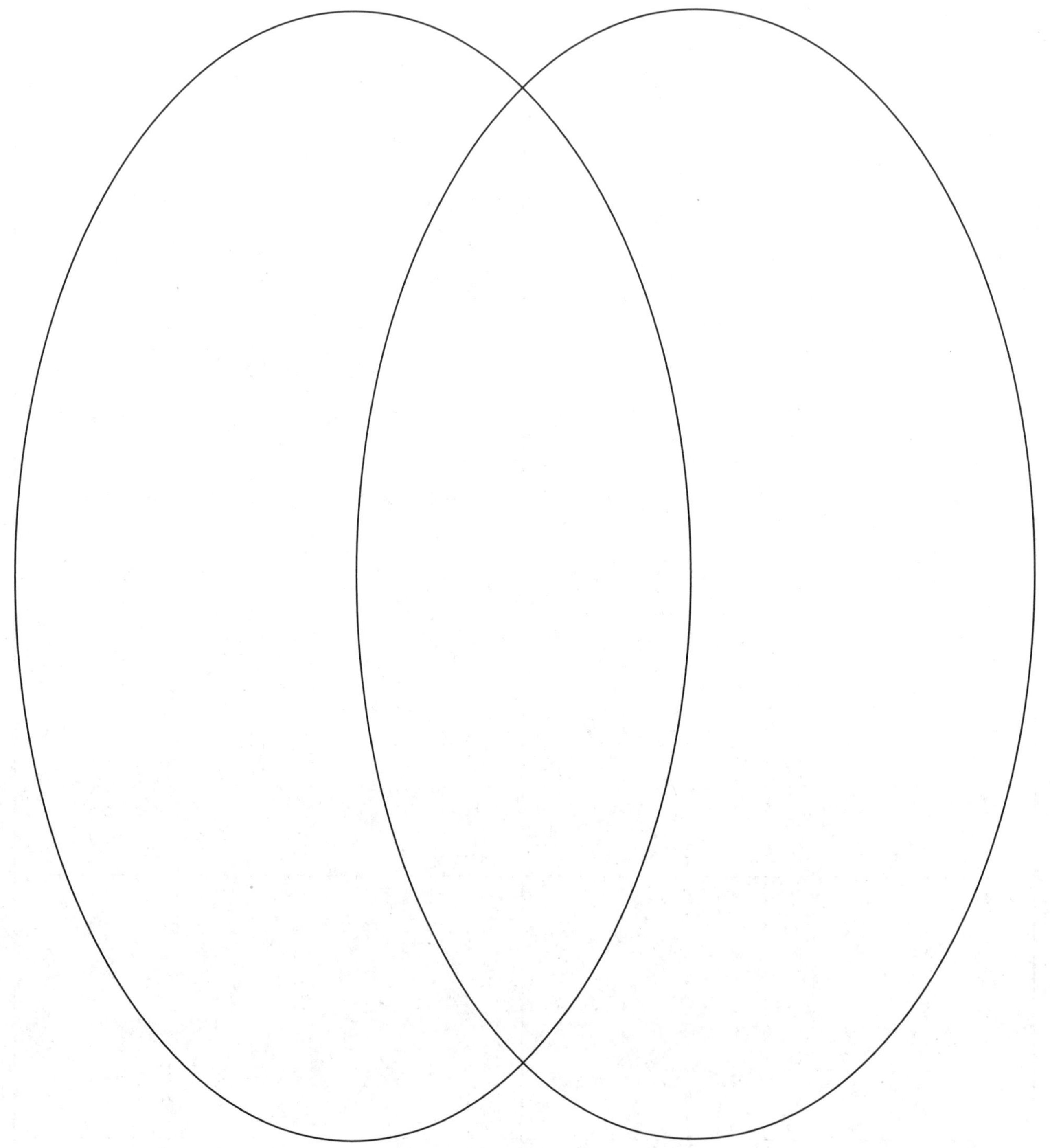

CAUSE-AND-EFFECT CHART

Name ______________________ **Date** ____________ **Class** ____________

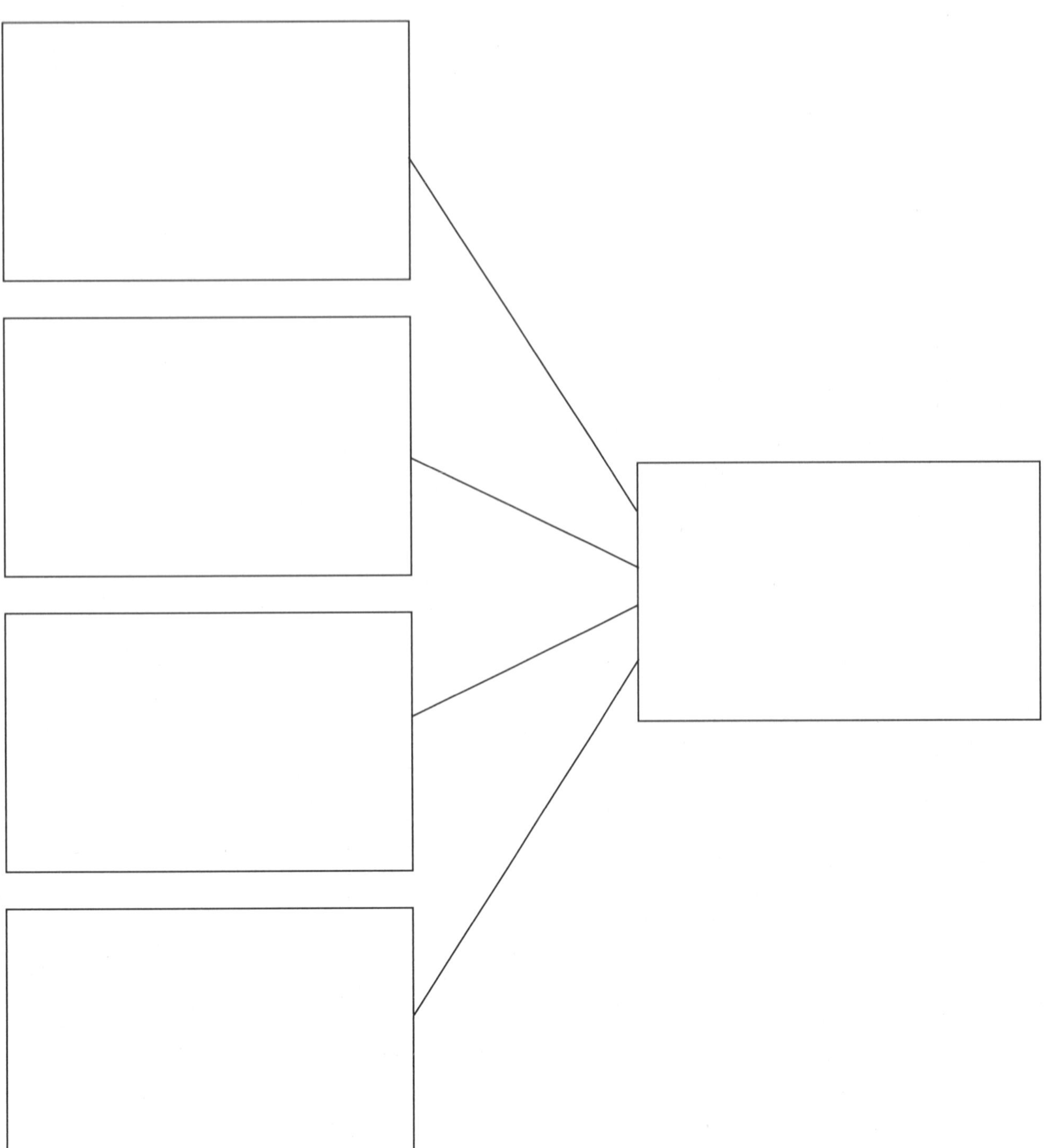

Name ______________________ Date ____________ Class ____________

Word	
Definition	
Examples	Non-Examples

K-W-L-H CHART

Name ____________________ **Date** __________ **Class** __________

What I Know	What I Want to Know	What I Learned	How Can I Learn More

A

acknowledge accept or note the existence of

affects (verb) influences

analogy comparison of two things that are similar in some way

analyze closely examine

apply be connected to

approach how an author presents a subject

appropriate especially suitable or proper for a particular circumstance

argument reasons given to persuade an audience on a position

assumption fact or idea that is accepted as true

audience group of people who will read, see, or hear something

author's intention what a writer hopes the reader will take away after reading his or her text

author's purpose author's reason for writing a text

autobiography the story of a person's life written and narrated by himself or herself

B

biased showing unreasoned judgment or prejudice

biography the story of a person's life, written by another

C

cause-and-effect structure an organizational pattern that presents why something happened

character person in a novel, story, or play

characteristics features that identify something

characterization the way an author reveals characters' traits

chronological in time order

cite make reference to

claim statement that something is true

collaboration the act of working together with others

compare identify the ways in which two things are alike

complement complete or add to something

complex complicated or difficult to understand

comprehensive complete; including most or all

concise brief and to the point

conclusion 1. reasonable judgment; 2. final section of a text; ending

conflict struggle between opposing forces in a story or play, usually resolved by the end of the work

conflicting in opposition to

connected linked or joined together

connotative suggested by a word or phrase

contestable disputable; subject to differences of opinion

context 1. circumstances or conditions in which something exists or occurs; 2. the words, phrases, and sentences that surround a word

contradictory inconsistent; suggesting the opposite

contrast identify the ways in which two things differ

convey express; communicate

criteria measures that are used to evaluate something

D

deduce figure out

deductions conclusions reached through logical reasoning

depicts describes in words

description statement of what someone or something is like

details items of information

determine identify through investigation or reasoning

differentiate distinguish

dispute debate; call into question

distinguish notice a difference

drama a story written to be performed on the stage

dynamic showing change or growth

E

effect (noun) result; impression

effective producing the desired result

emotions feelings

emphasize stress or highlight

enumeration listing or specifying one after another

essay a composition giving the author's analysis, interpretation, or perspective on a particular topic

evidence details that support a claim

examine inspect in detail; investigate carefully

explicit clearly stated

F

faulty not valid; ineffective

fiction literary work, usually written in prose, based on the imagination and not necessarily on fact

figurative meaning more than its literal sense

flashback interruption of a time sequence to tell what happened earlier

folk tale a story passed down (usually orally) in a culture

format order and form in which a text is arranged or presented

G

generalization broad statement

genre category of writing with certain identifiable characteristics

graphic organizer diagram or illustration of ideas in a visual format

H

hearsay rumor; information based on another's statement

homophones words that sound the same but are spelled differently and have different meanings

I

identify find; pinpoint

impact 1. (noun) effect or impression; 2. (verb) have an effect on

implicitly not directly

implied expressed indirectly

imply suggest

infer come to a conclusion based on evidence and prior knowledge

inference logical guess based on stated details in the text and prior knowledge

informational text passage meant to explain, describe, instruct, or persuade

interpret explain the meaning of something; understand something

irrelevant pointless; inappropriate; unnecessary

L

literary techniques methods authors use to convey their messages

literary text passage based on imagination or reality that tells a story

logic reasoned thought or argument; valid reasoning

logical evidence clear and reasonable support for a claim

M

main idea most important idea in a paragraph or passage

memo short form of *memorandum*; a record or written statement of something, especially in a business setting

metaphor figure of speech in which a word or phrase is applied to something that it does not denote in order to imply a similarity

mood emotions a reader feels while reading a text

N

narrative story

neutral not favoring one side or position

O

observe watch carefully

opinion 1. belief; point of view; 2. statement of the reasons and principles upon which a legal decision is based

opposing conflicting or contrasting

organization the way text is arranged

outcome result; effect

P

parallel plots a narrative device in which two characters experience similar or contrasting stories at the same time in the narrative

paraphrase restate information in one's own words

perspective particular standpoint or point of view

persuade convince someone to agree

plot series of events that make up a story

poetry literature written in stanzas; verse

point of view writer's attitude toward a topic

position an author's opinion on a specific issue or question

predict foretell

prior knowledge familiarity or awareness you already have about a topic

problem-and-solution structure an organizational pattern that presents something that needs to be dealt with and how to deal with it

process series of actions leading to an end

proof evidence establishing a fact

proponents people who argue in favor of something

prose text written in sentences and paragraphs

proximity closeness, quality of being near or next to

R

reasoning process of thinking, understanding, and forming conclusions

refute claim, argue, or show as inaccurate or wrong

reiterate repeat for emphasis or clarity

relevant related

rhetoric the art of effective or persuasive (speaking or) writing, especially using figures of speech and composition techniques

rhetorical device language technique that writers or speakers use to create an effect

S

satire humor that mocks a person, event, or situation

scan read quickly, looking for specific information

scope breadth; area covered

scrutiny close examination

sequence order

setting time and place in which the action of a story occurs

signal words words and phrases that clarify relationships between ideas within and between sentences and paragraphs

similar alike but not identical

similes comparisons that use "like" or "as"

skim read quickly, looking for main ideas and key details

solidify make stronger and more certain

sound error-free; logical; based on thorough knowledge or experience

specific concrete; distinct

stanzas groups of lines in a poem

stated explained directly

storyboard series of sketches showing key events or scenes in a plot

style writer's use of language

sufficient enough

summarize to describe the main points in a concise manner

support confirm

supporting details facts, opinions, examples, or other details that help explain the main idea

supporting evidence facts, reasons, and examples that back up a claim

suppositions ideas or theories believed to be true even though there is no proof of them

symbolism use of objects or actions to represent something else

synthesize combine parts or elements to form a new whole

text structure pattern a writer uses to organize ideas in a text

textual consisting of words

theme underlying message in a work of fiction

time line diagram that shows events in the order they occurred

tone expression of a writer's attitude through stylistic choices

topic subject

topic sentence statement of the main idea of a paragraph or passage

transition change or movement from one event or idea to another, within and between sentences and paragraphs in a text

transmit pass on; convey; relay; disseminate

underlying supporting; forming the foundation of (an idea, process, etc.)

unstated suggested but not directly explained

valid justified; appropriate; meaningful

validity the quality of being logically or factually reliable

verifiable capable of being confirmed as accurate

visual consisting of images

visualize form a mental picture

word choice use of specific words in speaking or writing for description and effect

H

I

J

K

L

M